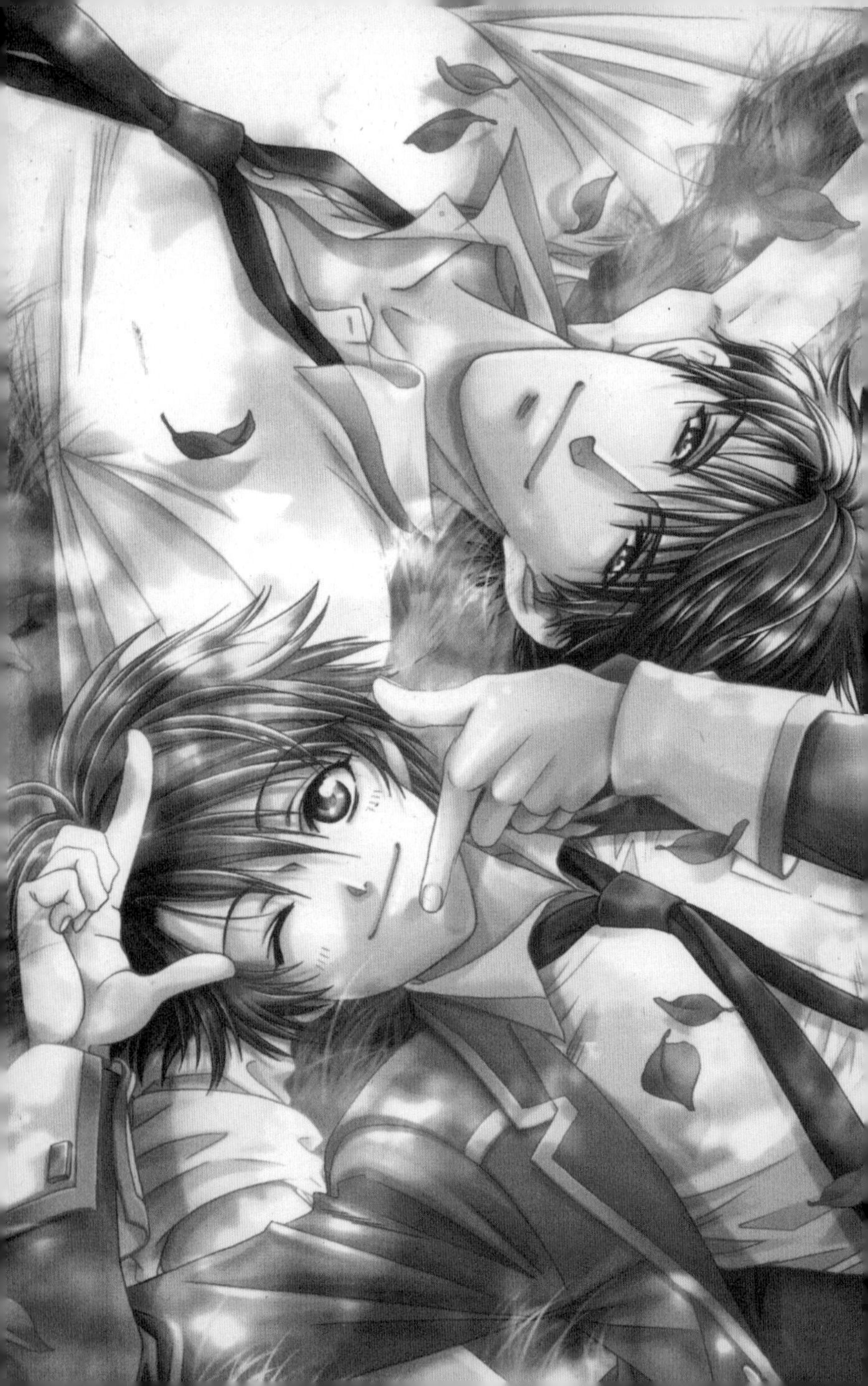

Gakuen Heaven
You Higuri   Original Work/SPRAY

GAKUEN HEAVEN
CONTENTS

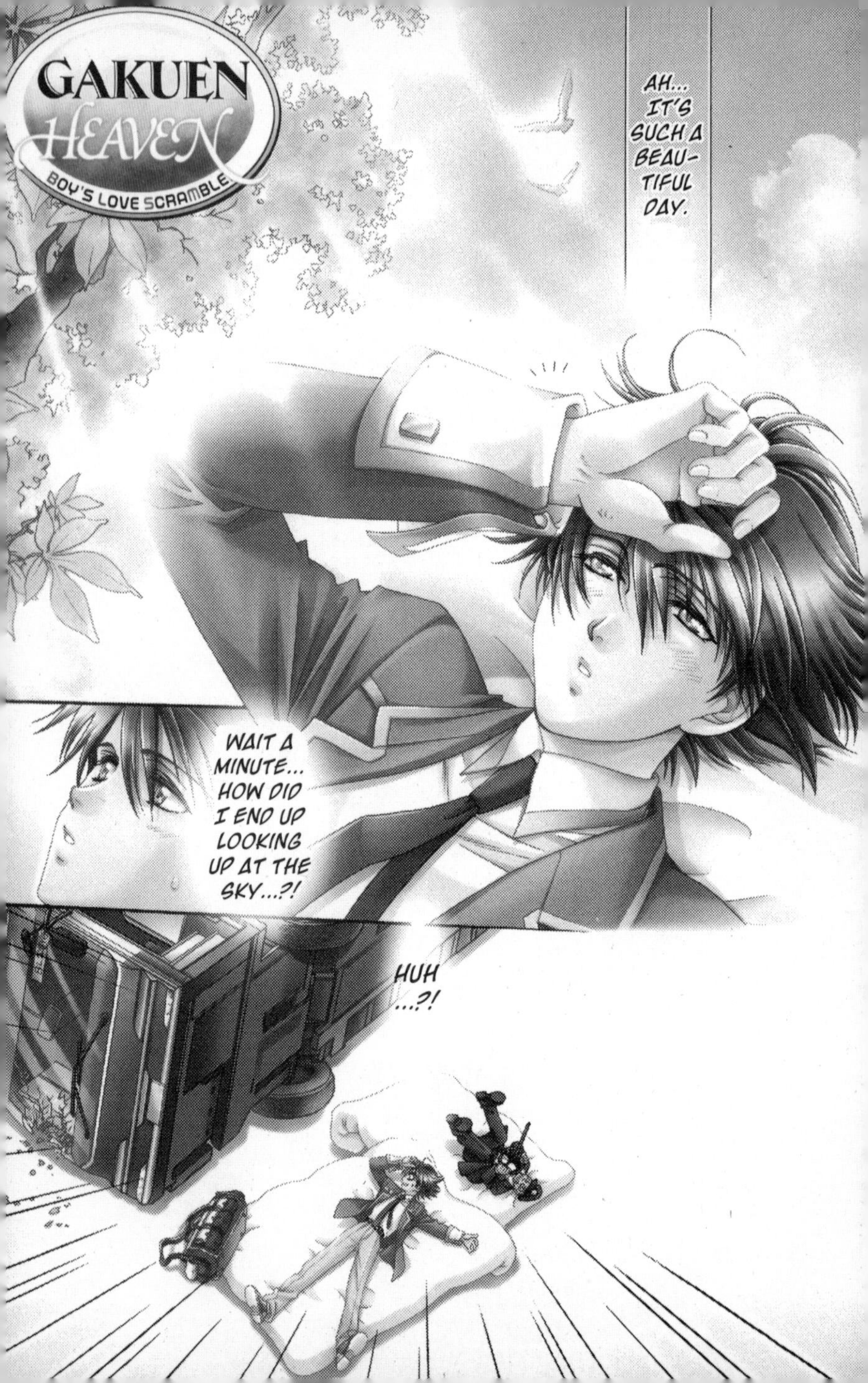
GAKUEN HEAVEN
BOY'S LOVE SCRAMBLE
AH... IT'S SUCH A BEAU-TIFUL DAY.
WAIT A MINUTE... HOW DID I END UP LOOKING UP AT THE SKY...?!
HUH ...?!

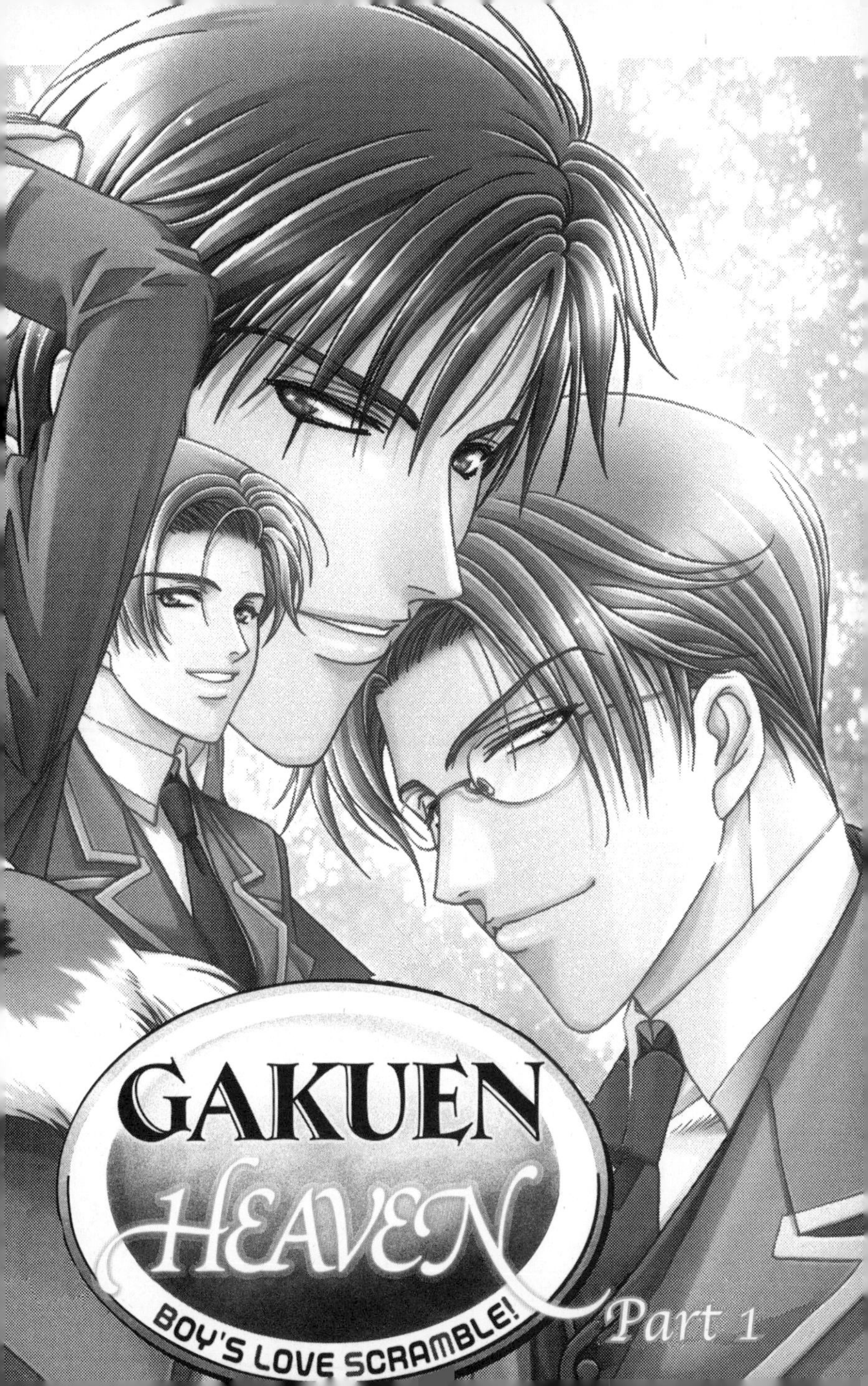
GAKUEN
HEAVEN
BOY'S LOVE SCRAMBLE!
Part 1

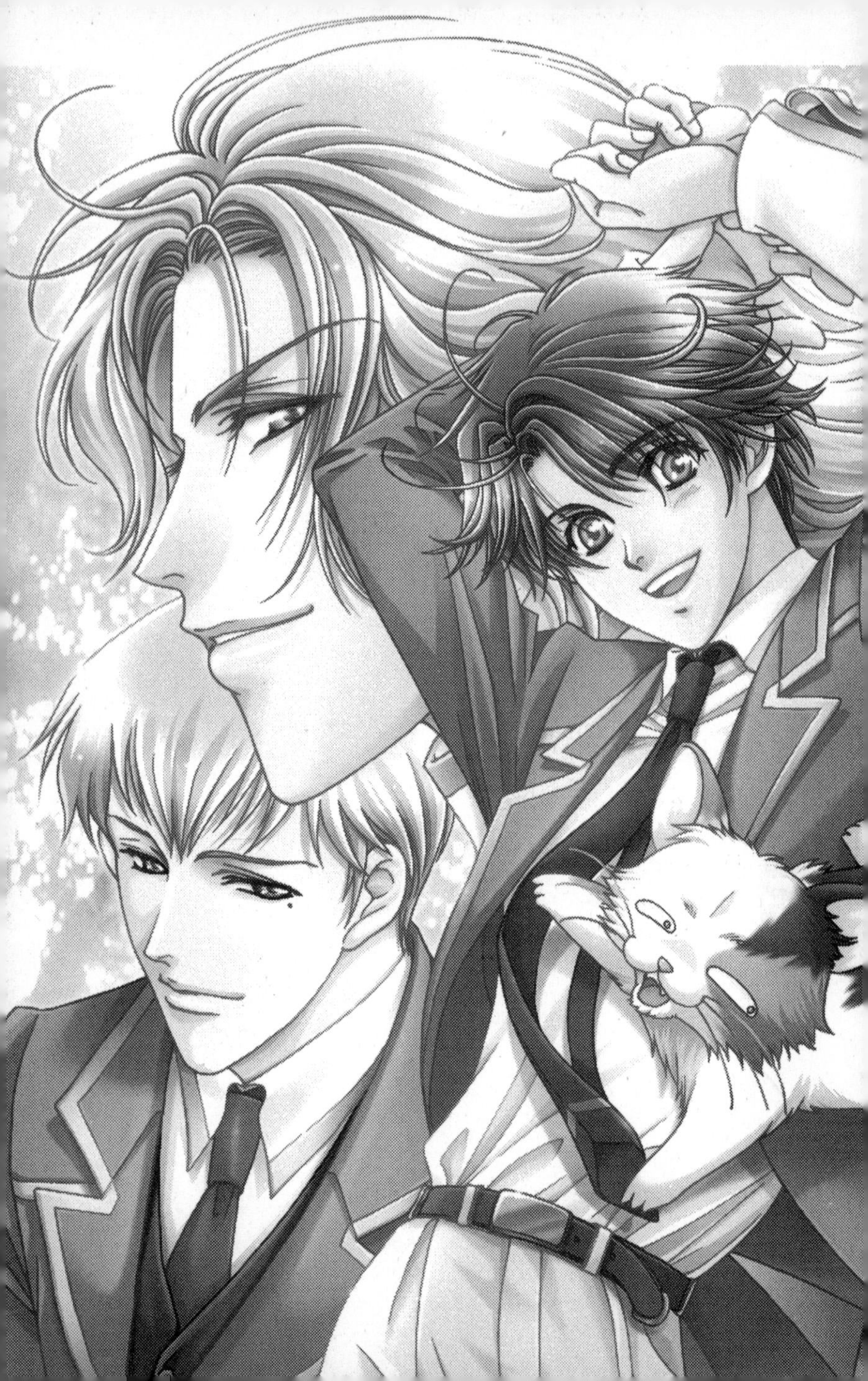

GAKUEN *HEAVEN*

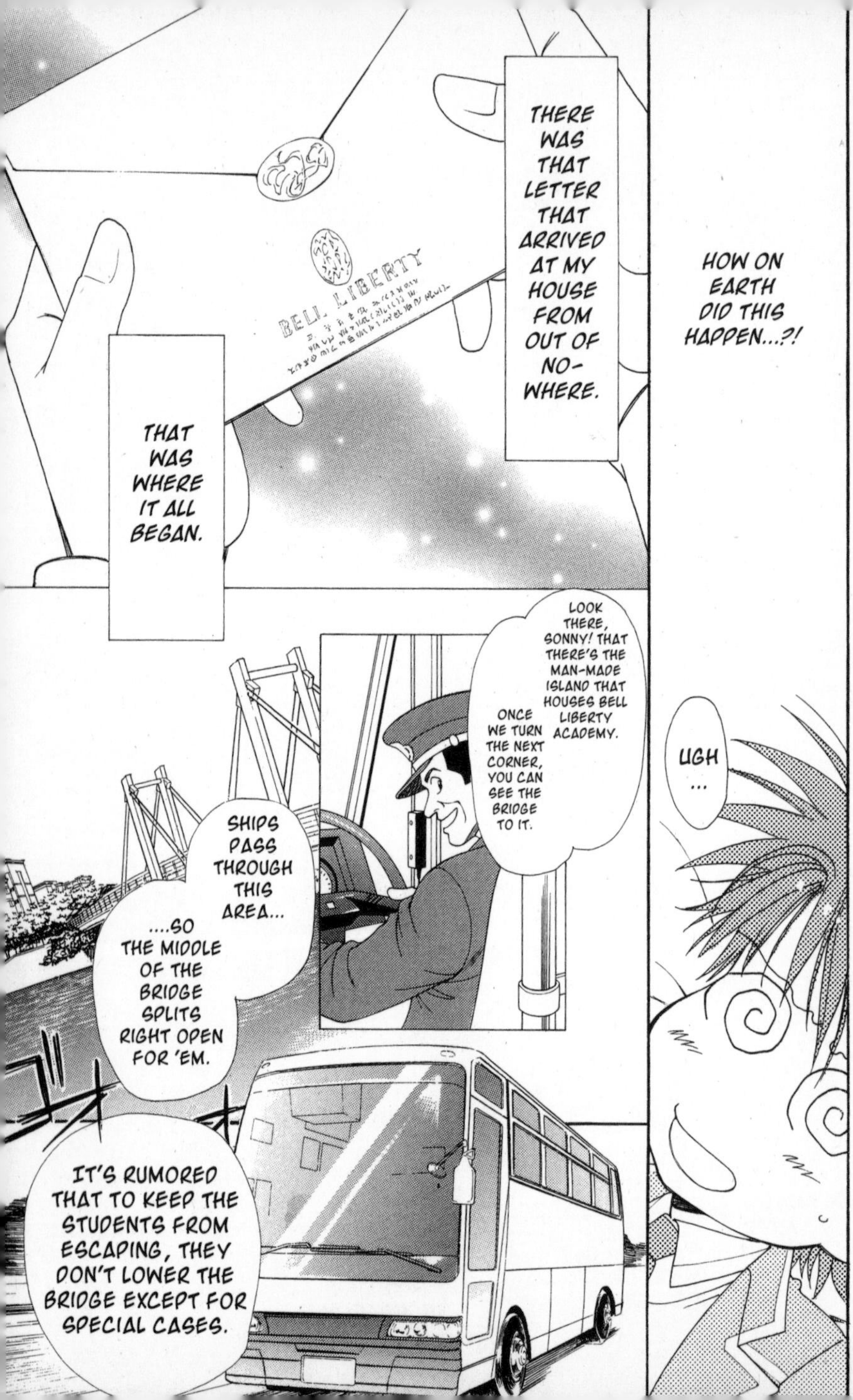
HOW ON EARTH DID THIS HAPPEN...?!
UGH...
THERE WAS THAT LETTER THAT ARRIVED AT MY HOUSE FROM OUT OF NO-WHERE.
BELL LIBERTY
THAT WAS WHERE IT ALL BEGAN.
LOOK THERE, SONNY! THAT THERE'S THE MAN-MADE ISLAND THAT HOUSES BELL LIBERTY ACADEMY.
ONCE WE TURN THE NEXT CORNER, YOU CAN SEE THE BRIDGE TO IT.
SHIPS PASS THROUGH THIS AREA...
...SO THE MIDDLE OF THE BRIDGE SPLITS RIGHT OPEN FOR 'EM.
IT'S RUMORED THAT TO KEEP THE STUDENTS FROM ESCAPING, THEY DON'T LOWER THE BRIDGE EXCEPT FOR SPECIAL CASES.

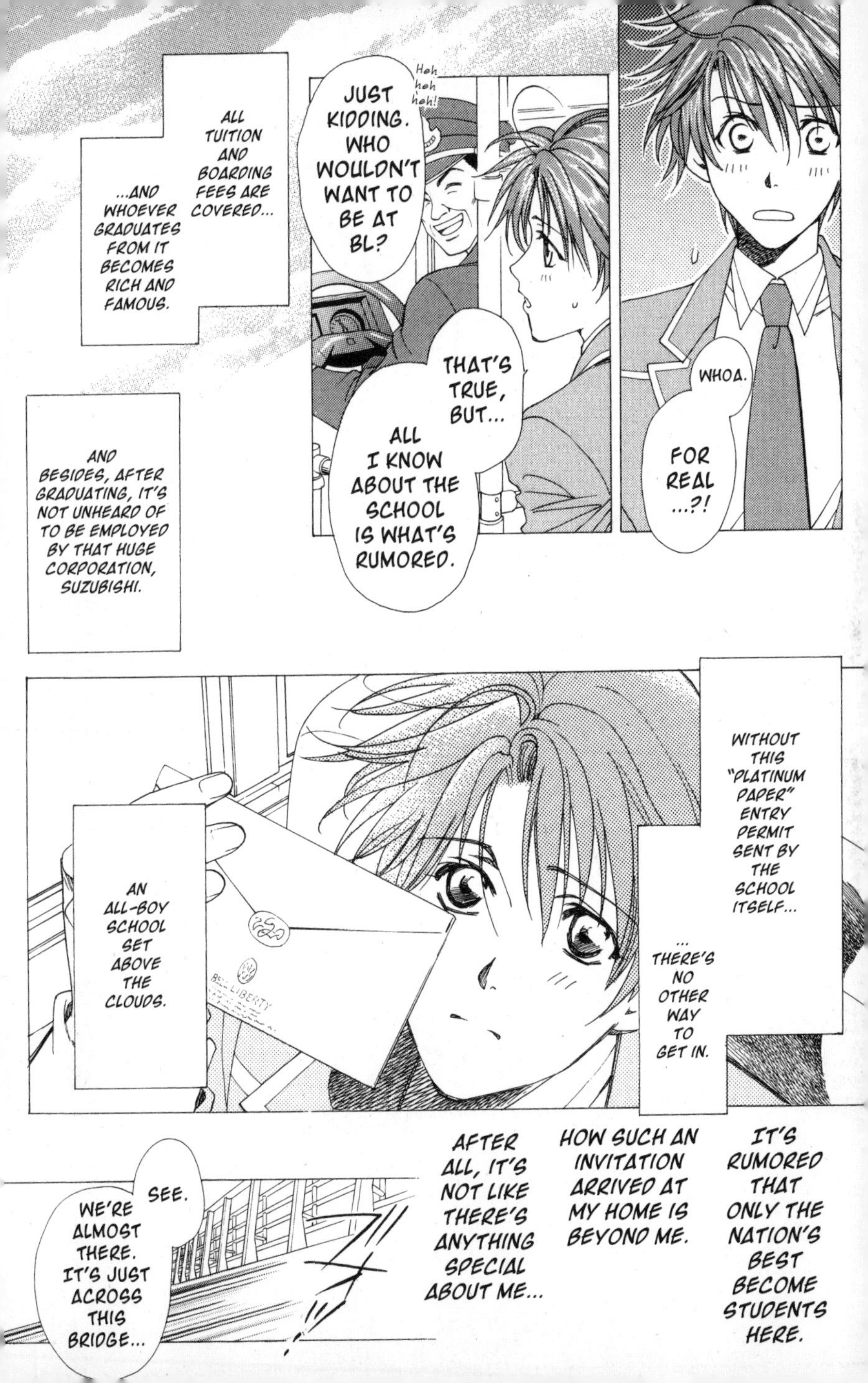
WHOA.
FOR REAL ...?!
Heh heh heh!
JUST KIDDING. WHO WOULDN'T WANT TO BE AT BL?
THAT'S TRUE, BUT...
ALL I KNOW ABOUT THE SCHOOL IS WHAT'S RUMORED.
ALL TUITION AND BOARDING FEES ARE COVERED...
...AND WHOEVER GRADUATES FROM IT BECOMES RICH AND FAMOUS.
AND BESIDES, AFTER GRADUATING, IT'S NOT UNHEARD OF TO BE EMPLOYED BY THAT HUGE CORPORATION, SUZUBISHI.
WITHOUT THIS "PLATINUM PAPER" ENTRY PERMIT SENT BY THE SCHOOL ITSELF...
...THERE'S NO OTHER WAY TO GET IN.
AN ALL-BOY SCHOOL SET ABOVE THE CLOUDS.
BELL LIBERTY
IT'S RUMORED THAT ONLY THE NATION'S BEST BECOME STUDENTS HERE.
HOW SUCH AN INVITATION ARRIVED AT MY HOME IS BEYOND ME.
AFTER ALL, IT'S NOT LIKE THERE'S ANYTHING SPECIAL ABOUT ME...
SEE.
WE'RE ALMOST THERE. IT'S JUST ACROSS THIS BRIDGE...

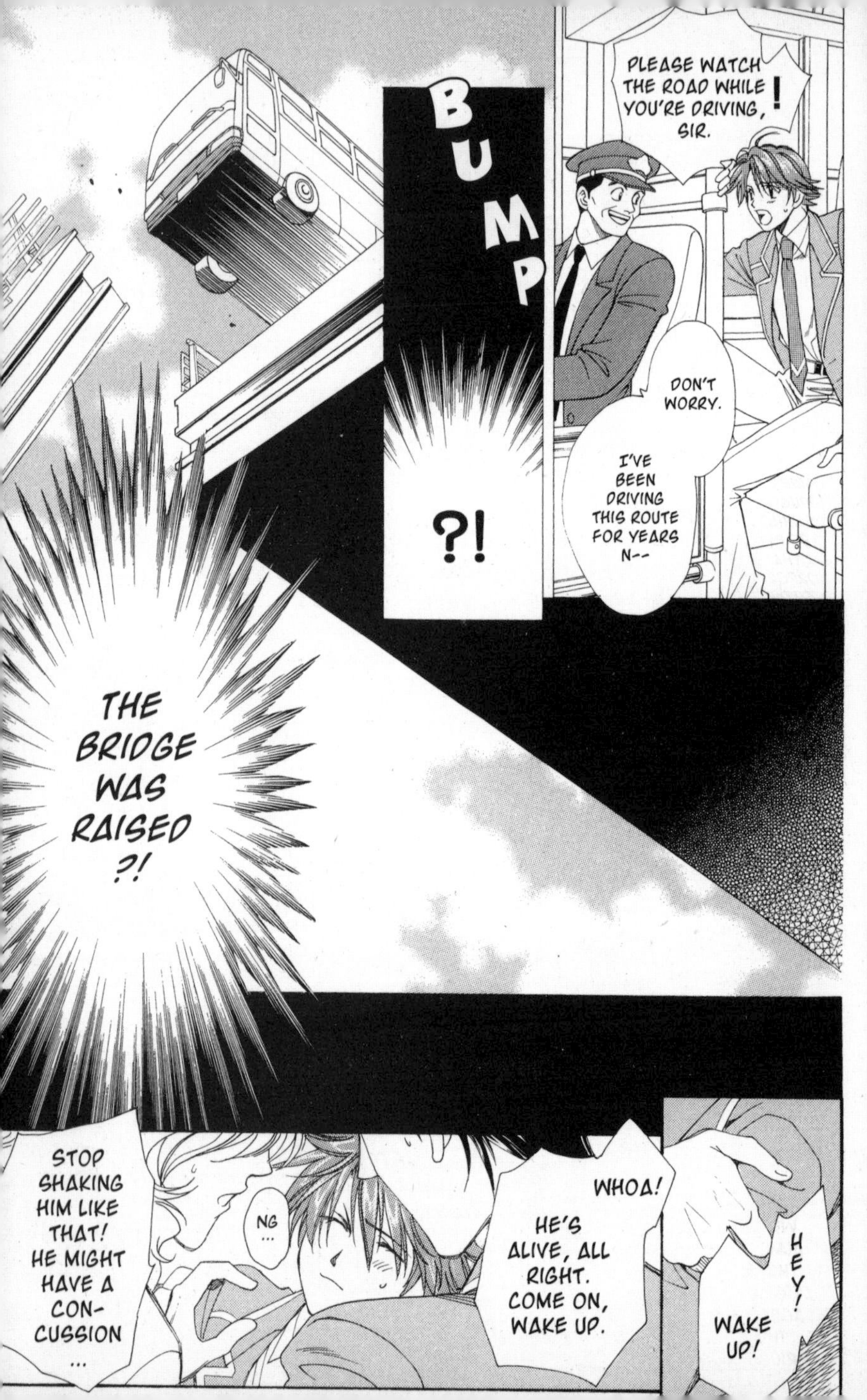
PLEASE WATCH THE ROAD WHILE YOU'RE DRIVING, SIR.
!
DON'T WORRY.
I'VE BEEN DRIVING THIS ROUTE FOR YEARS N--
BUMP
?!
THE BRIDGE WAS RAISED ?!
HEY!
WAKE UP!
WHOA!
HE'S ALIVE, ALL RIGHT. COME ON, WAKE UP.
NG ...
STOP SHAKING HIM LIKE THAT! HE MIGHT HAVE A CON-CUSSION ...

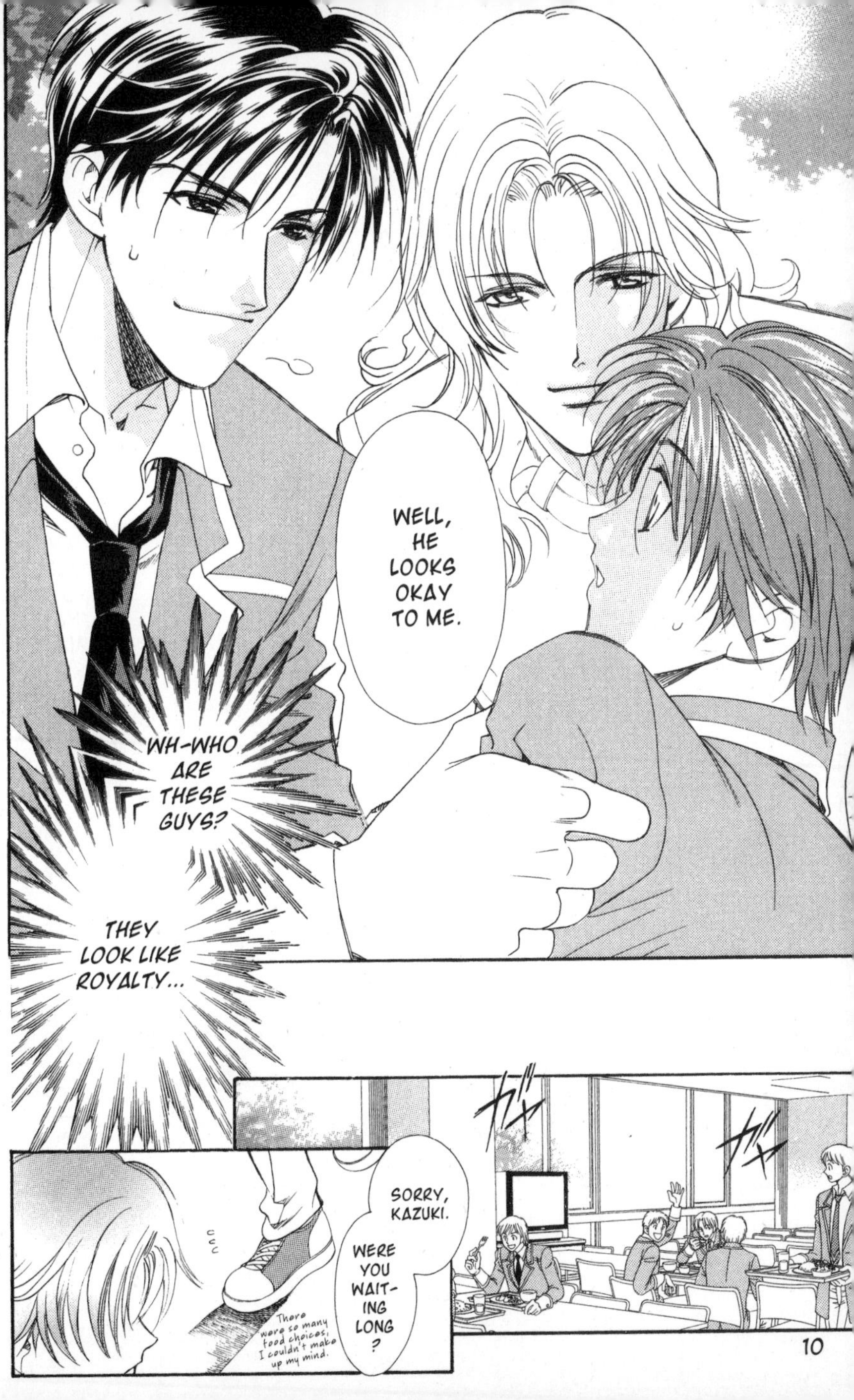
WELL, HE LOOKS OKAY TO ME.
WH-WHO ARE THESE GUYS?
THEY LOOK LIKE ROYALTY...
SORRY, KAZUKI.
WERE YOU WAITING LONG?
There were so many food choices, I couldn't make up my mind.

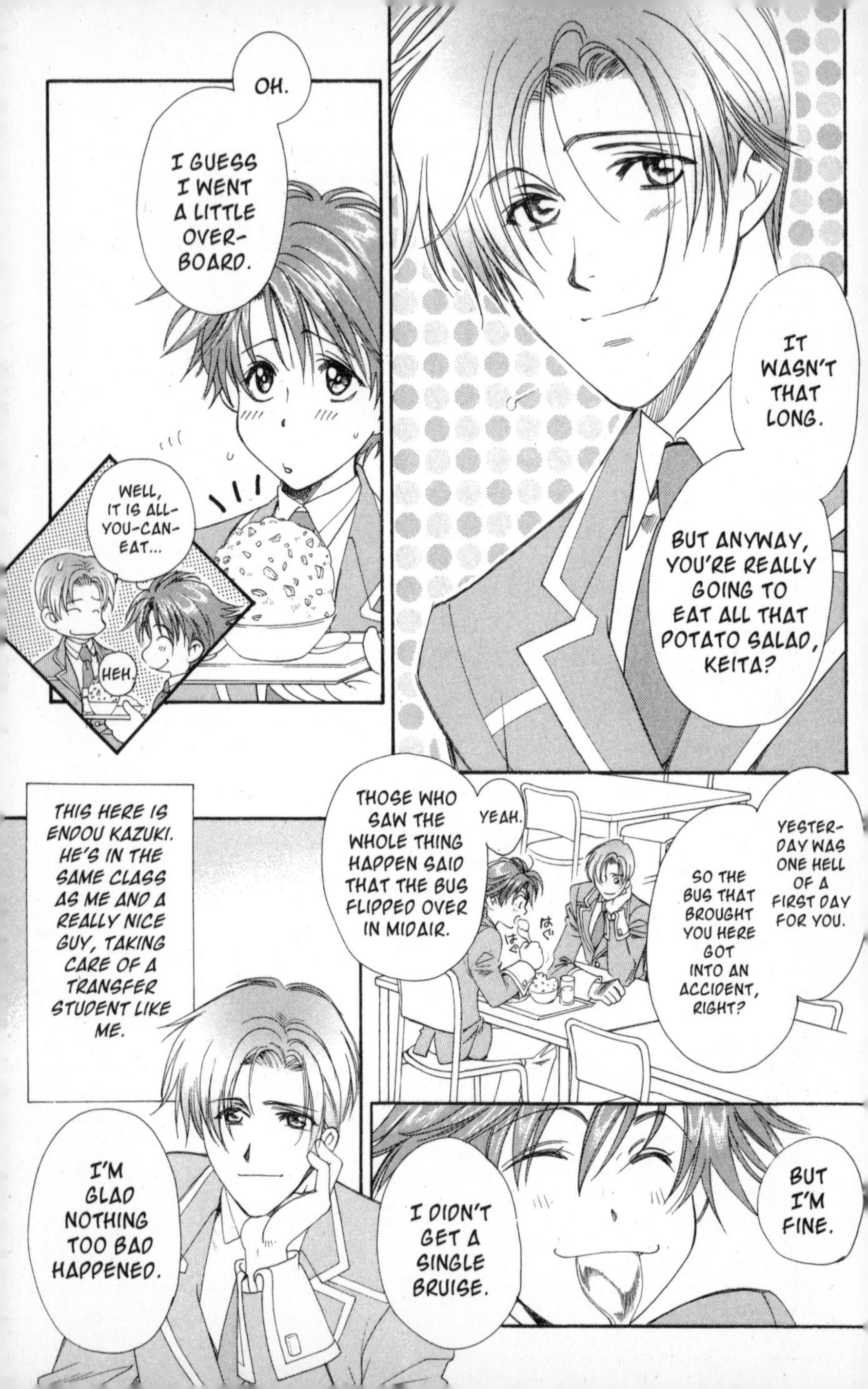

IT WASN'T THAT LONG.
BUT ANYWAY, YOU'RE REALLY GOING TO EAT ALL THAT POTATO SALAD, KEITA?
OH.
I GUESS I WENT A LITTLE OVER-BOARD.
WELL, IT IS ALL-YOU-CAN-EAT...
HEH.
YESTER-DAY WAS ONE HELL OF A FIRST DAY FOR YOU.
SO THE BUS THAT BROUGHT YOU HERE GOT INTO AN ACCIDENT, RIGHT?
YEAH.
THOSE WHO SAW THE WHOLE THING HAPPEN SAID THAT THE BUS FLIPPED OVER IN MIDAIR.
THIS HERE IS ENDOU KAZUKI. HE'S IN THE SAME CLASS AS ME AND A REALLY NICE GUY, TAKING CARE OF A TRANSFER STUDENT LIKE ME.
BUT I'M FINE.
I DIDN'T GET A SINGLE BRUISE.
I'M GLAD NOTHING TOO BAD HAPPENED.

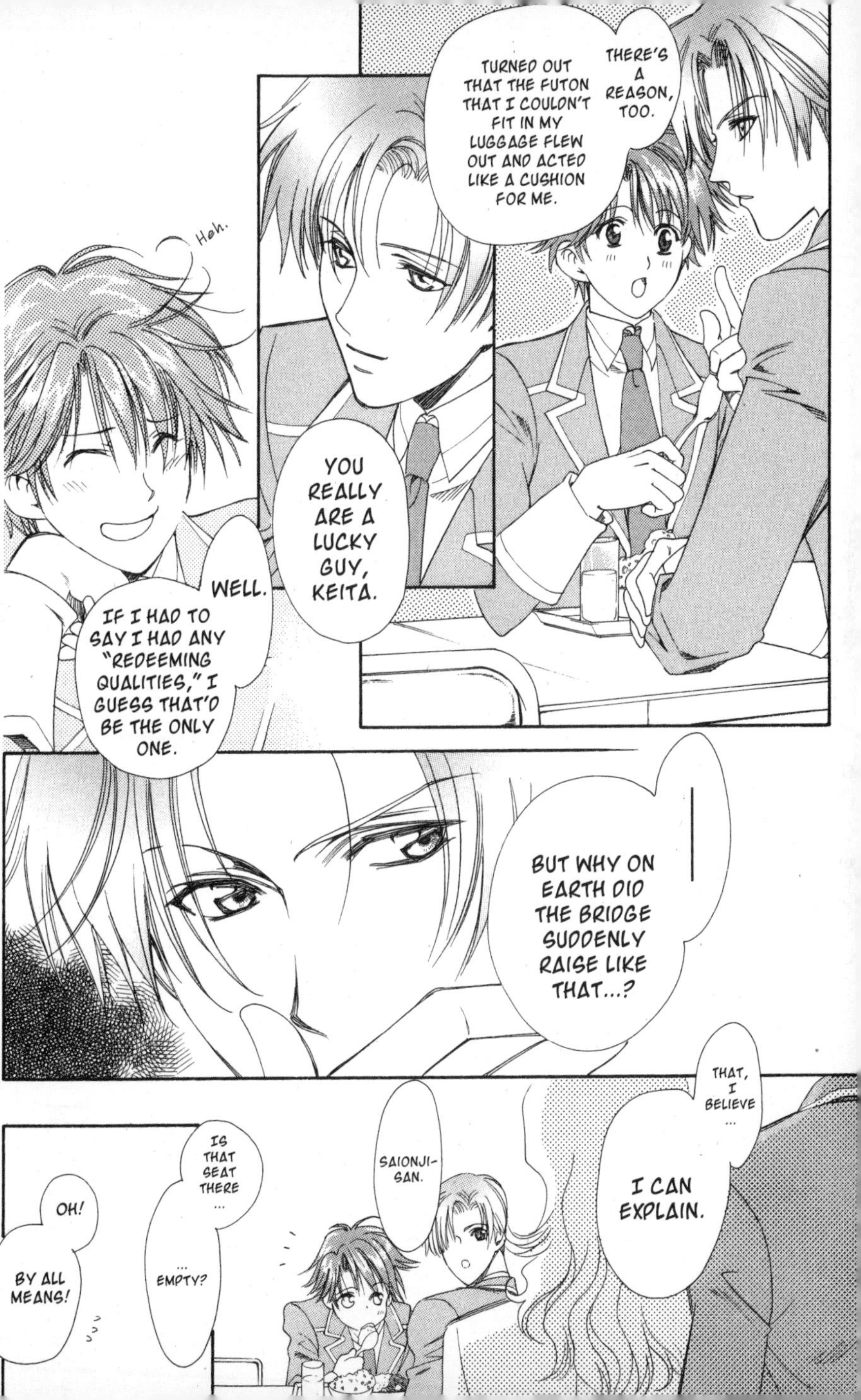
THERE'S A REASON, TOO.
TURNED OUT THAT THE FUTON THAT I COULDN'T FIT IN MY LUGGAGE FLEW OUT AND ACTED LIKE A CUSHION FOR ME.
YOU REALLY ARE A LUCKY GUY, KEITA.
Heh.
WELL.
IF I HAD TO SAY I HAD ANY "REDEEMING QUALITIES," I GUESS THAT'D BE THE ONLY ONE.
BUT WHY ON EARTH DID THE BRIDGE SUDDENLY RAISE LIKE THAT...?
THAT, I BELIEVE ...
I CAN EXPLAIN.
SAIONJI-SAN.
IS THAT SEAT THERE ...
... EMPTY?
OH!
BY ALL MEANS!

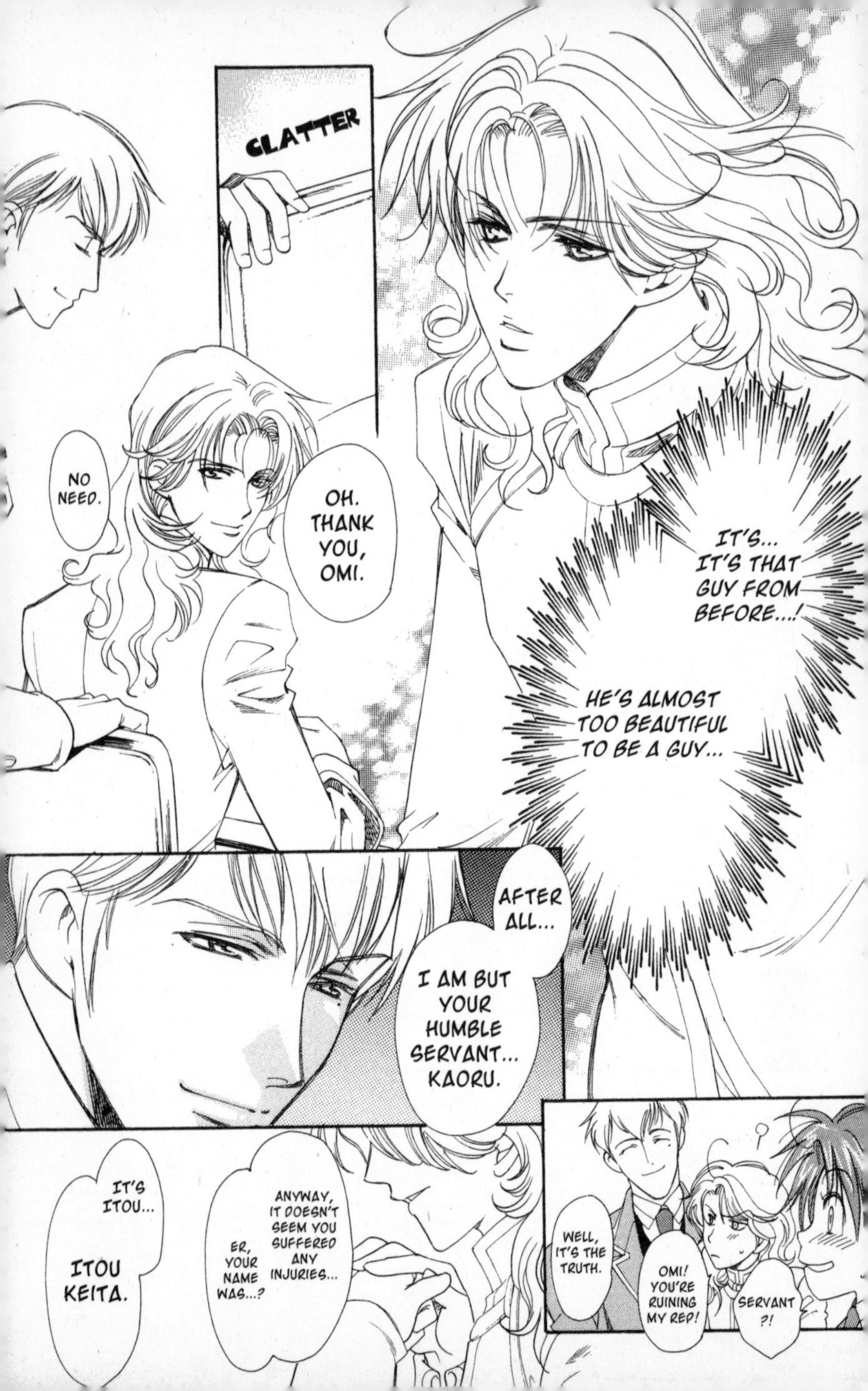
IT'S... IT'S THAT GUY FROM BEFORE...!
HE'S ALMOST TOO BEAUTIFUL TO BE A GUY...
CLATTER
OH. THANK YOU, OMI.
NO NEED.
AFTER ALL...
I AM BUT YOUR HUMBLE SERVANT... KAORU.
SERVANT ?!
OMI! YOU'RE RUINING MY REP!
WELL, IT'S THE TRUTH.
ANYWAY, IT DOESN'T SEEM YOU SUFFERED ANY INJURIES...
ER, YOUR NAME WAS...?
IT'S ITOU...
ITOU KEITA.

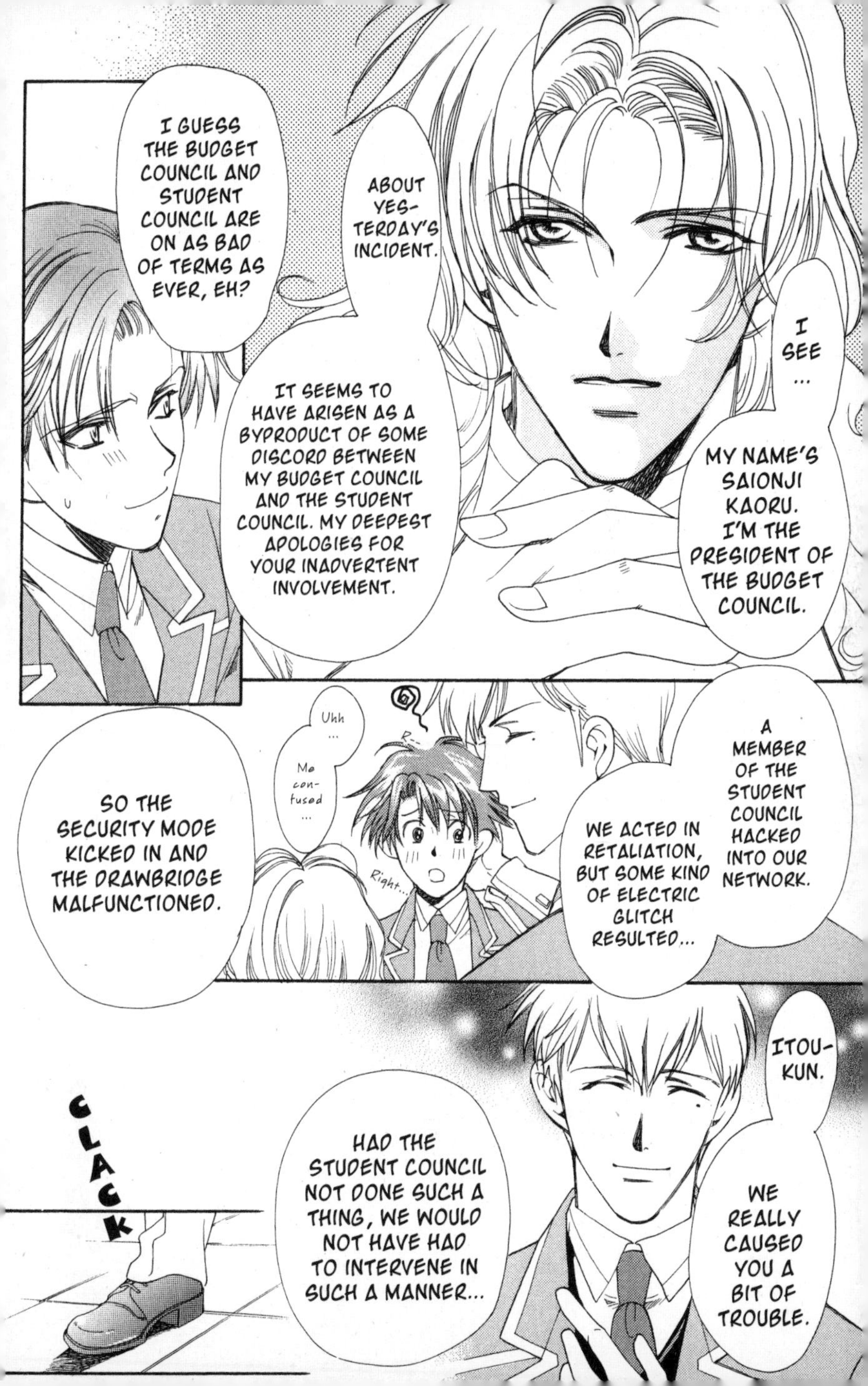
I SEE ...
MY NAME'S SAIONJI KAORU. I'M THE PRESIDENT OF THE BUDGET COUNCIL.
ABOUT YES-TERDAY'S INCIDENT.
IT SEEMS TO HAVE ARISEN AS A BYPRODUCT OF SOME DISCORD BETWEEN MY BUDGET COUNCIL AND THE STUDENT COUNCIL. MY DEEPEST APOLOGIES FOR YOUR INADVERTENT INVOLVEMENT.
I GUESS THE BUDGET COUNCIL AND STUDENT COUNCIL ARE ON AS BAD OF TERMS AS EVER, EH?
A MEMBER OF THE STUDENT COUNCIL HACKED INTO OUR NETWORK.
WE ACTED IN RETALIATION, BUT SOME KIND OF ELECTRIC GLITCH RESULTED...
Uhh ...
Me con-fused ...
Right...
SO THE SECURITY MODE KICKED IN AND THE DRAWBRIDGE MALFUNCTIONED.
ITOU-KUN.
WE REALLY CAUSED YOU A BIT OF TROUBLE.
HAD THE STUDENT COUNCIL NOT DONE SUCH A THING, WE WOULD NOT HAVE HAD TO INTERVENE IN SUCH A MANNER...
CLACK

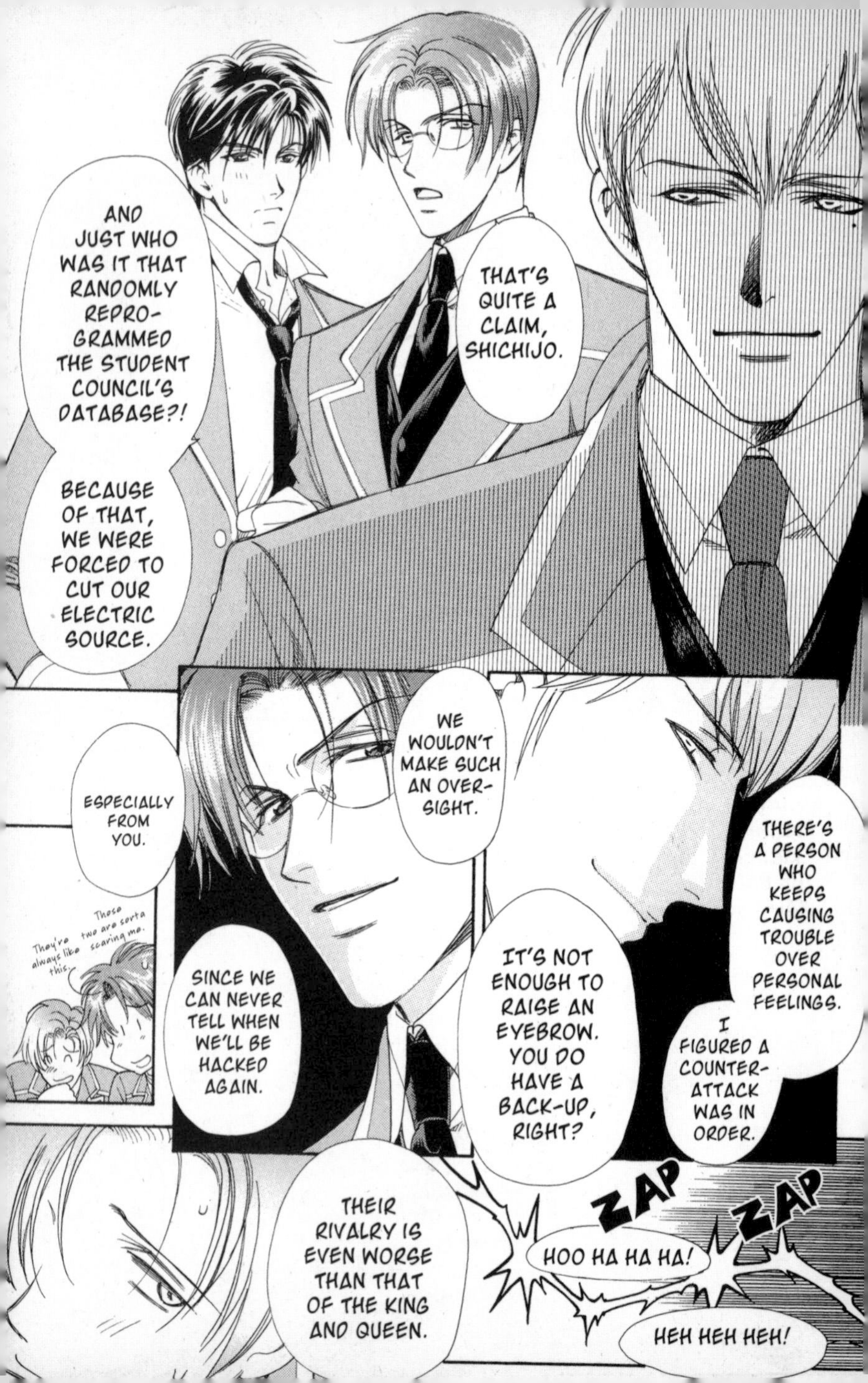
THAT'S QUITE A CLAIM, SHICHIJO.
AND JUST WHO WAS IT THAT RANDOMLY REPRO-GRAMMED THE STUDENT COUNCIL'S DATABASE?!
BECAUSE OF THAT, WE WERE FORCED TO CUT OUR ELECTRIC SOURCE.
THERE'S A PERSON WHO KEEPS CAUSING TROUBLE OVER PERSONAL FEELINGS.
I FIGURED A COUNTER-ATTACK WAS IN ORDER.
IT'S NOT ENOUGH TO RAISE AN EYEBROW. YOU DO HAVE A BACK-UP, RIGHT?
WE WOULDN'T MAKE SUCH AN OVER-SIGHT.
ESPECIALLY FROM YOU.
SINCE WE CAN NEVER TELL WHEN WE'LL BE HACKED AGAIN.
Those two are sorta scaring me.
They're always like this...
ZAP
ZAP
HOO HA HA HA!
HEH HEH HEH!
THEIR RIVALRY IS EVEN WORSE THAN THAT OF THE KING AND QUEEN.

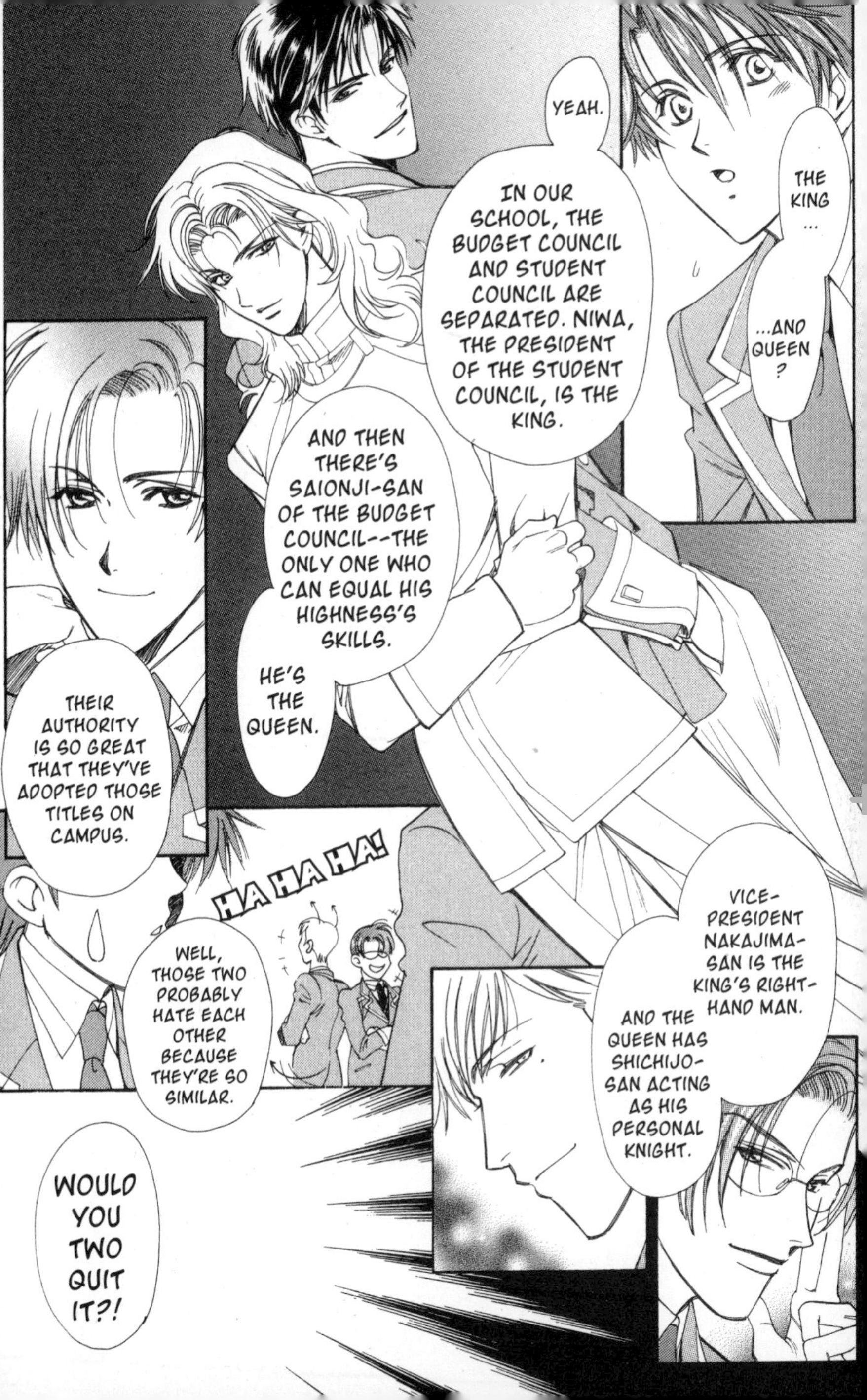
THE KING ...
...AND QUEEN ?
YEAH.
IN OUR SCHOOL, THE BUDGET COUNCIL AND STUDENT COUNCIL ARE SEPARATED. NIWA, THE PRESIDENT OF THE STUDENT COUNCIL, IS THE KING.
AND THEN THERE'S SAIONJI-SAN OF THE BUDGET COUNCIL--THE ONLY ONE WHO CAN EQUAL HIS HIGHNESS'S SKILLS.
HE'S THE QUEEN.
THEIR AUTHORITY IS SO GREAT THAT THEY'VE ADOPTED THOSE TITLES ON CAMPUS.
VICE-PRESIDENT NAKAJIMA-SAN IS THE KING'S RIGHT-HAND MAN.
AND THE QUEEN HAS SHICHIJO-SAN ACTING AS HIS PERSONAL KNIGHT.
HA HA HA!
WELL, THOSE TWO PROBABLY HATE EACH OTHER BECAUSE THEY'RE SO SIMILAR.
WOULD YOU TWO QUIT IT?!

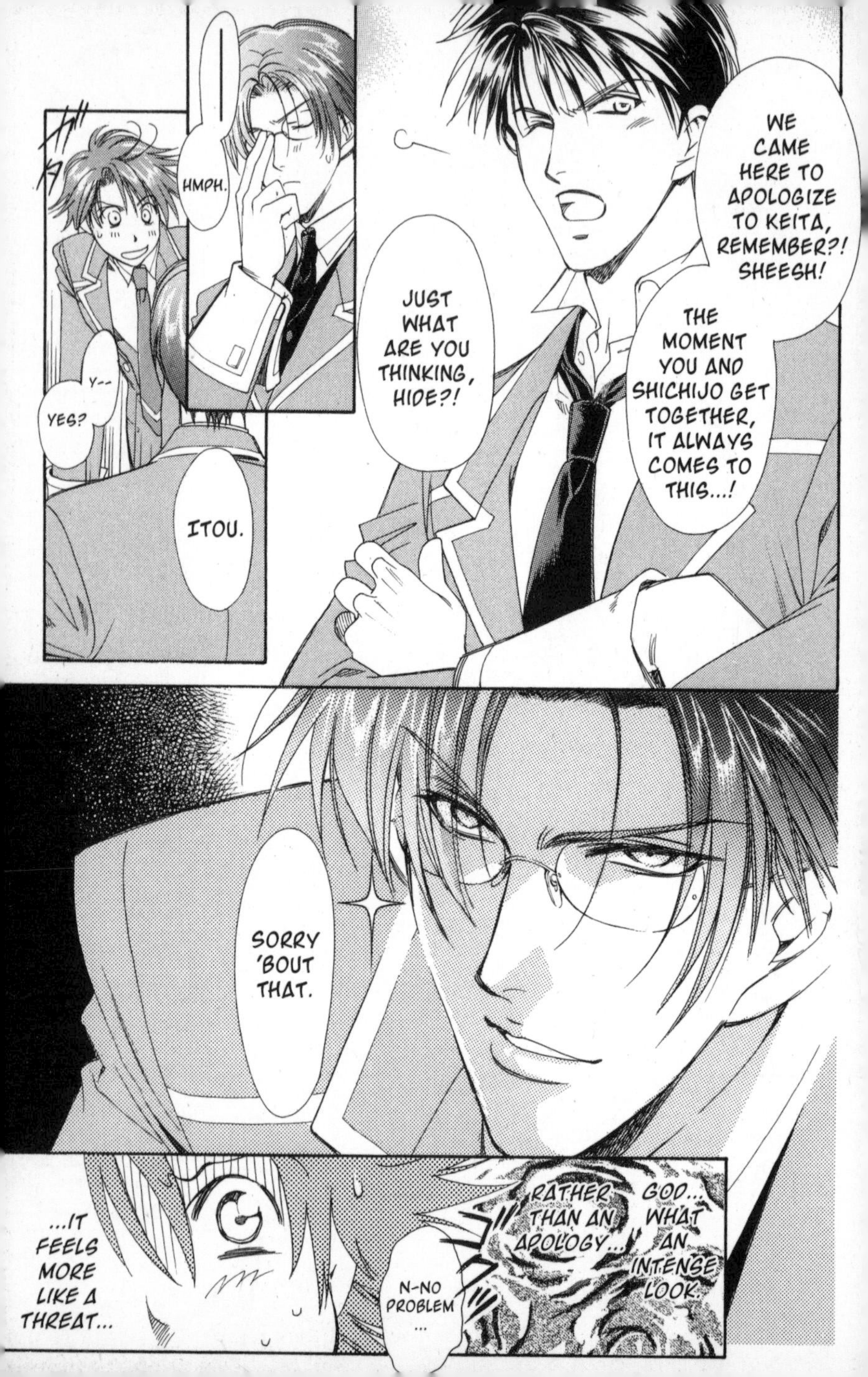
WE CAME HERE TO APOLOGIZE TO KEITA, REMEMBER?! SHEESH!
THE MOMENT YOU AND SHICHIJO GET TOGETHER, IT ALWAYS COMES TO THIS...!
JUST WHAT ARE YOU THINKING, HIDE?!
...
HMPH.
ITOU.
Y-- YES?
SORRY 'BOUT THAT.
GOD... WHAT AN INTENSE LOOK
RATHER THAN AN APOLOGY...
N-NO PROBLEM ...
...IT FEELS MORE LIKE A THREAT...

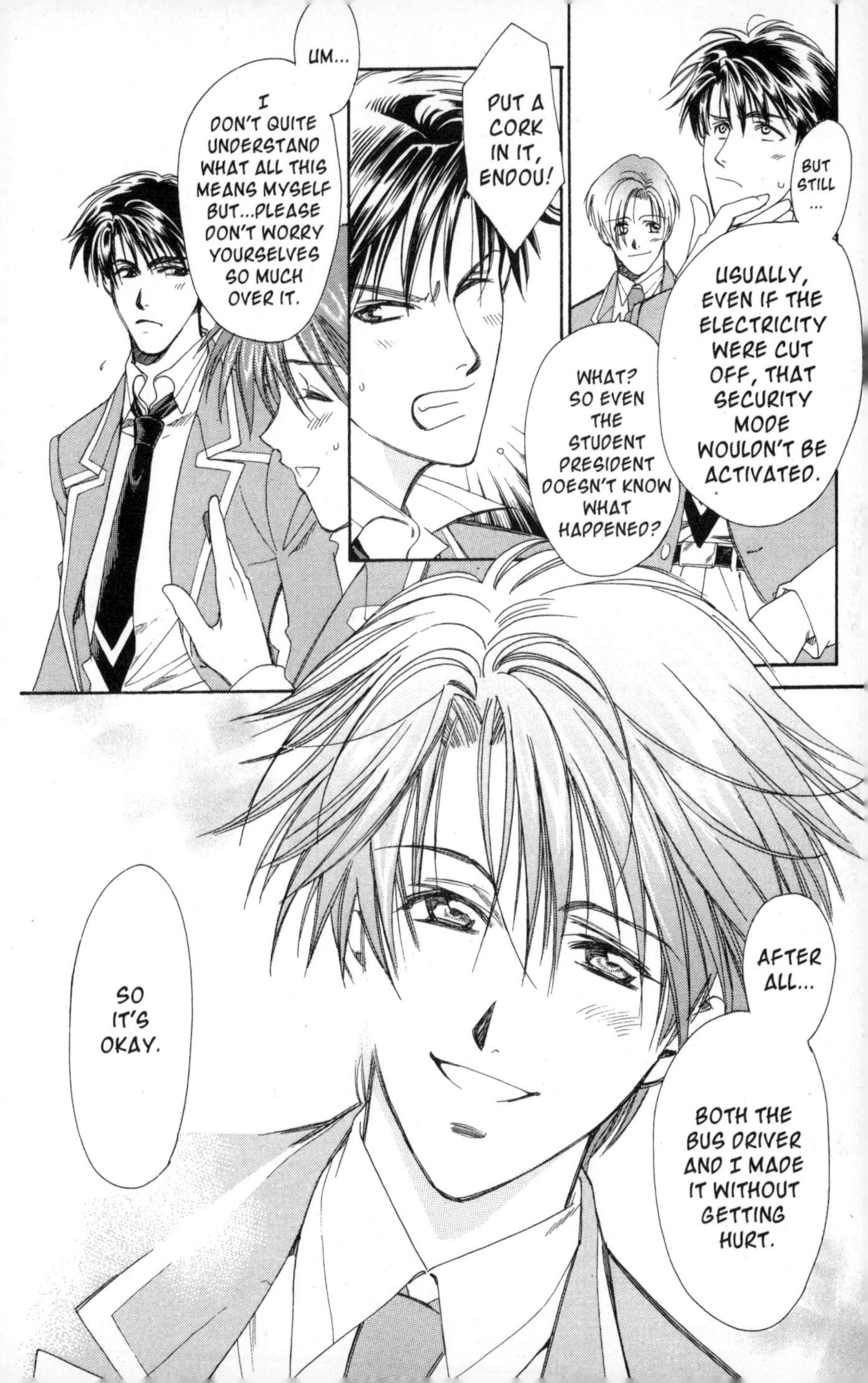
BUT STILL...
USUALLY, EVEN IF THE ELECTRICITY WERE CUT OFF, THAT SECURITY MODE WOULDN'T BE ACTIVATED.
WHAT? SO EVEN THE STUDENT PRESIDENT DOESN'T KNOW WHAT HAPPENED?
PUT A CORK IN IT, ENDOU!
UM...
I DON'T QUITE UNDERSTAND WHAT ALL THIS MEANS MYSELF BUT...PLEASE DON'T WORRY YOURSELVES SO MUCH OVER IT.
AFTER ALL...
BOTH THE BUS DRIVER AND I MADE IT WITHOUT GETTING HURT.
SO IT'S OKAY.

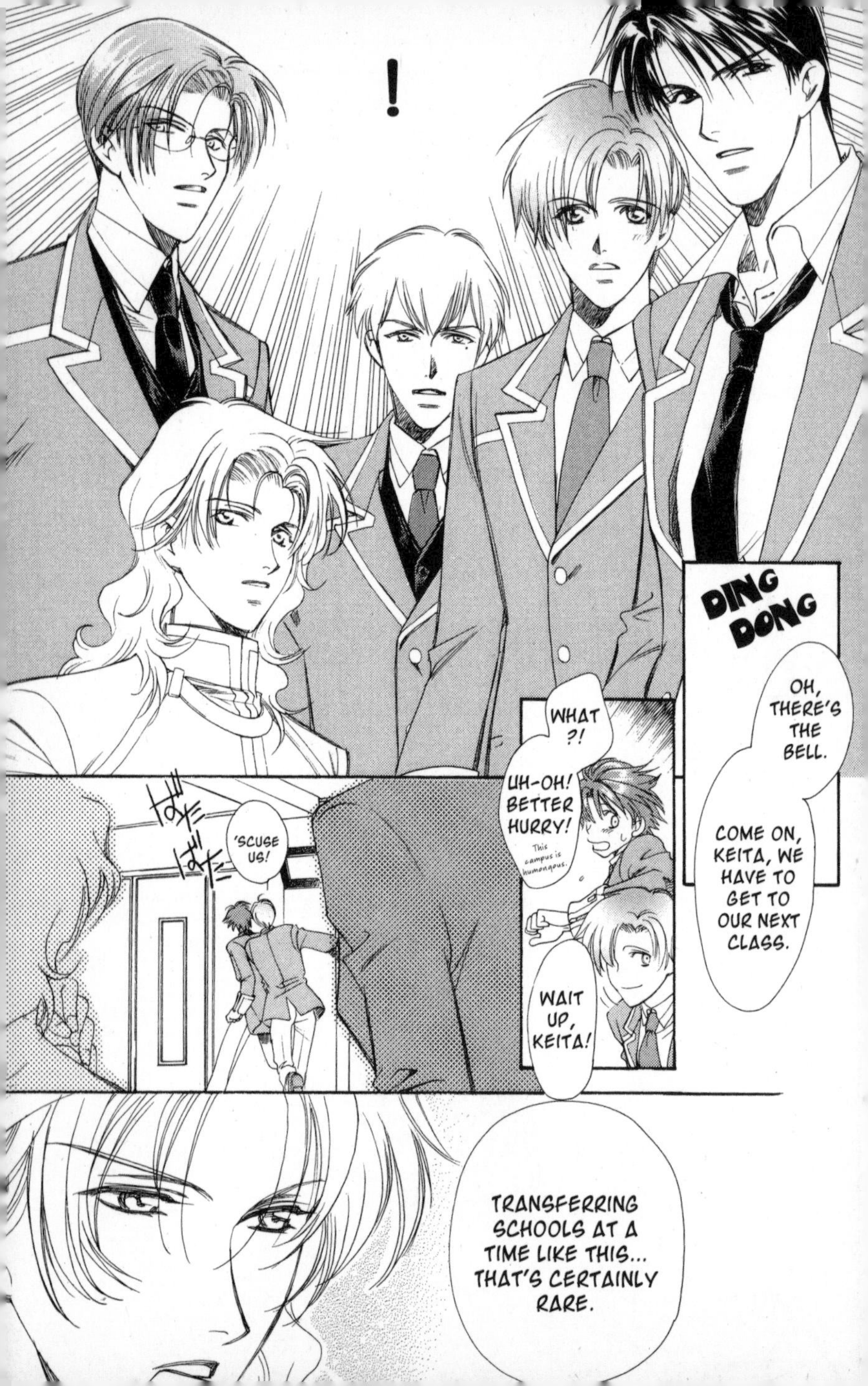
!
DING DONG
OH, THERE'S THE BELL.
COME ON, KEITA, WE HAVE TO GET TO OUR NEXT CLASS.
WHAT ?!
UH-OH! BETTER HURRY!
This campus is humongous.
WAIT UP, KEITA!
'SCUSE US!
TRANSFERRING SCHOOLS AT A TIME LIKE THIS... THAT'S CERTAINLY RARE.

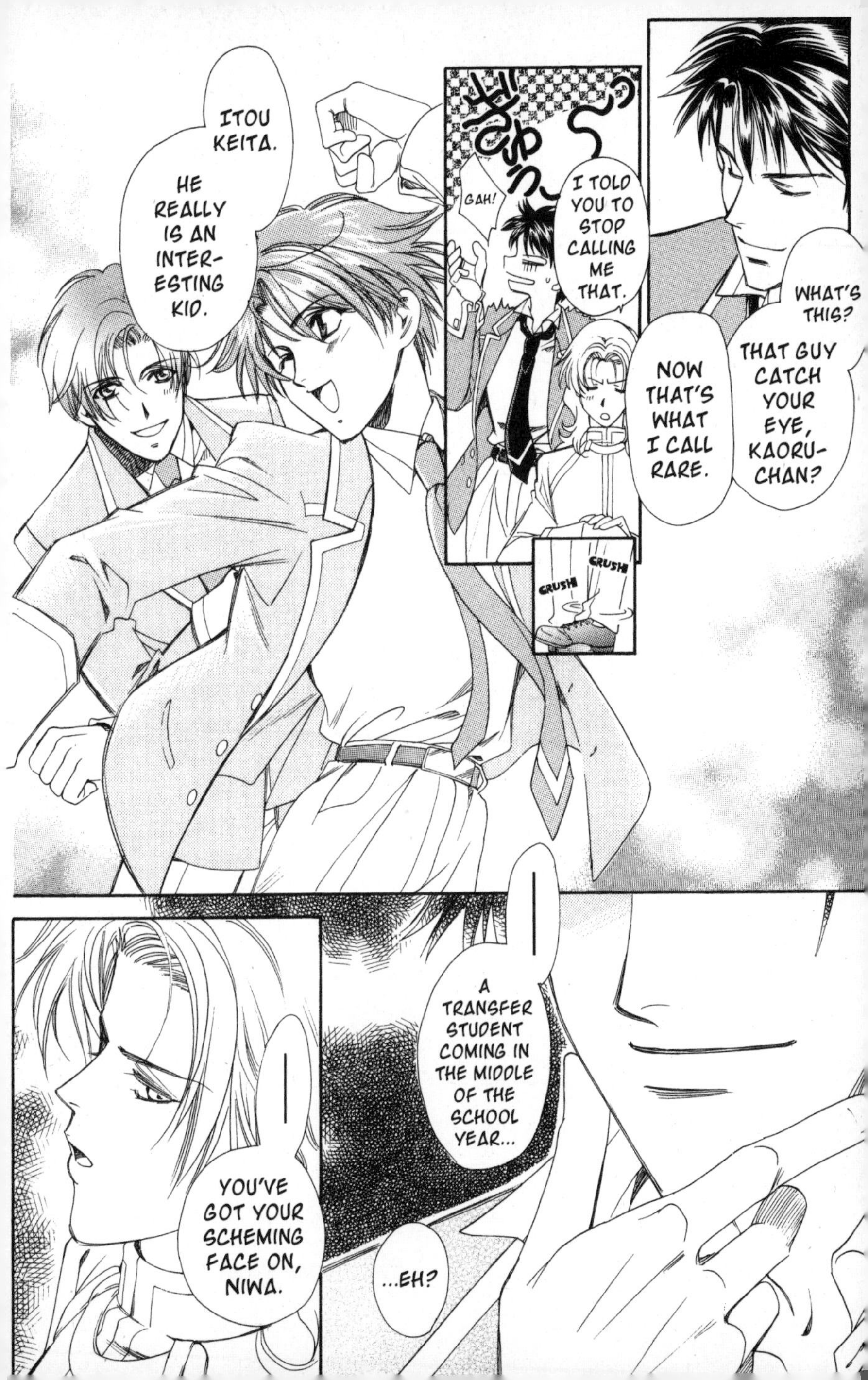
WHAT'S THIS?
THAT GUY CATCH YOUR EYE, KAORU-CHAN?
NOW THAT'S WHAT I CALL RARE.
ぎゅう～
GAH!
I TOLD YOU TO STOP CALLING ME THAT.
CRUSH
CRUSH
ITOU KEITA.
HE REALLY IS AN INTERESTING KID.
A TRANSFER STUDENT COMING IN THE MIDDLE OF THE SCHOOL YEAR...
...EH?
YOU'VE GOT YOUR SCHEMING FACE ON, NIWA.

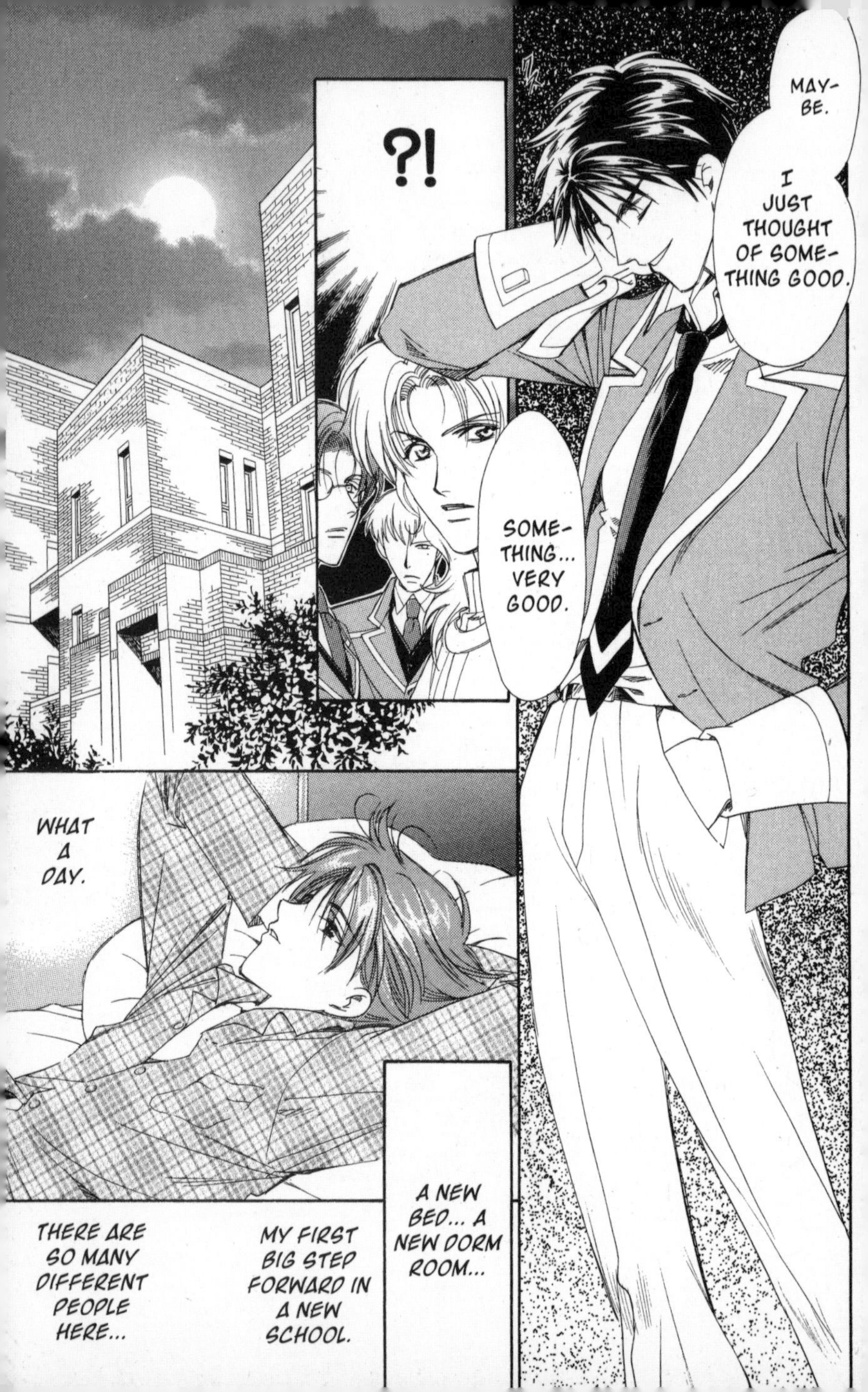
MAY-BE.
I JUST THOUGHT OF SOME-THING GOOD.
SOME-THING... VERY GOOD.
?!
WHAT A DAY.
A NEW BED... A NEW DORM ROOM...
MY FIRST BIG STEP FORWARD IN A NEW SCHOOL.
THERE ARE SO MANY DIFFERENT PEOPLE HERE...

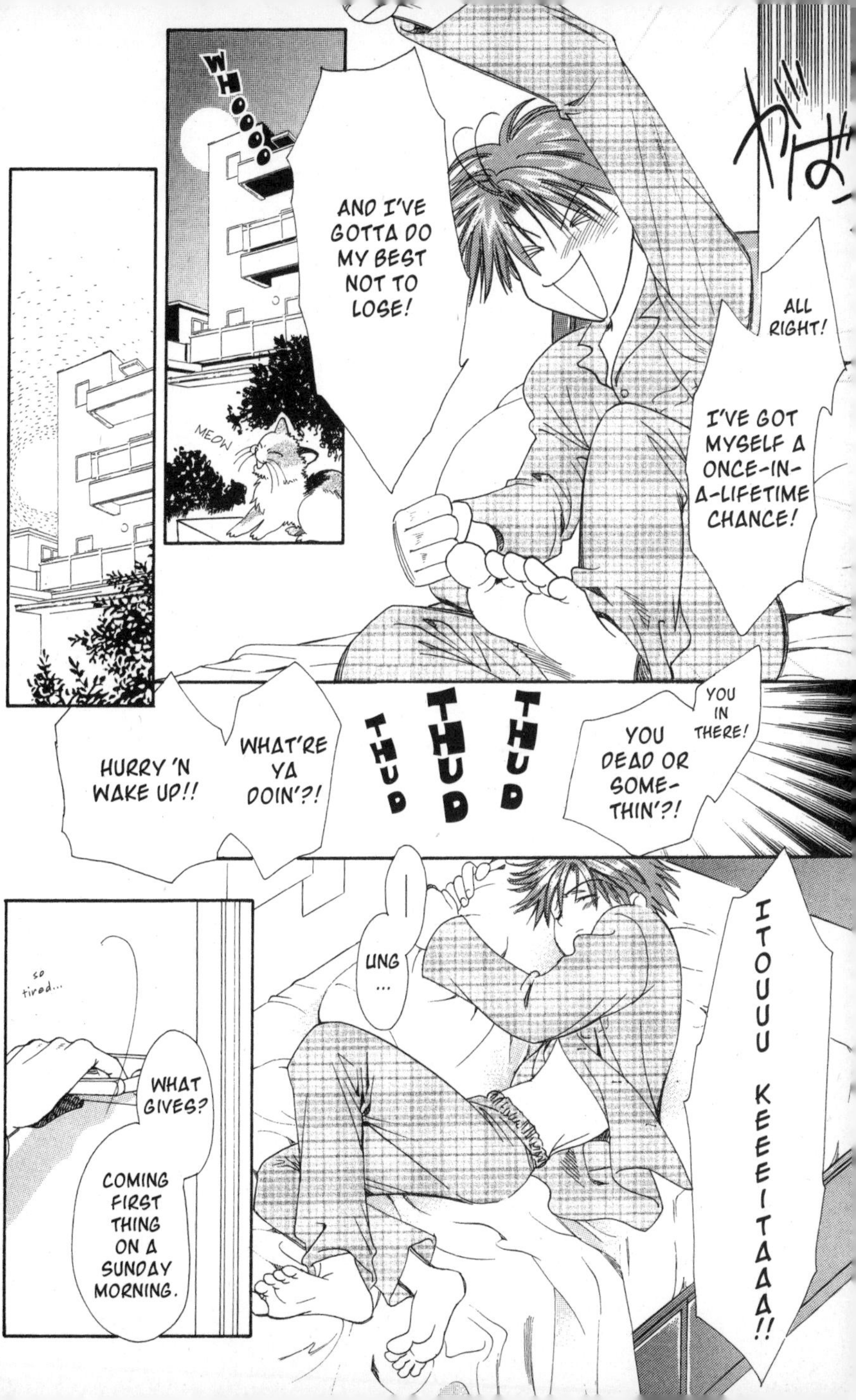
がばっ
ALL RIGHT!
I'VE GOT MYSELF A ONCE-IN-A-LIFETIME CHANCE!
AND I'VE GOTTA DO MY BEST NOT TO LOSE!
WHOOOOO
MEOW
YOU IN THERE!
YOU DEAD OR SOMETHIN'?!
THUD THUD THUD
WHAT'RE YA DOIN'?!
HURRY 'N WAKE UP!!
ITOUUU KEEEITAAA!!
UNG ...
so tired...
WHAT GIVES?
COMING FIRST THING ON A SUNDAY MORNING.

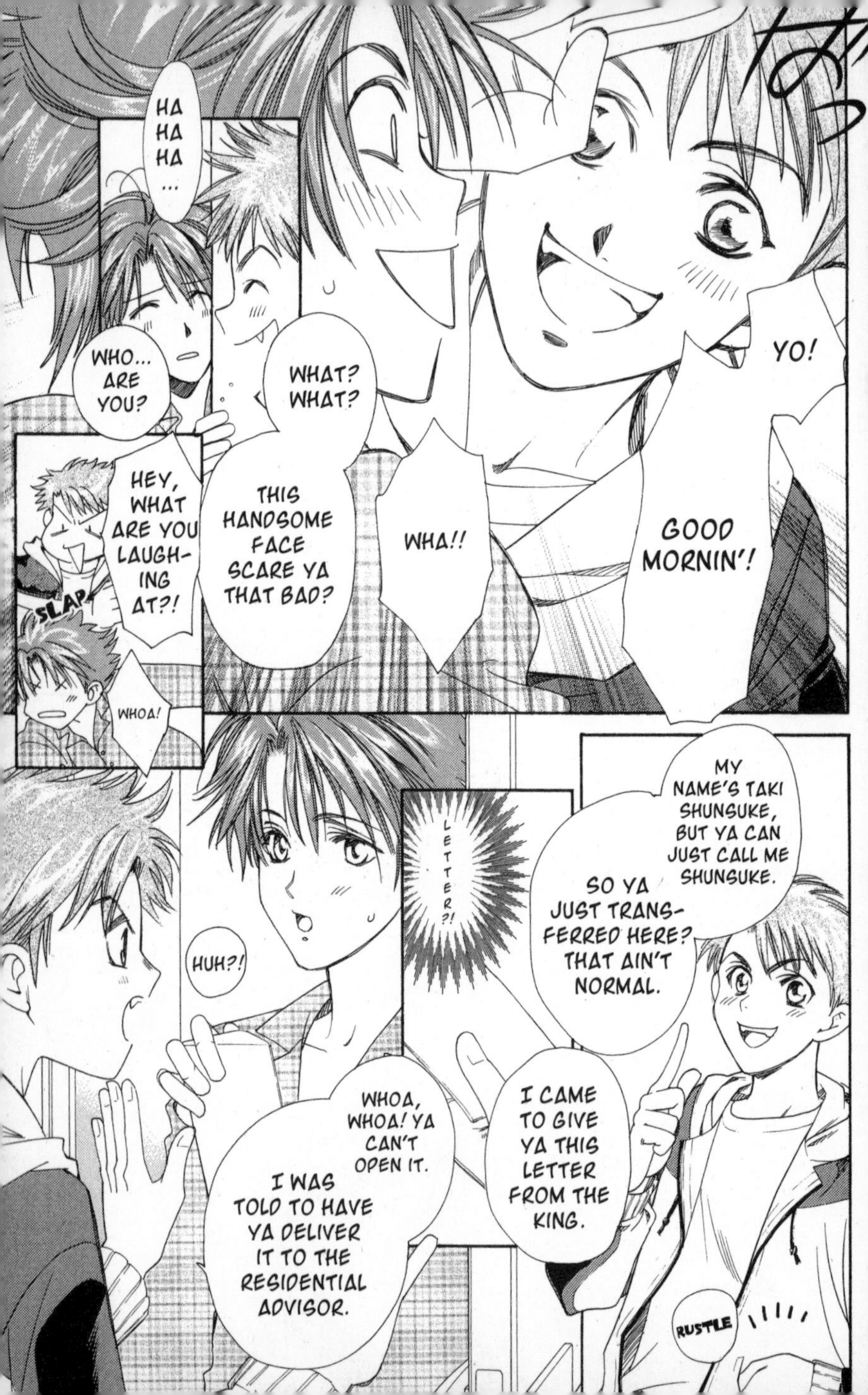
YO!
GOOD MORNIN'!
WHA!!
HA HA HA ...
WHO... ARE YOU?
WHAT? WHAT?
THIS HANDSOME FACE SCARE YA THAT BAD?
HEY, WHAT ARE YOU LAUGH-ING AT?!
SLAP
WHOA!
MY NAME'S TAKI SHUNSUKE, BUT YA CAN JUST CALL ME SHUNSUKE.
SO YA JUST TRANS-FERRED HERE? THAT AIN'T NORMAL.
I CAME TO GIVE YA THIS LETTER FROM THE KING.
RUSTLE
LETTER?!
HUH?!
WHOA, WHOA! YA CAN'T OPEN IT.
I WAS TOLD TO HAVE YA DELIVER IT TO THE RESIDENTIAL ADVISOR.

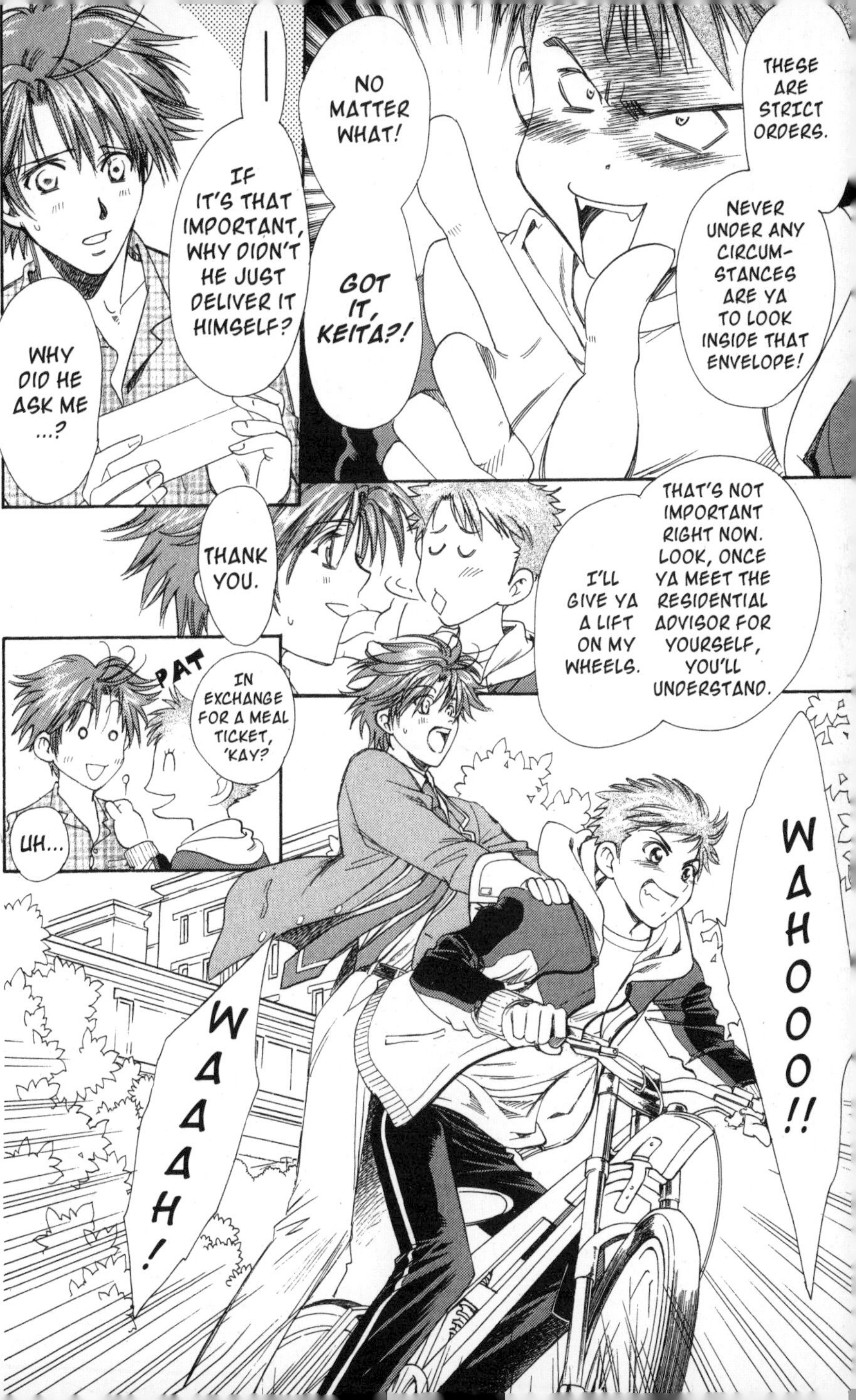
THESE ARE STRICT ORDERS.
NEVER UNDER ANY CIRCUM-STANCES ARE YA TO LOOK INSIDE THAT ENVELOPE!
NO MATTER WHAT!
GOT IT, KEITA?!
—
IF IT'S THAT IMPORTANT, WHY DIDN'T HE JUST DELIVER IT HIMSELF?
WHY DID HE ASK ME ...?
THAT'S NOT IMPORTANT RIGHT NOW. LOOK, ONCE YA MEET THE RESIDENTIAL ADVISOR FOR YOURSELF, YOU'LL UNDERSTAND.
I'LL GIVE YA A LIFT ON MY WHEELS.
THANK YOU.
PAT
IN EXCHANGE FOR A MEAL TICKET, 'KAY?
UH...
WAHOOOO!!
WAAAAH!

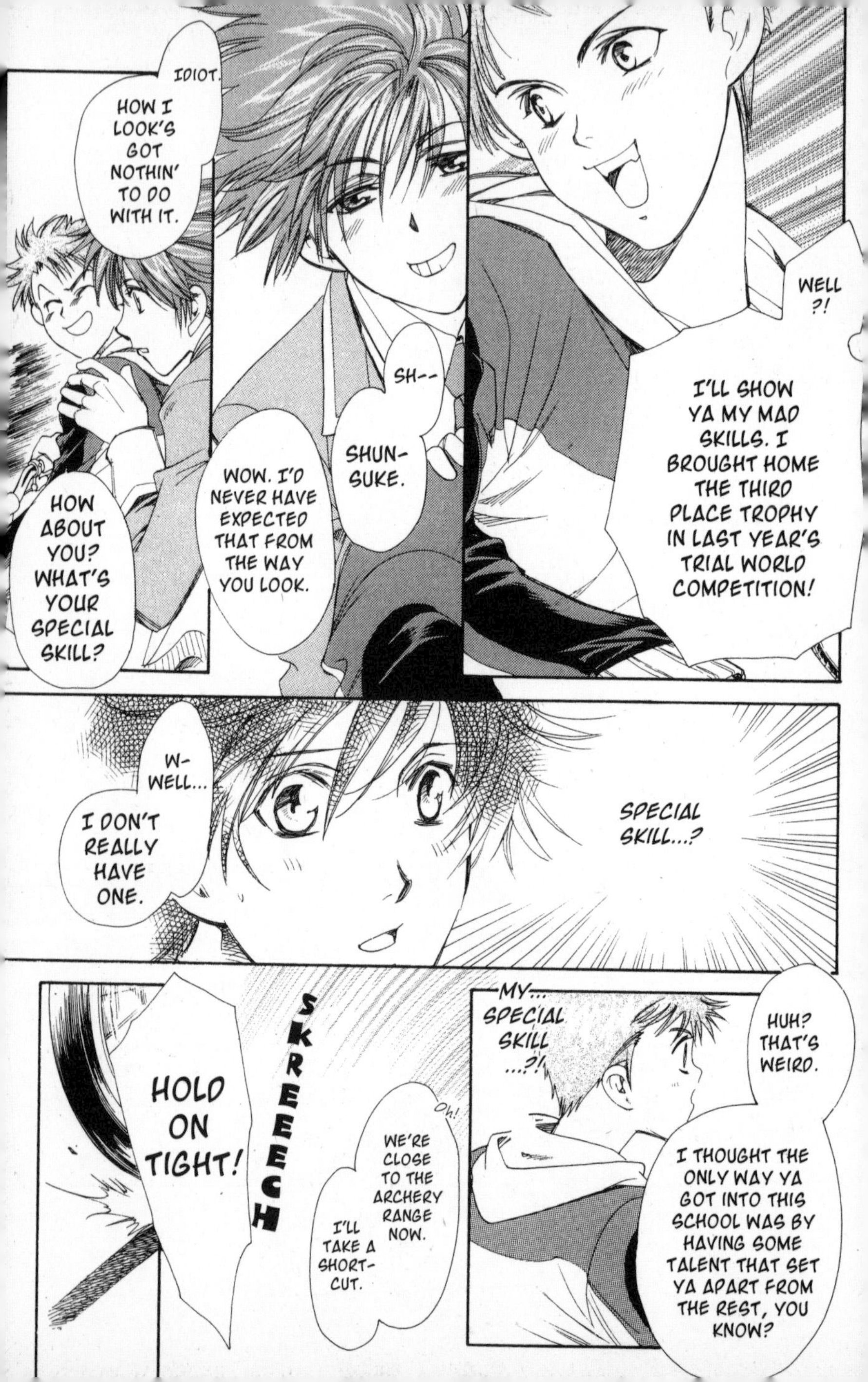
WELL ?!
I'LL SHOW YA MY MAD SKILLS. I BROUGHT HOME THE THIRD PLACE TROPHY IN LAST YEAR'S TRIAL WORLD COMPETITION!
SH--
SHUN-SUKE.
WOW. I'D NEVER HAVE EXPECTED THAT FROM THE WAY YOU LOOK.
IDIOT.
HOW I LOOK'S GOT NOTHIN' TO DO WITH IT.
HOW ABOUT YOU? WHAT'S YOUR SPECIAL SKILL?
SPECIAL SKILL...?
W-WELL...
I DON'T REALLY HAVE ONE.
HUH? THAT'S WEIRD.
I THOUGHT THE ONLY WAY YA GOT INTO THIS SCHOOL WAS BY HAVING SOME TALENT THAT SET YA APART FROM THE REST, YOU KNOW?
MY... SPECIAL SKILL ...?!
Oh!
WE'RE CLOSE TO THE ARCHERY RANGE NOW.
I'LL TAKE A SHORT-CUT.
SKREEECH
HOLD ON TIGHT!

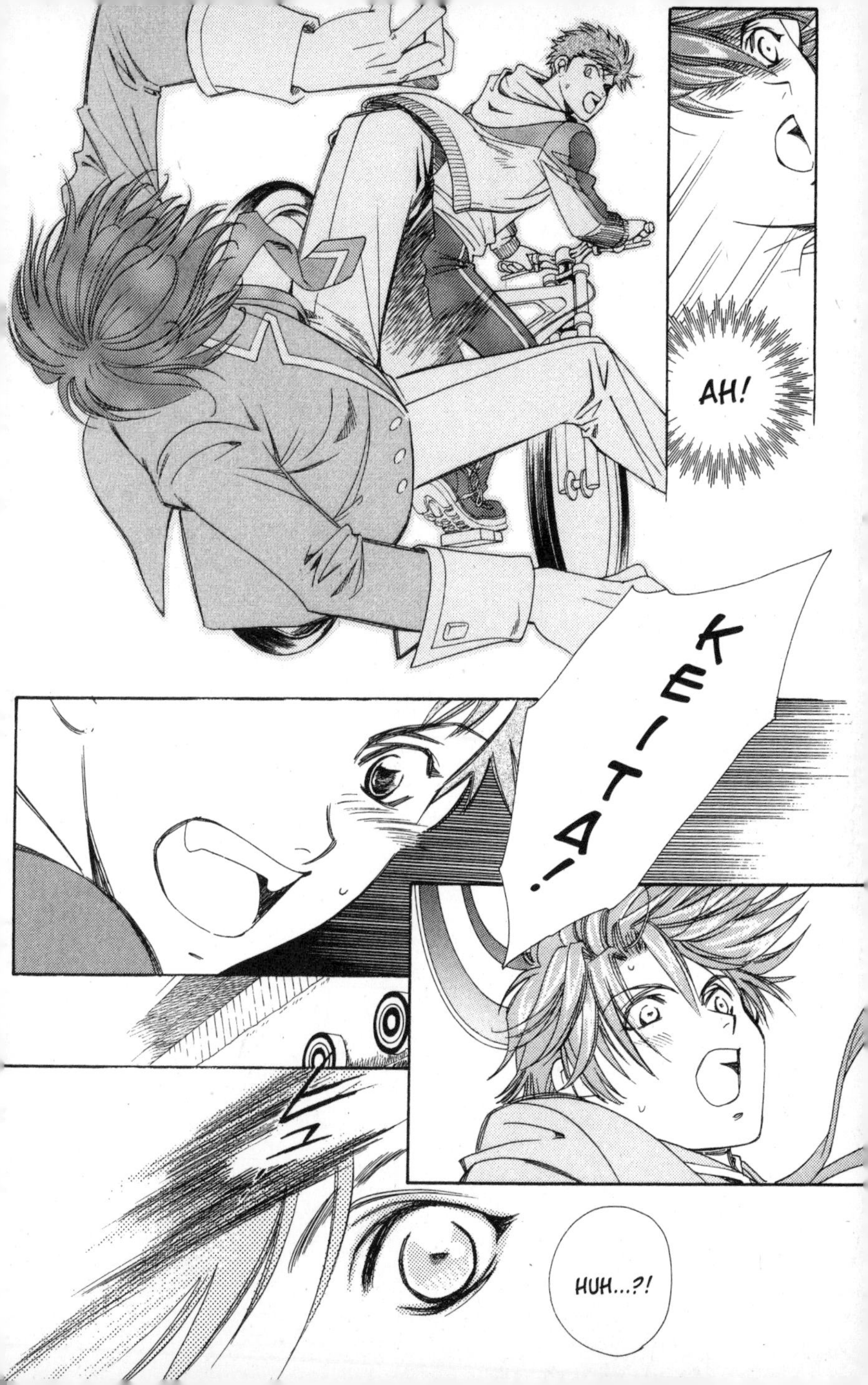
AH!
KEITA-!
HUH...?!

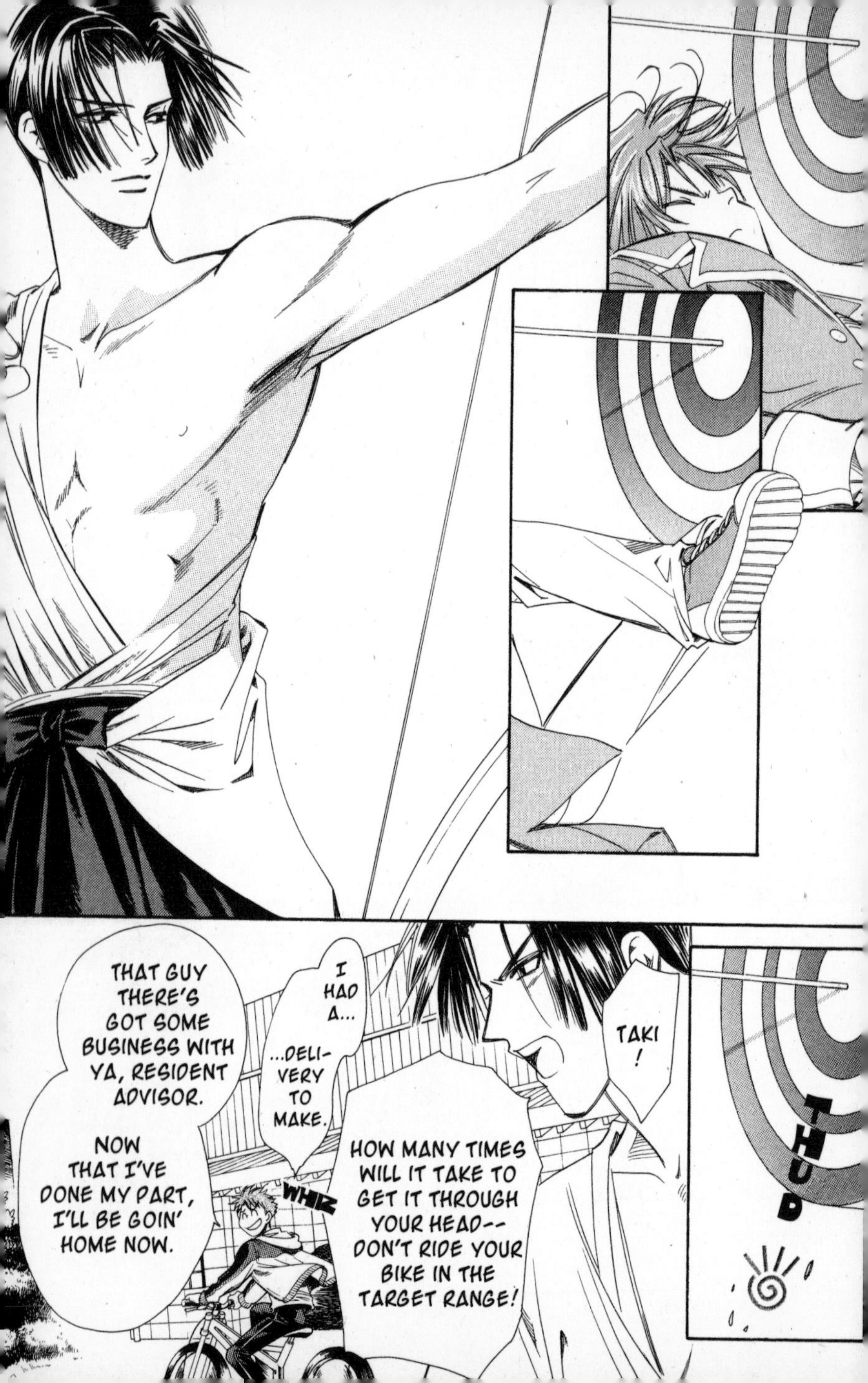
THUD
TAKI!
HOW MANY TIMES WILL IT TAKE TO GET IT THROUGH YOUR HEAD-- DON'T RIDE YOUR BIKE IN THE TARGET RANGE!
I HAD A...
...DELI-VERY TO MAKE.
WHIZ
THAT GUY THERE'S GOT SOME BUSINESS WITH YA, RESIDENT ADVISOR.
NOW THAT I'VE DONE MY PART, I'LL BE GOIN' HOME NOW.

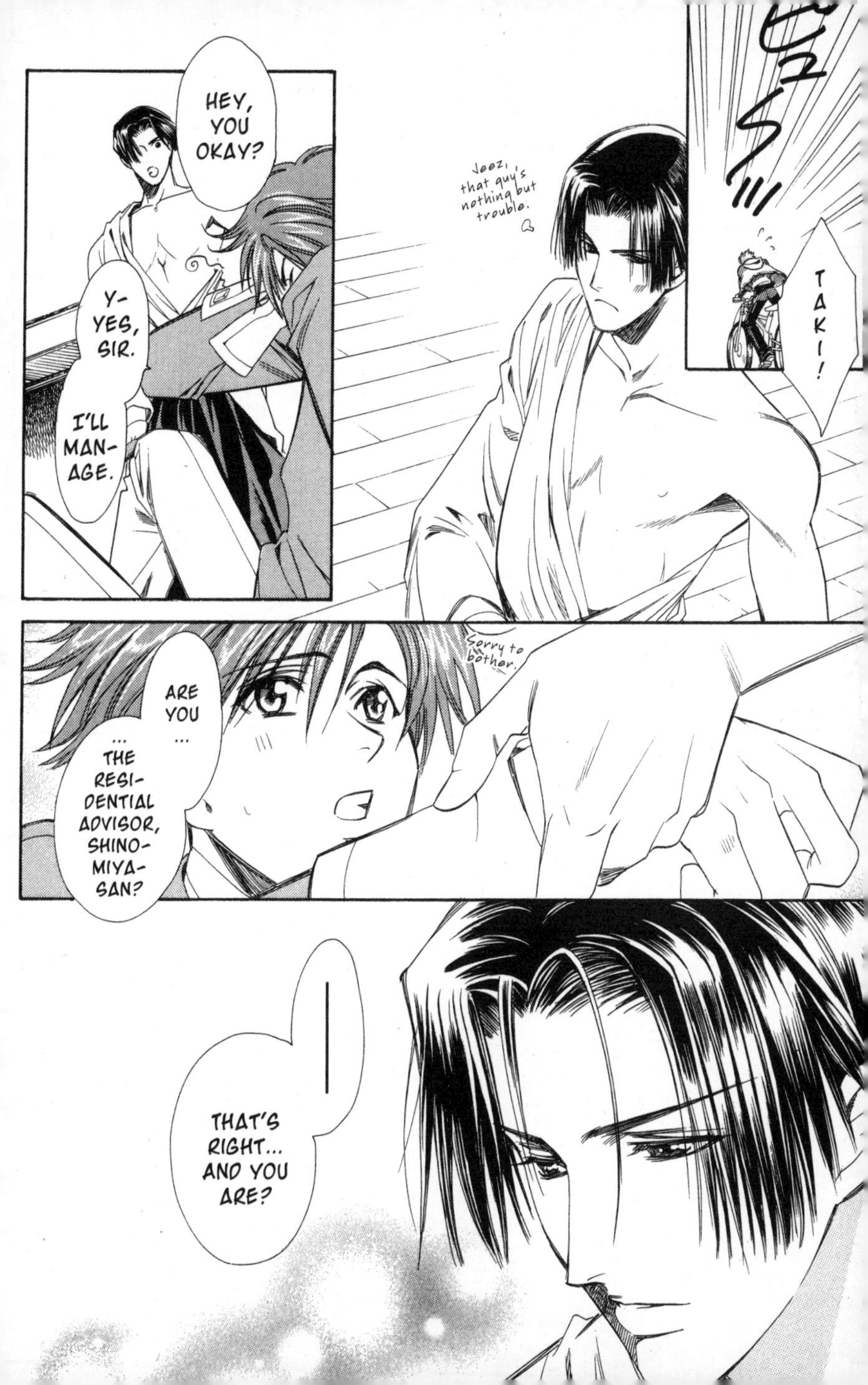
TAKI!
Jeez, that guy's nothing but trouble.
HEY, YOU OKAY?
Y-YES, SIR.
I'LL MANAGE.
Sorry to bother.
ARE YOU ... THE RESIDENTIAL ADVISOR, SHINOMIYA-SAN?
— THAT'S RIGHT... AND YOU ARE?

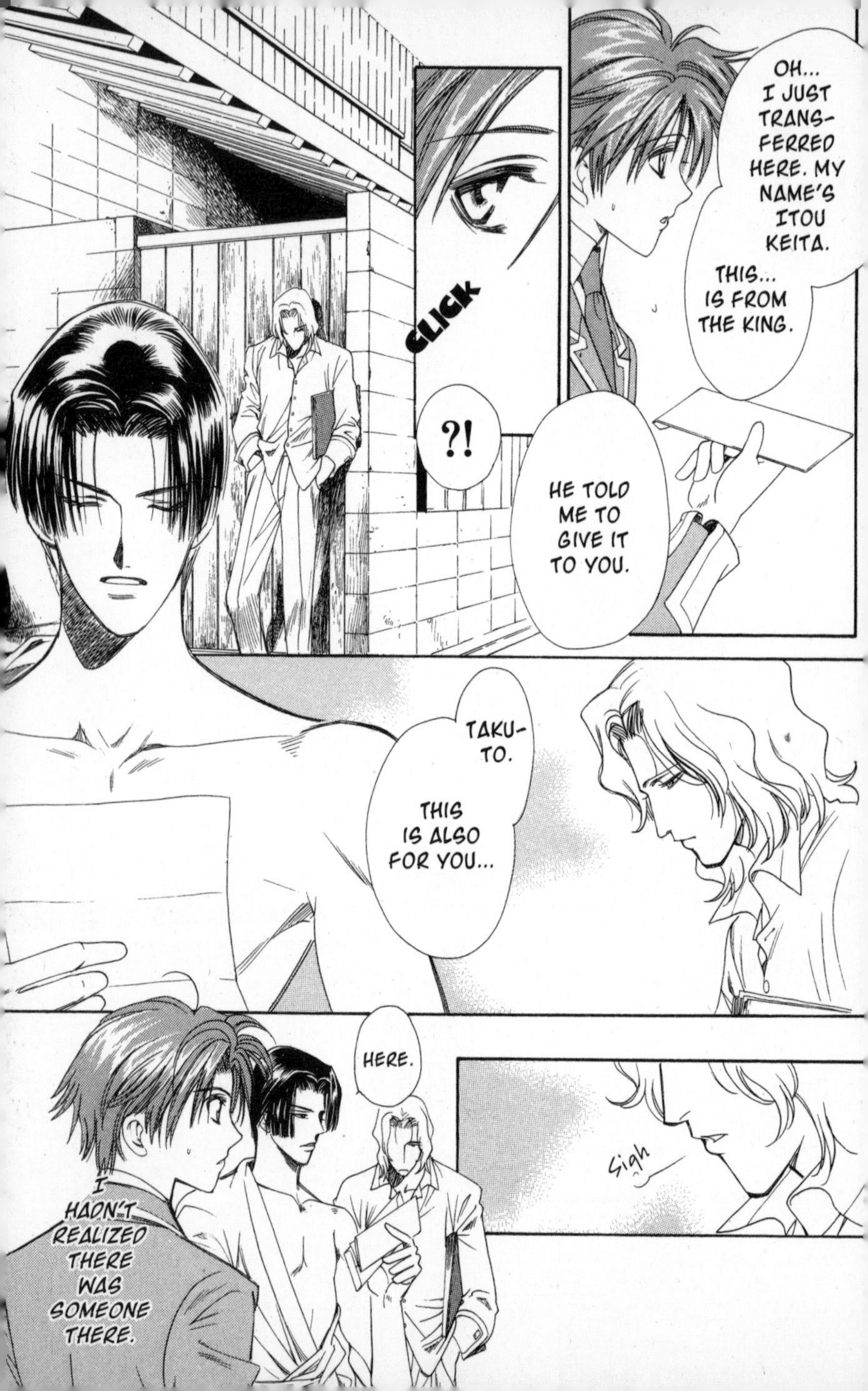
OH... I JUST TRANS-FERRED HERE. MY NAME'S ITOU KEITA.
THIS... IS FROM THE KING.
HE TOLD ME TO GIVE IT TO YOU.
CLICK
?!
TAKU-TO.
THIS IS ALSO FOR YOU...
Sigh
HERE.
I HADN'T REALIZED THERE WAS SOMEONE THERE.

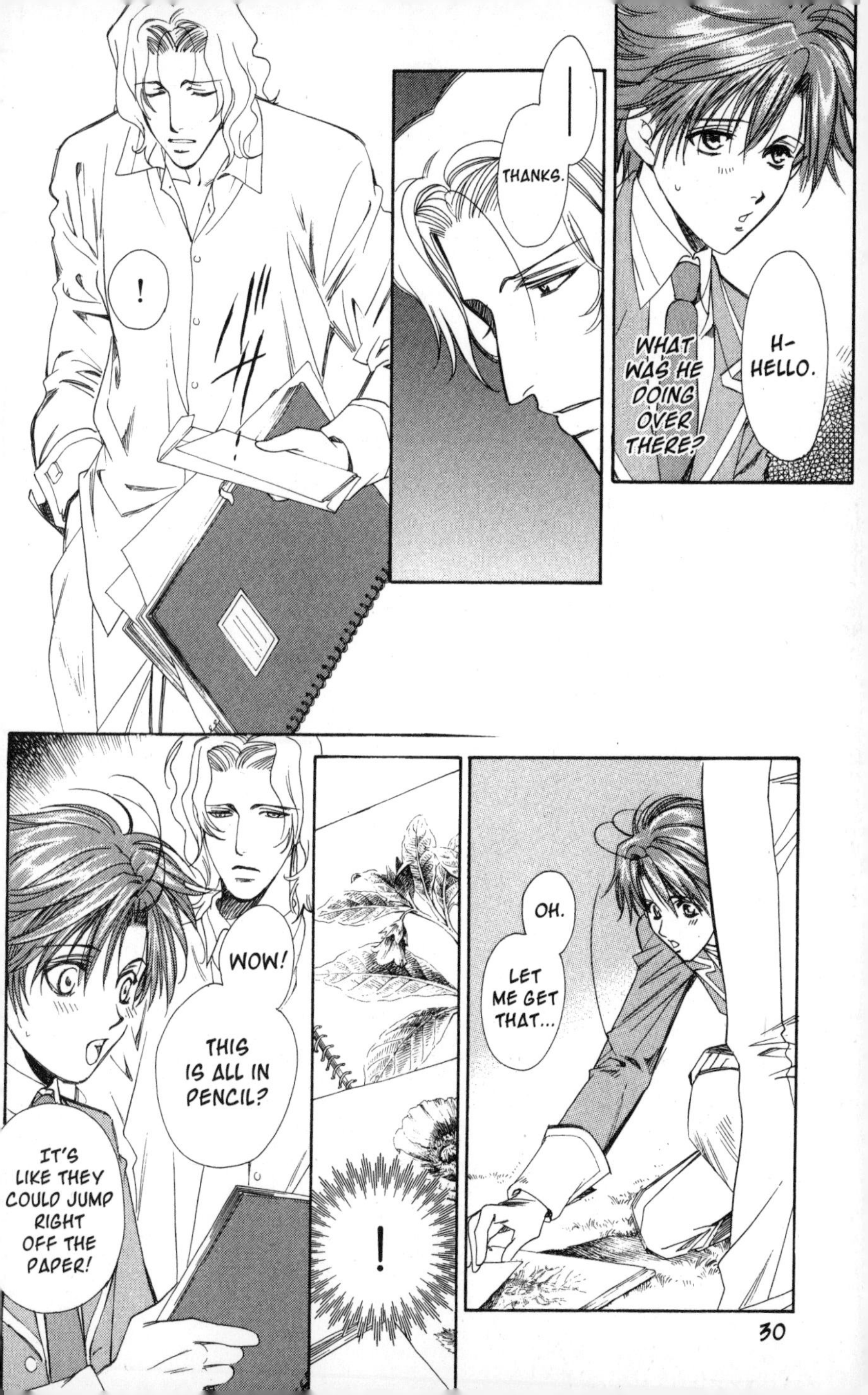
H-HELLO.
WHAT WAS HE DOING OVER THERE?
— THANKS.
!
OH.
LET ME GET THAT...
!
WOW!
THIS IS ALL IN PENCIL?
IT'S LIKE THEY COULD JUMP RIGHT OFF THE PAPER!

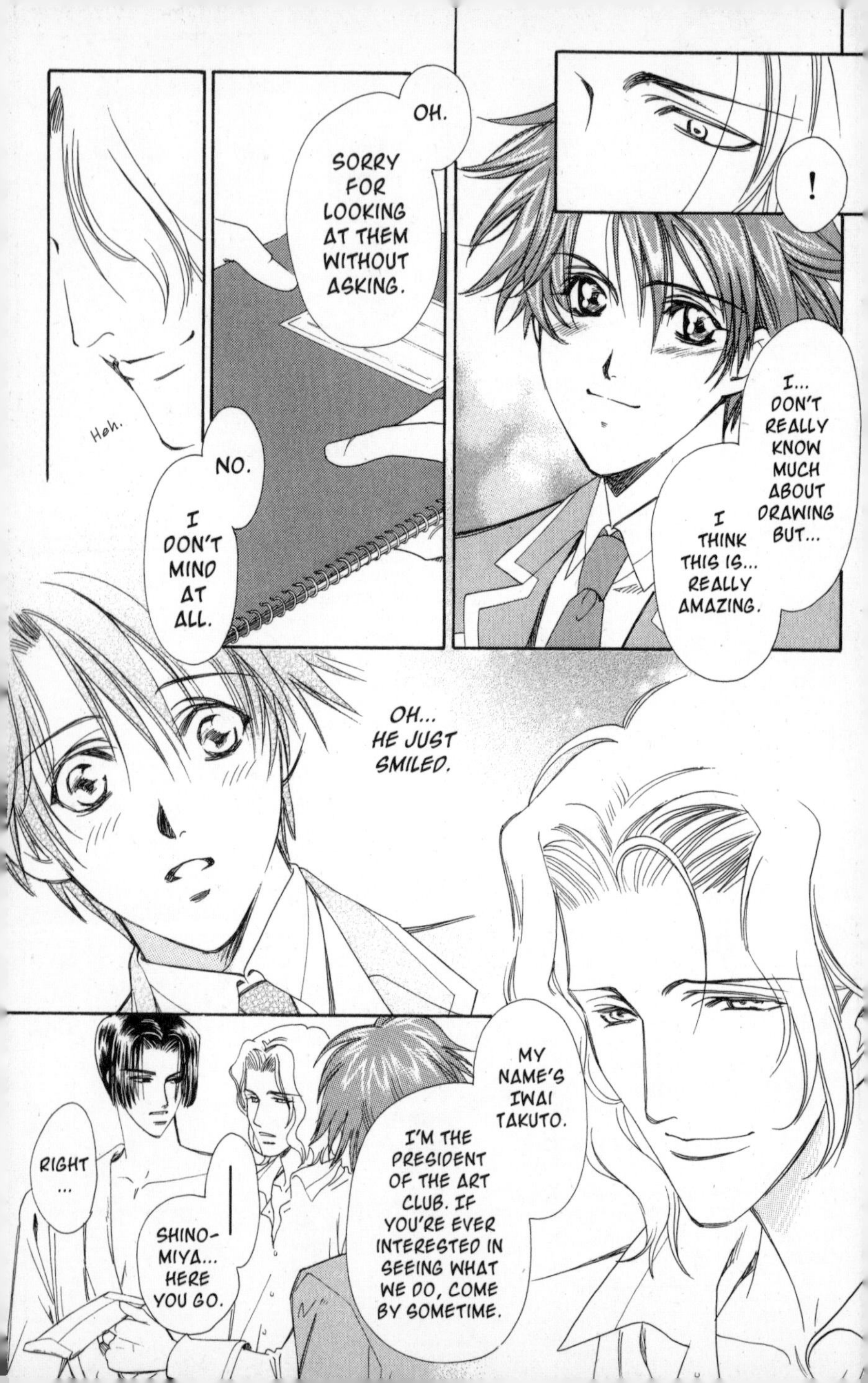
!
I... DON'T REALLY KNOW MUCH ABOUT DRAWING BUT...
I THINK THIS IS... REALLY AMAZING.
OH.
SORRY FOR LOOKING AT THEM WITHOUT ASKING.
NO.
I DON'T MIND AT ALL.
Heh.
OH... HE JUST SMILED.
MY NAME'S IWAI TAKUTO.
I'M THE PRESIDENT OF THE ART CLUB. IF YOU'RE EVER INTERESTED IN SEEING WHAT WE DO, COME BY SOMETIME.
SHINOMIYA... HERE YOU GO.
RIGHT...

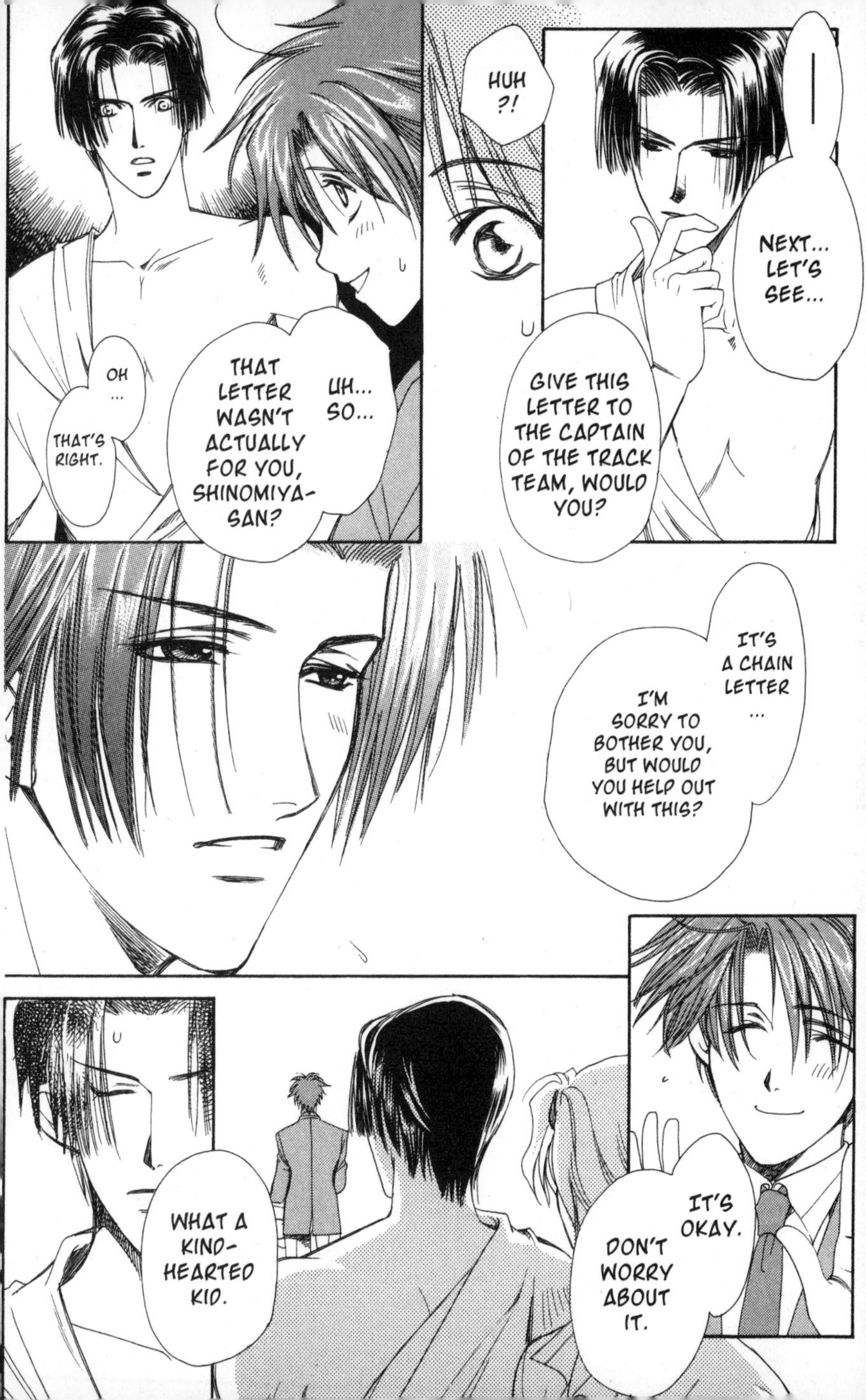
NEXT... LET'S SEE...
GIVE THIS LETTER TO THE CAPTAIN OF THE TRACK TEAM, WOULD YOU?
HUH ?!
UH... SO...
THAT LETTER WASN'T ACTUALLY FOR YOU, SHINOMIYA-SAN?
OH ... THAT'S RIGHT.
IT'S A CHAIN LETTER ...
I'M SORRY TO BOTHER YOU, BUT WOULD YOU HELP OUT WITH THIS?
IT'S OKAY.
DON'T WORRY ABOUT IT.
WHAT A KIND-HEARTED KID.

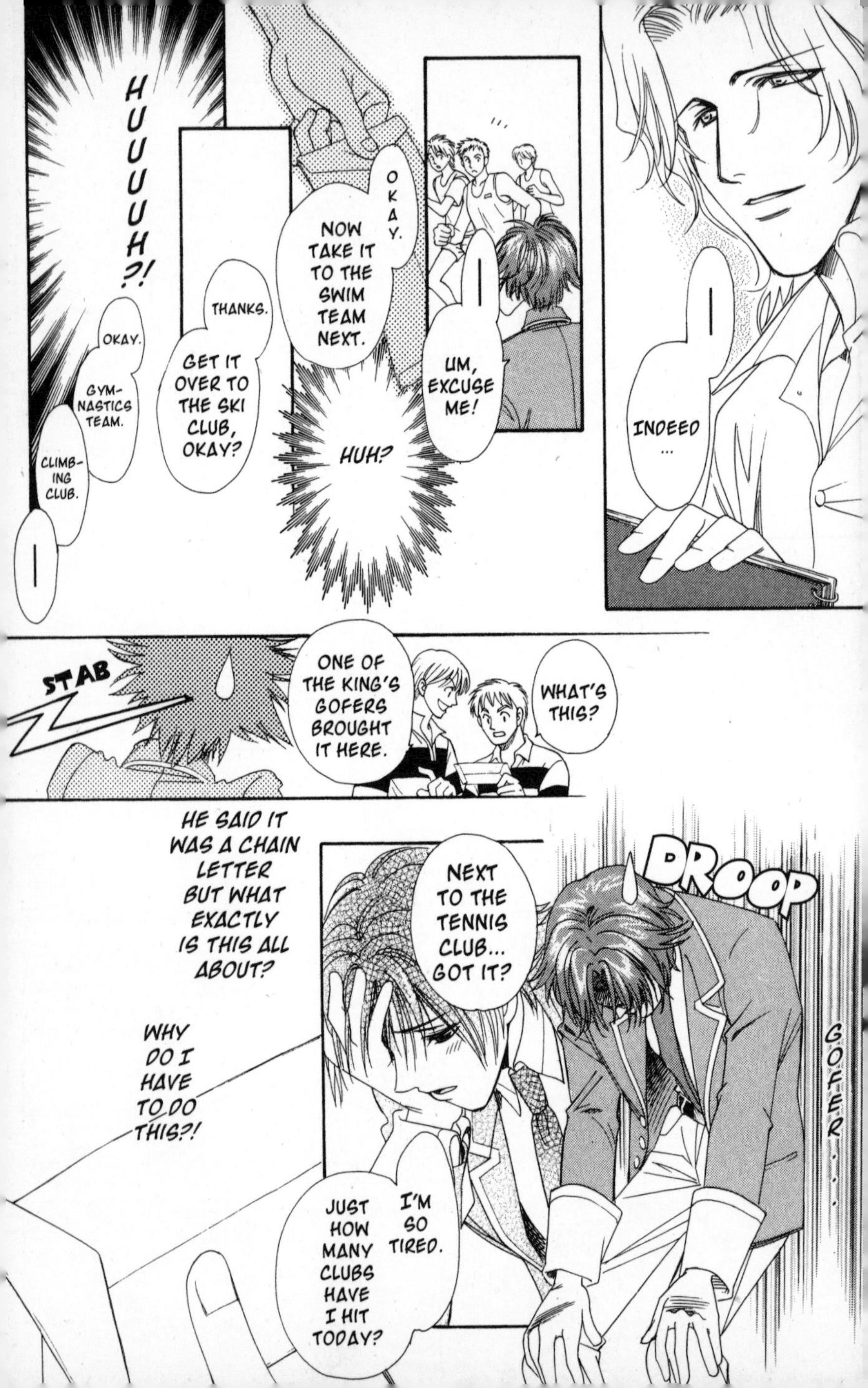
INDEED ...
UM, EXCUSE ME!
OKAY.
NOW TAKE IT TO THE SWIM TEAM NEXT.
HUH?
THANKS.
GET IT OVER TO THE SKI CLUB, OKAY?
OKAY.
GYM-NASTICS TEAM.
CLIMB-ING CLUB.
HUUUUUH?!
WHAT'S THIS?
ONE OF THE KING'S GOFERS BROUGHT IT HERE.
STAB
DROOP
GOFER...
NEXT TO THE TENNIS CLUB... GOT IT?
HE SAID IT WAS A CHAIN LETTER BUT WHAT EXACTLY IS THIS ALL ABOUT?
WHY DO I HAVE TO DO THIS?!
I'M SO TIRED.
JUST HOW MANY CLUBS HAVE I HIT TODAY?

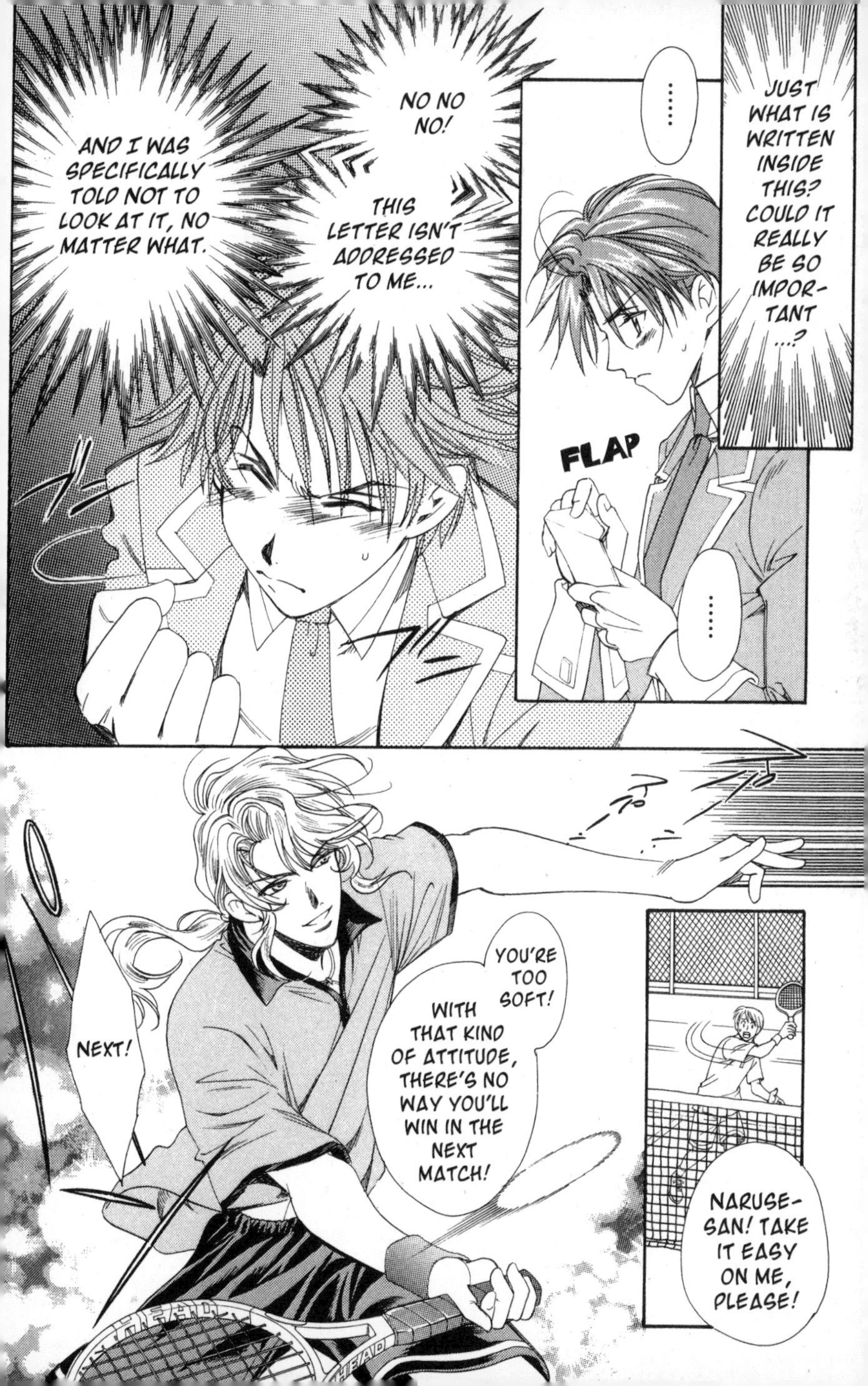
JUST WHAT IS WRITTEN INSIDE THIS? COULD IT REALLY BE SO IMPOR-TANT ...?
......
FLAP
......
NO NO NO!
THIS LETTER ISN'T ADDRESSED TO ME...
AND I WAS SPECIFICALLY TOLD NOT TO LOOK AT IT, NO MATTER WHAT.
NARUSE-SAN! TAKE IT EASY ON ME, PLEASE!
YOU'RE TOO SOFT!
WITH THAT KIND OF ATTITUDE, THERE'S NO WAY YOU'LL WIN IN THE NEXT MATCH!
NEXT!

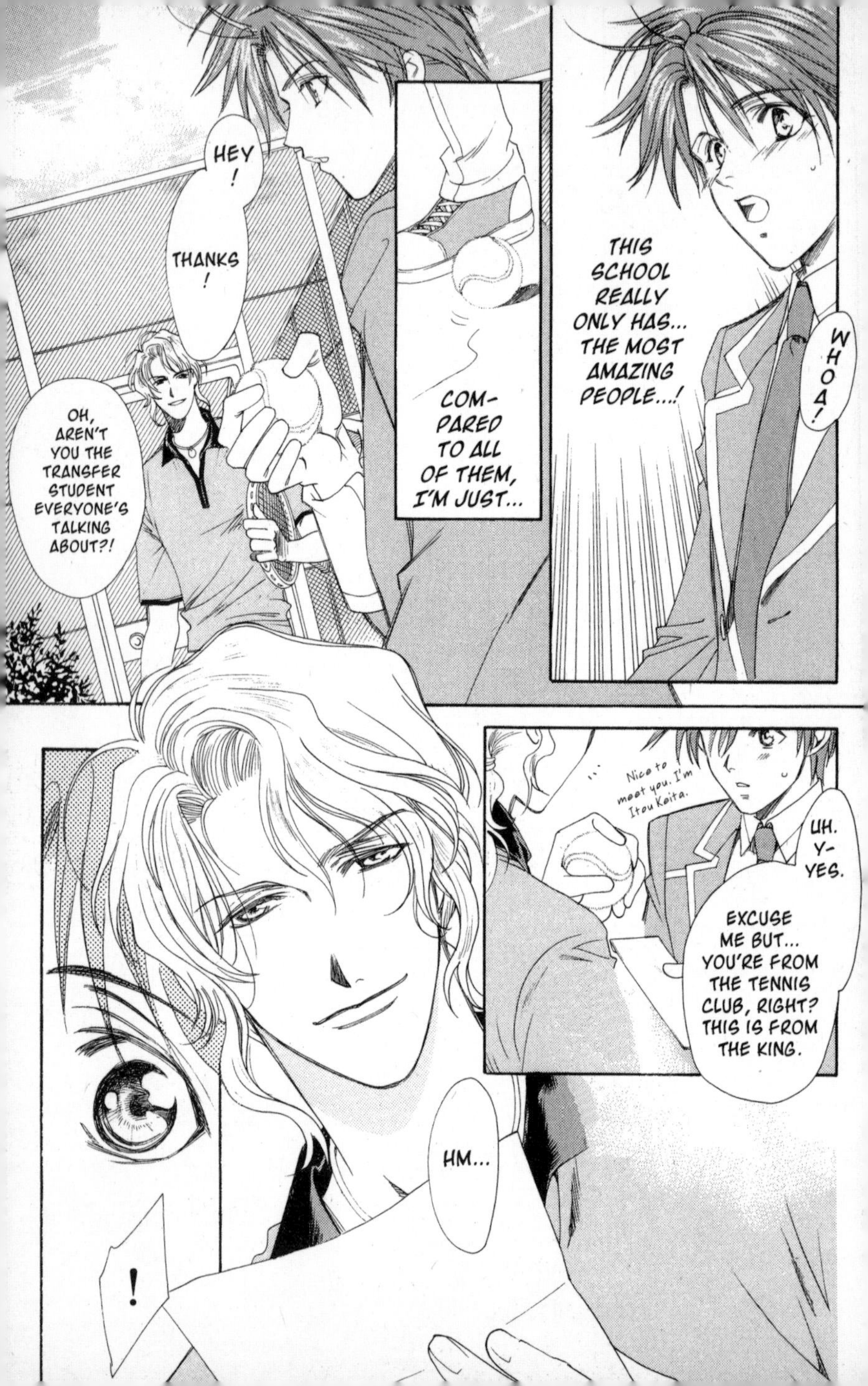
WHOA!
THIS SCHOOL REALLY ONLY HAS... THE MOST AMAZING PEOPLE...!
COMPARED TO ALL OF THEM, I'M JUST...
HEY!
THANKS!
OH, AREN'T YOU THE TRANSFER STUDENT EVERYONE'S TALKING ABOUT?!
UH. Y-YES.
EXCUSE ME BUT... YOU'RE FROM THE TENNIS CLUB, RIGHT? THIS IS FROM THE KING.
Nice to meet you. I'm Itou Keita.
HM...
!

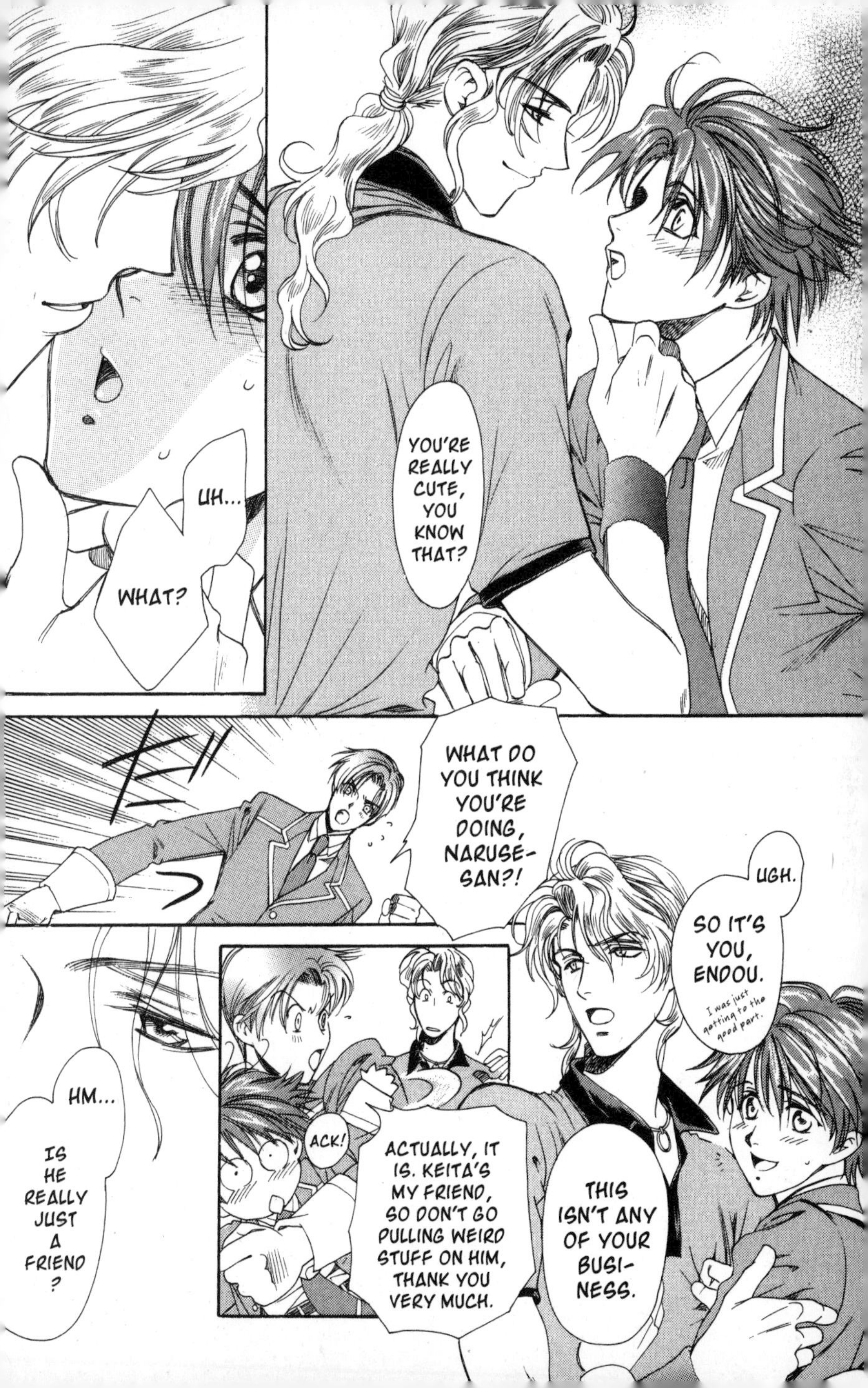
YOU'RE REALLY CUTE, YOU KNOW THAT?
UH...
WHAT?
WHAT DO YOU THINK YOU'RE DOING, NARUSE-SAN?!
UGH.
SO IT'S YOU, ENDOU.
I was just getting to the good part.
THIS ISN'T ANY OF YOUR BUSI-NESS.
ACK!
ACTUALLY, IT IS. KEITA'S MY FRIEND, SO DON'T GO PULLING WEIRD STUFF ON HIM, THANK YOU VERY MUCH.
HM...
IS HE REALLY JUST A FRIEND?

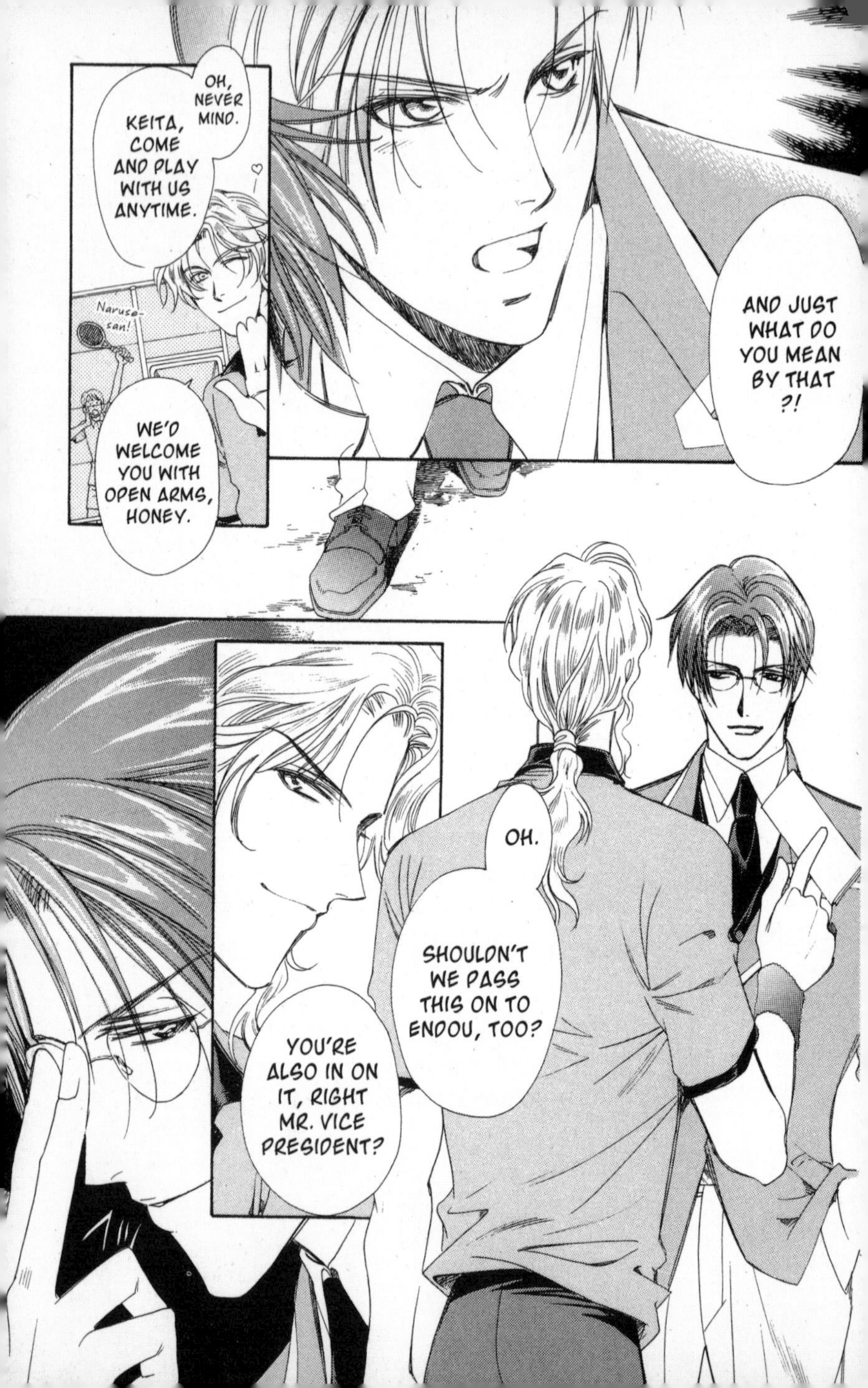
AND JUST WHAT DO YOU MEAN BY THAT?!
OH, NEVER MIND.
KEITA, COME AND PLAY WITH US ANYTIME.
Naruse-san!
WE'D WELCOME YOU WITH OPEN ARMS, HONEY.
OH.
SHOULDN'T WE PASS THIS ON TO ENDOU, TOO?
YOU'RE ALSO IN ON IT, RIGHT MR. VICE PRESIDENT?

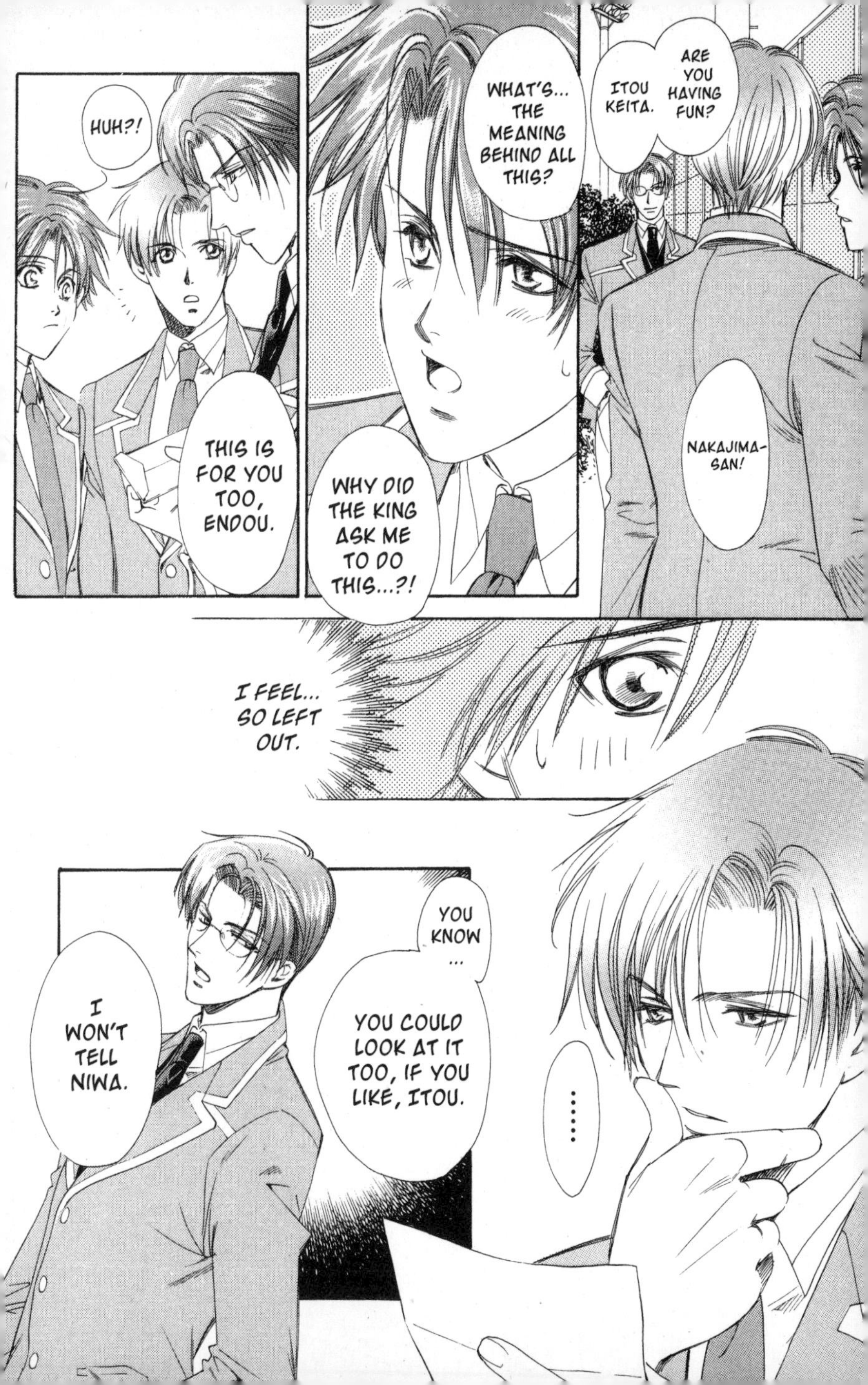
ARE YOU HAVING FUN?
ITOU KEITA.
NAKAJIMA-SAN!
WHAT'S... THE MEANING BEHIND ALL THIS?
WHY DID THE KING ASK ME TO DO THIS...?!
HUH?!
THIS IS FOR YOU TOO, ENDOU.
I FEEL... SO LEFT OUT.
......
YOU KNOW ...
YOU COULD LOOK AT IT TOO, IF YOU LIKE, ITOU.
I WON'T TELL NIWA.

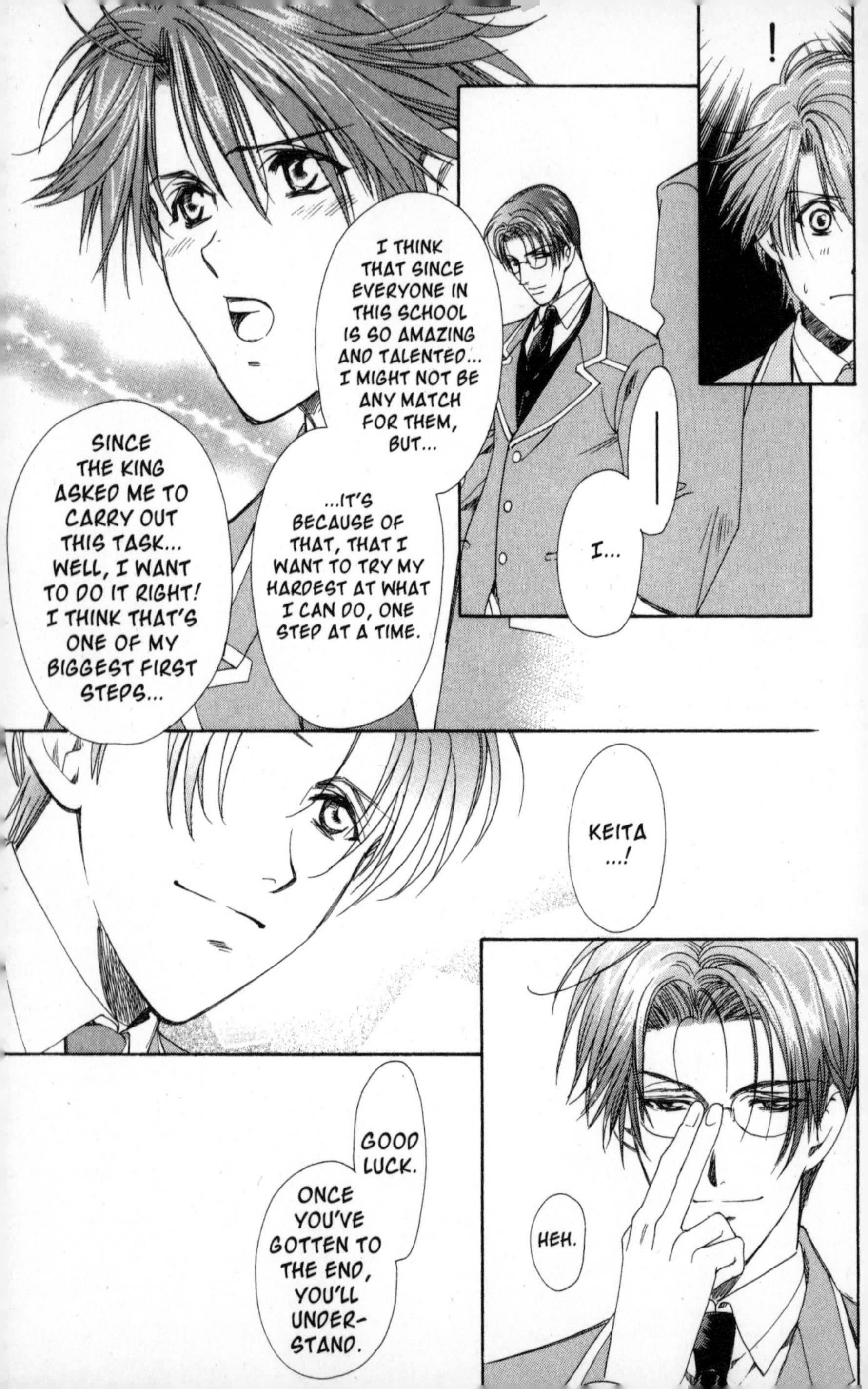
!
I...
I THINK THAT SINCE EVERYONE IN THIS SCHOOL IS SO AMAZING AND TALENTED... I MIGHT NOT BE ANY MATCH FOR THEM, BUT...
...IT'S BECAUSE OF THAT, THAT I WANT TO TRY MY HARDEST AT WHAT I CAN DO, ONE STEP AT A TIME.
SINCE THE KING ASKED ME TO CARRY OUT THIS TASK... WELL, I WANT TO DO IT RIGHT! I THINK THAT'S ONE OF MY BIGGEST FIRST STEPS...
KEITA ...!
HEH.
GOOD LUCK.
ONCE YOU'VE GOTTEN TO THE END, YOU'LL UNDER-STAND.

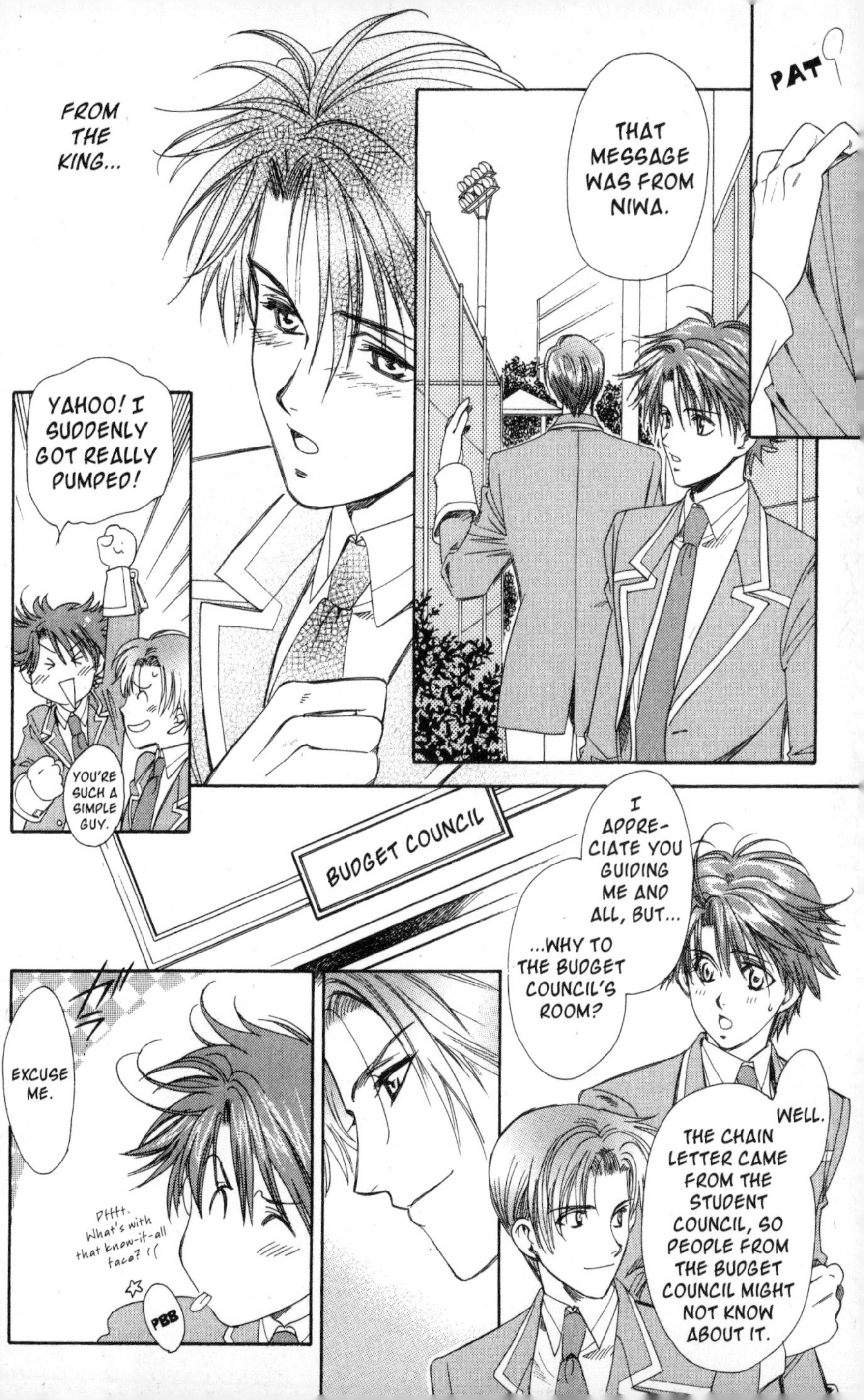
PAT
THAT MESSAGE WAS FROM NIWA.
FROM THE KING...
YAHOO! I SUDDENLY GOT REALLY PUMPED!
YOU'RE SUCH A SIMPLE GUY.
BUDGET COUNCIL
I APPRECIATE YOU GUIDING ME AND ALL, BUT...
...WHY TO THE BUDGET COUNCIL'S ROOM?
WELL.
THE CHAIN LETTER CAME FROM THE STUDENT COUNCIL, SO PEOPLE FROM THE BUDGET COUNCIL MIGHT NOT KNOW ABOUT IT.
EXCUSE ME.
Pfftt. What's with that know-it-all face?
PBB

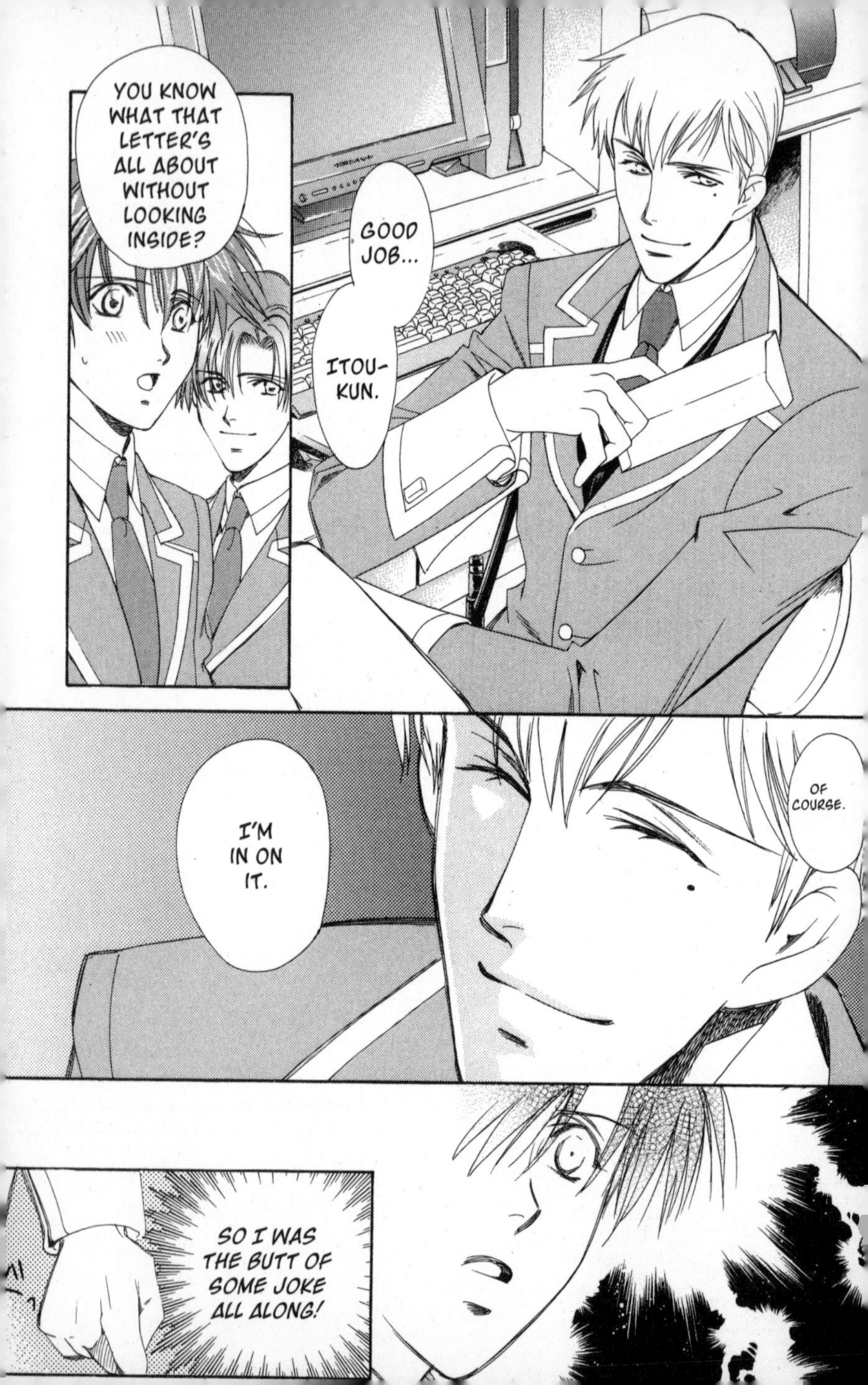
GOOD JOB...
ITOU-KUN.
YOU KNOW WHAT THAT LETTER'S ALL ABOUT WITHOUT LOOKING INSIDE?
OF COURSE.
I'M IN ON IT.
SO I WAS THE BUTT OF SOME JOKE ALL ALONG!

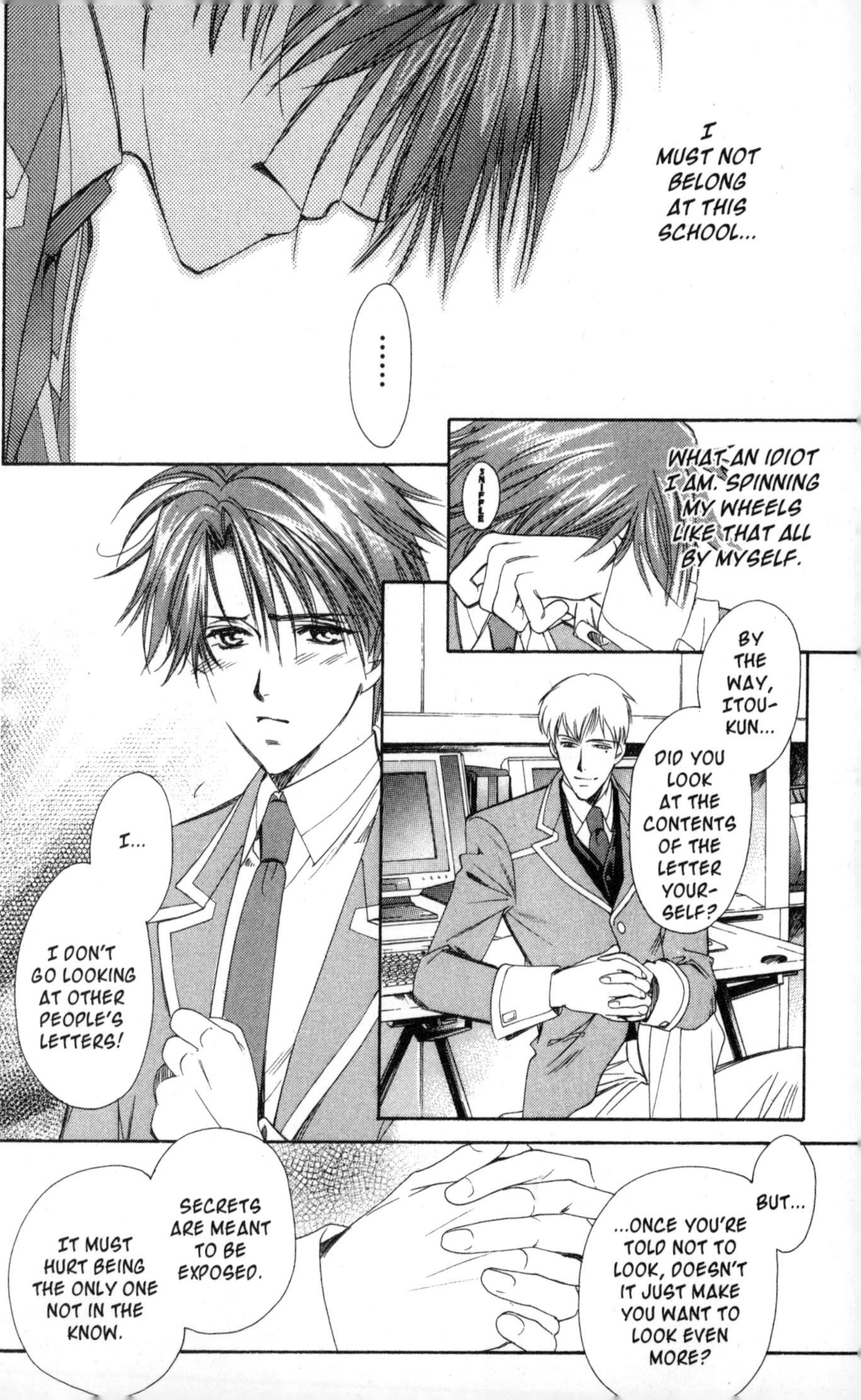
I MUST NOT BELONG AT THIS SCHOOL...
......
WHAT AN IDIOT I AM. SPINNING MY WHEELS LIKE THAT ALL BY MYSELF.
SNIFFLE
BY THE WAY, ITOU-KUN...
DID YOU LOOK AT THE CONTENTS OF THE LETTER YOURSELF?
I...
I DON'T GO LOOKING AT OTHER PEOPLE'S LETTERS!
BUT...
...ONCE YOU'RE TOLD NOT TO LOOK, DOESN'T IT JUST MAKE YOU WANT TO LOOK EVEN MORE?
SECRETS ARE MEANT TO BE EXPOSED.
IT MUST HURT BEING THE ONLY ONE NOT IN THE KNOW.

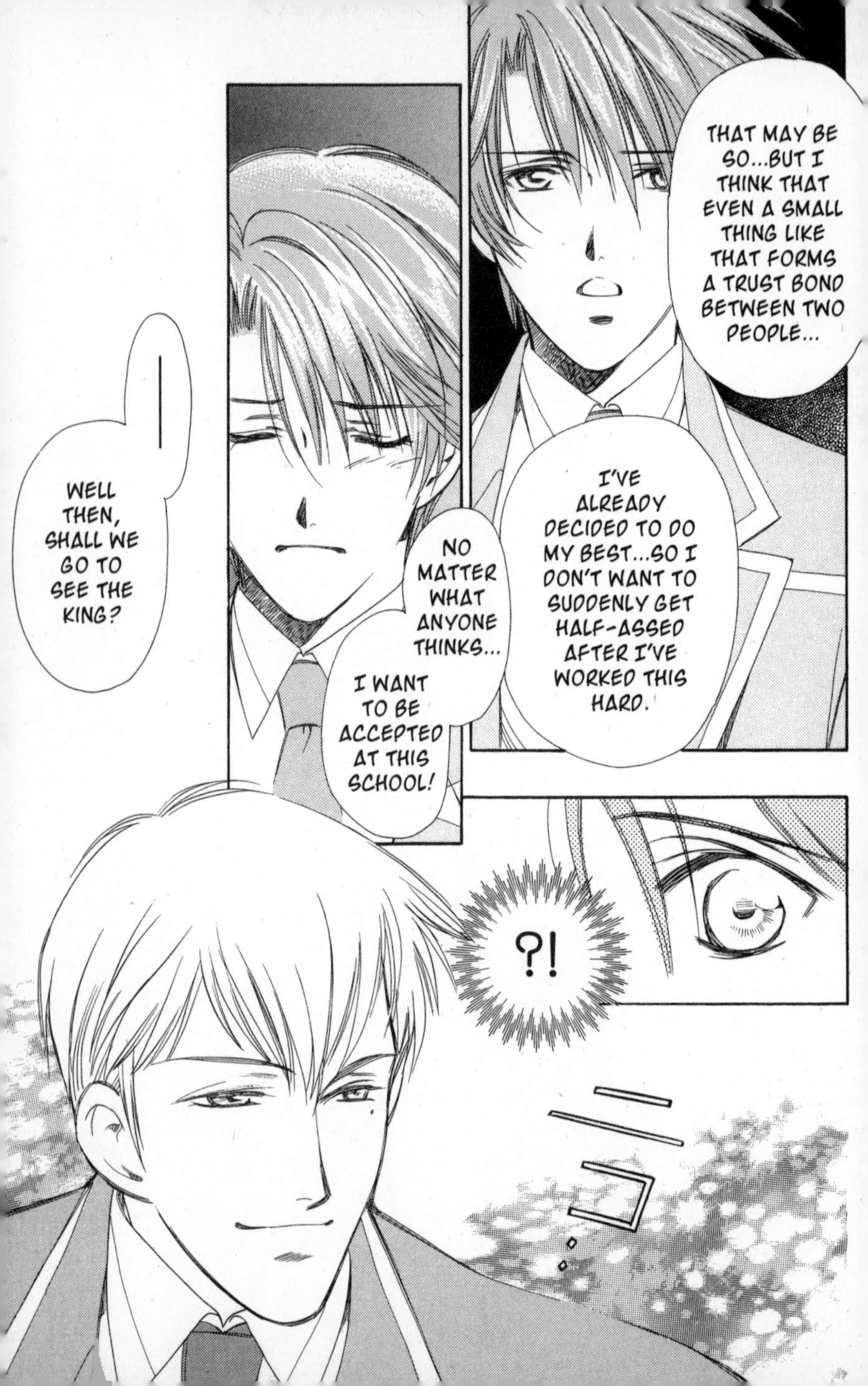
THAT MAY BE SO...BUT I THINK THAT EVEN A SMALL THING LIKE THAT FORMS A TRUST BOND BETWEEN TWO PEOPLE...
I'VE ALREADY DECIDED TO DO MY BEST...SO I DON'T WANT TO SUDDENLY GET HALF-ASSED AFTER I'VE WORKED THIS HARD.
NO MATTER WHAT ANYONE THINKS...
I WANT TO BE ACCEPTED AT THIS SCHOOL!
—
WELL THEN, SHALL WE GO TO SEE THE KING?
?!

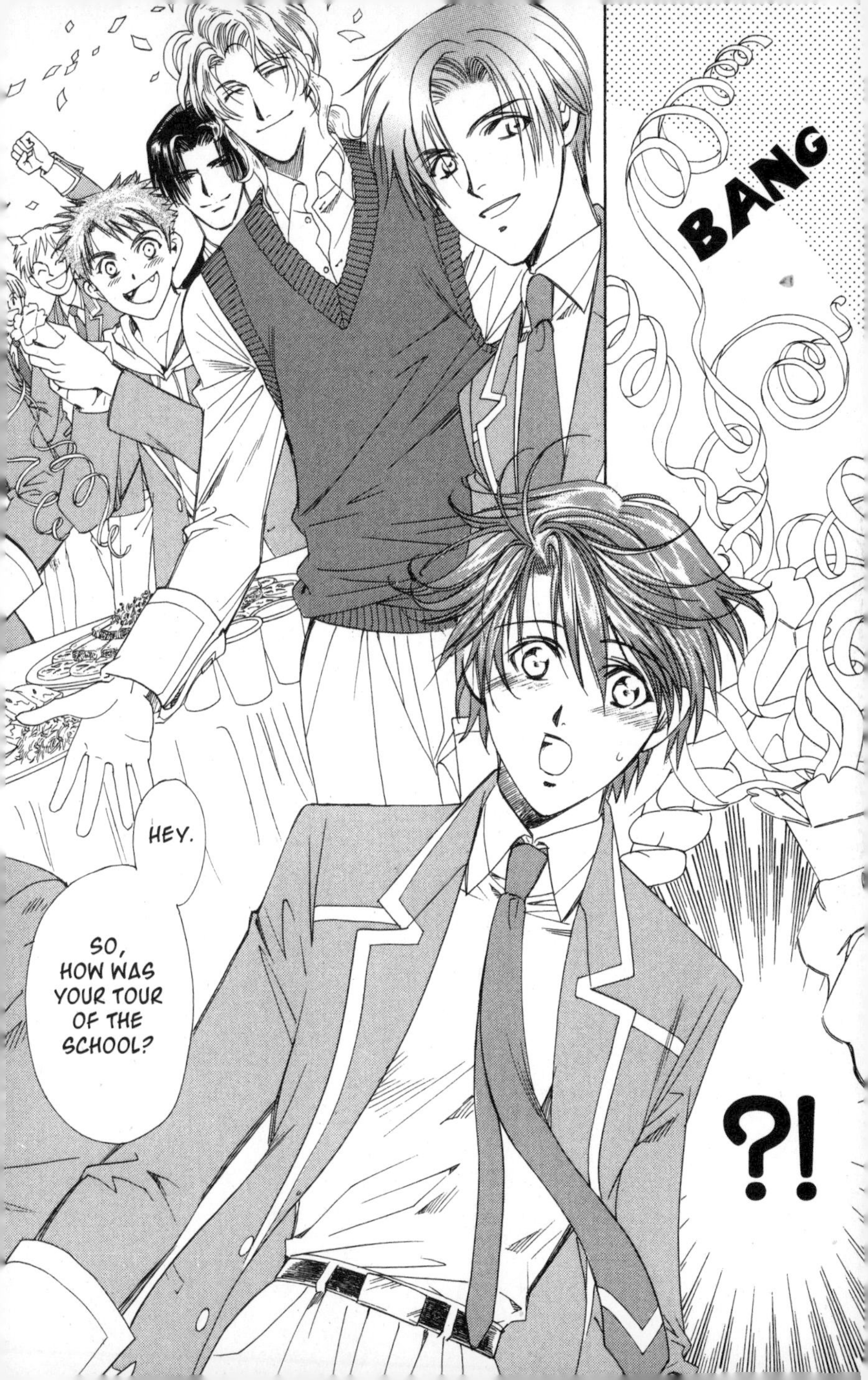
BANG
?!
HEY.
SO, HOW WAS YOUR TOUR OF THE SCHOOL?

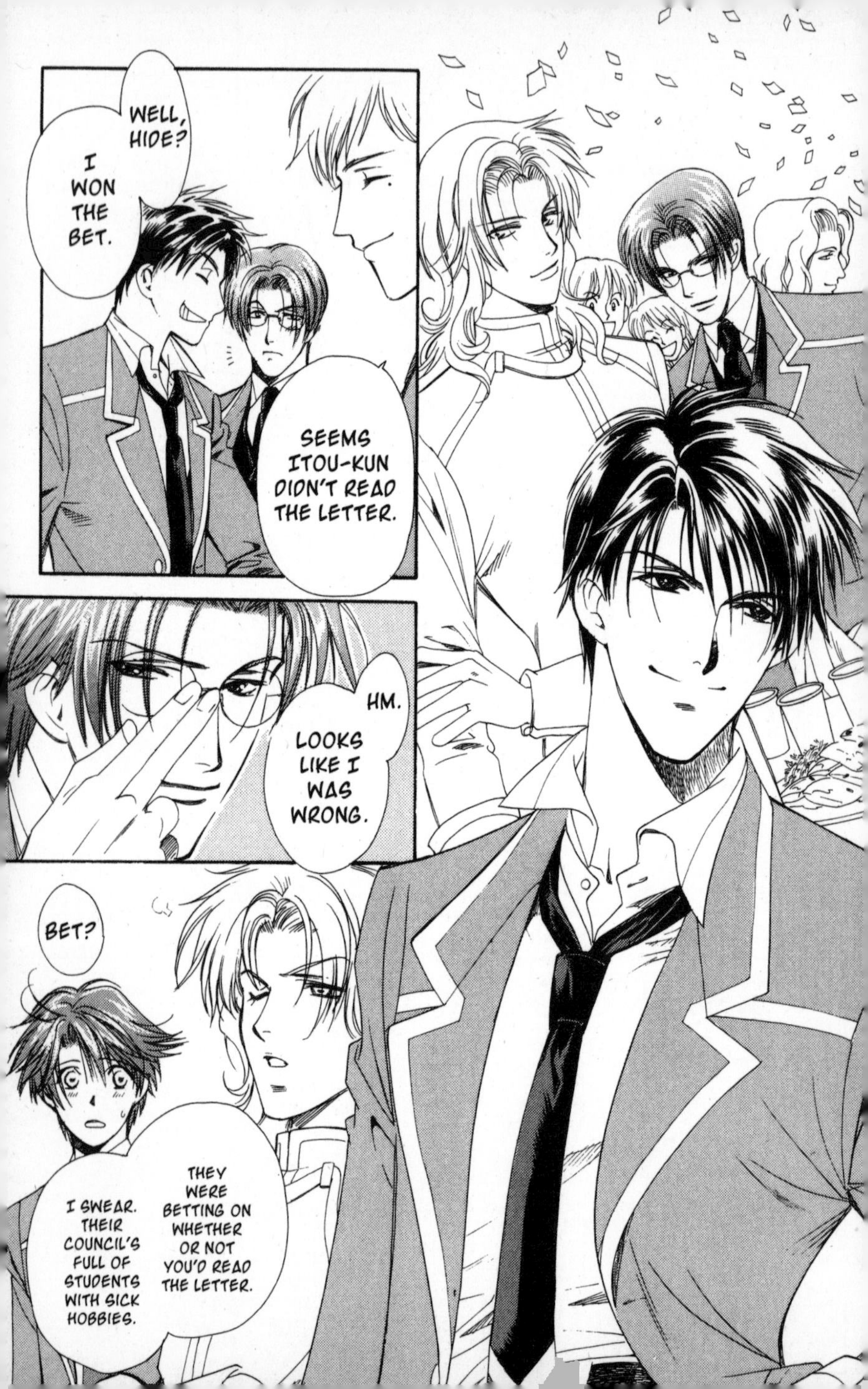

WELL, HIDE? I WON THE BET.
SEEMS ITOU-KUN DIDN'T READ THE LETTER.
HM. LOOKS LIKE I WAS WRONG.
BET?
THEY WERE BETTING ON WHETHER OR NOT YOU'D READ THE LETTER.
I SWEAR. THEIR COUNCIL'S FULL OF STUDENTS WITH SICK HOBBIES.

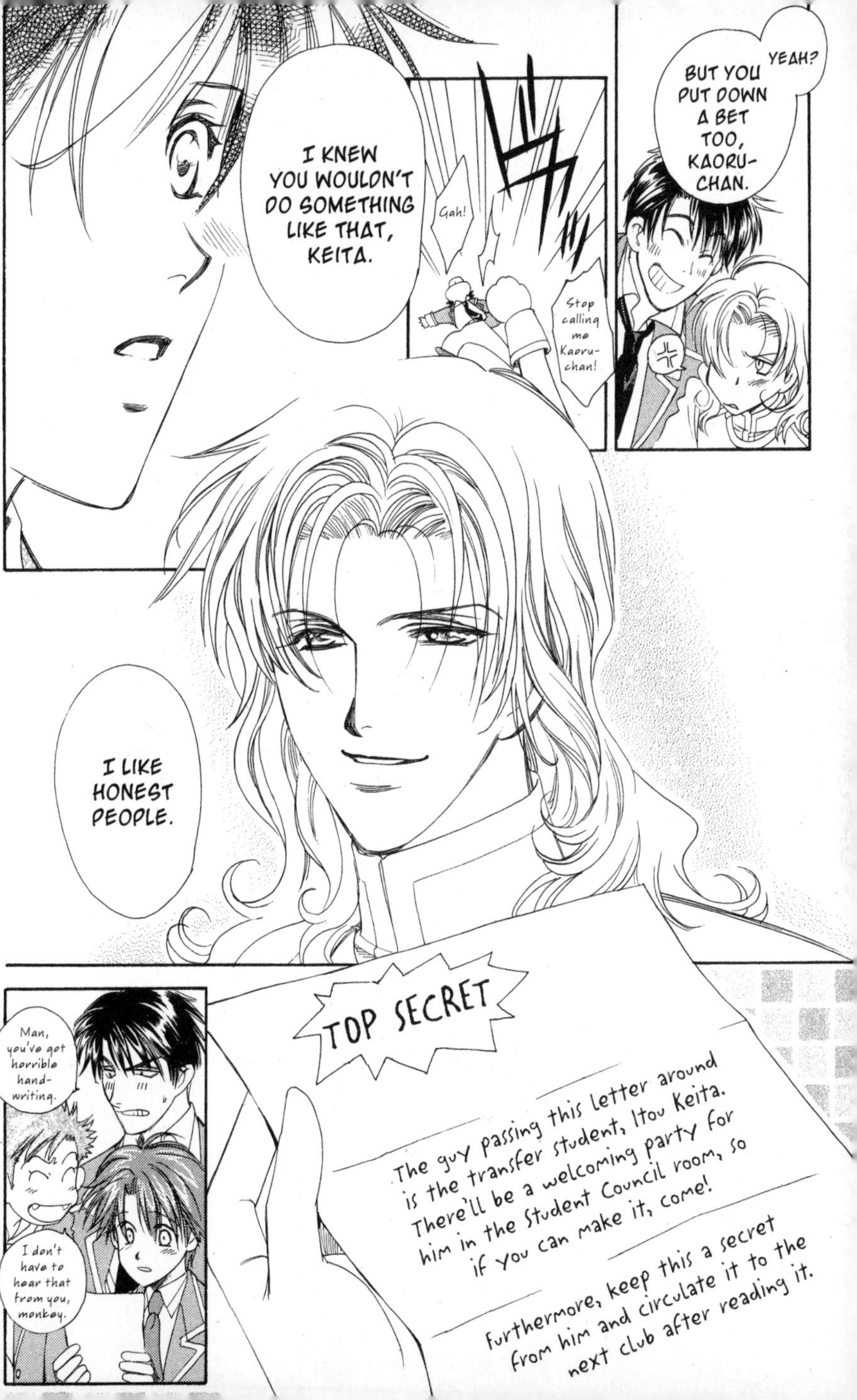
YEAH?
BUT YOU PUT DOWN A BET TOO, KAORU-CHAN.
Stop calling me Kaoru-chan!
Gah!
I KNEW YOU WOULDN'T DO SOMETHING LIKE THAT, KEITA.
I LIKE HONEST PEOPLE.
TOP SECRET
The guy passing this letter around is the transfer student, Itou Keita. There'll be a welcoming party for him in the Student Council room, so if you can make it, come!
Furthermore, keep this a secret from him and circulate it to the next club after reading it.
Man, you've got horrible hand-writing.
I don't have to hear that from you, monkey.

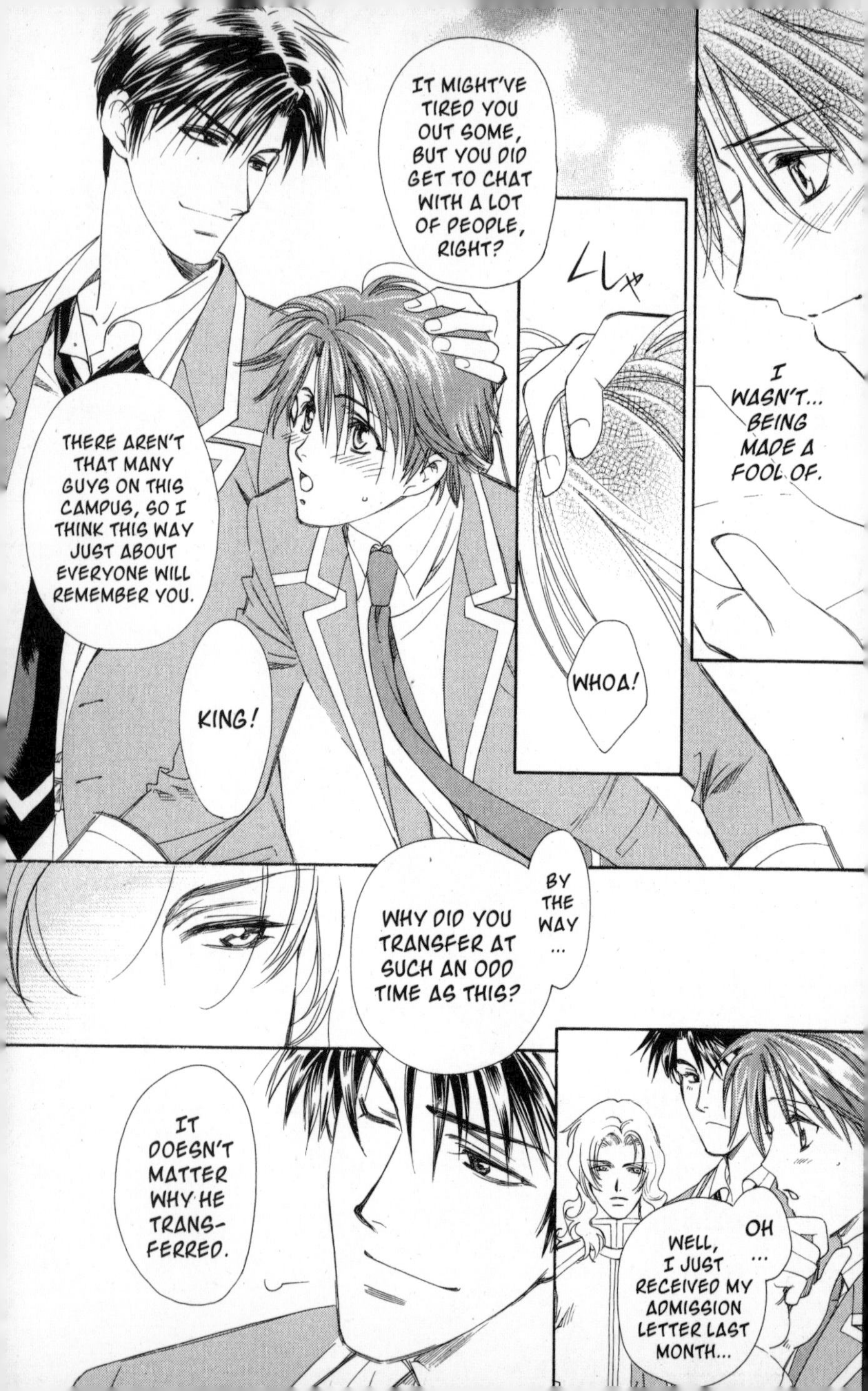
I WASN'T... BEING MADE A FOOL OF.
くしゃ
WHOA!
IT MIGHT'VE TIRED YOU OUT SOME, BUT YOU DID GET TO CHAT WITH A LOT OF PEOPLE, RIGHT?
THERE AREN'T THAT MANY GUYS ON THIS CAMPUS, SO I THINK THIS WAY JUST ABOUT EVERYONE WILL REMEMBER YOU.
KING!
BY THE WAY ...
WHY DID YOU TRANSFER AT SUCH AN ODD TIME AS THIS?
OH ...
WELL, I JUST RECEIVED MY ADMISSION LETTER LAST MONTH...
IT DOESN'T MATTER WHY HE TRANSFERRED.

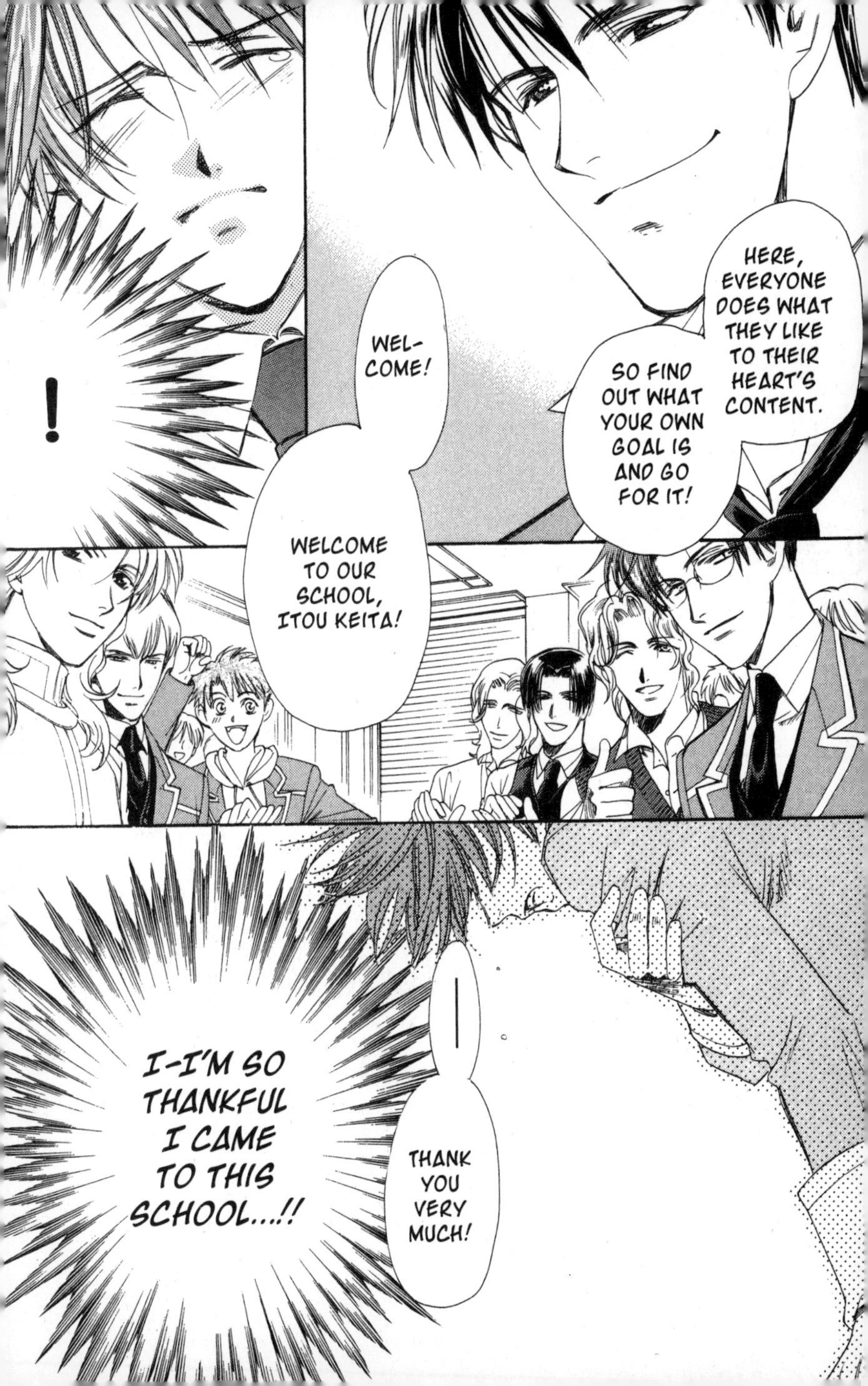
HERE, EVERYONE DOES WHAT THEY LIKE TO THEIR HEART'S CONTENT.
SO FIND OUT WHAT YOUR OWN GOAL IS AND GO FOR IT!
!
WEL-COME!
WELCOME TO OUR SCHOOL, ITOU KEITA!
THANK YOU VERY MUCH!
I-I'M SO THANKFUL I CAME TO THIS SCHOOL...!!

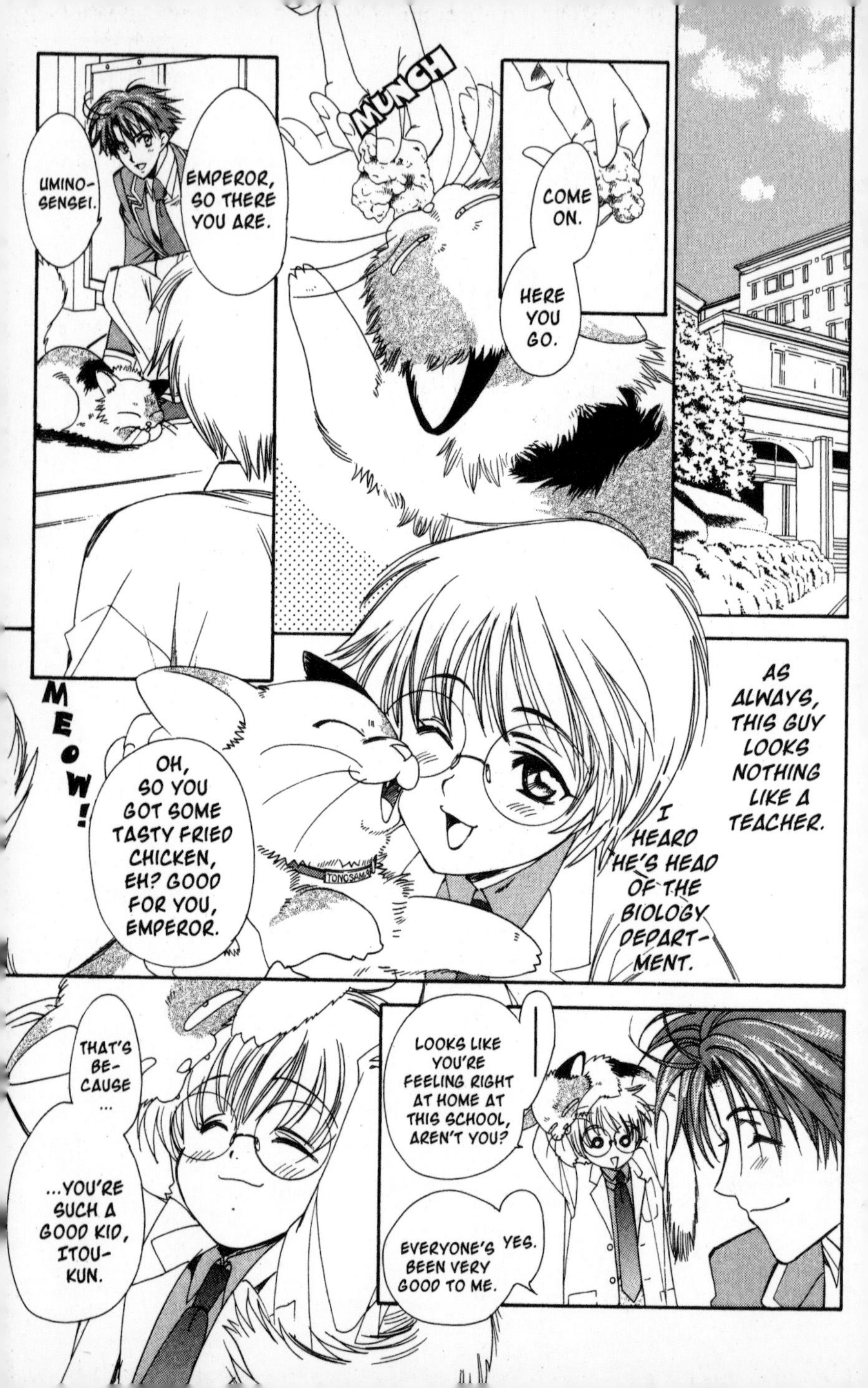
COME ON.
HERE YOU GO.
MUNCH
EMPEROR, SO THERE YOU ARE.
UMINO-SENSEI.
AS ALWAYS, THIS GUY LOOKS NOTHING LIKE A TEACHER.
I HEARD HE'S HEAD OF THE BIOLOGY DEPART-MENT.
TONOSAMA
OH, SO YOU GOT SOME TASTY FRIED CHICKEN, EH? GOOD FOR YOU, EMPEROR.
MEOW!
LOOKS LIKE YOU'RE FEELING RIGHT AT HOME AT THIS SCHOOL, AREN'T YOU?
YES.
EVERYONE'S BEEN VERY GOOD TO ME.
THAT'S BE-CAUSE...
...YOU'RE SUCH A GOOD KID, ITOU-KUN.

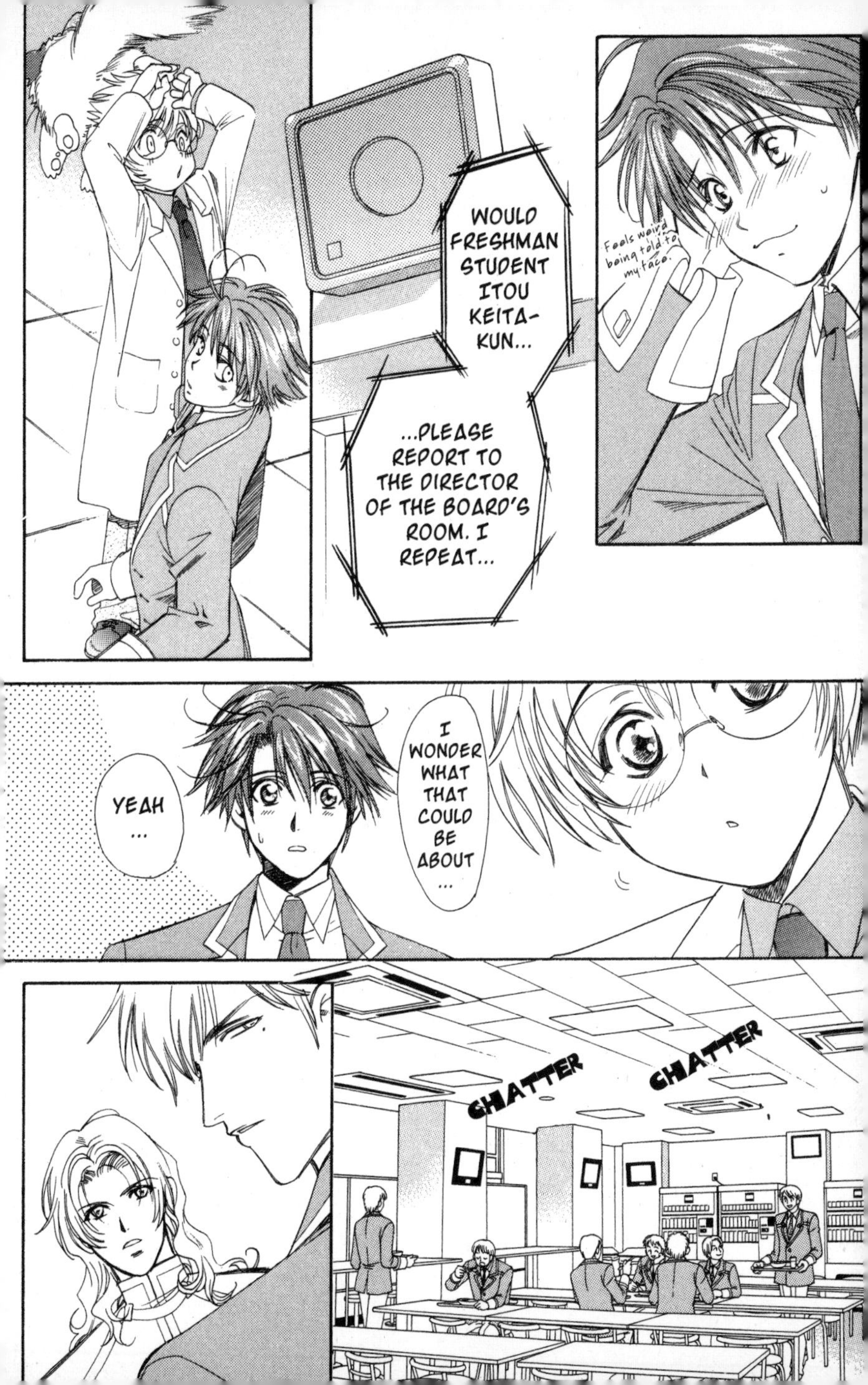
Feels weird being told to my face.
WOULD FRESHMAN STUDENT ITOU KEITA-KUN...
...PLEASE REPORT TO THE DIRECTOR OF THE BOARD'S ROOM. I REPEAT...
I WONDER WHAT THAT COULD BE ABOUT ...
YEAH ...
CHATTER
CHATTER

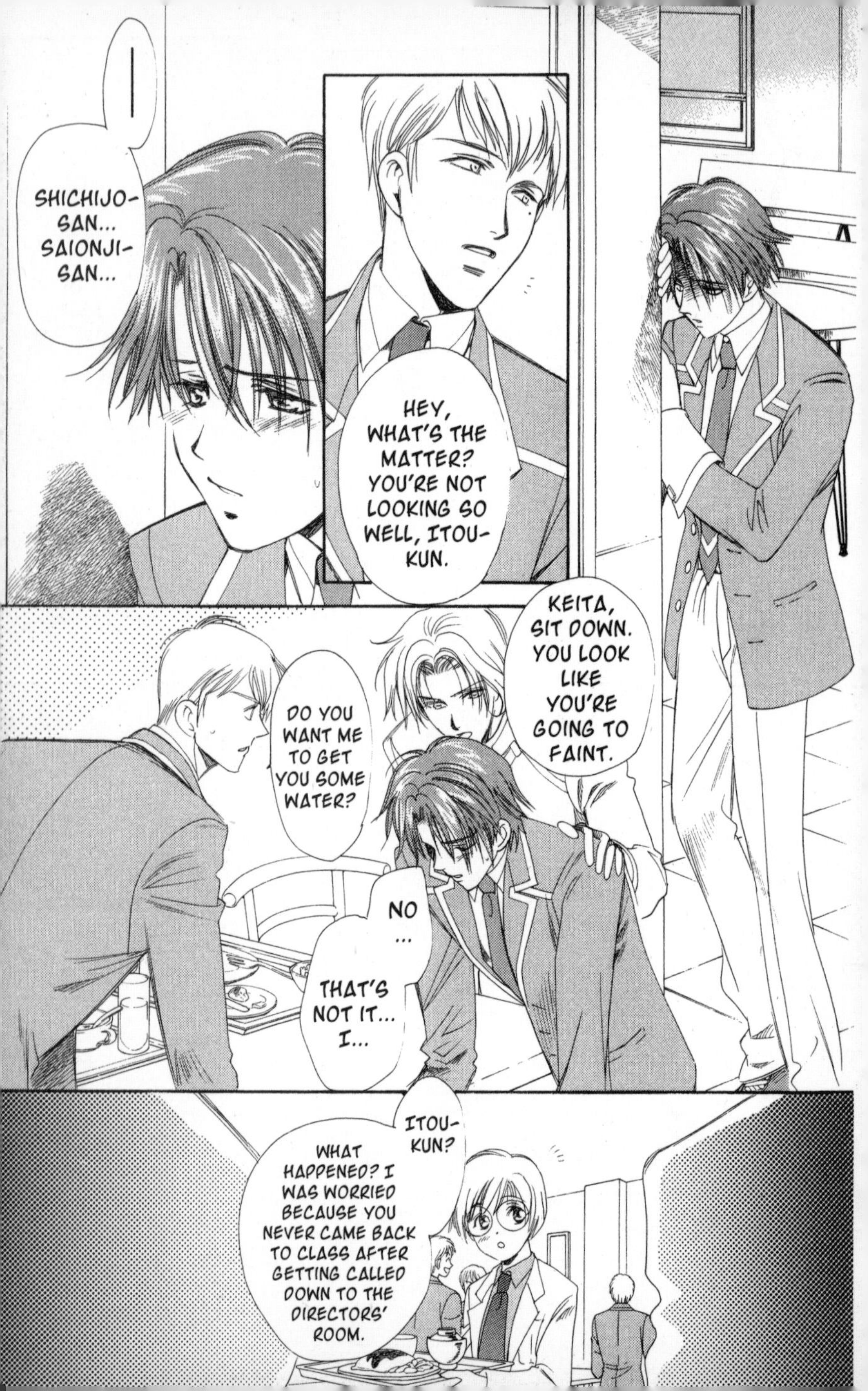
HEY, WHAT'S THE MATTER? YOU'RE NOT LOOKING SO WELL, ITOU-KUN.
!
SHICHIJO-SAN... SAIONJI-SAN...
KEITA, SIT DOWN. YOU LOOK LIKE YOU'RE GOING TO FAINT.
DO YOU WANT ME TO GET YOU SOME WATER?
NO ...
THAT'S NOT IT... I...
ITOU-KUN?
WHAT HAPPENED? I WAS WORRIED BECAUSE YOU NEVER CAME BACK TO CLASS AFTER GETTING CALLED DOWN TO THE DIRECTORS' ROOM.

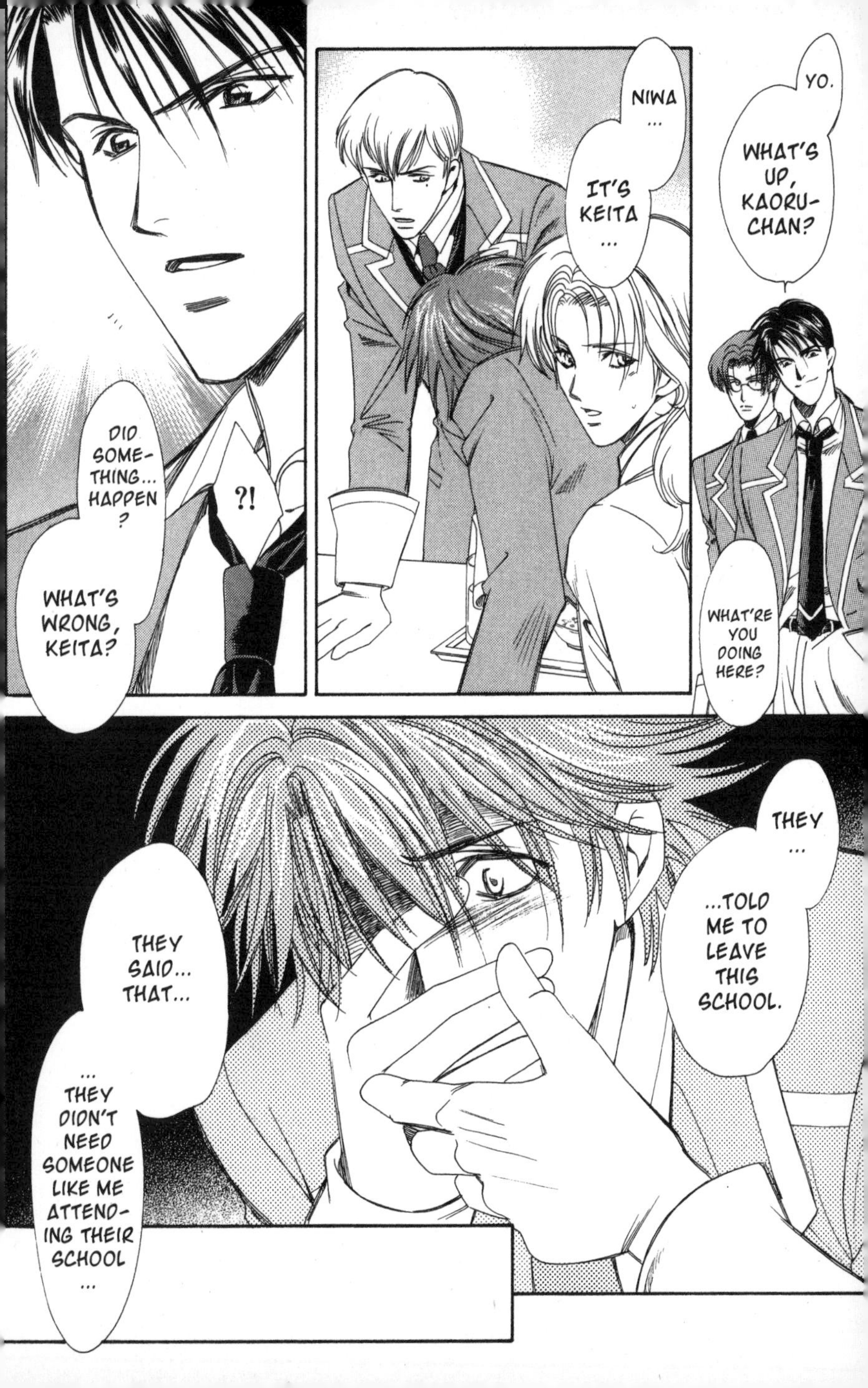
YO.
WHAT'S UP, KAORU-CHAN?
WHAT'RE YOU DOING HERE?
NIWA ...
IT'S KEITA ...
?!
DID SOMETHING... HAPPEN?
WHAT'S WRONG, KEITA?
THEY ...
...TOLD ME TO LEAVE THIS SCHOOL.
THEY SAID... THAT...
... THEY DIDN'T NEED SOMEONE LIKE ME ATTENDING THEIR SCHOOL ...

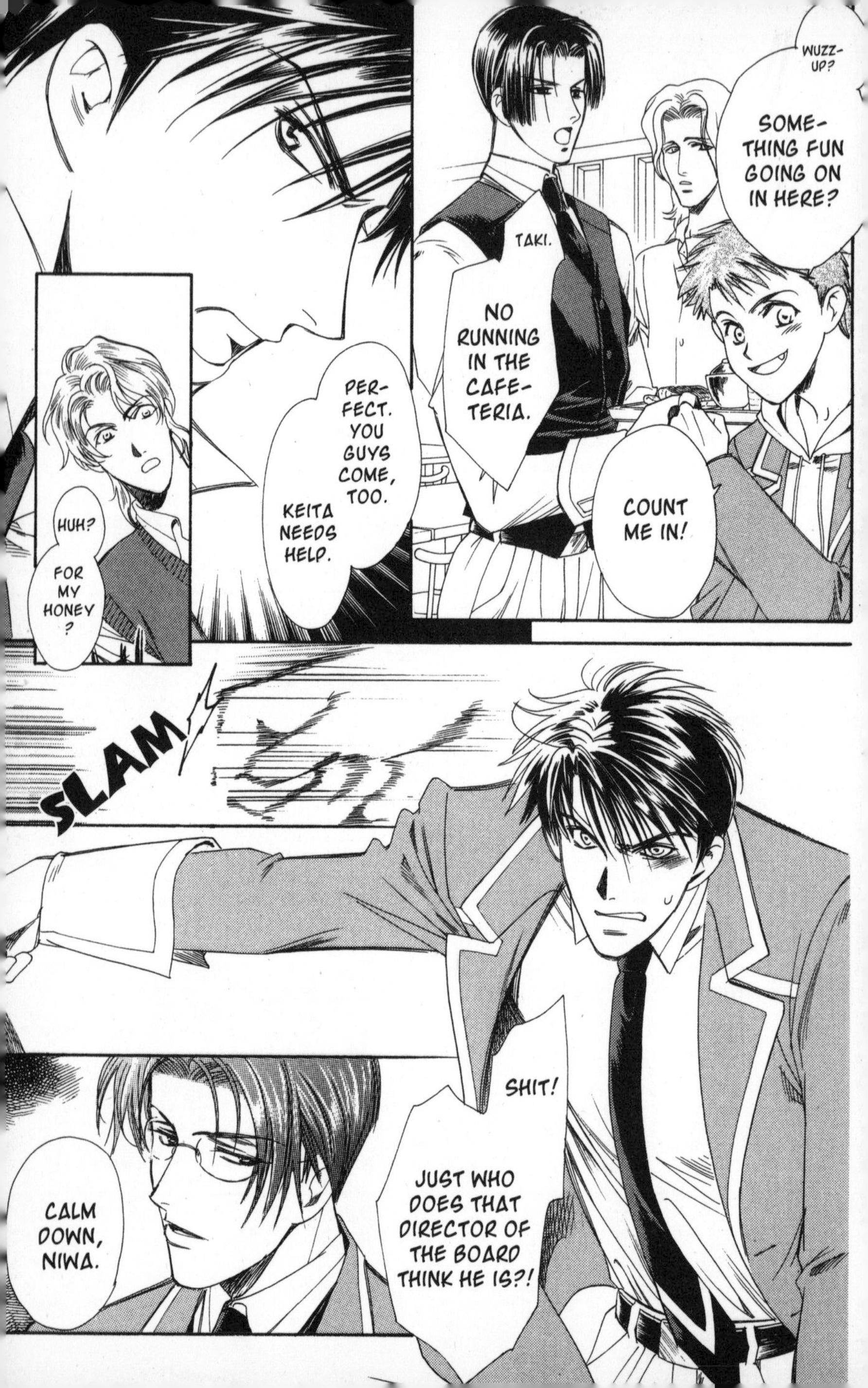
WUZZ-UP?
SOME-THING FUN GOING ON IN HERE?
TAKI.
NO RUNNING IN THE CAFE-TERIA.
COUNT ME IN!
PER-FECT. YOU GUYS COME, TOO.
KEITA NEEDS HELP.
HUH?
FOR MY HONEY?
SLAM
SHIT!
JUST WHO DOES THAT DIRECTOR OF THE BOARD THINK HE IS?!
CALM DOWN, NIWA.

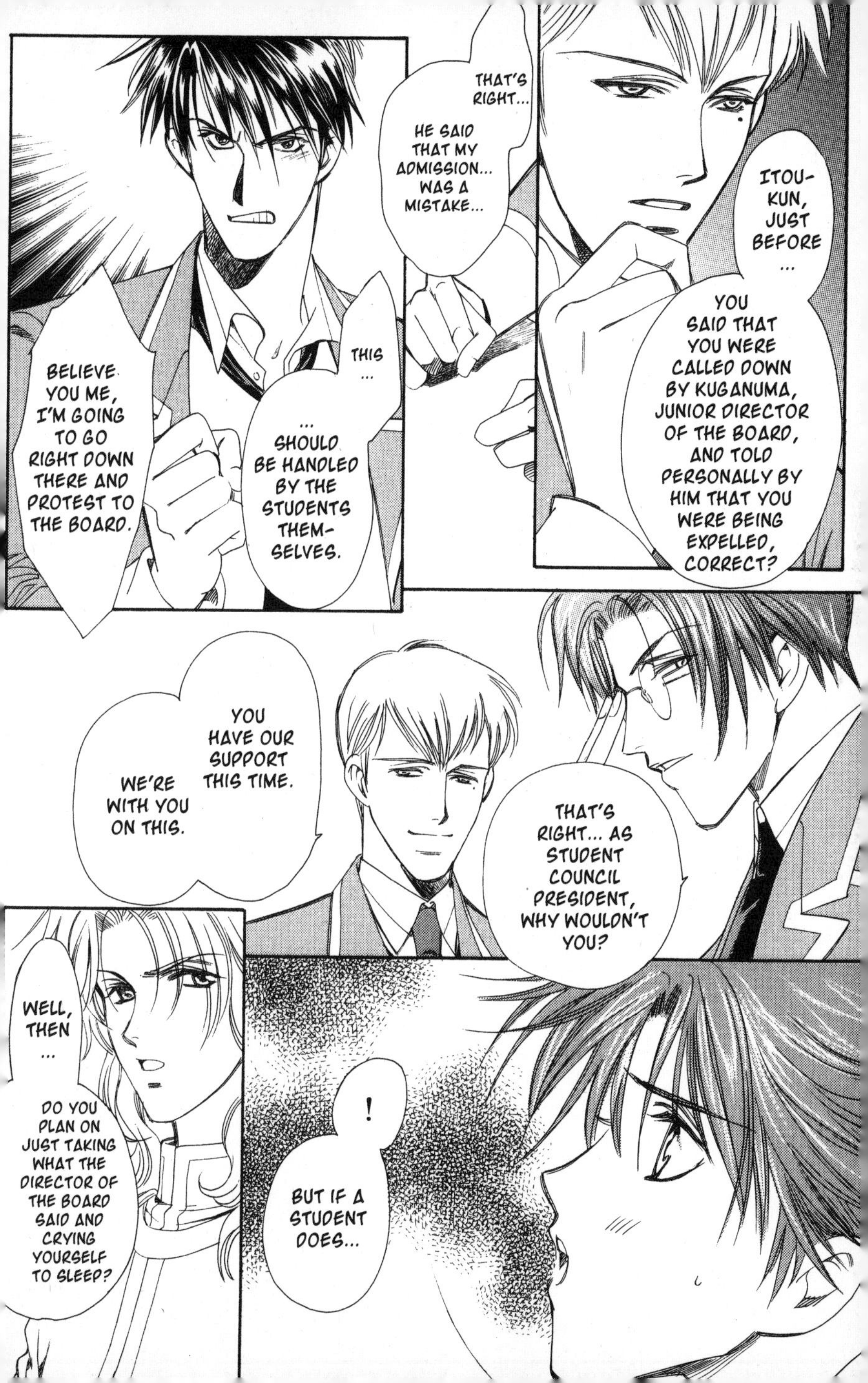
ITOU-KUN, JUST BEFORE...
YOU SAID THAT YOU WERE CALLED DOWN BY KUGANUMA, JUNIOR DIRECTOR OF THE BOARD, AND TOLD PERSONALLY BY HIM THAT YOU WERE BEING EXPELLED, CORRECT?
THAT'S RIGHT...
HE SAID THAT MY ADMISSION... WAS A MISTAKE...
THIS...
...SHOULD BE HANDLED BY THE STUDENTS THEM-SELVES.
BELIEVE YOU ME, I'M GOING TO GO RIGHT DOWN THERE AND PROTEST TO THE BOARD.
THAT'S RIGHT... AS STUDENT COUNCIL PRESIDENT, WHY WOULDN'T YOU?
YOU HAVE OUR SUPPORT THIS TIME.
WE'RE WITH YOU ON THIS.
!
BUT IF A STUDENT DOES...
WELL, THEN...
DO YOU PLAN ON JUST TAKING WHAT THE DIRECTOR OF THE BOARD SAID AND CRYING YOURSELF TO SLEEP?

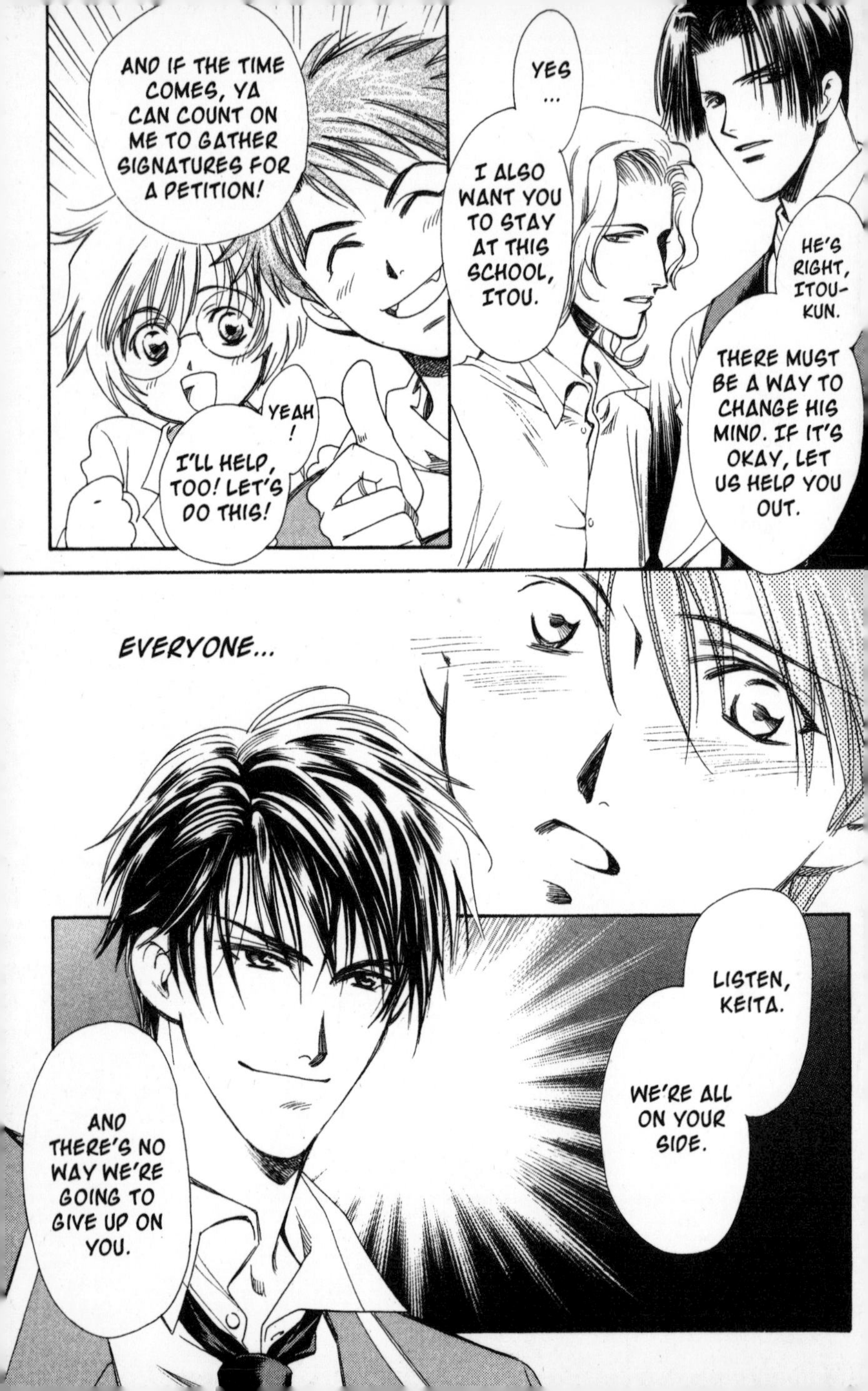
YES ...
I ALSO WANT YOU TO STAY AT THIS SCHOOL, ITOU.
HE'S RIGHT, ITOU-KUN.
THERE MUST BE A WAY TO CHANGE HIS MIND. IF IT'S OKAY, LET US HELP YOU OUT.
AND IF THE TIME COMES, YA CAN COUNT ON ME TO GATHER SIGNATURES FOR A PETITION!
YEAH!
I'LL HELP, TOO! LET'S DO THIS!
EVERYONE...
LISTEN, KEITA.
WE'RE ALL ON YOUR SIDE.
AND THERE'S NO WAY WE'RE GOING TO GIVE UP ON YOU.

GAKUEN *HEAVEN*

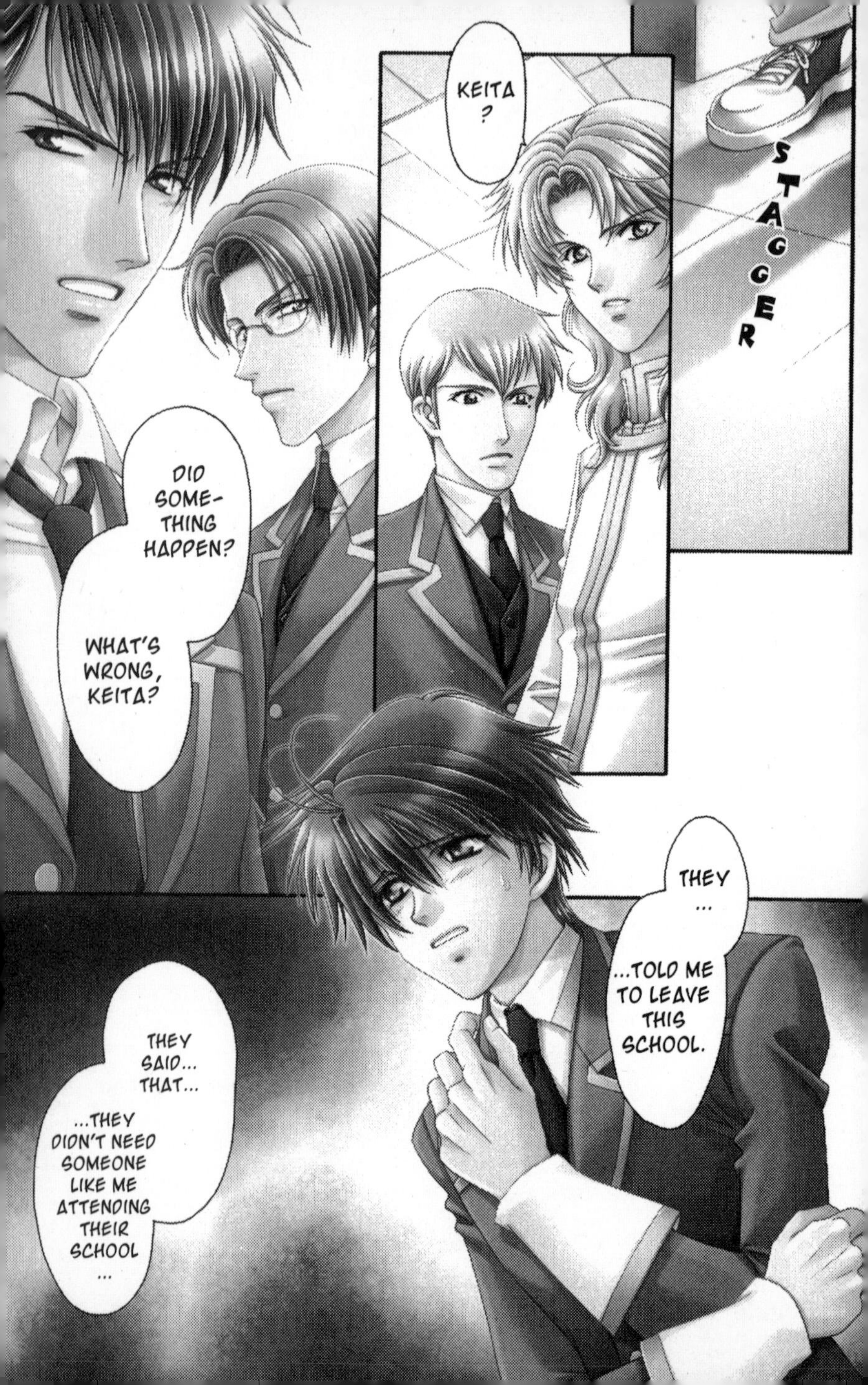
STAGGER
KEITA ?
DID SOMETHING HAPPEN?
WHAT'S WRONG, KEITA?
THEY ...
...TOLD ME TO LEAVE THIS SCHOOL.
THEY SAID... THAT...
...THEY DIDN'T NEED SOMEONE LIKE ME ATTENDING THEIR SCHOOL ...

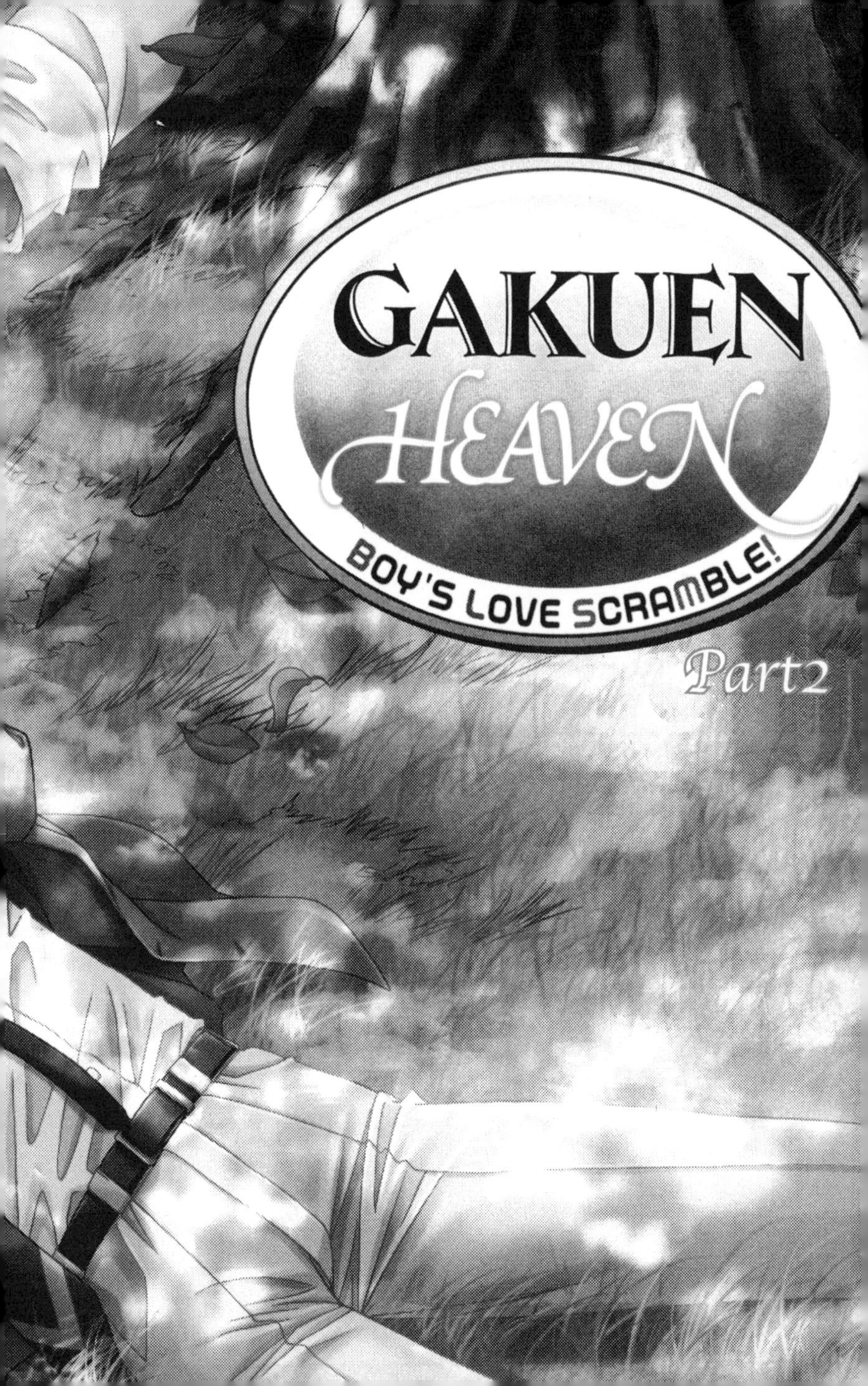
GAKUEN HEAVEN
BOY'S LOVE SCRAMBLE!
Part2

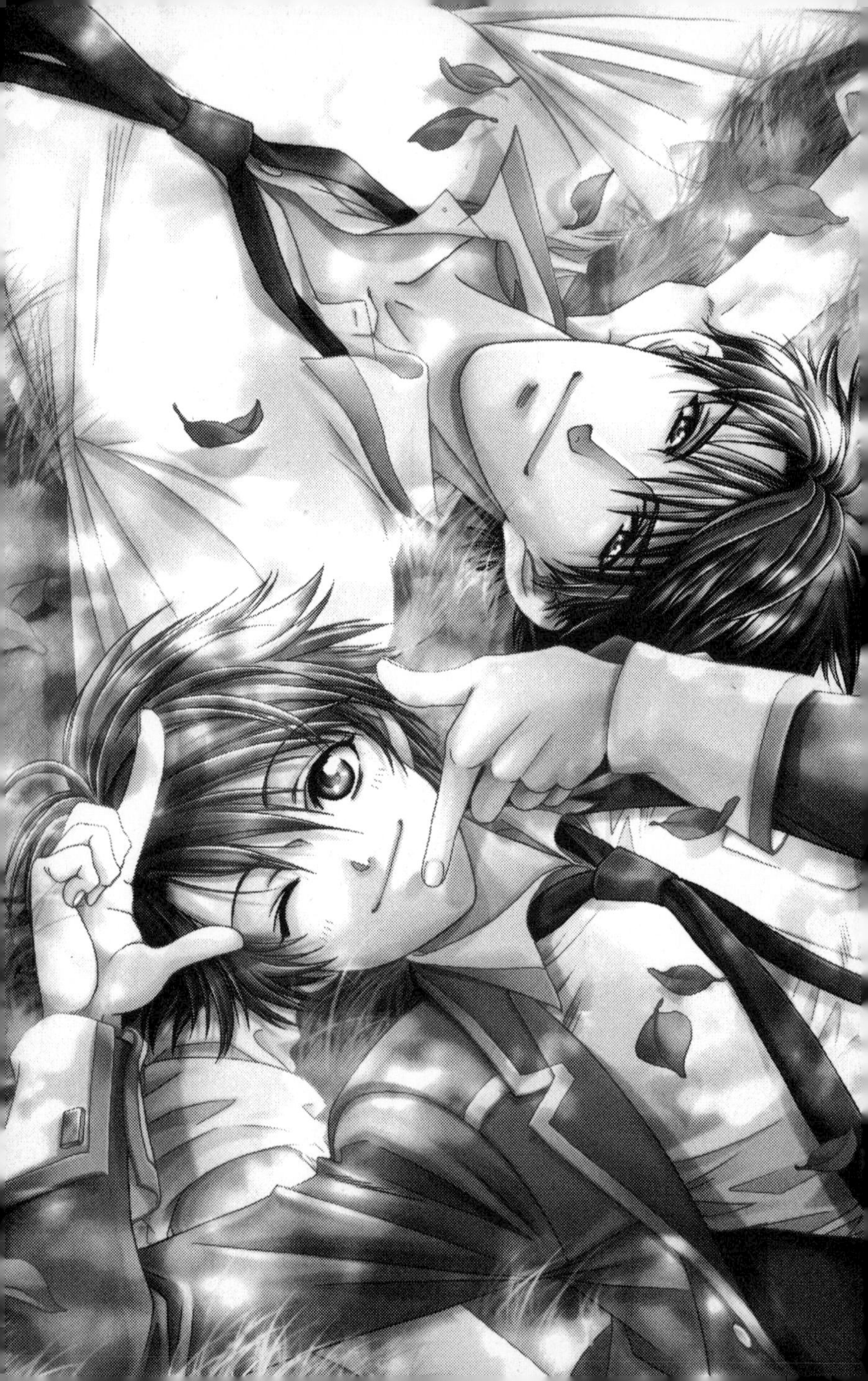

GAKUEN *HEAVEN*

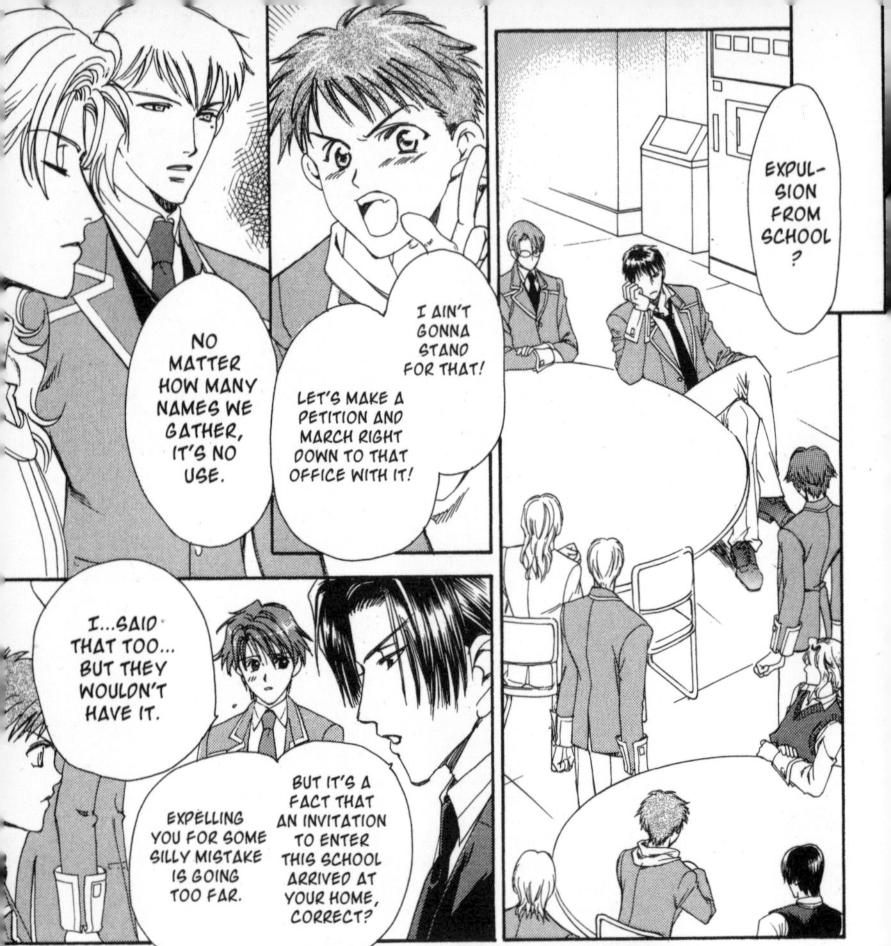
EXPUL-SION FROM SCHOOL?
I AIN'T GONNA STAND FOR THAT!
LET'S MAKE A PETITION AND MARCH RIGHT DOWN TO THAT OFFICE WITH IT!
NO MATTER HOW MANY NAMES WE GATHER, IT'S NO USE.
I...SAID THAT TOO... BUT THEY WOULDN'T HAVE IT.
BUT IT'S A FACT THAT AN INVITATION TO ENTER THIS SCHOOL ARRIVED AT YOUR HOME, CORRECT?
EXPELLING YOU FOR SOME SILLY MISTAKE IS GOING TOO FAR.

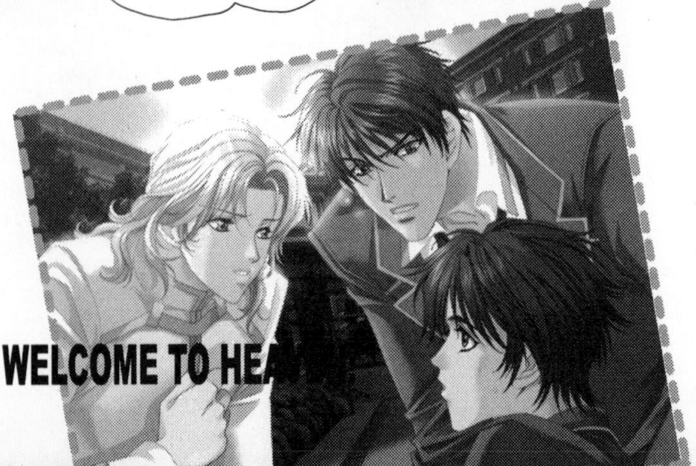
WELCOME TO HEA

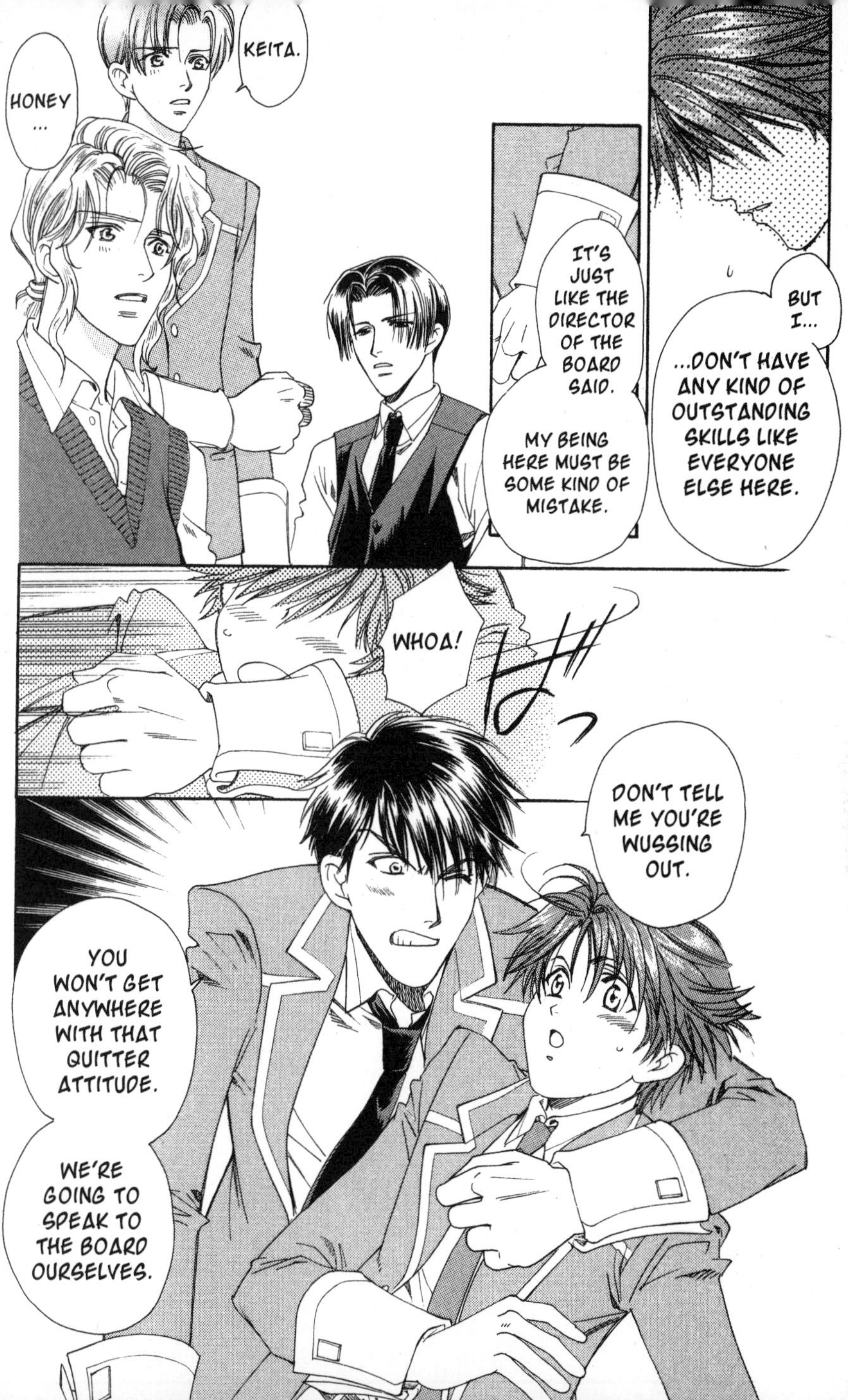
BUT I...
...DON'T HAVE ANY KIND OF OUTSTANDING SKILLS LIKE EVERYONE ELSE HERE.
IT'S JUST LIKE THE DIRECTOR OF THE BOARD SAID.
MY BEING HERE MUST BE SOME KIND OF MISTAKE.
KEITA.
HONEY ...
WHOA!
ばっ
DON'T TELL ME YOU'RE WUSSING OUT.
YOU WON'T GET ANYWHERE WITH THAT QUITTER ATTITUDE.
WE'RE GOING TO SPEAK TO THE BOARD OURSELVES.

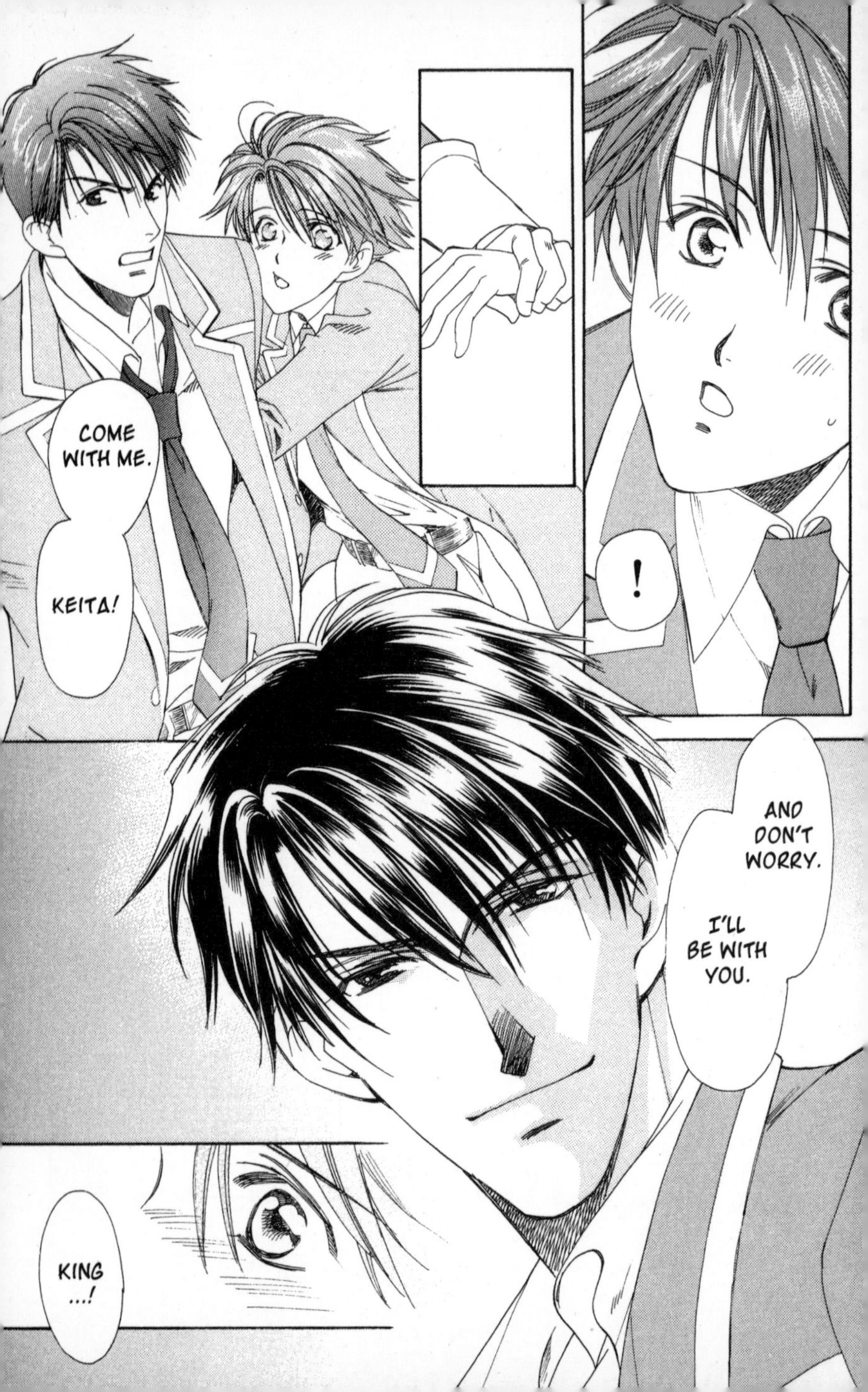
!
COME WITH ME.
KEITA!
AND DON'T WORRY.
I'LL BE WITH YOU.
KING ...!

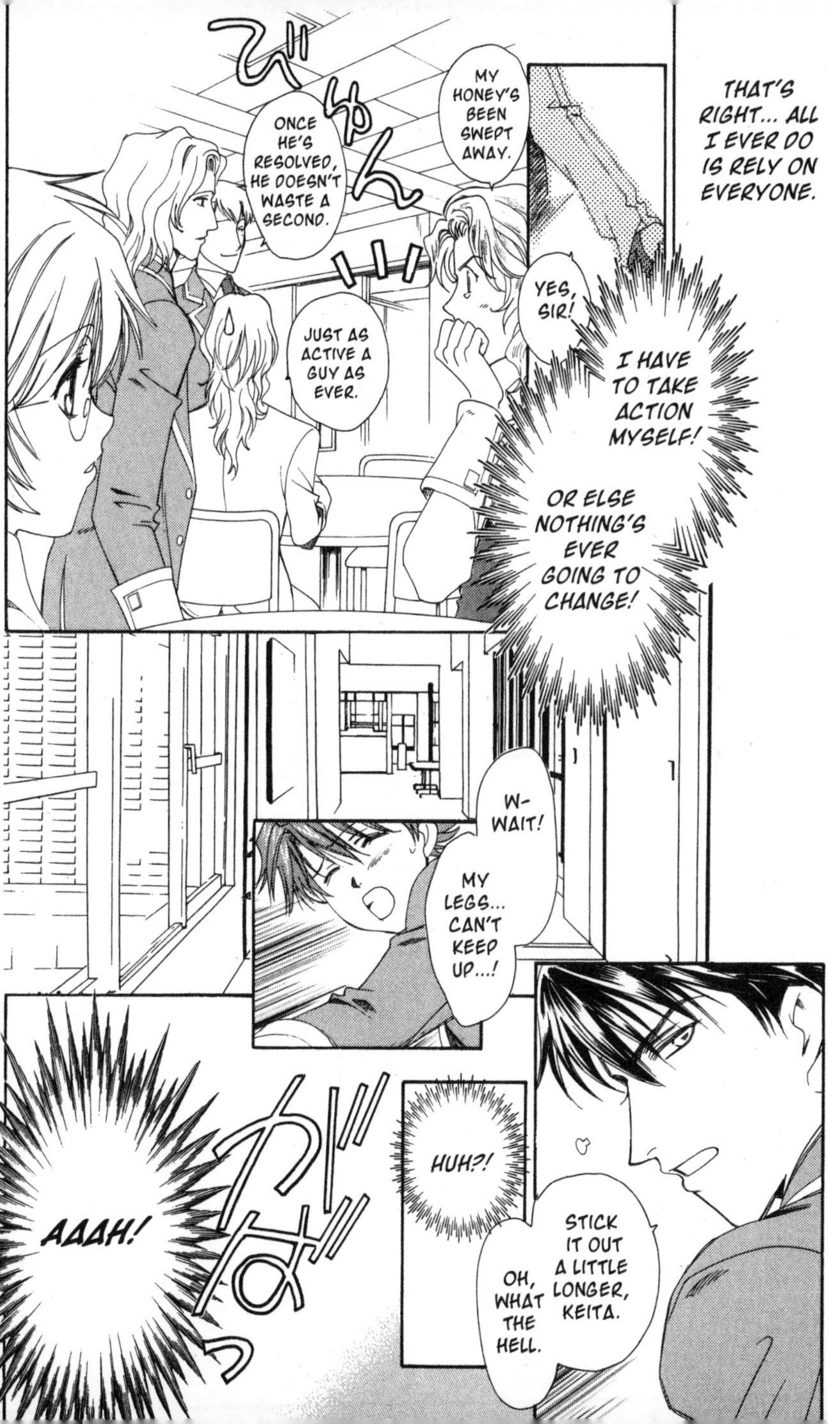
THAT'S RIGHT... ALL I EVER DO IS RELY ON EVERYONE.
MY HONEY'S BEEN SWEPT AWAY.
ONCE HE'S RESOLVED, HE DOESN'T WASTE A SECOND.
びゅん
YES, SIR!
JUST AS ACTIVE A GUY AS EVER.
I HAVE TO TAKE ACTION MYSELF!
OR ELSE NOTHING'S EVER GOING TO CHANGE!
W-WAIT!
MY LEGS... CAN'T KEEP UP...!
STICK IT OUT A LITTLE LONGER, KEITA.
OH, WHAT THE HELL.
HUH?!
AAAH!
がばっ

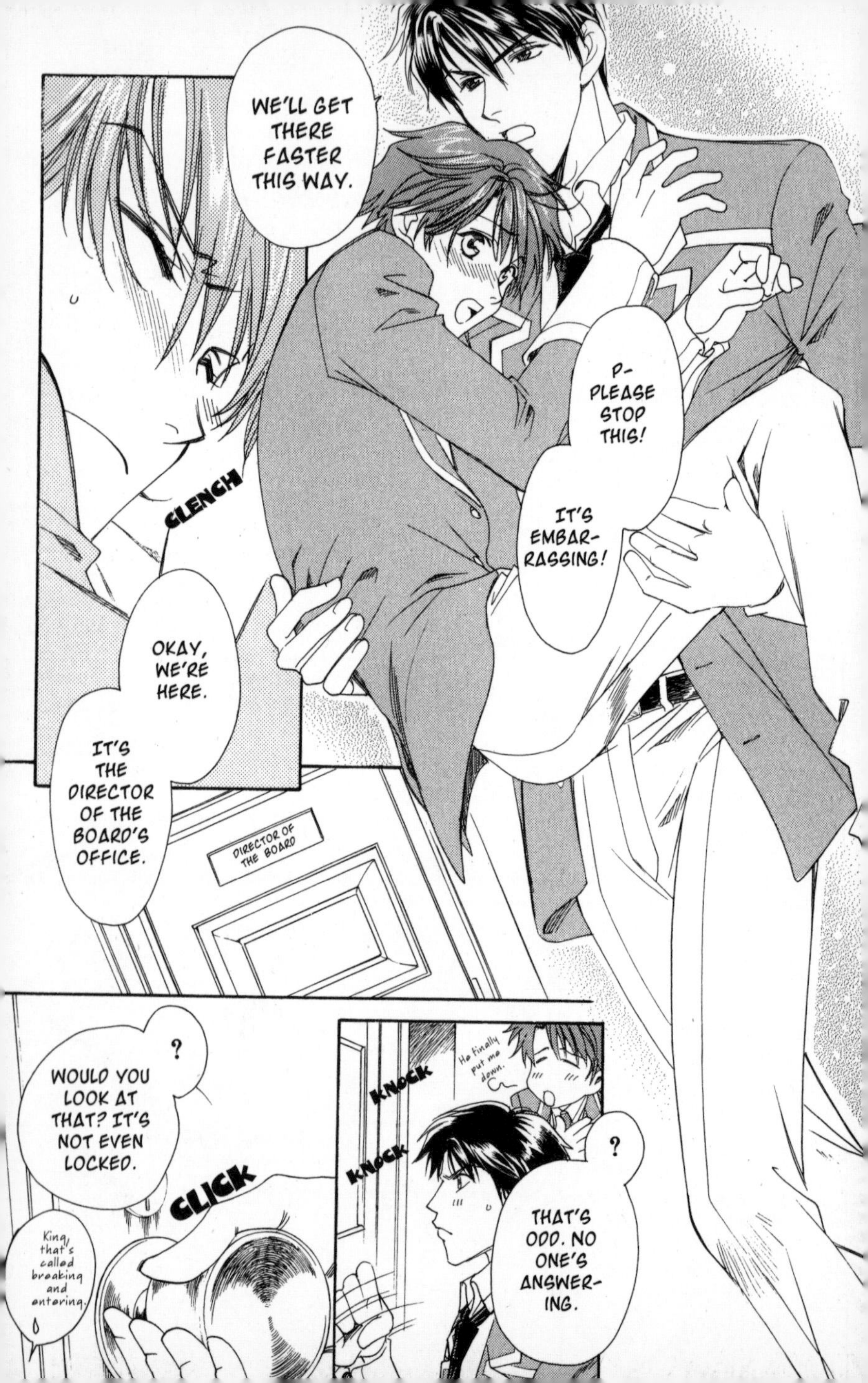
WE'LL GET THERE FASTER THIS WAY.
P-PLEASE STOP THIS!
IT'S EMBARRASSING!
CLENCH
OKAY, WE'RE HERE.
IT'S THE DIRECTOR OF THE BOARD'S OFFICE.
DIRECTOR OF THE BOARD
He finally put me down.
KNOCK
KNOCK
?
THAT'S ODD. NO ONE'S ANSWERING.
?
WOULD YOU LOOK AT THAT? IT'S NOT EVEN LOCKED.
CLICK
King, that's called breaking and entering.

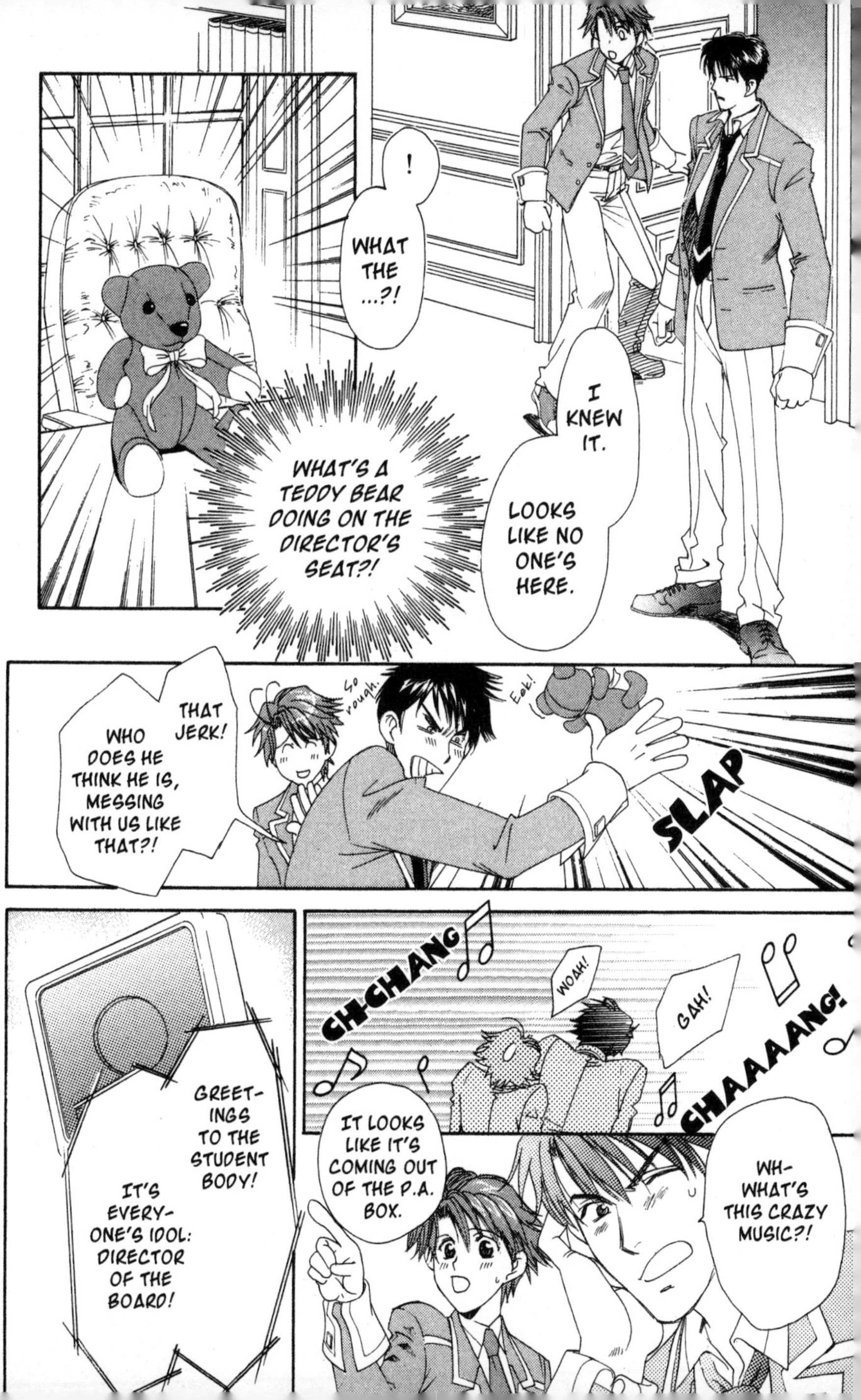
I KNEW IT.
LOOKS LIKE NO ONE'S HERE.
!
WHAT THE ...?!
WHAT'S A TEDDY BEAR DOING ON THE DIRECTOR'S SEAT?!
SLAP
Eek!
So rough.
THAT JERK!
WHO DOES HE THINK HE IS, MESSING WITH US LIKE THAT?!
CH-CHANG
WOAH!
GAH!
CHAAAANG!
WH-WHAT'S THIS CRAZY MUSIC?!
IT LOOKS LIKE IT'S COMING OUT OF THE P.A. BOX.
GREET-INGS TO THE STUDENT BODY!
IT'S EVERY-ONE'S IDOL: DIRECTOR OF THE BOARD!

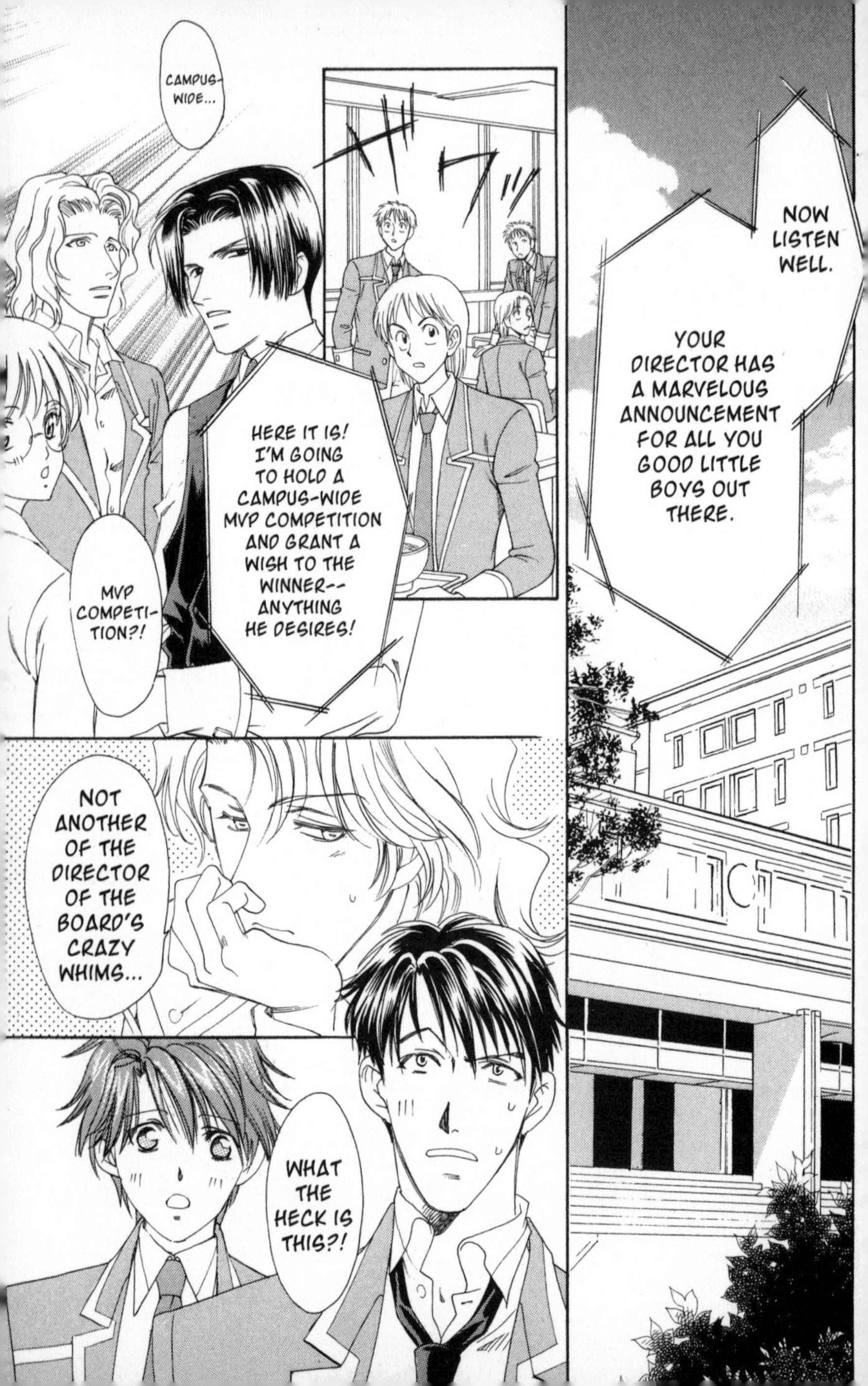
NOW LISTEN WELL.
YOUR DIRECTOR HAS A MARVELOUS ANNOUNCEMENT FOR ALL YOU GOOD LITTLE BOYS OUT THERE.
HERE IT IS! I'M GOING TO HOLD A CAMPUS-WIDE MVP COMPETITION AND GRANT A WISH TO THE WINNER--ANYTHING HE DESIRES!
CAMPUS-WIDE...
MVP COMPETITION?!
NOT ANOTHER OF THE DIRECTOR OF THE BOARD'S CRAZY WHIMS...
WHAT THE HECK IS THIS?!

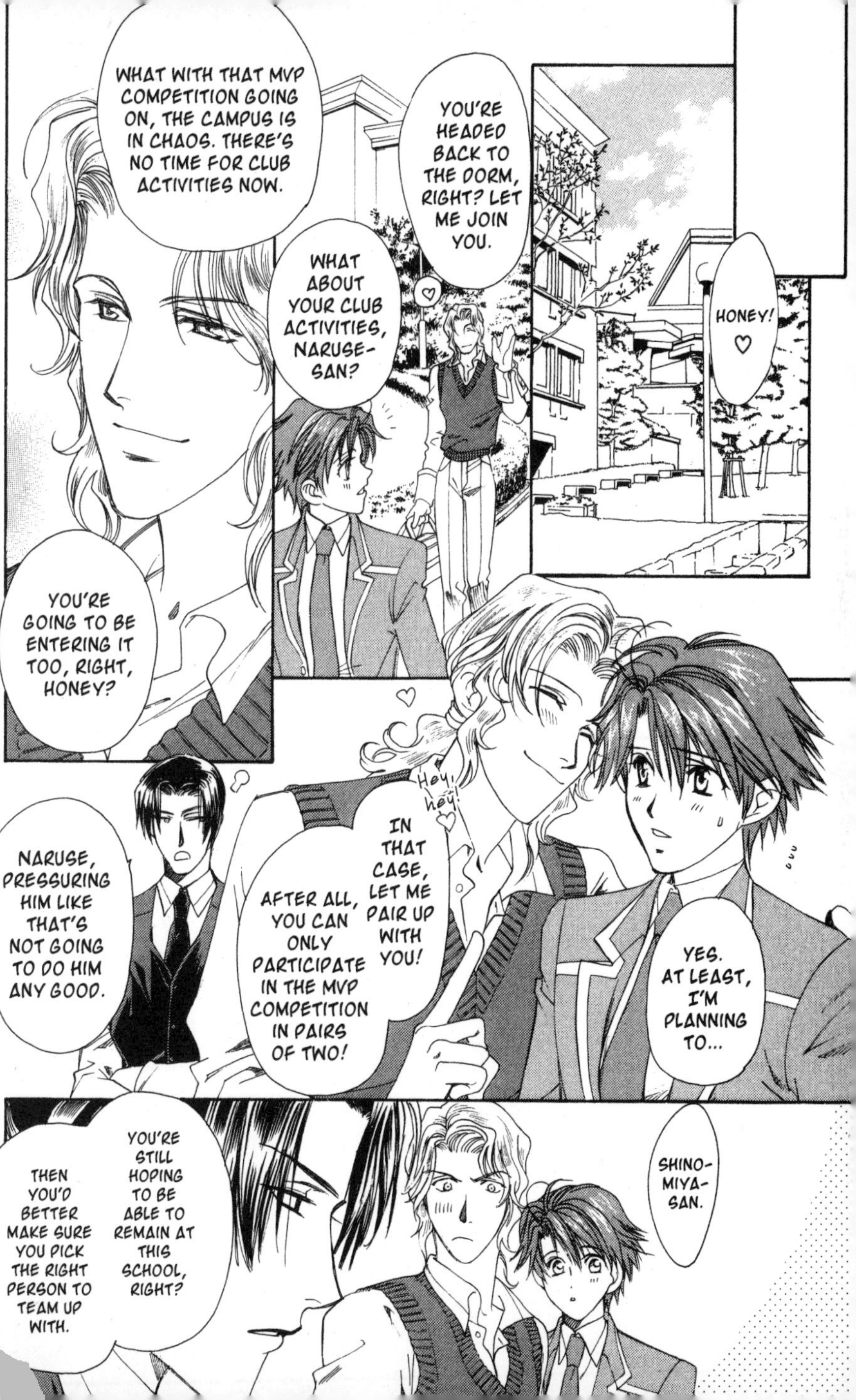
HONEY! ♡
YOU'RE HEADED BACK TO THE DORM, RIGHT? LET ME JOIN YOU.
WHAT ABOUT YOUR CLUB ACTIVITIES, NARUSE-SAN?
WHAT WITH THAT MVP COMPETITION GOING ON, THE CAMPUS IS IN CHAOS. THERE'S NO TIME FOR CLUB ACTIVITIES NOW.
YOU'RE GOING TO BE ENTERING IT TOO, RIGHT, HONEY?
YES. AT LEAST, I'M PLANNING TO...
Hey, hey! ♡
IN THAT CASE, LET ME PAIR UP WITH YOU!
AFTER ALL, YOU CAN ONLY PARTICIPATE IN THE MVP COMPETITION IN PAIRS OF TWO!
NARUSE, PRESSURING HIM LIKE THAT'S NOT GOING TO DO HIM ANY GOOD.
SHINOMIYA-SAN.
YOU'RE STILL HOPING TO BE ABLE TO REMAIN AT THIS SCHOOL, RIGHT?
THEN YOU'D BETTER MAKE SURE YOU PICK THE RIGHT PERSON TO TEAM UP WITH.

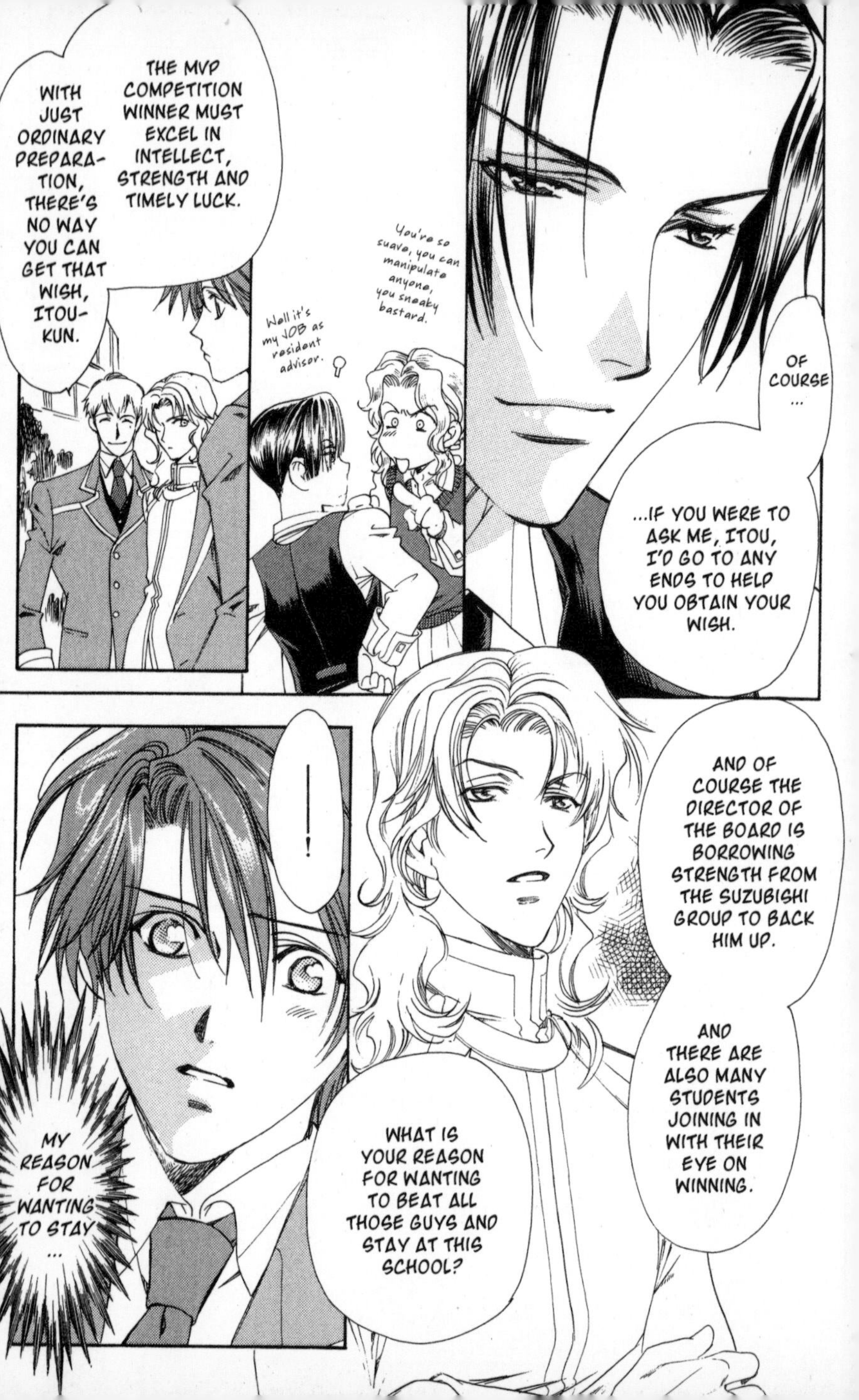
OF COURSE ...
...IF YOU WERE TO ASK ME, ITOU, I'D GO TO ANY ENDS TO HELP YOU OBTAIN YOUR WISH.
You're so suave, you can manipulate anyone, you sneaky bastard.
Well it's my JOB as resident advisor.
THE MVP COMPETITION WINNER MUST EXCEL IN INTELLECT, STRENGTH AND TIMELY LUCK.
WITH JUST ORDINARY PREPARA-TION, THERE'S NO WAY YOU CAN GET THAT WISH, ITOU-KUN.
AND OF COURSE THE DIRECTOR OF THE BOARD IS BORROWING STRENGTH FROM THE SUZUBISHI GROUP TO BACK HIM UP.
AND THERE ARE ALSO MANY STUDENTS JOINING IN WITH THEIR EYE ON WINNING.
WHAT IS YOUR REASON FOR WANTING TO BEAT ALL THOSE GUYS AND STAY AT THIS SCHOOL?
!
MY REASON FOR WANTING TO STAY ...

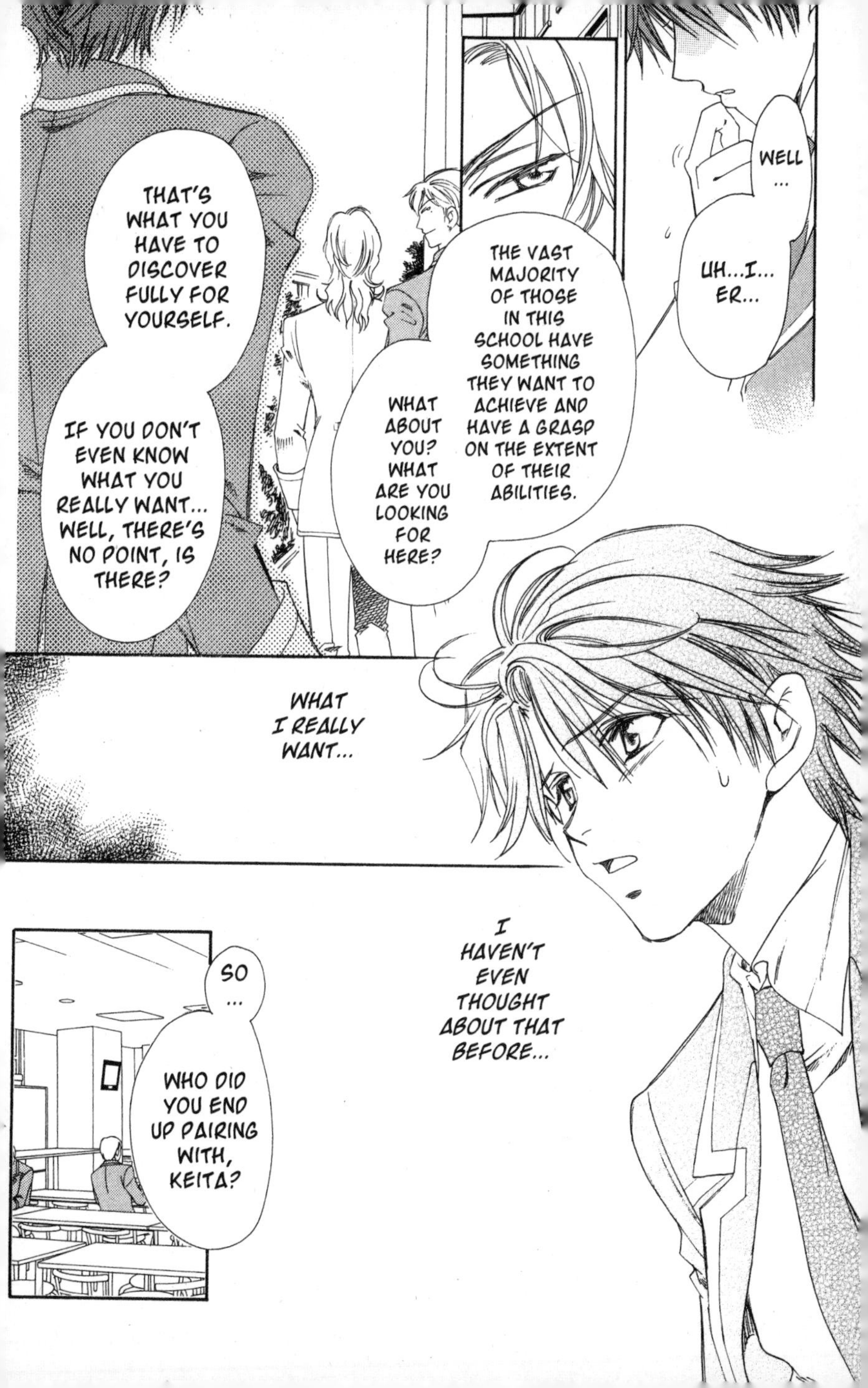
THE VAST MAJORITY OF THOSE IN THIS SCHOOL HAVE SOMETHING THEY WANT TO ACHIEVE AND HAVE A GRASP ON THE EXTENT OF THEIR ABILITIES.
WHAT ABOUT YOU? WHAT ARE YOU LOOKING FOR HERE?
WELL...
UH...I... ER...
THAT'S WHAT YOU HAVE TO DISCOVER FULLY FOR YOURSELF.
IF YOU DON'T EVEN KNOW WHAT YOU REALLY WANT... WELL, THERE'S NO POINT, IS THERE?
WHAT I REALLY WANT...
I HAVEN'T EVEN THOUGHT ABOUT THAT BEFORE...
SO...
WHO DID YOU END UP PAIRING WITH, KEITA?

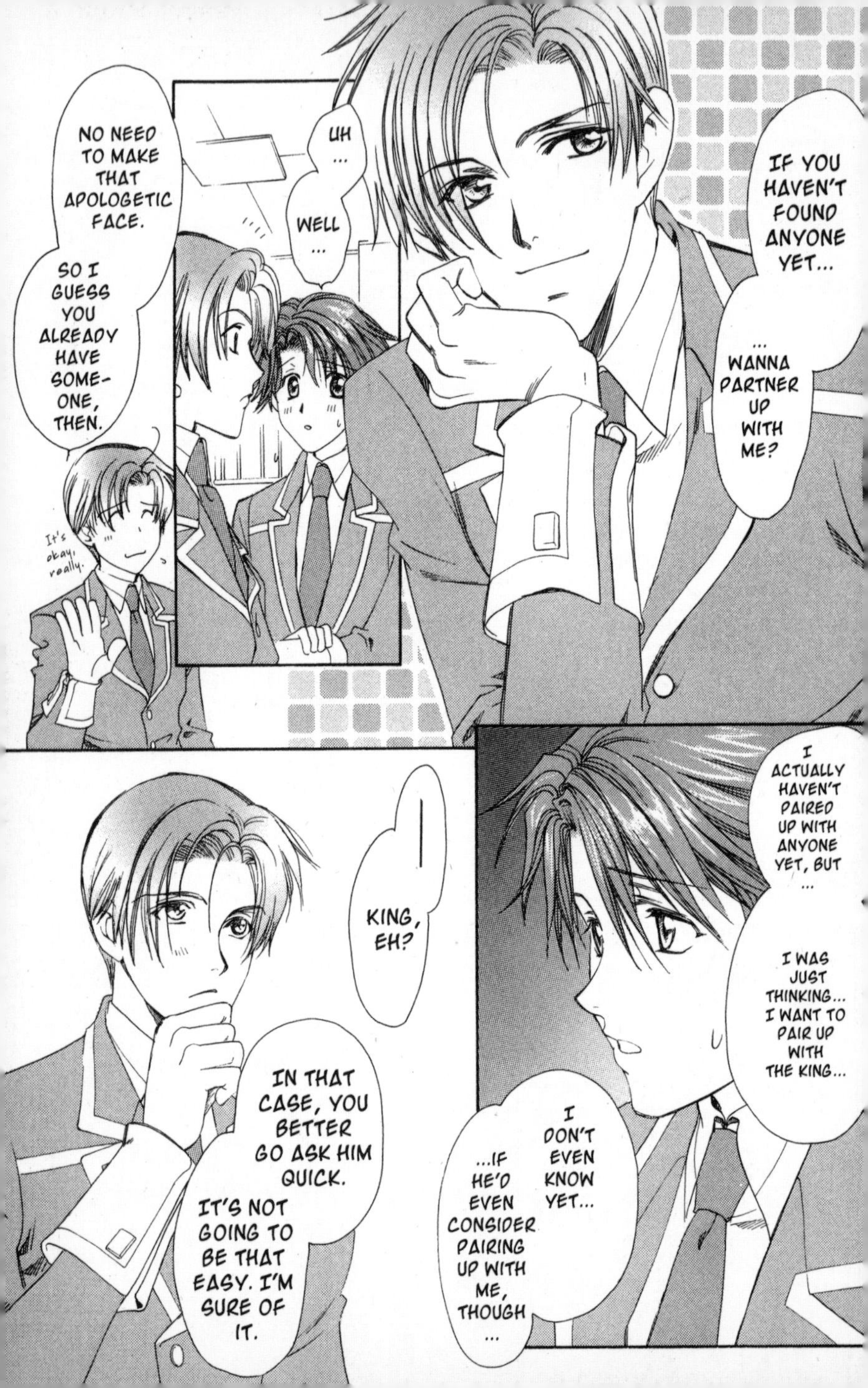
IF YOU HAVEN'T FOUND ANYONE YET...
... WANNA PARTNER UP WITH ME?
UH ...
WELL ...
NO NEED TO MAKE THAT APOLOGETIC FACE.
SO I GUESS YOU ALREADY HAVE SOME-ONE, THEN.
It's okay, really.
I ACTUALLY HAVEN'T PAIRED UP WITH ANYONE YET, BUT ...
I WAS JUST THINKING... I WANT TO PAIR UP WITH THE KING...
I DON'T EVEN KNOW YET...
...IF HE'D EVEN CONSIDER PAIRING UP WITH ME, THOUGH ...
—
KING, EH?
IN THAT CASE, YOU BETTER GO ASK HIM QUICK.
IT'S NOT GOING TO BE THAT EASY. I'M SURE OF IT.

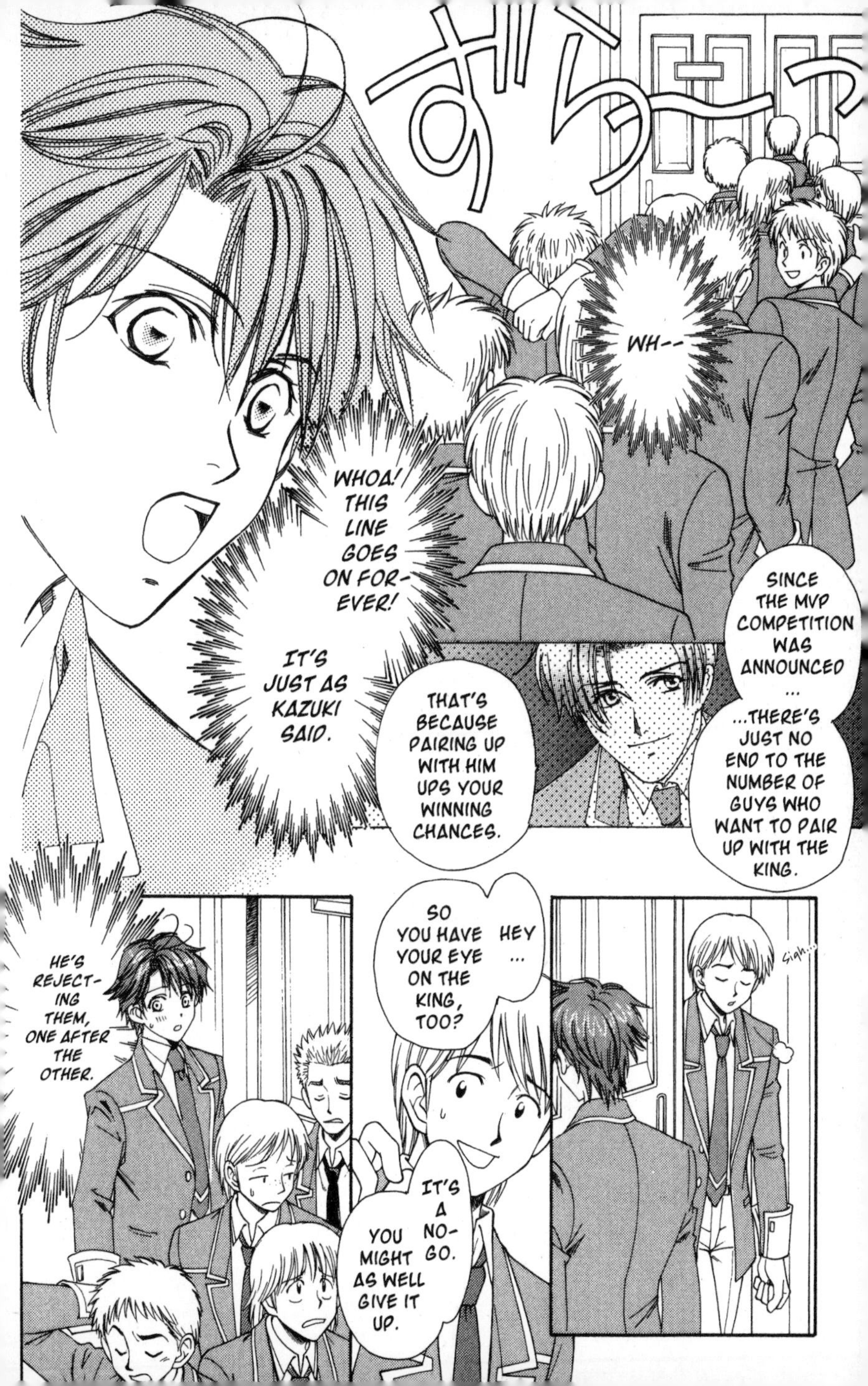
ずらー
WH--
WHOA! THIS LINE GOES ON FOR-EVER!
IT'S JUST AS KAZUKI SAID.
SINCE THE MVP COMPETITION WAS ANNOUNCED ...
...THERE'S JUST NO END TO THE NUMBER OF GUYS WHO WANT TO PAIR UP WITH THE KING.
THAT'S BECAUSE PAIRING UP WITH HIM UPS YOUR WINNING CHANCES.
Sigh...
HEY ...
SO YOU HAVE YOUR EYE ON THE KING, TOO?
IT'S A NO-GO.
YOU MIGHT AS WELL GIVE IT UP.
HE'S REJECT-ING THEM, ONE AFTER THE OTHER.

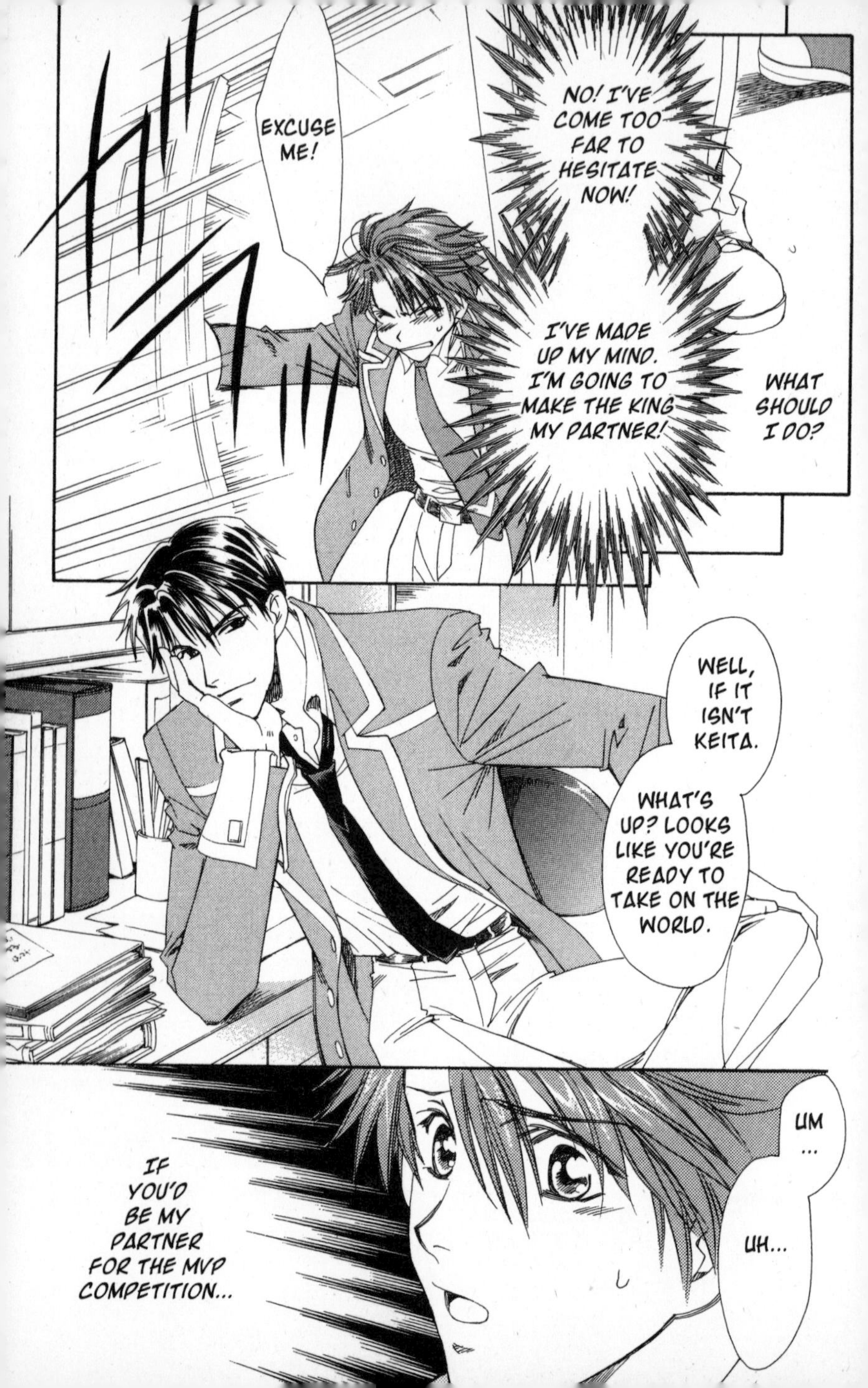
WHAT SHOULD I DO?
NO! I'VE COME TOO FAR TO HESITATE NOW!
I'VE MADE UP MY MIND. I'M GOING TO MAKE THE KING MY PARTNER!
EXCUSE ME!
WELL, IF IT ISN'T KEITA.
WHAT'S UP? LOOKS LIKE YOU'RE READY TO TAKE ON THE WORLD.
UM ...
UH...
IF YOU'D BE MY PARTNER FOR THE MVP COMPETITION...

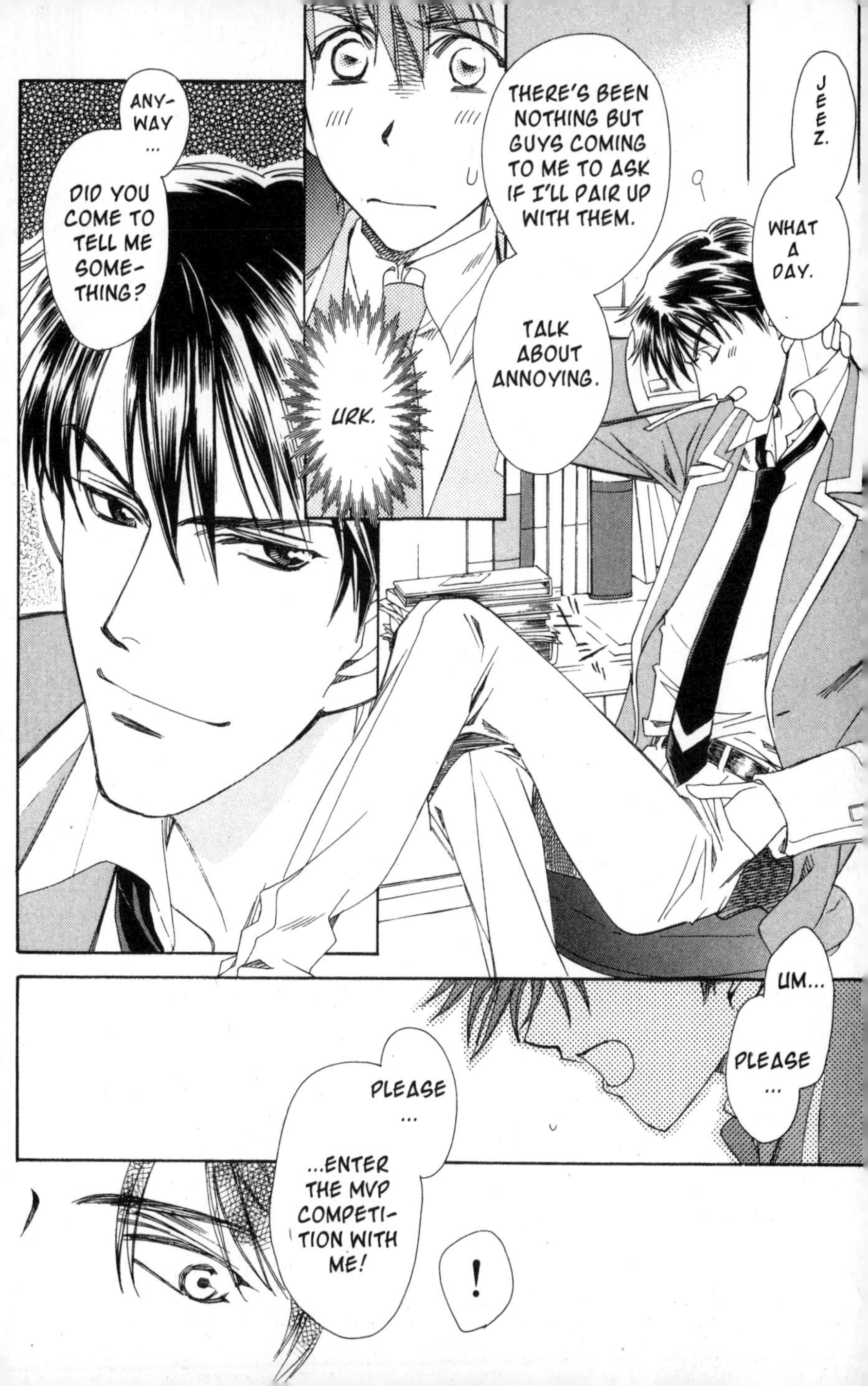
JEEZ.
WHAT A DAY.
THERE'S BEEN NOTHING BUT GUYS COMING TO ME TO ASK IF I'LL PAIR UP WITH THEM.
TALK ABOUT ANNOYING.
URK.
ANY-WAY ...
DID YOU COME TO TELL ME SOME-THING?
UM...
PLEASE ...
PLEASE ...
...ENTER THE MVP COMPETI-TION WITH ME!
!

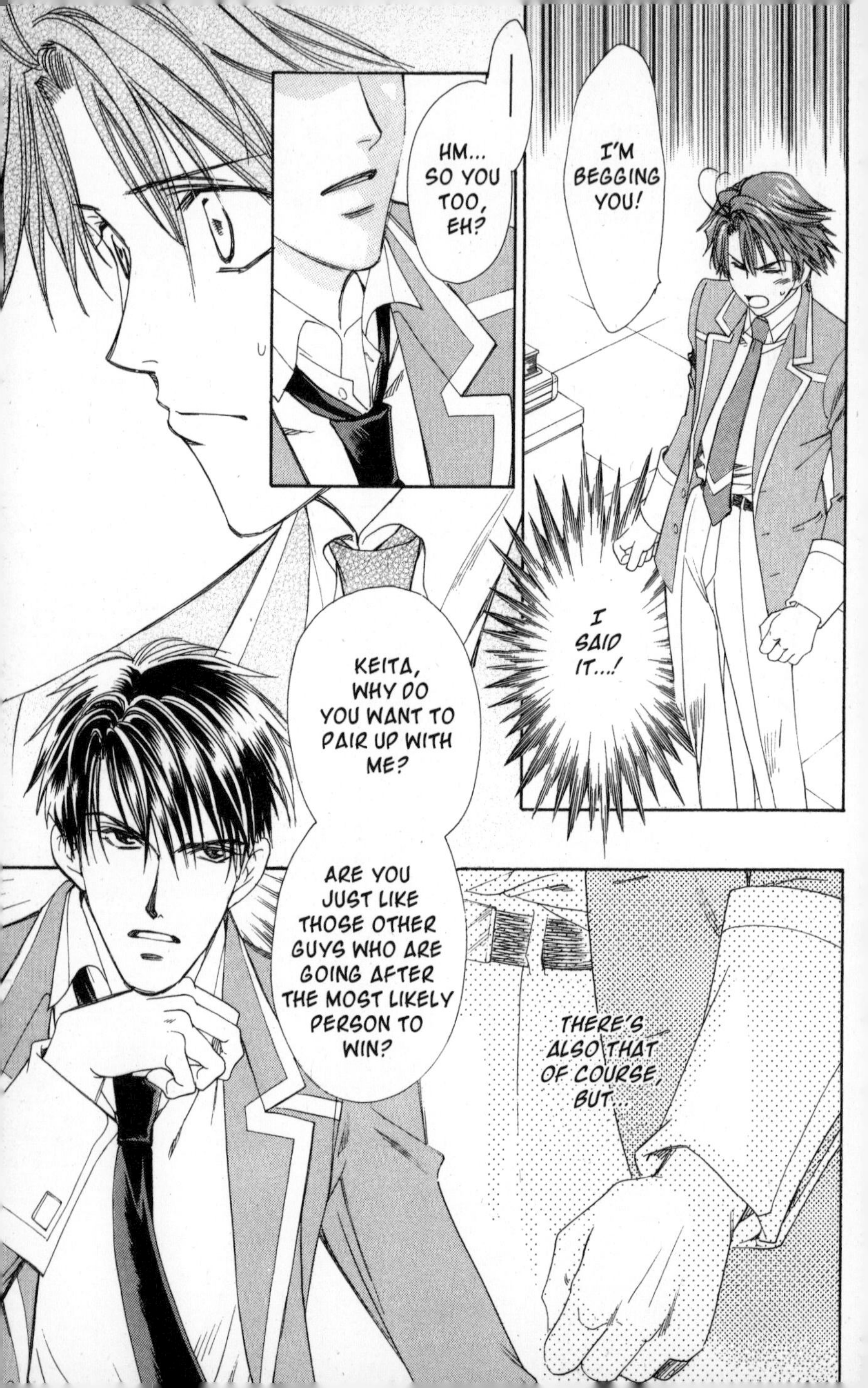
I'M BEGGING YOU!
I SAID IT...!
HM... SO YOU TOO, EH?
KEITA, WHY DO YOU WANT TO PAIR UP WITH ME?
ARE YOU JUST LIKE THOSE OTHER GUYS WHO ARE GOING AFTER THE MOST LIKELY PERSON TO WIN?
THERE'S ALSO THAT OF COURSE, BUT...

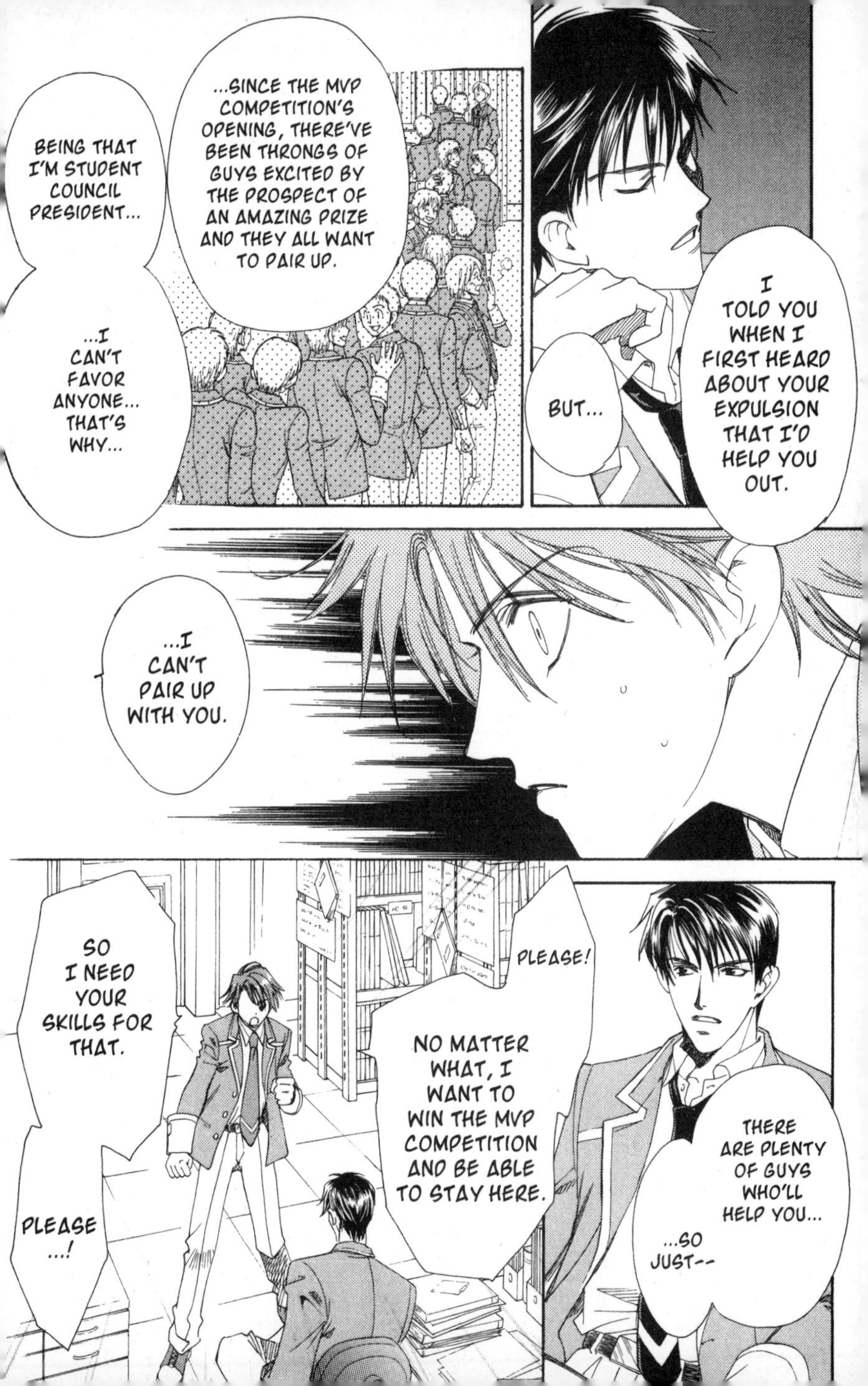
I TOLD YOU WHEN I FIRST HEARD ABOUT YOUR EXPULSION THAT I'D HELP YOU OUT.
BUT...
...SINCE THE MVP COMPETITION'S OPENING, THERE'VE BEEN THRONGS OF GUYS EXCITED BY THE PROSPECT OF AN AMAZING PRIZE AND THEY ALL WANT TO PAIR UP.
BEING THAT I'M STUDENT COUNCIL PRESIDENT...
...I CAN'T FAVOR ANYONE... THAT'S WHY...
...I CAN'T PAIR UP WITH YOU.
THERE ARE PLENTY OF GUYS WHO'LL HELP YOU...
...SO JUST--
PLEASE!
NO MATTER WHAT, I WANT TO WIN THE MVP COMPETITION AND BE ABLE TO STAY HERE.
SO I NEED YOUR SKILLS FOR THAT.
PLEASE ...!

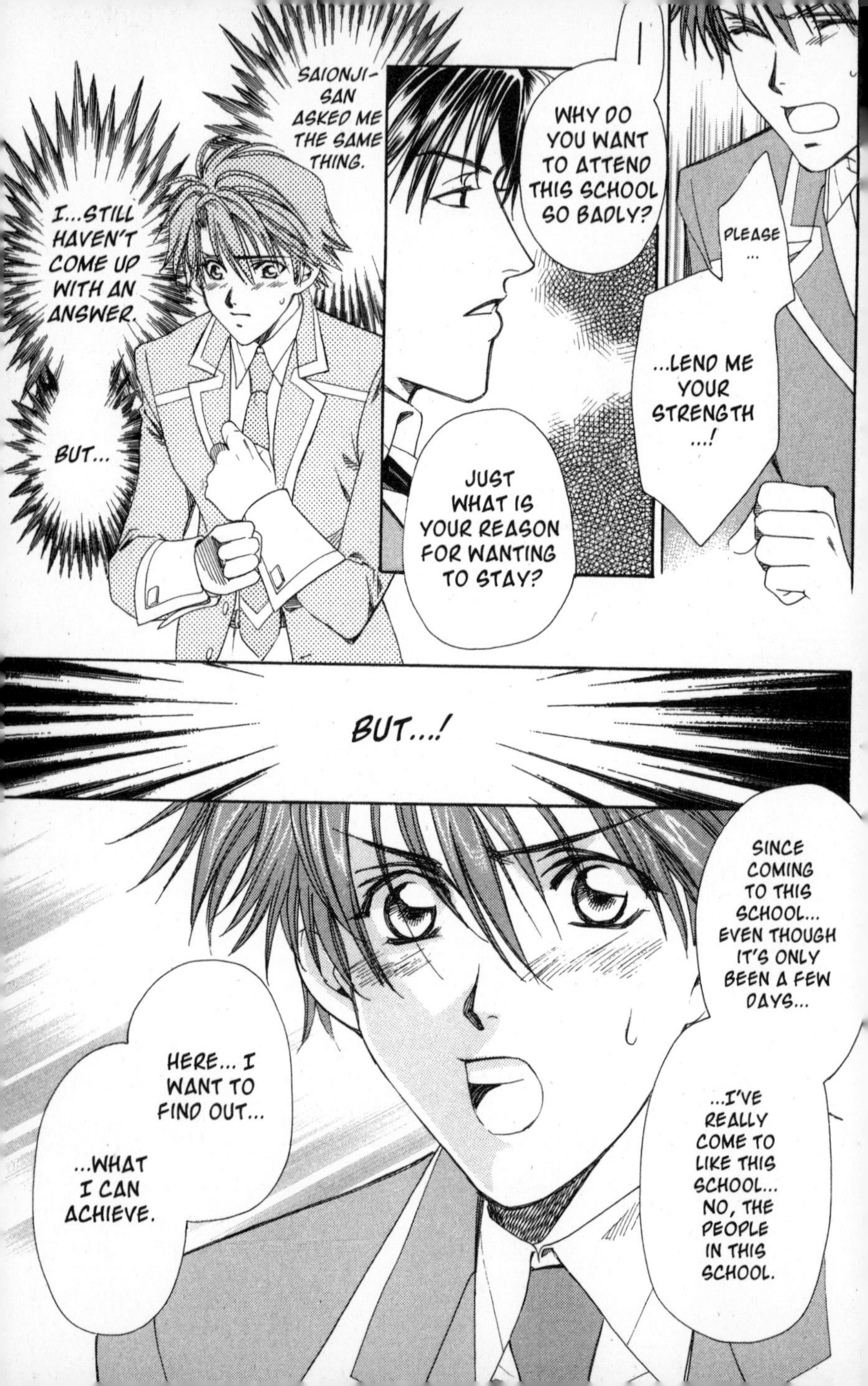
PLEASE...
...LEND ME YOUR STRENGTH...!
WHY DO YOU WANT TO ATTEND THIS SCHOOL SO BADLY?
JUST WHAT IS YOUR REASON FOR WANTING TO STAY?
SAIONJI-SAN ASKED ME THE SAME THING.
I...STILL HAVEN'T COME UP WITH AN ANSWER.
BUT...
BUT...!
SINCE COMING TO THIS SCHOOL... EVEN THOUGH IT'S ONLY BEEN A FEW DAYS...
...I'VE REALLY COME TO LIKE THIS SCHOOL... NO, THE PEOPLE IN THIS SCHOOL.
HERE... I WANT TO FIND OUT...
...WHAT I CAN ACHIEVE.

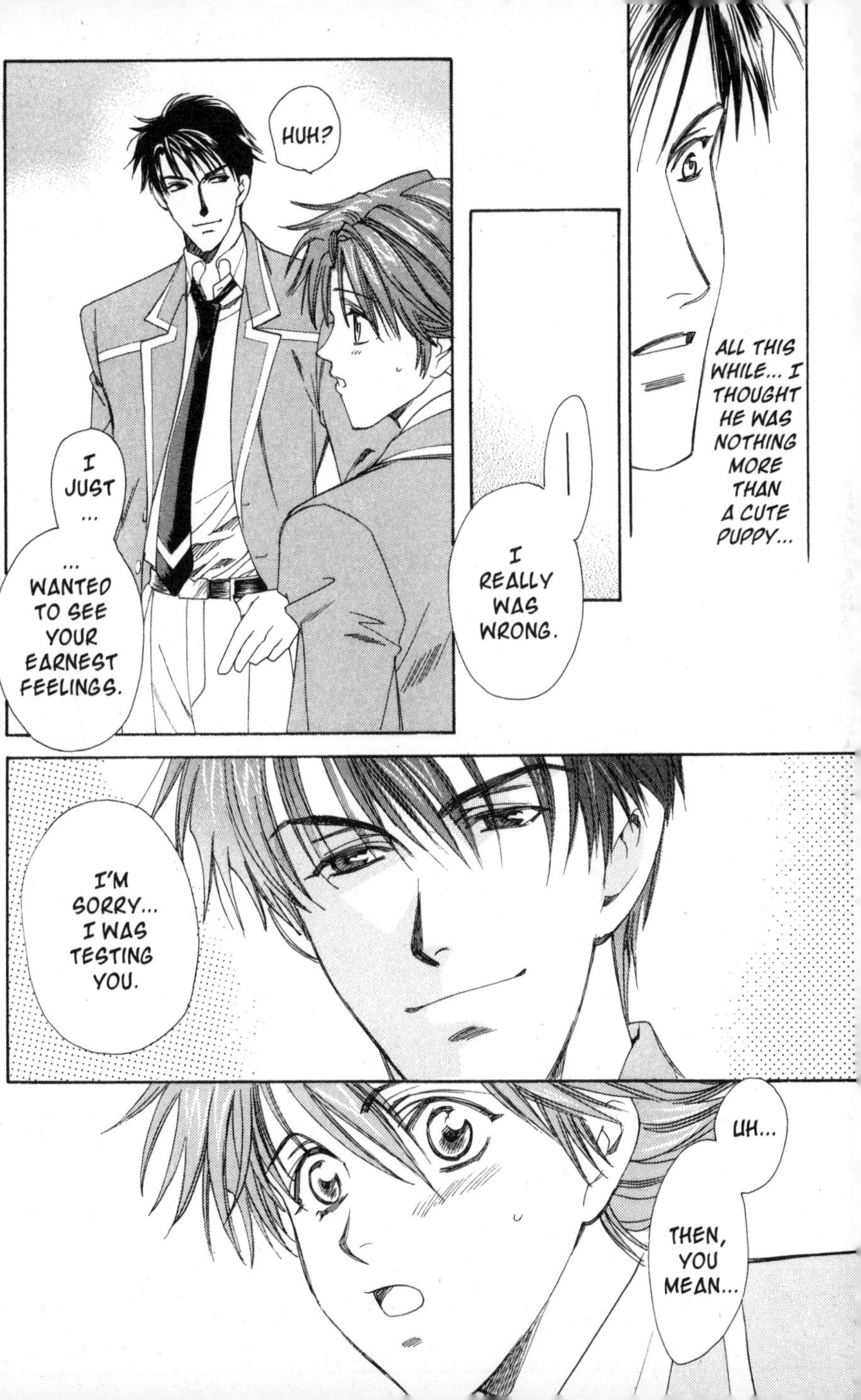
ALL THIS WHILE... I THOUGHT HE WAS NOTHING MORE THAN A CUTE PUPPY...
I REALLY WAS WRONG.
HUH?
I JUST ...
... WANTED TO SEE YOUR EARNEST FEELINGS.
I'M SORRY... I WAS TESTING YOU.
UH...
THEN, YOU MEAN...

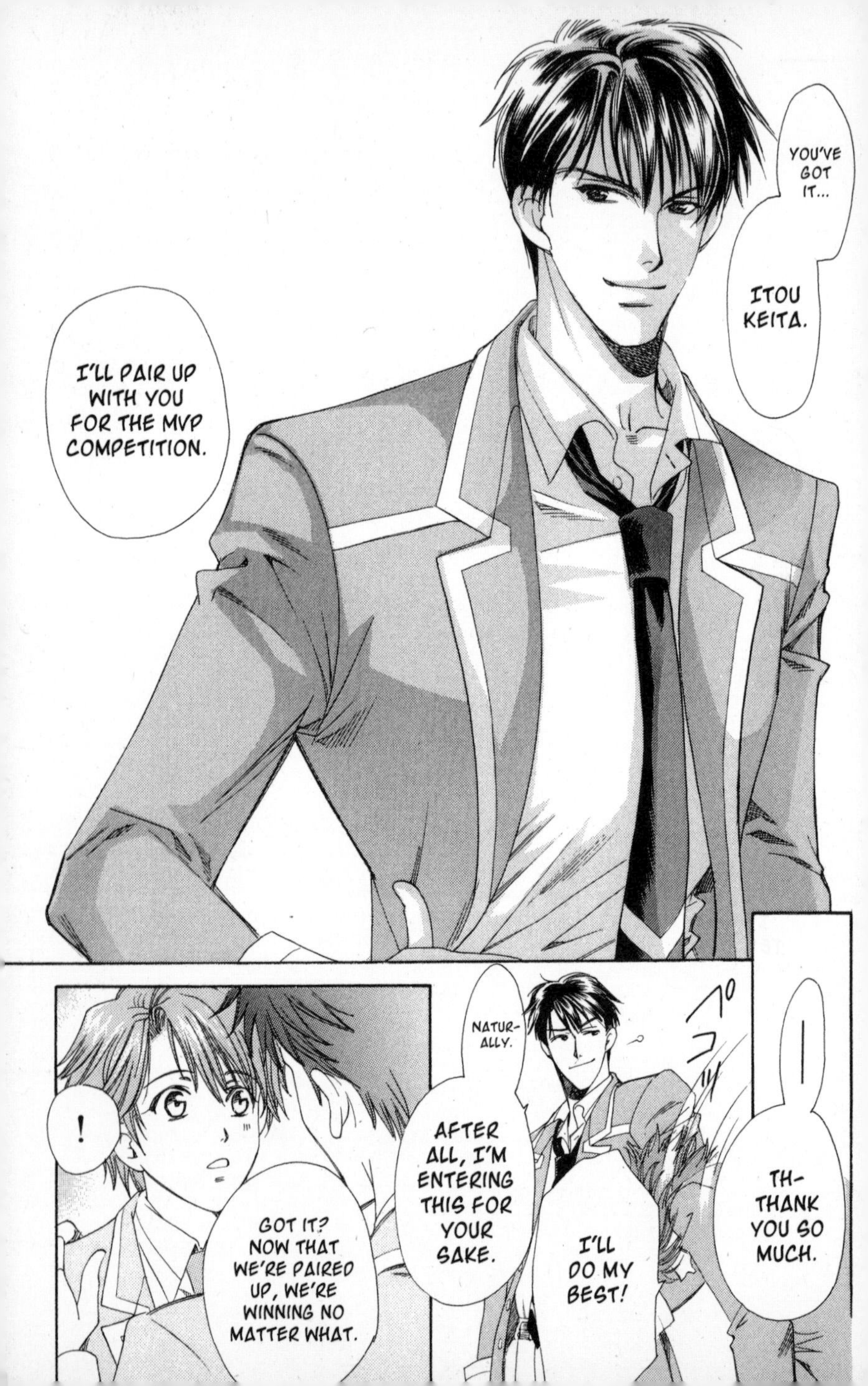
YOU'VE GOT IT...
ITOU KEITA.
I'LL PAIR UP WITH YOU FOR THE MVP COMPETITION.
TH- THANK YOU SO MUCH.
NATUR- ALLY.
AFTER ALL, I'M ENTERING THIS FOR YOUR SAKE.
I'LL DO MY BEST!
!
GOT IT? NOW THAT WE'RE PAIRED UP, WE'RE WINNING NO MATTER WHAT.

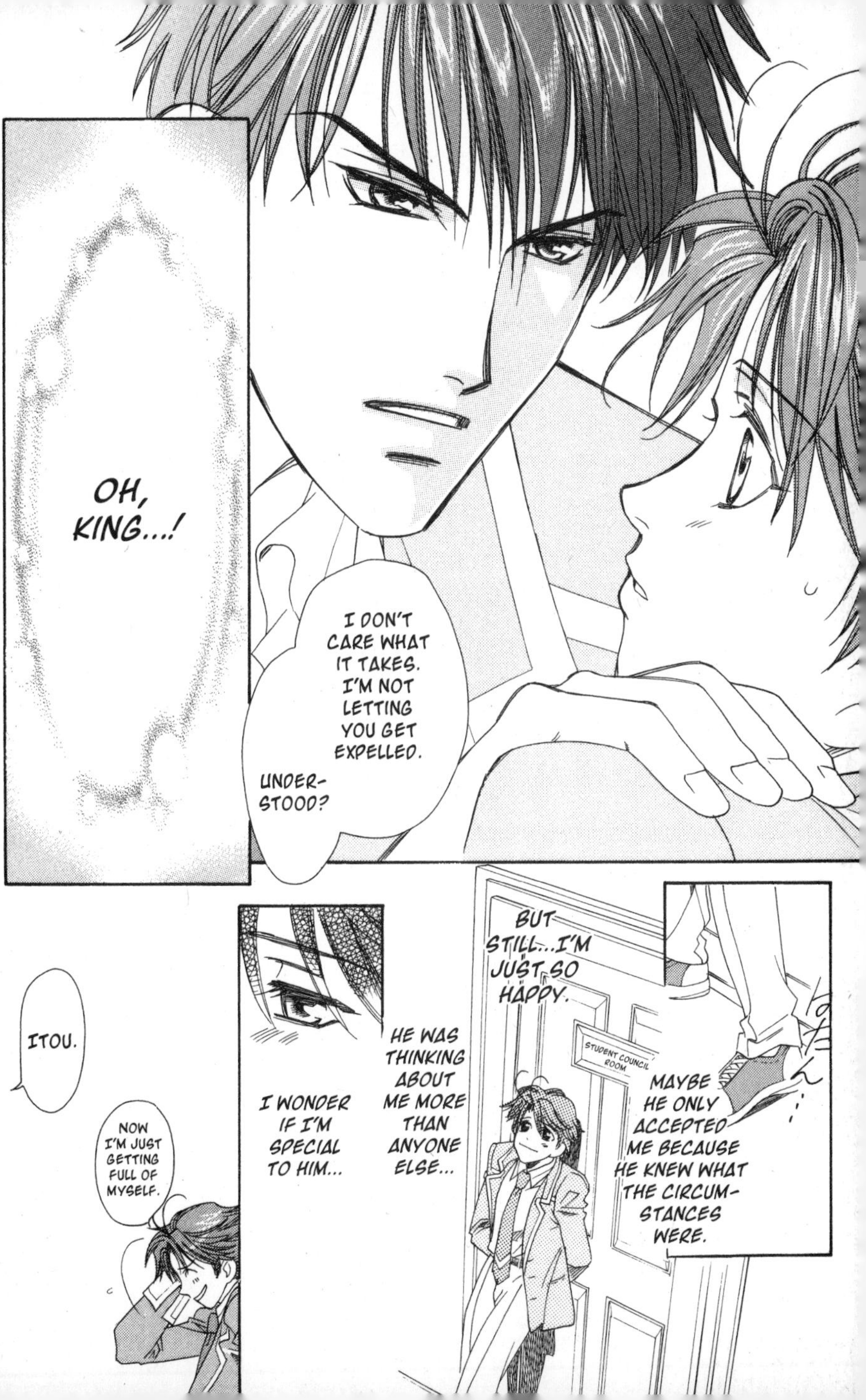
I DON'T CARE WHAT IT TAKES. I'M NOT LETTING YOU GET EXPELLED.
UNDER-STOOD?
OH, KING...!
MAYBE HE ONLY ACCEPTED ME BECAUSE HE KNEW WHAT THE CIRCUM-STANCES WERE.
BUT STILL...I'M JUST SO HAPPY.
STUDENT COUNCIL ROOM
HE WAS THINKING ABOUT ME MORE THAN ANYONE ELSE...
I WONDER IF I'M SPECIAL TO HIM...
NOW I'M JUST GETTING FULL OF MYSELF.
ITOU.

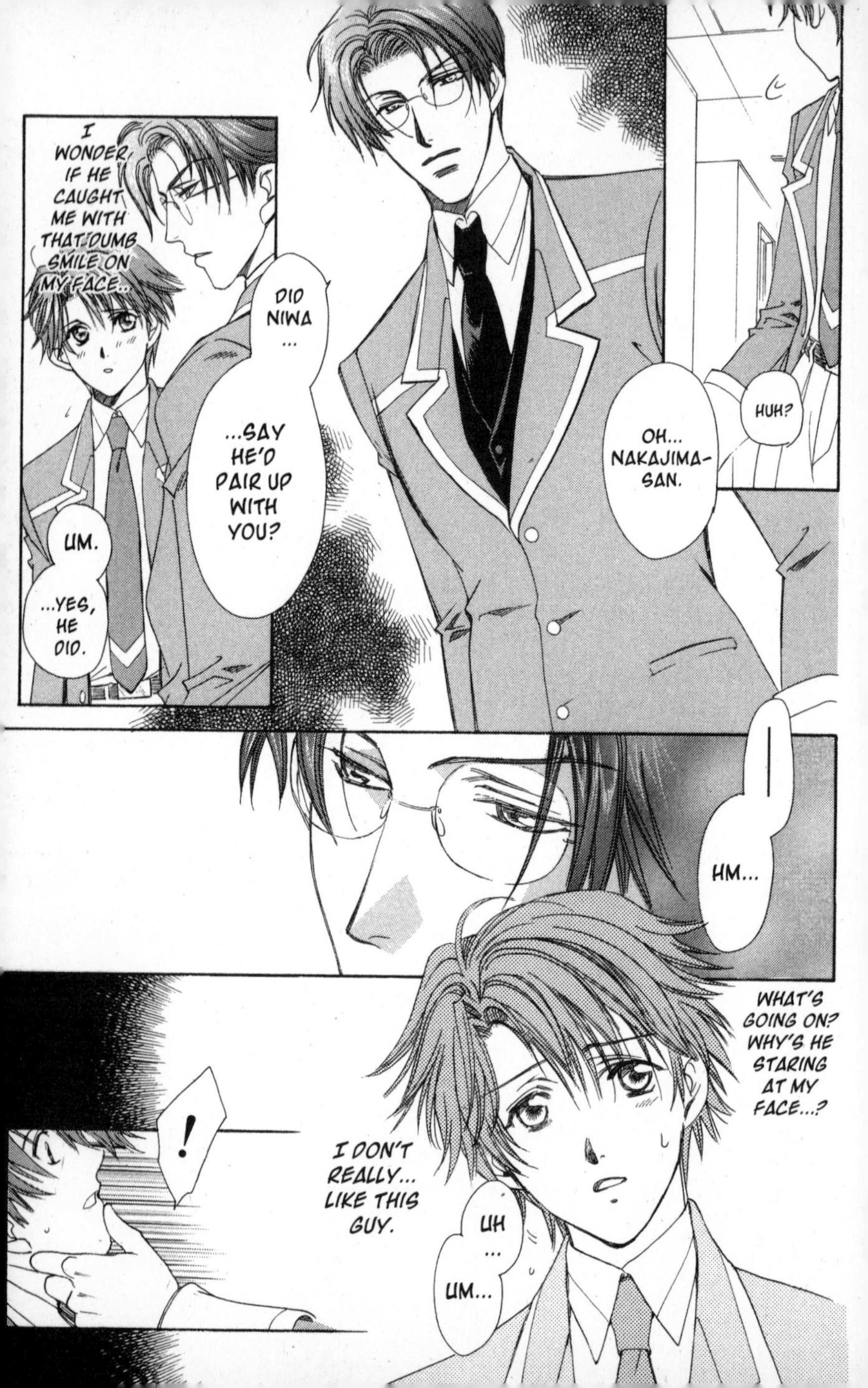
HUH?
OH... NAKAJIMA-SAN.
I WONDER IF HE CAUGHT ME WITH THAT DUMB SMILE ON MY FACE...
DID NIWA ...
...SAY HE'D PAIR UP WITH YOU?
UM.
...YES, HE DID.
HM...
WHAT'S GOING ON? WHY'S HE STARING AT MY FACE...?
I DON'T REALLY... LIKE THIS GUY.
UH ...
UM...
!

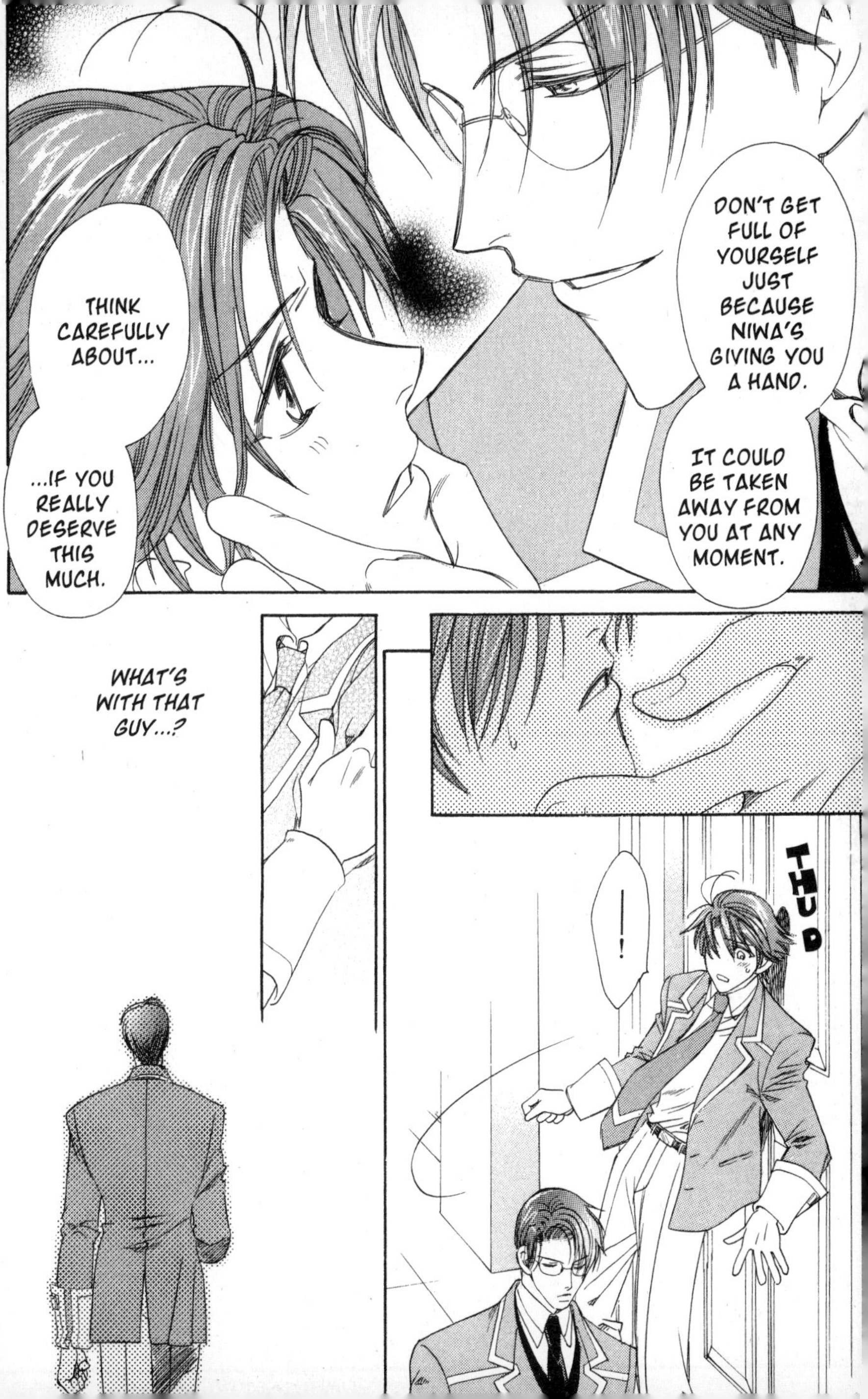
DON'T GET FULL OF YOURSELF JUST BECAUSE NIWA'S GIVING YOU A HAND.
IT COULD BE TAKEN AWAY FROM YOU AT ANY MOMENT.
THINK CAREFULLY ABOUT...
...IF YOU REALLY DESERVE THIS MUCH.
THUD
!
WHAT'S WITH THAT GUY...?

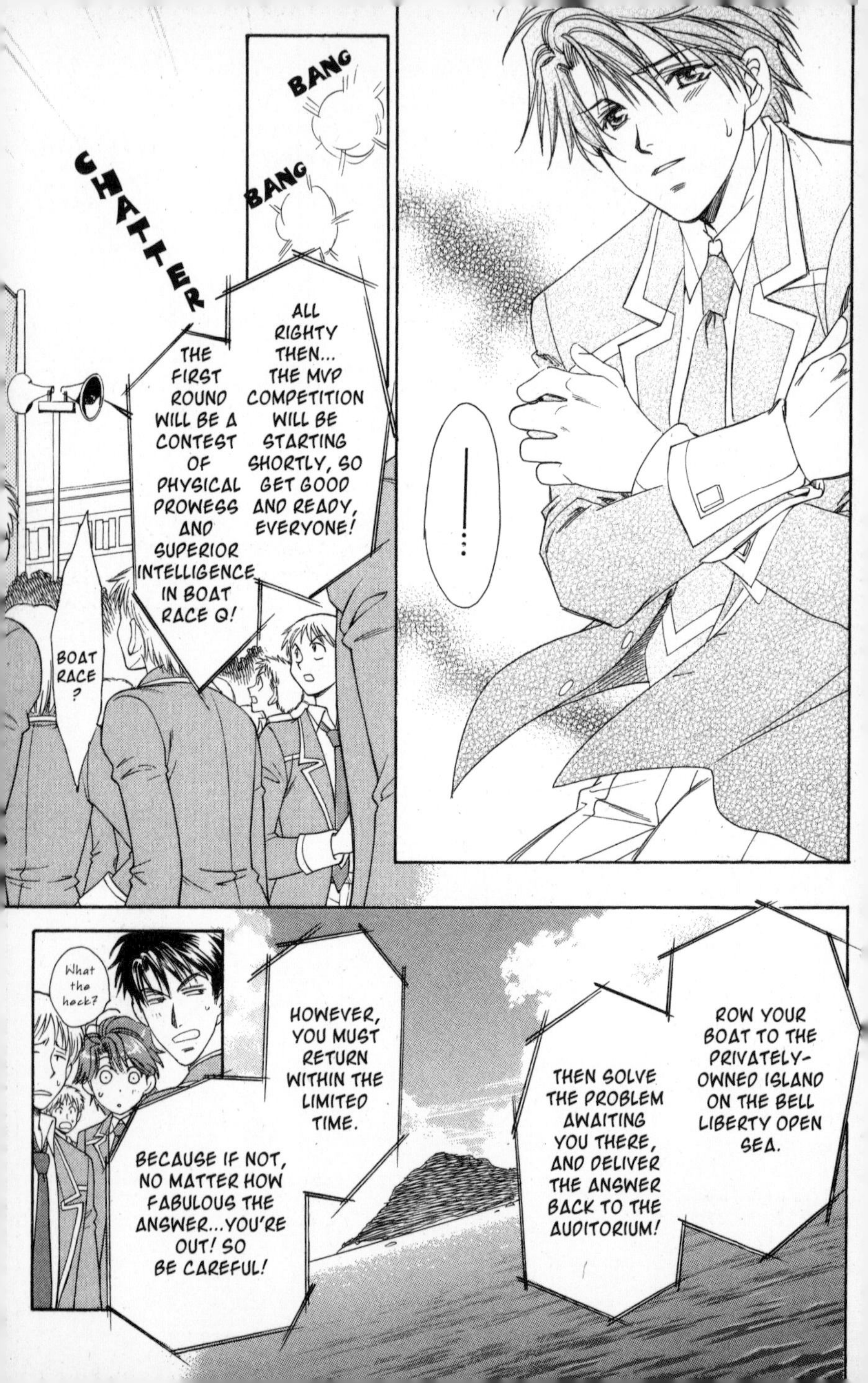
!...
BANG
BANG
CHATTER
ALL RIGHTY THEN... THE MVP COMPETITION WILL BE STARTING SHORTLY, SO GET GOOD AND READY, EVERYONE!
THE FIRST ROUND WILL BE A CONTEST OF PHYSICAL PROWESS AND SUPERIOR INTELLIGENCE IN BOAT RACE Q!
BOAT RACE?
ROW YOUR BOAT TO THE PRIVATELY-OWNED ISLAND ON THE BELL LIBERTY OPEN SEA.
THEN SOLVE THE PROBLEM AWAITING YOU THERE, AND DELIVER THE ANSWER BACK TO THE AUDITORIUM!
HOWEVER, YOU MUST RETURN WITHIN THE LIMITED TIME.
BECAUSE IF NOT, NO MATTER HOW FABULOUS THE ANSWER...YOU'RE OUT! SO BE CAREFUL!
What the heck?

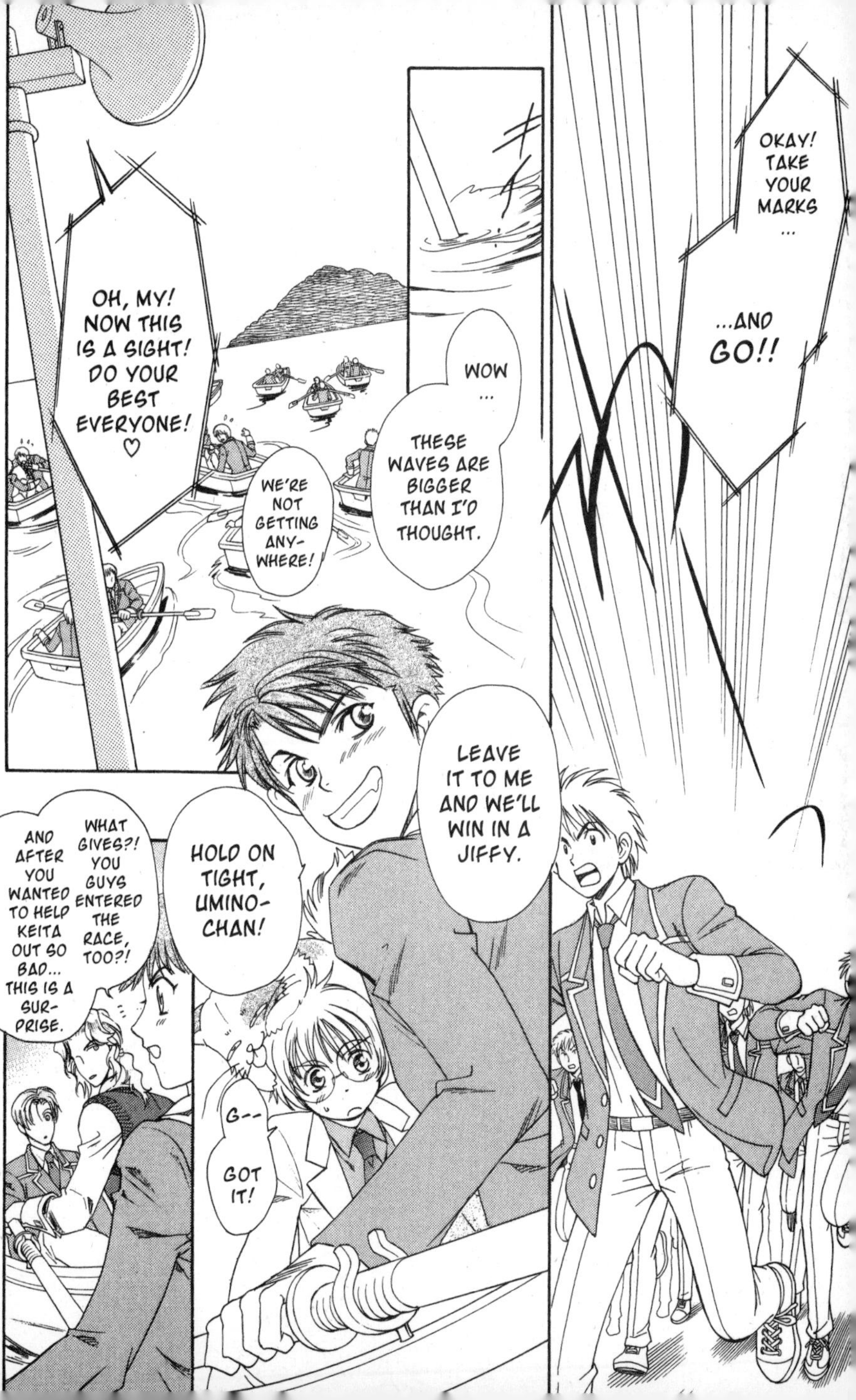
OKAY! TAKE YOUR MARKS ...
...AND GO!!
OH, MY! NOW THIS IS A SIGHT! DO YOUR BEST EVERYONE! ♡
WOW ...
THESE WAVES ARE BIGGER THAN I'D THOUGHT.
WE'RE NOT GETTING ANY-WHERE!
LEAVE IT TO ME AND WE'LL WIN IN A JIFFY.
HOLD ON TIGHT, UMINO-CHAN!
G--
GOT IT!
WHAT GIVES?! YOU GUYS ENTERED THE RACE, TOO?!
AND AFTER YOU WANTED TO HELP KEITA OUT SO BAD... THIS IS A SUR-PRISE.

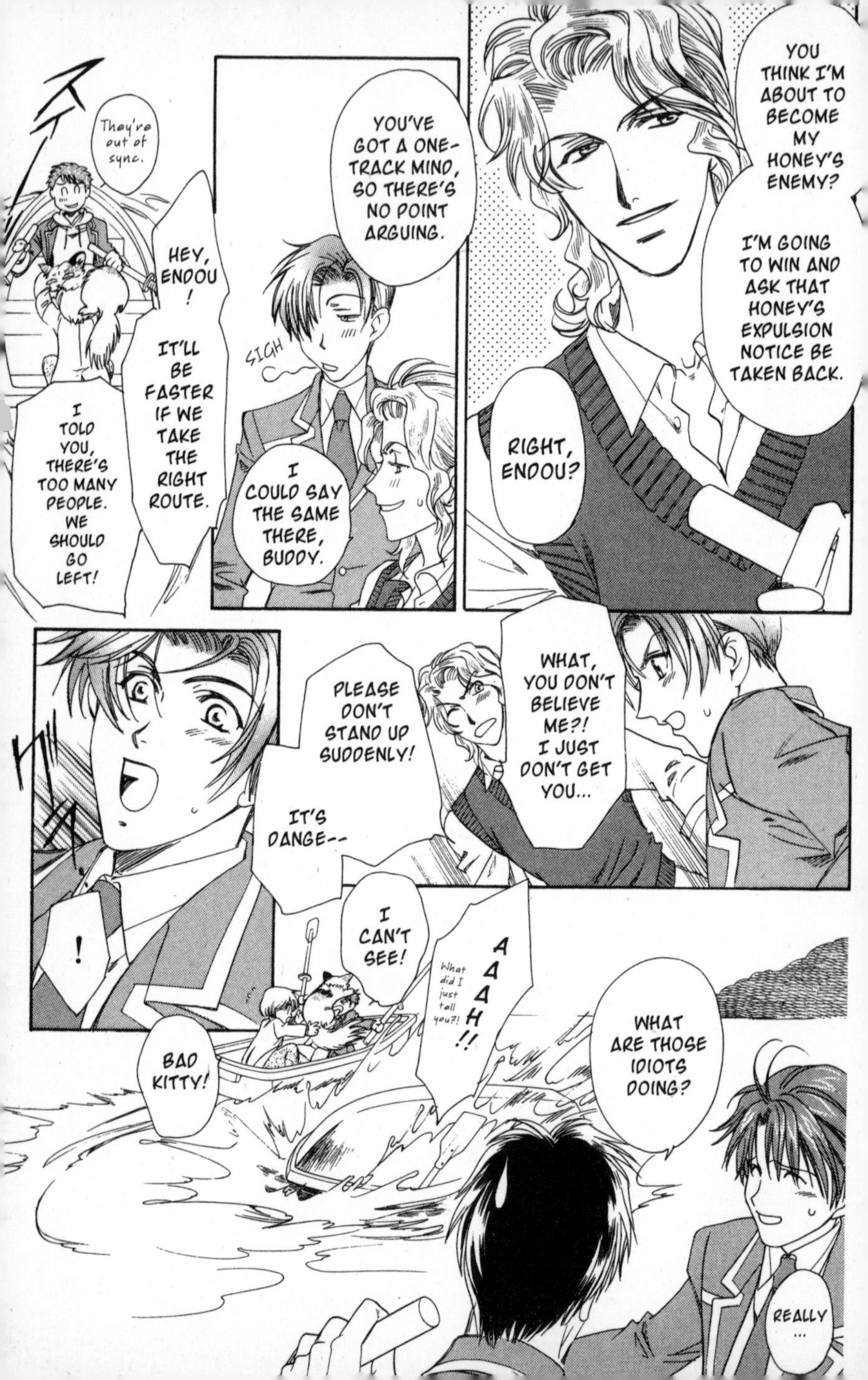
YOU THINK I'M ABOUT TO BECOME MY HONEY'S ENEMY?
I'M GOING TO WIN AND ASK THAT HONEY'S EXPULSION NOTICE BE TAKEN BACK.
RIGHT, ENDOU?
YOU'VE GOT A ONE-TRACK MIND, SO THERE'S NO POINT ARGUING.
SIGH
I COULD SAY THE SAME THERE, BUDDY.
HEY, ENDOU!
IT'LL BE FASTER IF WE TAKE THE RIGHT ROUTE.
They're out of sync.
I TOLD YOU, THERE'S TOO MANY PEOPLE. WE SHOULD GO LEFT!
WHAT, YOU DON'T BELIEVE ME?! I JUST DON'T GET YOU...
PLEASE DON'T STAND UP SUDDENLY!
IT'S DANGE--
!
I CAN'T SEE!
AAAAH!!
What did I just tell you?!
BAD KITTY!
WHAT ARE THOSE IDIOTS DOING?
REALLY...

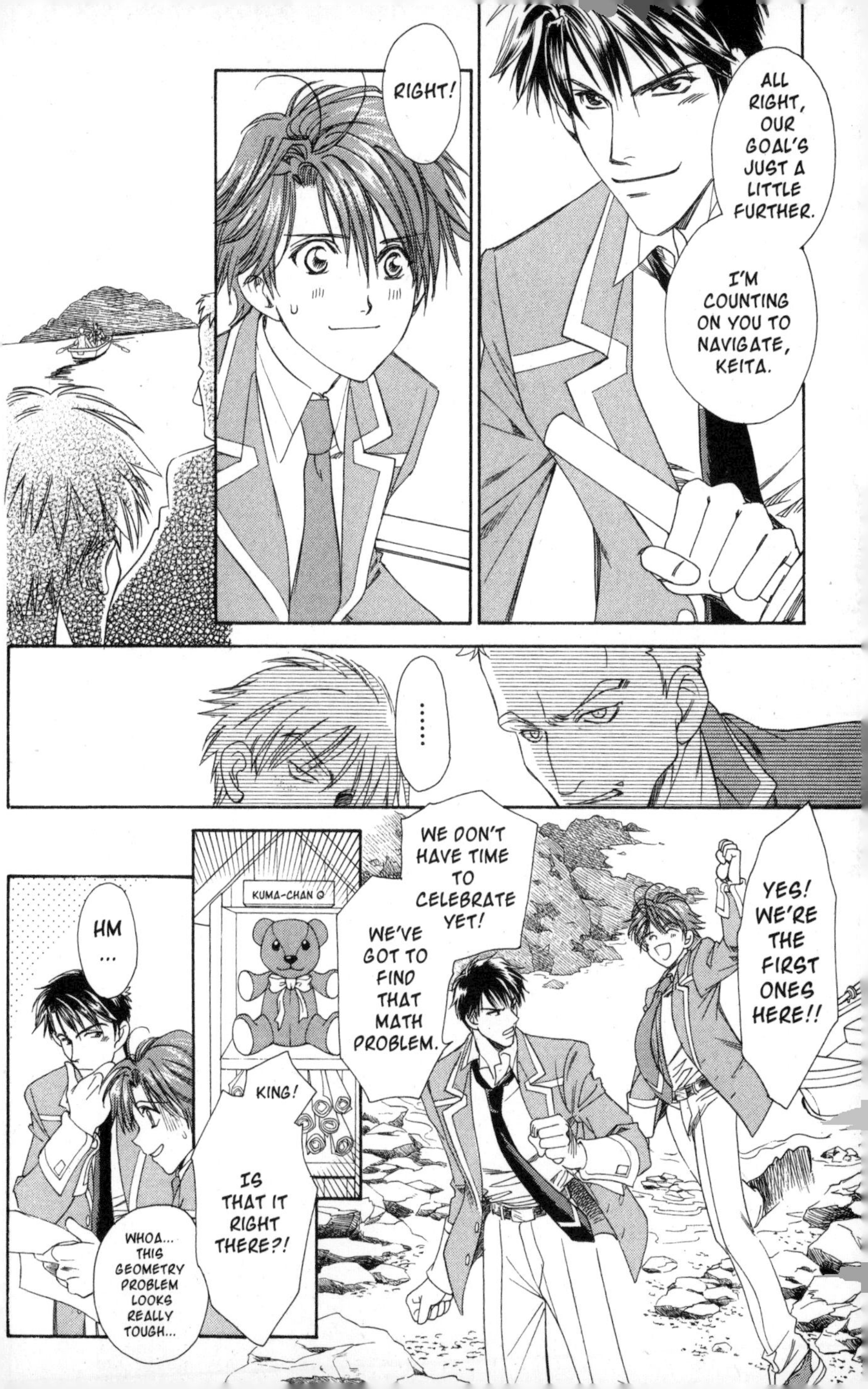
ALL RIGHT, OUR GOAL'S JUST A LITTLE FURTHER.
I'M COUNTING ON YOU TO NAVIGATE, KEITA.
RIGHT!
......
YES! WE'RE THE FIRST ONES HERE!!
WE DON'T HAVE TIME TO CELEBRATE YET!
WE'VE GOT TO FIND THAT MATH PROBLEM.
KUMA-CHAN
KING!
IS THAT IT RIGHT THERE?!
HM ...
WHOA... THIS GEOMETRY PROBLEM LOOKS REALLY TOUGH...

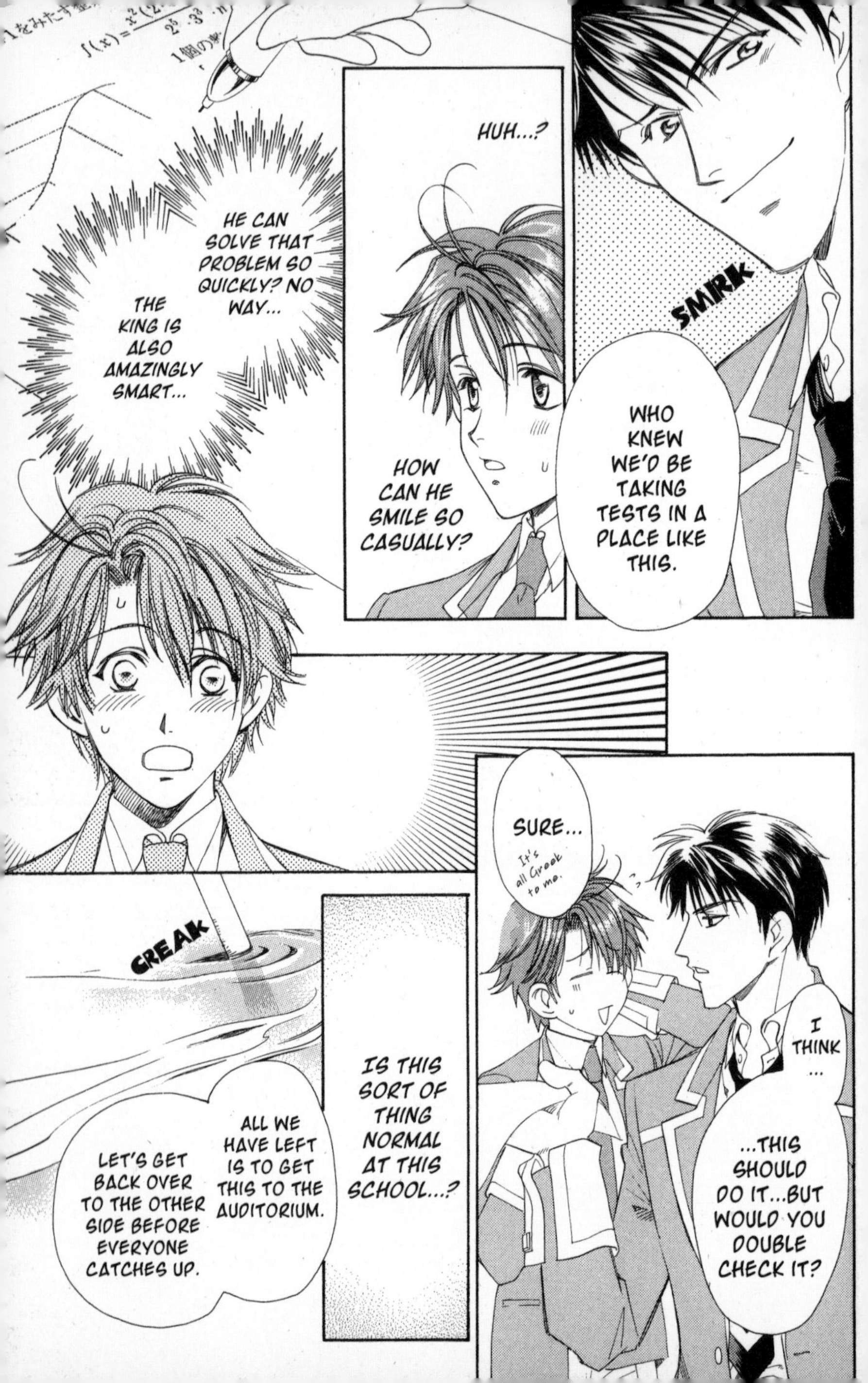
SMIRK
WHO KNEW WE'D BE TAKING TESTS IN A PLACE LIKE THIS.
HUH...?
HOW CAN HE SMILE SO CASUALLY?
HE CAN SOLVE THAT PROBLEM SO QUICKLY? NO WAY...
THE KING IS ALSO AMAZINGLY SMART...
I THINK...
...THIS SHOULD DO IT...BUT WOULD YOU DOUBLE CHECK IT?
SURE...
It's all Greek to me.
IS THIS SORT OF THING NORMAL AT THIS SCHOOL...?
CREAK
ALL WE HAVE LEFT IS TO GET THIS TO THE AUDITORIUM.
LET'S GET BACK OVER TO THE OTHER SIDE BEFORE EVERYONE CATCHES UP.

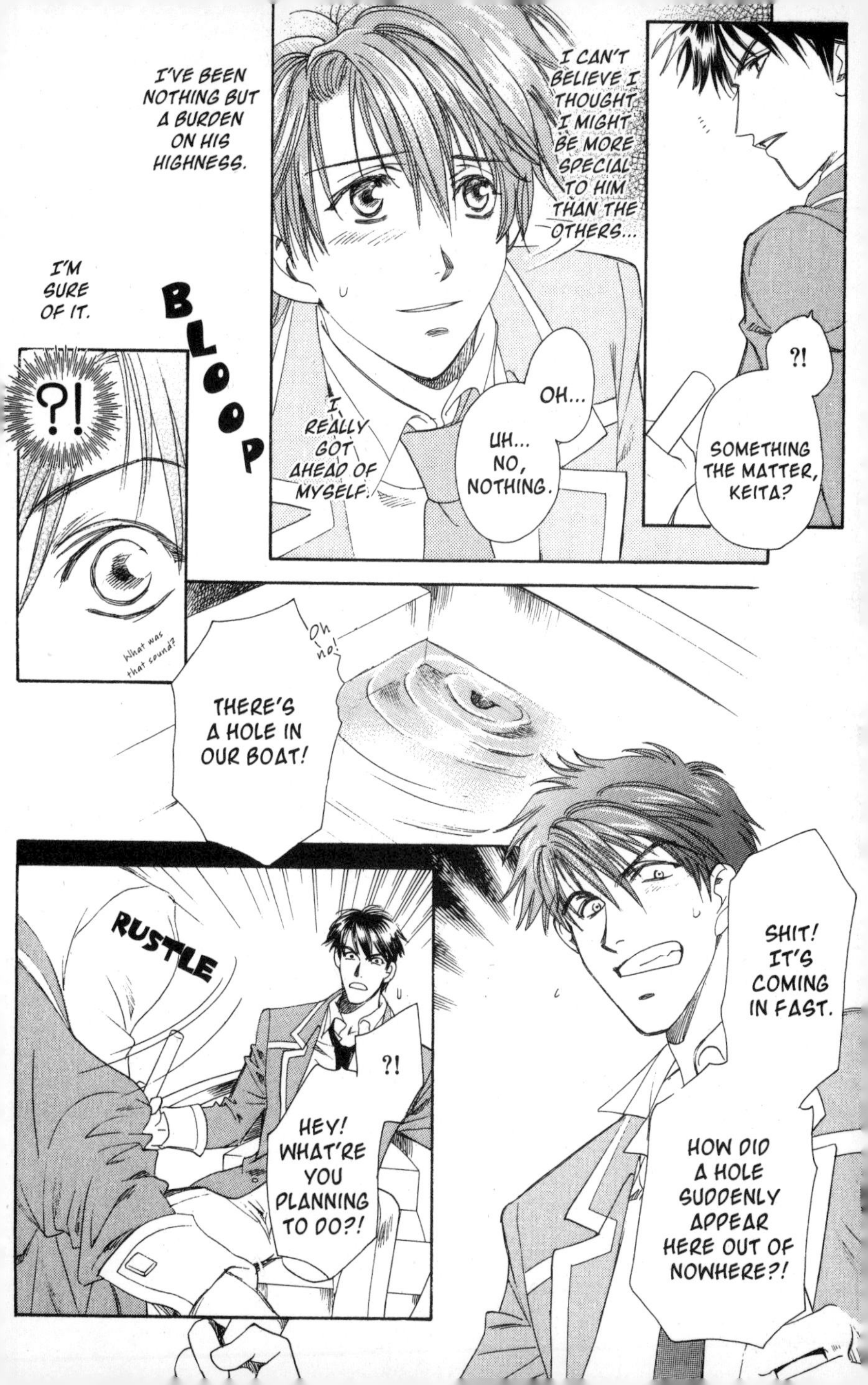
?!
SOMETHING THE MATTER, KEITA?
I CAN'T BELIEVE I THOUGHT I MIGHT BE MORE SPECIAL TO HIM THAN THE OTHERS...
OH...
UH... NO, NOTHING.
I REALLY GOT AHEAD OF MYSELF.
I'VE BEEN NOTHING BUT A BURDEN ON HIS HIGHNESS.
I'M SURE OF IT.
BLOOP
?!
What was that sound?
Oh no!
THERE'S A HOLE IN OUR BOAT!
SHIT! IT'S COMING IN FAST.
HOW DID A HOLE SUDDENLY APPEAR HERE OUT OF NOWHERE?!
RUSTLE
?!
HEY! WHAT'RE YOU PLANNING TO DO?!

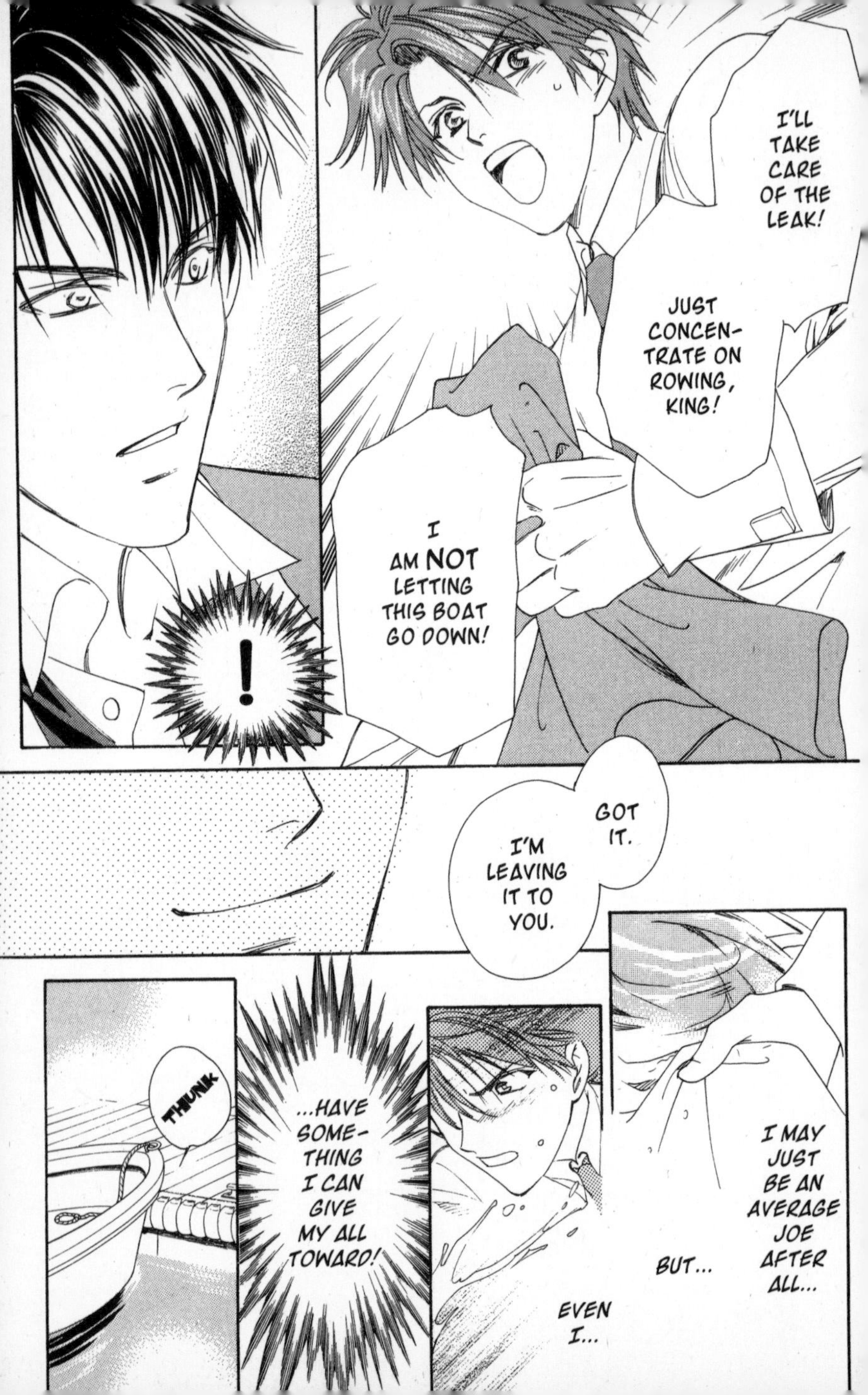
I'LL TAKE CARE OF THE LEAK!
JUST CONCENTRATE ON ROWING, KING!
I AM NOT LETTING THIS BOAT GO DOWN!
!
GOT IT.
I'M LEAVING IT TO YOU.
I MAY JUST BE AN AVERAGE JOE AFTER ALL...
BUT...
EVEN I...
...HAVE SOME-THING I CAN GIVE MY ALL TOWARD!
THUNK

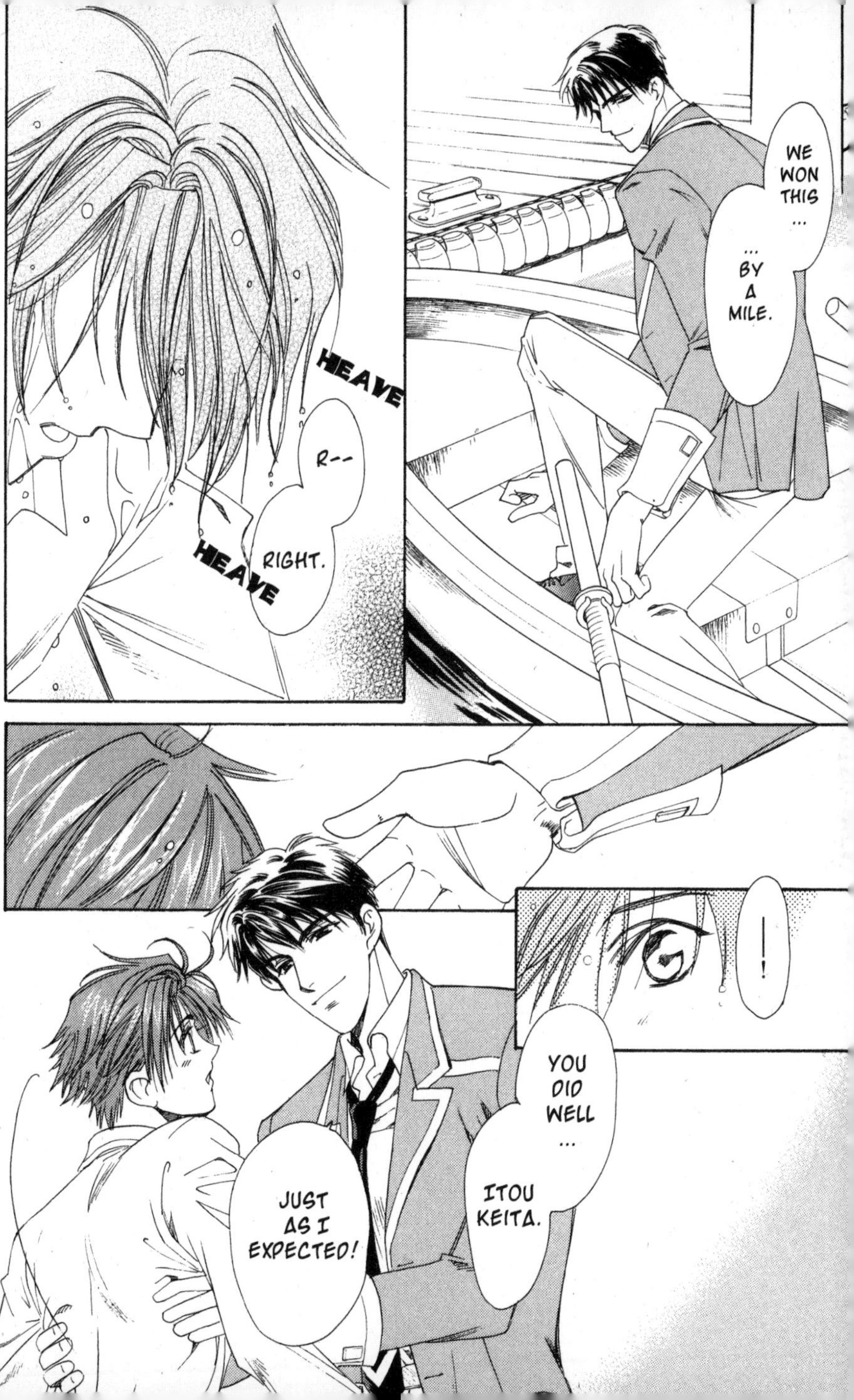
WE WON THIS ...
... BY A MILE.
HEAVE
R--
HEAVE
RIGHT.
!
YOU DID WELL ...
ITOU KEITA.
JUST AS I EXPECTED!

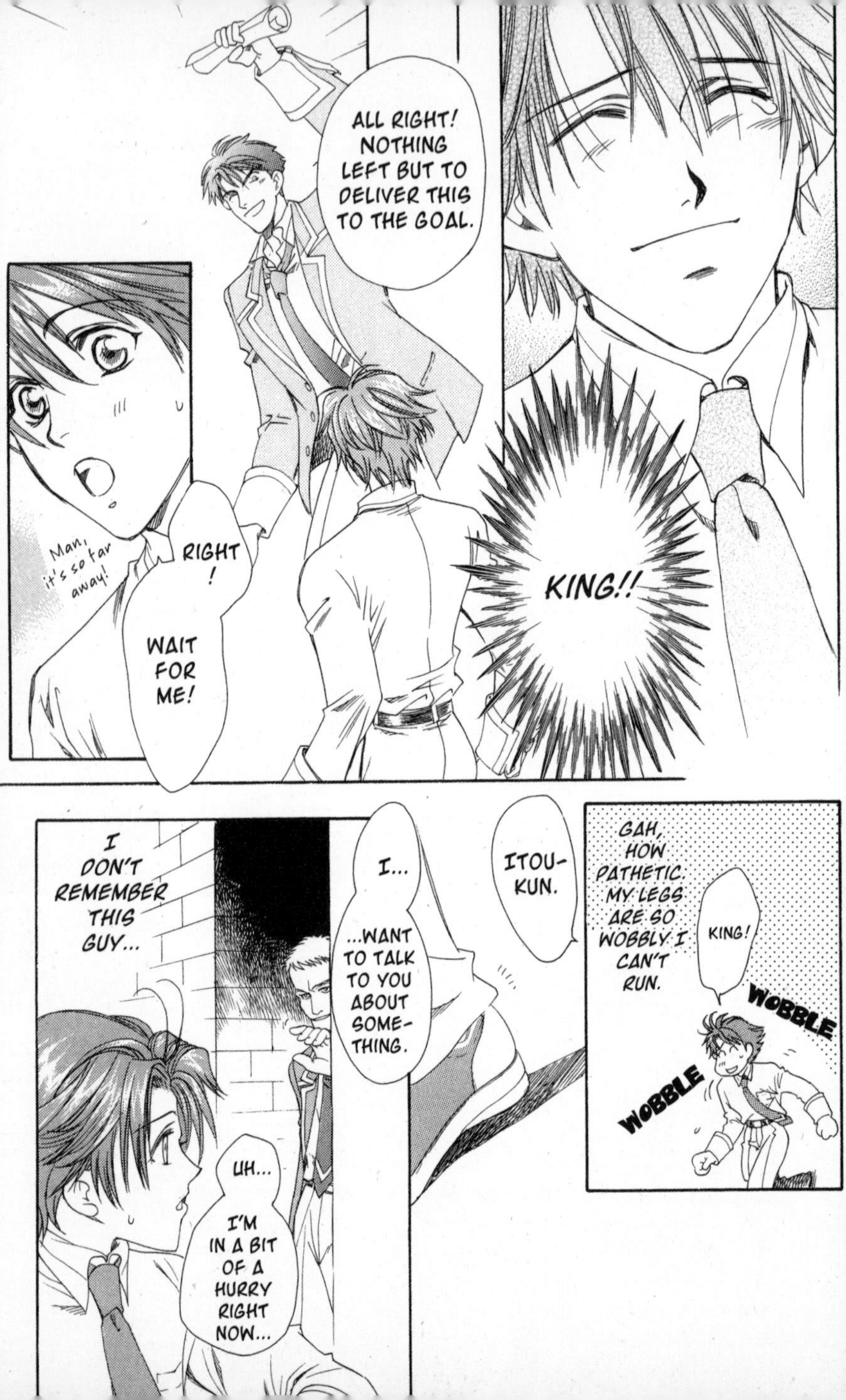
KING!!
ALL RIGHT! NOTHING LEFT BUT TO DELIVER THIS TO THE GOAL.
RIGHT!
WAIT FOR ME!
Man, it's so far away!
GAH, HOW PATHETIC. MY LEGS ARE SO WOBBLY I CAN'T RUN.
KING!
WOBBLE
WOBBLE
ITOU-KUN.
I...
...WANT TO TALK TO YOU ABOUT SOME-THING.
I DON'T REMEMBER THIS GUY...
UH...
I'M IN A BIT OF A HURRY RIGHT NOW...

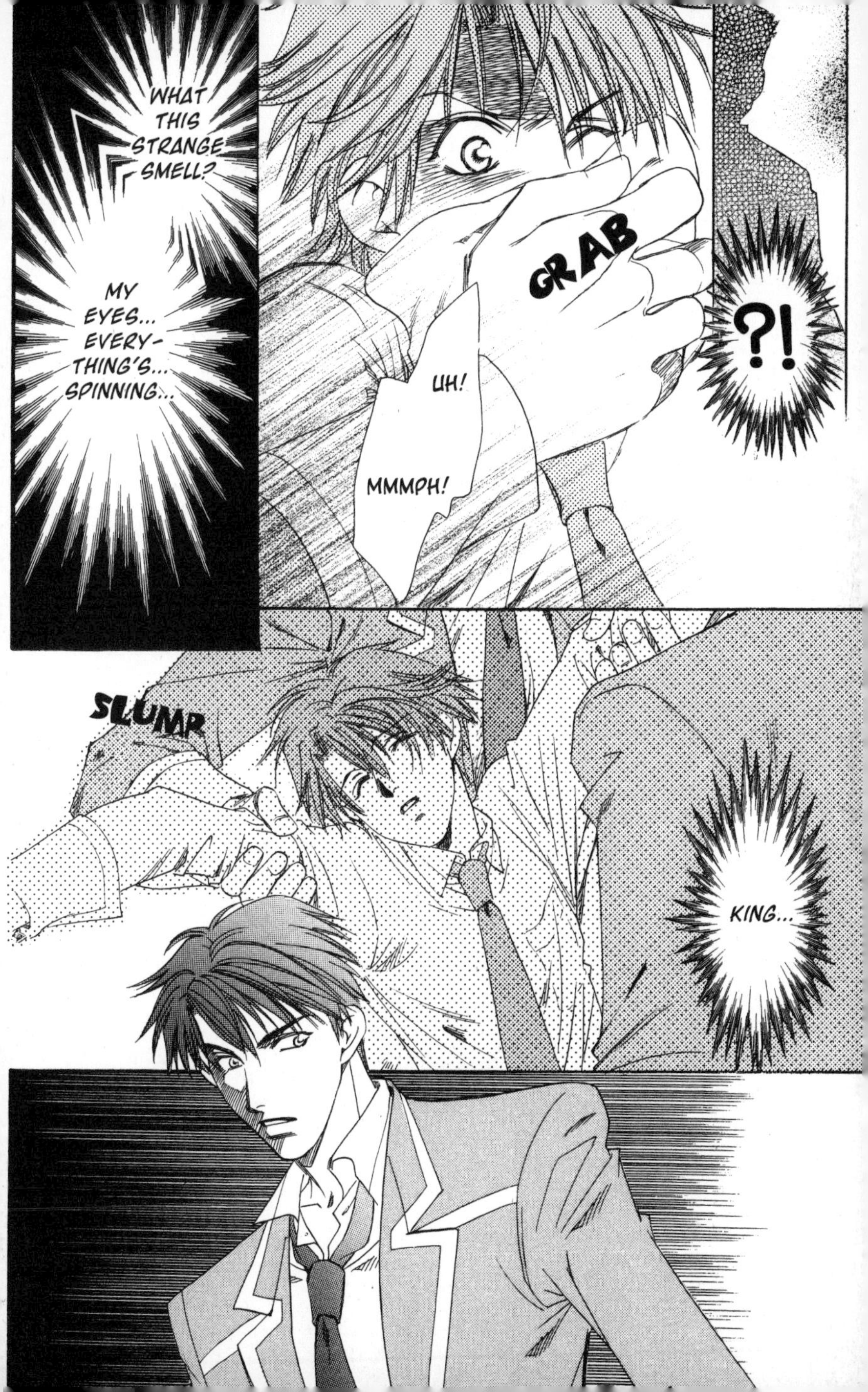
?!
GRAB
UH!
MMMPH!
WHAT THIS STRANGE SMELL?
MY EYES... EVERY-THING'S... SPINNING...
KING...
SLUMP

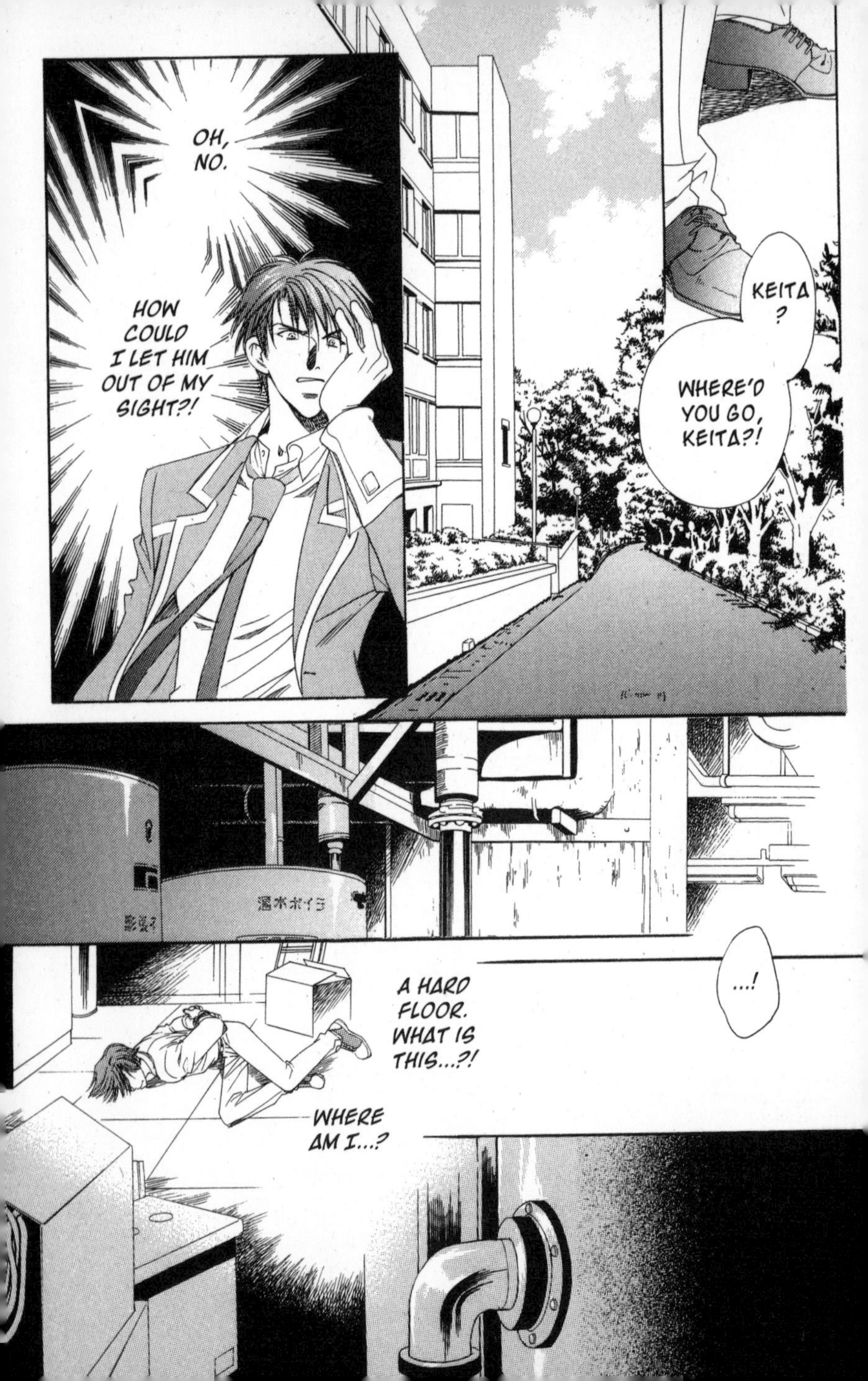
KEITA?
WHERE'D YOU GO, KEITA?!
OH, NO.
HOW COULD I LET HIM OUT OF MY SIGHT?!
温水ボイラ
...!
A HARD FLOOR. WHAT IS THIS...?!
WHERE AM I...?

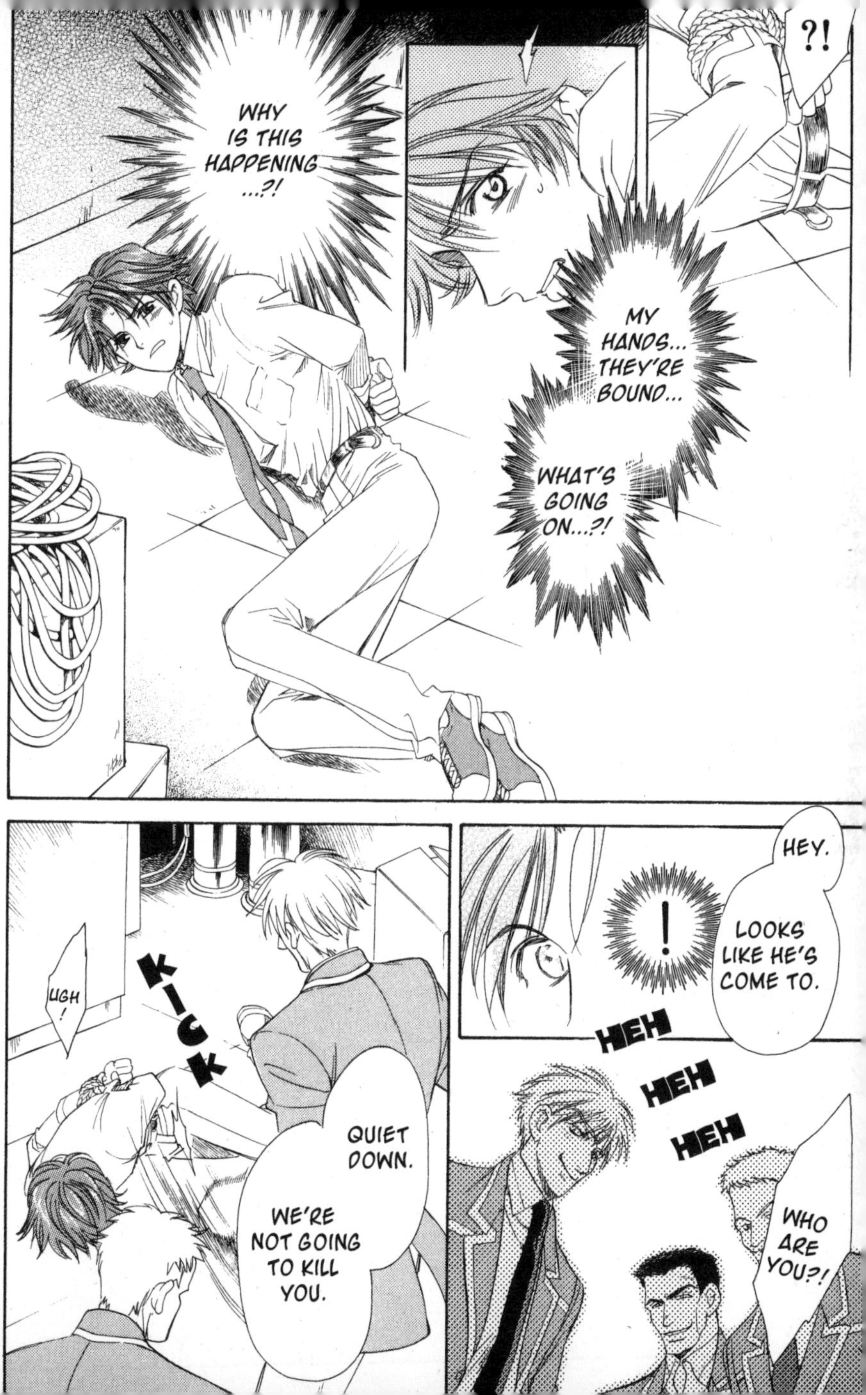
?!
MY HANDS... THEY'RE BOUND...
WHAT'S GOING ON...?!
WHY IS THIS HAPPENING ...?!
!
HEY.
LOOKS LIKE HE'S COME TO.
HEH HEH HEH
WHO ARE YOU?!
KICK
UGH!
QUIET DOWN.
WE'RE NOT GOING TO KILL YOU.

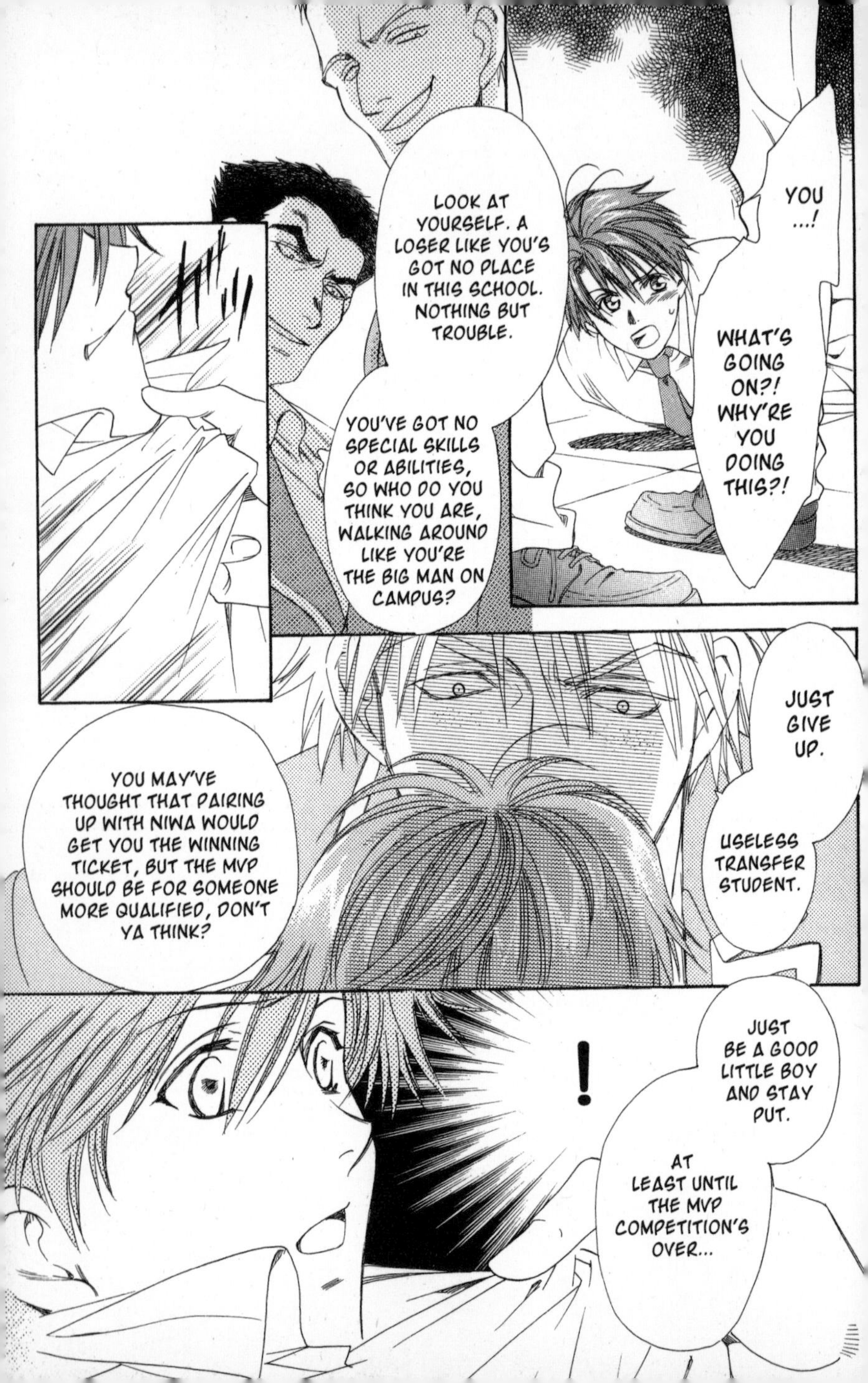
YOU ...!
WHAT'S GOING ON?! WHY'RE YOU DOING THIS?!
LOOK AT YOURSELF. A LOSER LIKE YOU'S GOT NO PLACE IN THIS SCHOOL. NOTHING BUT TROUBLE.
YOU'VE GOT NO SPECIAL SKILLS OR ABILITIES, SO WHO DO YOU THINK YOU ARE, WALKING AROUND LIKE YOU'RE THE BIG MAN ON CAMPUS?
JUST GIVE UP.
USELESS TRANSFER STUDENT.
YOU MAY'VE THOUGHT THAT PAIRING UP WITH NIWA WOULD GET YOU THE WINNING TICKET, BUT THE MVP SHOULD BE FOR SOMEONE MORE QUALIFIED, DON'T YA THINK?
!
JUST BE A GOOD LITTLE BOY AND STAY PUT.
AT LEAST UNTIL THE MVP COMPETITION'S OVER...

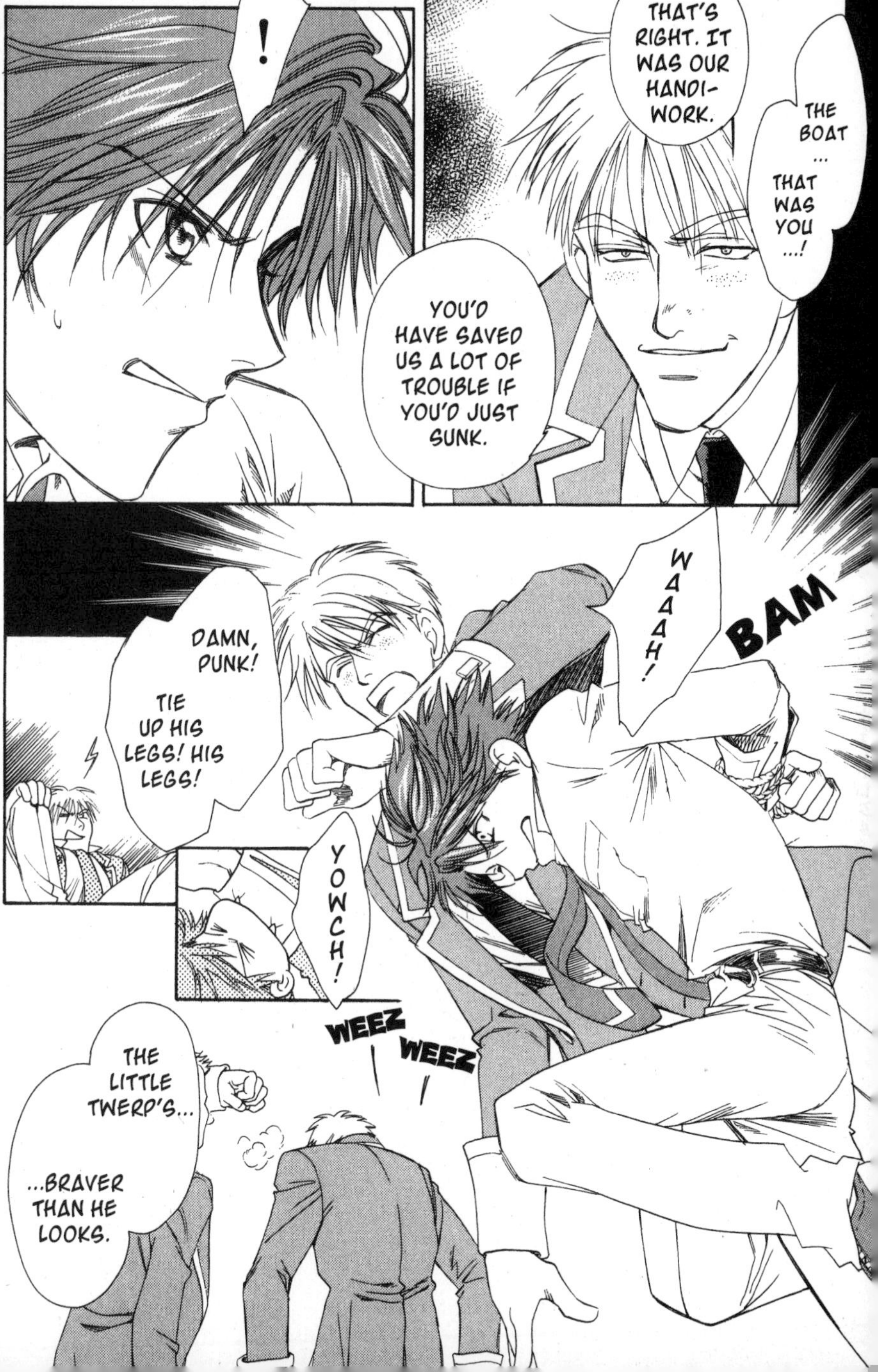

THE BOAT ... THAT WAS YOU ...!
THAT'S RIGHT. IT WAS OUR HANDI-WORK.
YOU'D HAVE SAVED US A LOT OF TROUBLE IF YOU'D JUST SUNK.
!
WAAAAH!
BAM
DAMN, PUNK!
TIE UP HIS LEGS! HIS LEGS!
YOWCH!
WEEZ
WEEZ
THE LITTLE TWERP'S...
...BRAVER THAN HE LOOKS.

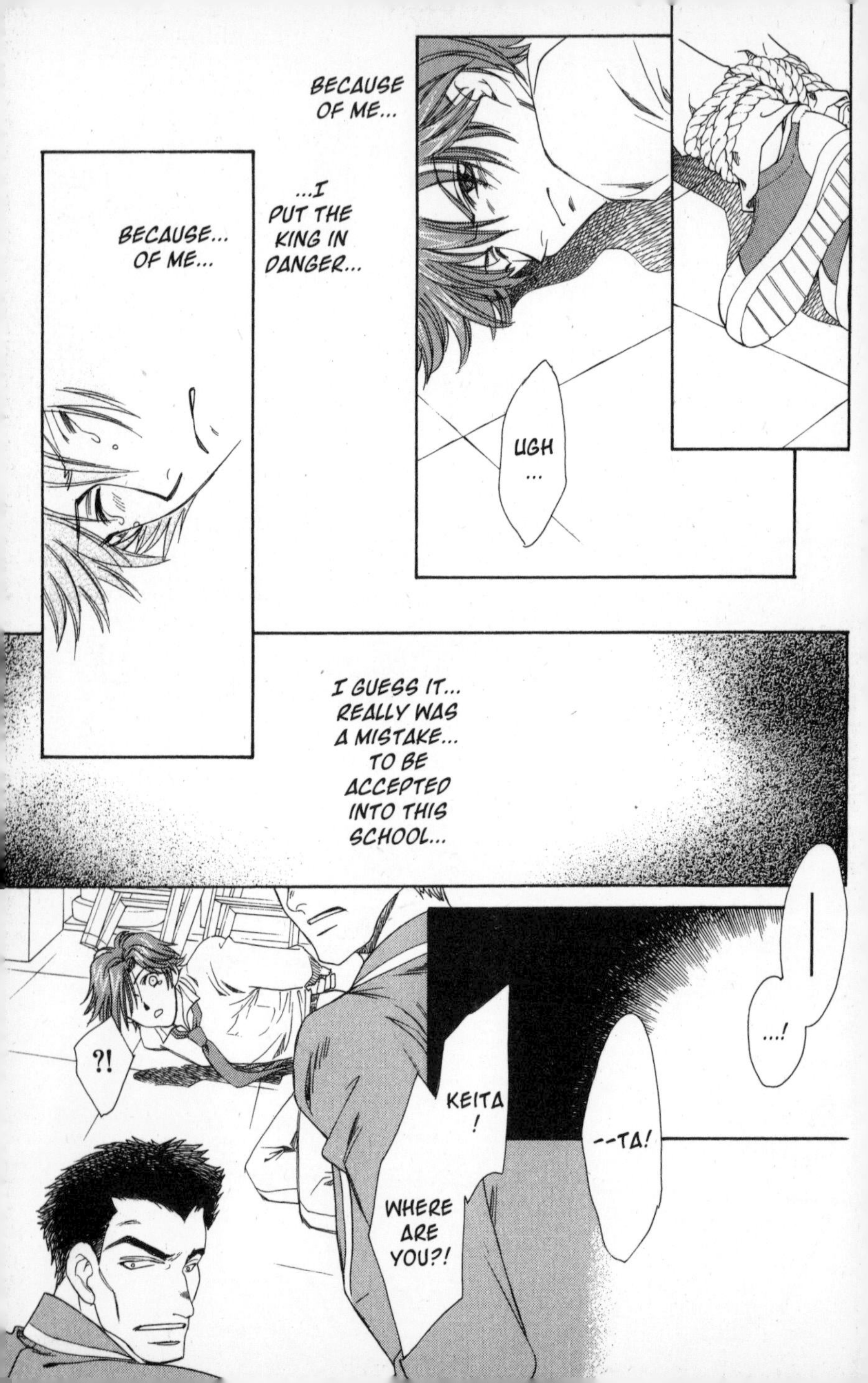
BECAUSE OF ME...
...I PUT THE KING IN DANGER...
UGH ...
BECAUSE... OF ME...
I GUESS IT... REALLY WAS A MISTAKE... TO BE ACCEPTED INTO THIS SCHOOL...
—
...!
--TA!
KEITA!
WHERE ARE YOU?!
?!

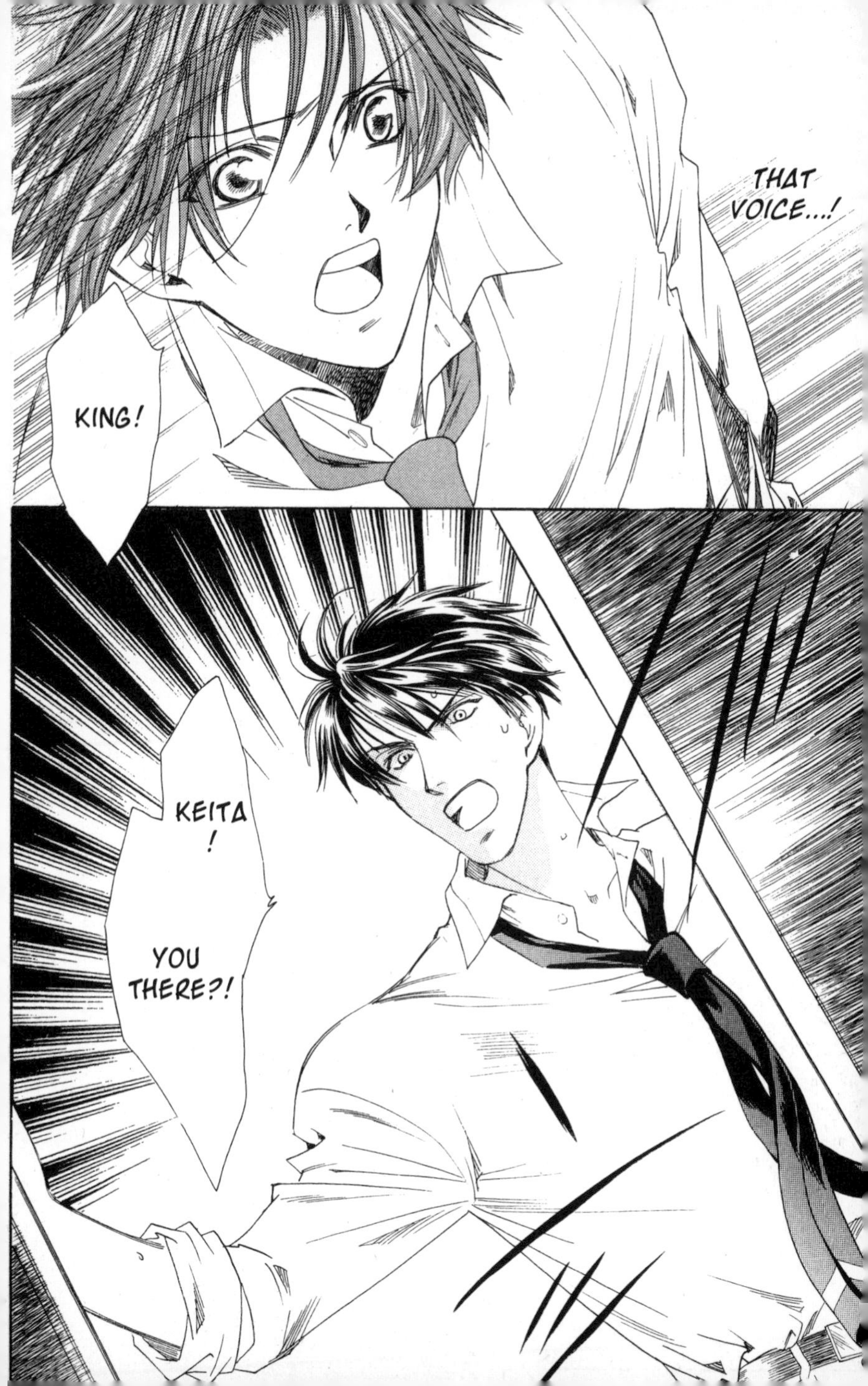
THAT VOICE...!
KING!
KEITA!
YOU THERE?!

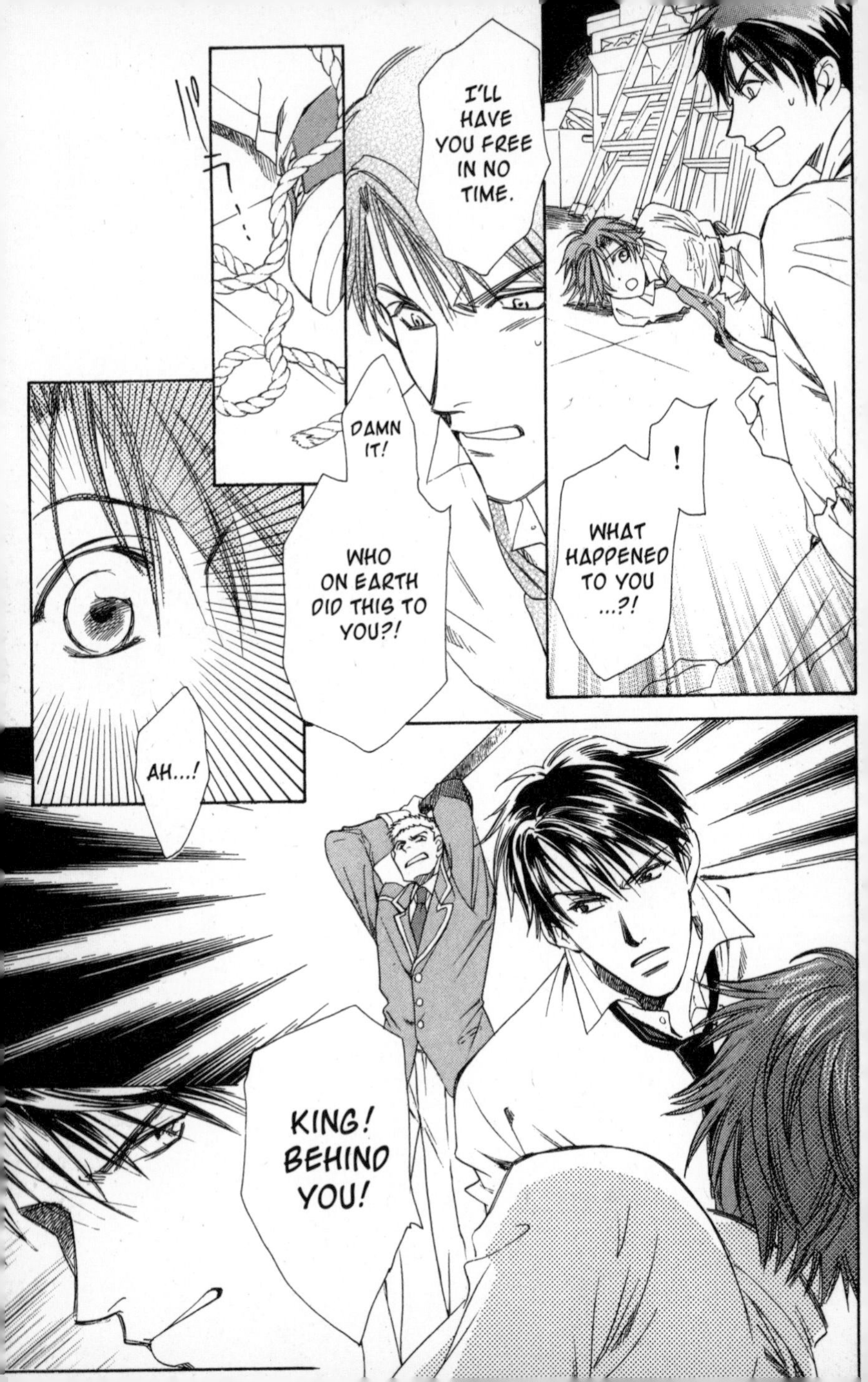
!
WHAT HAPPENED TO YOU ...?!
I'LL HAVE YOU FREE IN NO TIME.
DAMN IT!
WHO ON EARTH DID THIS TO YOU?!
AH...!
KING! BEHIND YOU!

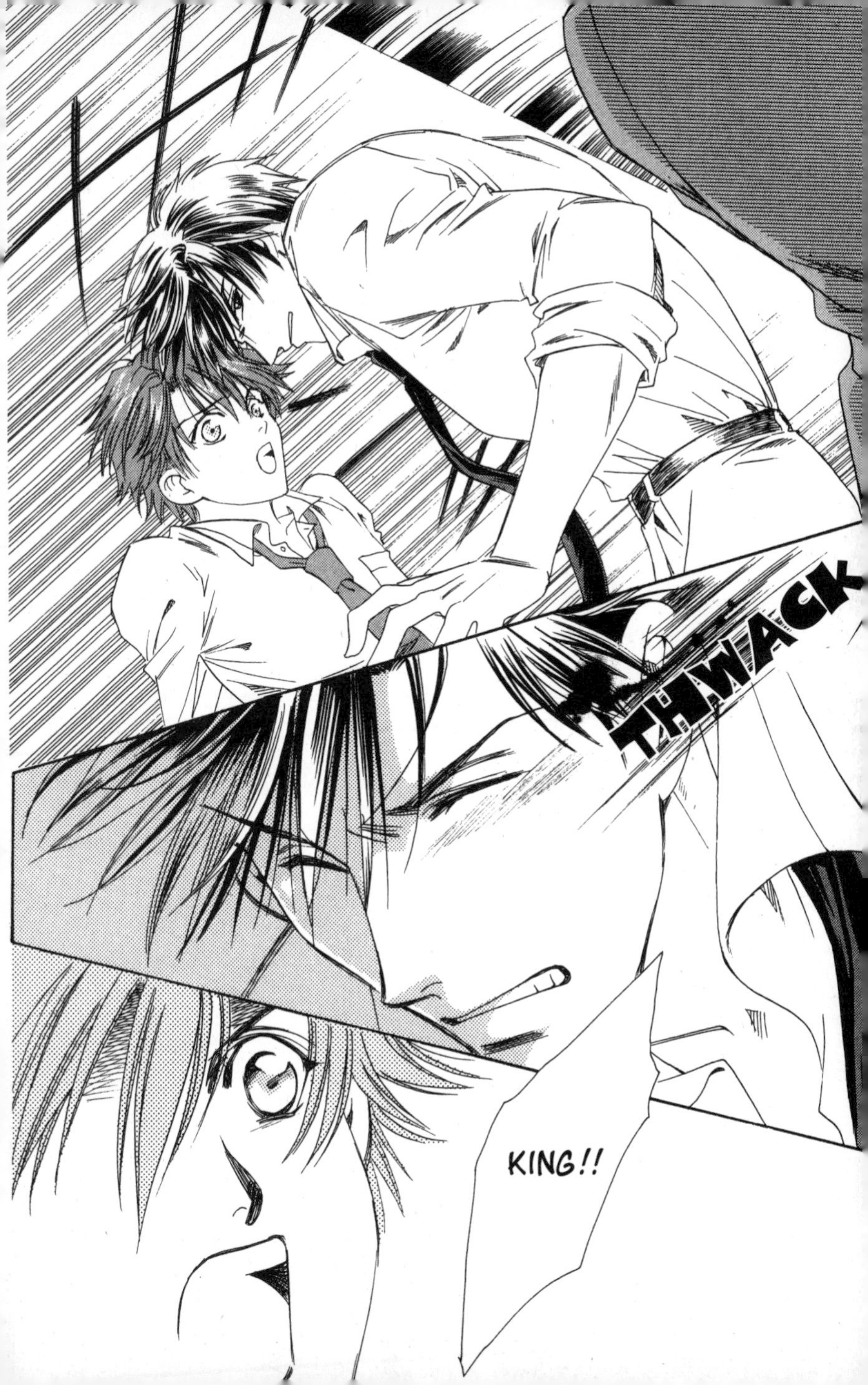
THWACK
KING!!

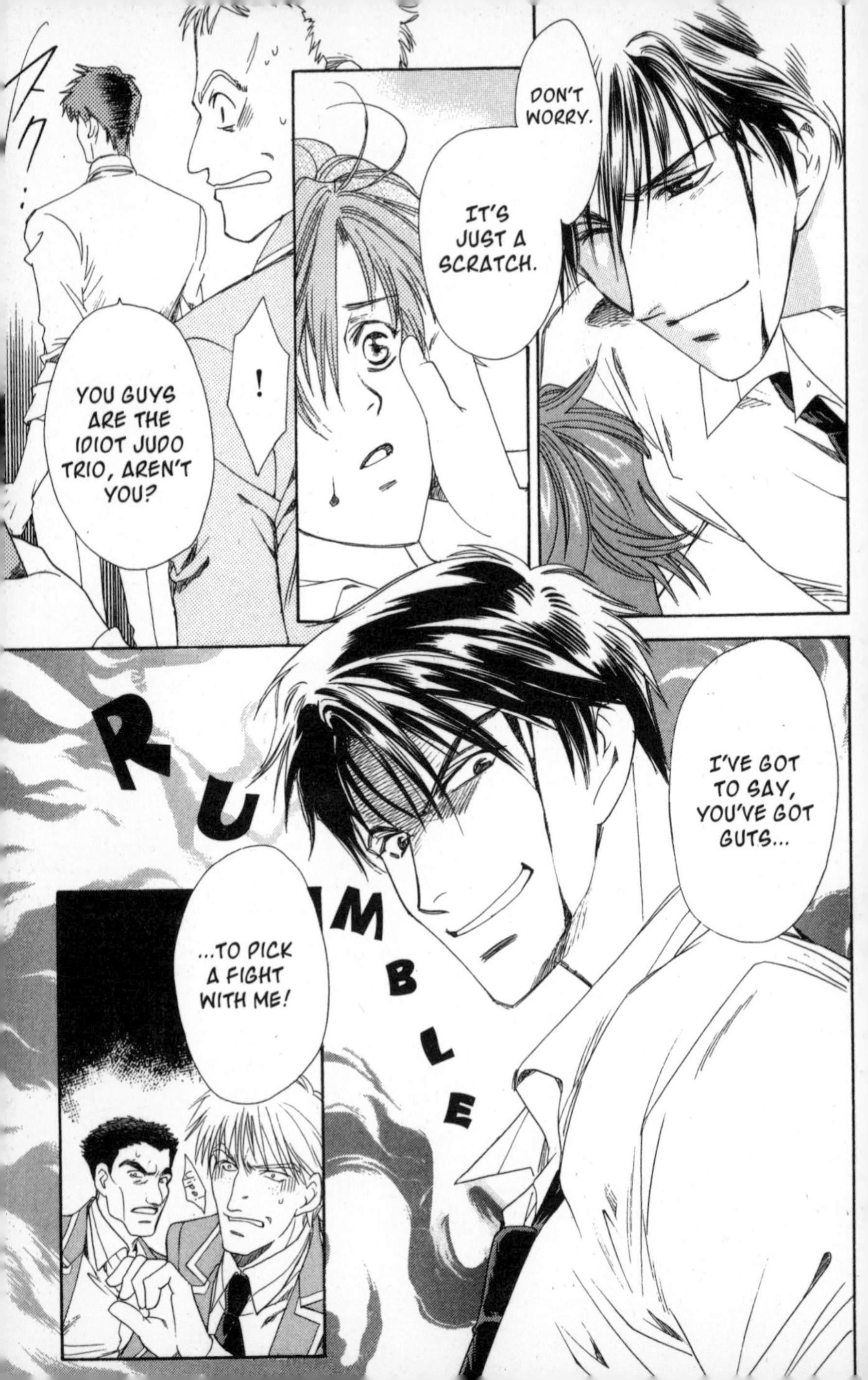
DON'T WORRY.
IT'S JUST A SCRATCH.
!
YOU GUYS ARE THE IDIOT JUDO TRIO, AREN'T YOU?
I'VE GOT TO SAY, YOU'VE GOT GUTS...
RUMBLE
...TO PICK A FIGHT WITH ME!

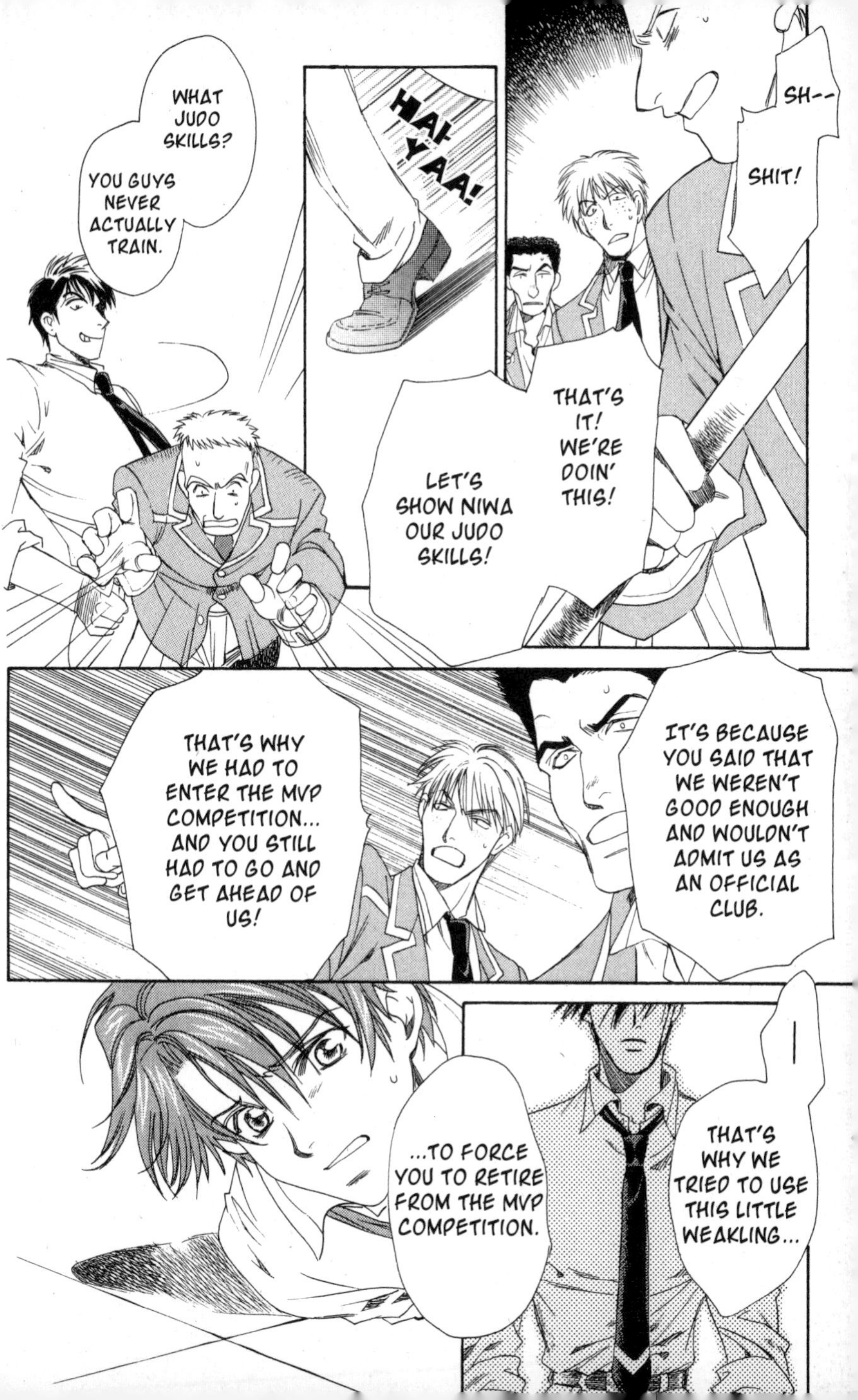
SH--
SHIT!
THAT'S IT! WE'RE DOIN' THIS!
LET'S SHOW NIWA OUR JUDO SKILLS!
HAI-YAA!
WHAT JUDO SKILLS?
YOU GUYS NEVER ACTUALLY TRAIN.
IT'S BECAUSE YOU SAID THAT WE WEREN'T GOOD ENOUGH AND WOULDN'T ADMIT US AS AN OFFICIAL CLUB.
THAT'S WHY WE HAD TO ENTER THE MVP COMPETITION... AND YOU STILL HAD TO GO AND GET AHEAD OF US!
THAT'S WHY WE TRIED TO USE THIS LITTLE WEAKLING...
...TO FORCE YOU TO RETIRE FROM THE MVP COMPETITION.

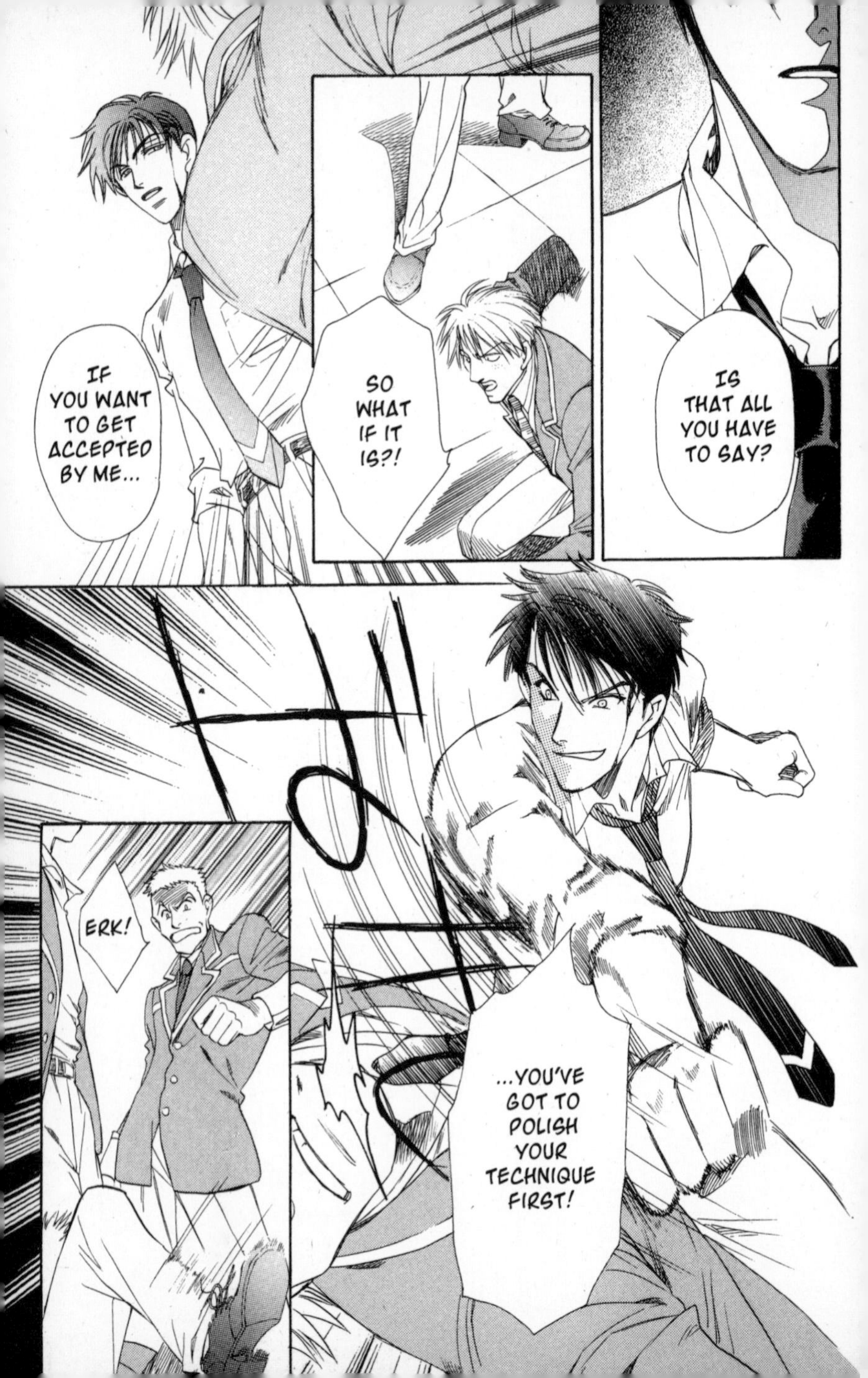
IS THAT ALL YOU HAVE TO SAY?
SO WHAT IF IT IS?!
IF YOU WANT TO GET ACCEPTED BY ME...
...YOU'VE GOT TO POLISH YOUR TECHNIQUE FIRST!
ERK!

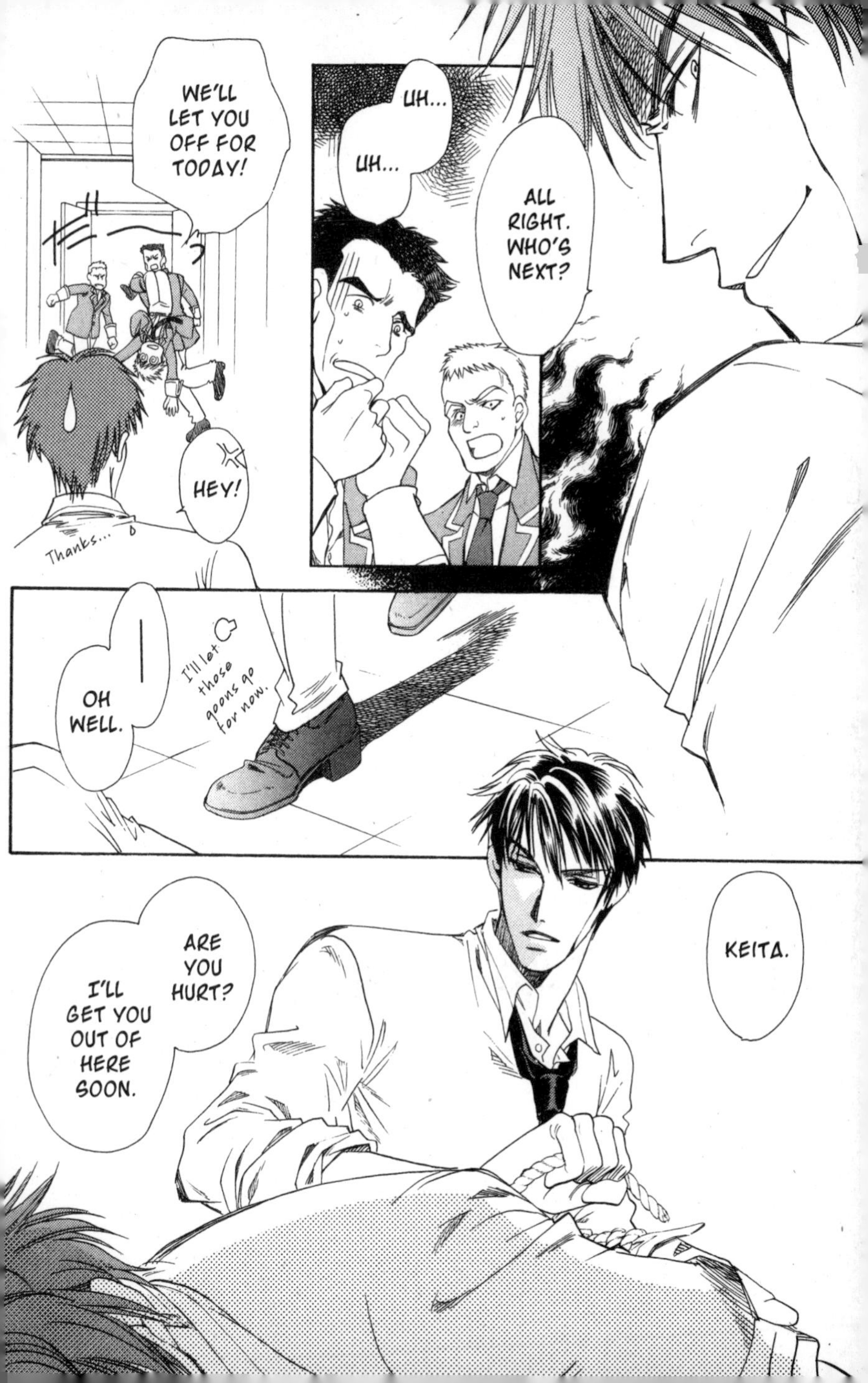

ALL RIGHT. WHO'S NEXT?
UH...
UH...
WE'LL LET YOU OFF FOR TODAY!
HEY!
Thanks...
OH WELL.
I'll let those goons go for now.
KEITA.
ARE YOU HURT?
I'LL GET YOU OUT OF HERE SOON.

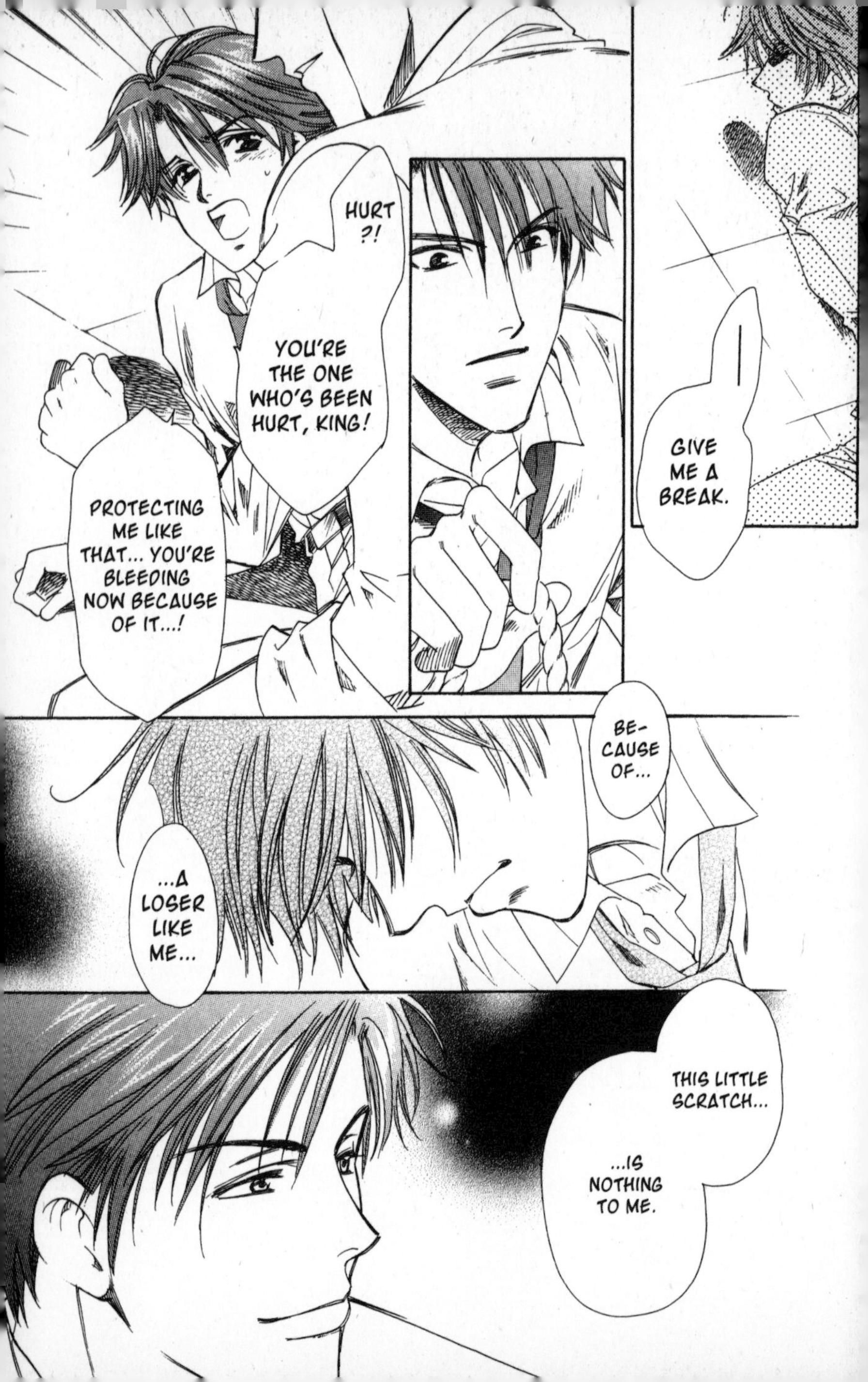
GIVE ME A BREAK.
HURT ?!
YOU'RE THE ONE WHO'S BEEN HURT, KING!
PROTECTING ME LIKE THAT... YOU'RE BLEEDING NOW BECAUSE OF IT...!
BE-CAUSE OF...
...A LOSER LIKE ME...
THIS LITTLE SCRATCH...
...IS NOTHING TO ME.

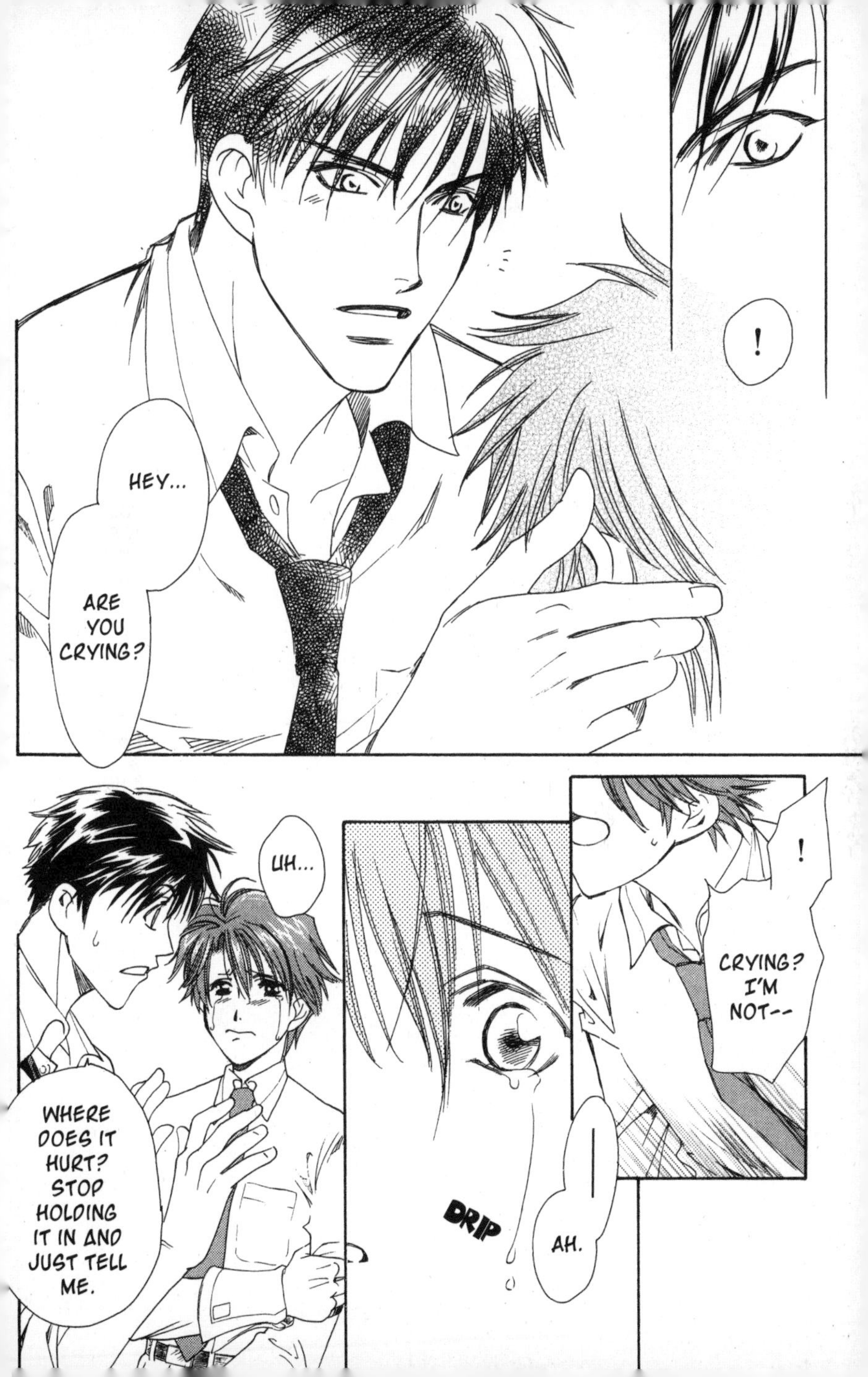
!
HEY...
ARE YOU CRYING?
!
CRYING? I'M NOT--
AH.
DRIP
UH...
WHERE DOES IT HURT? STOP HOLDING IT IN AND JUST TELL ME.

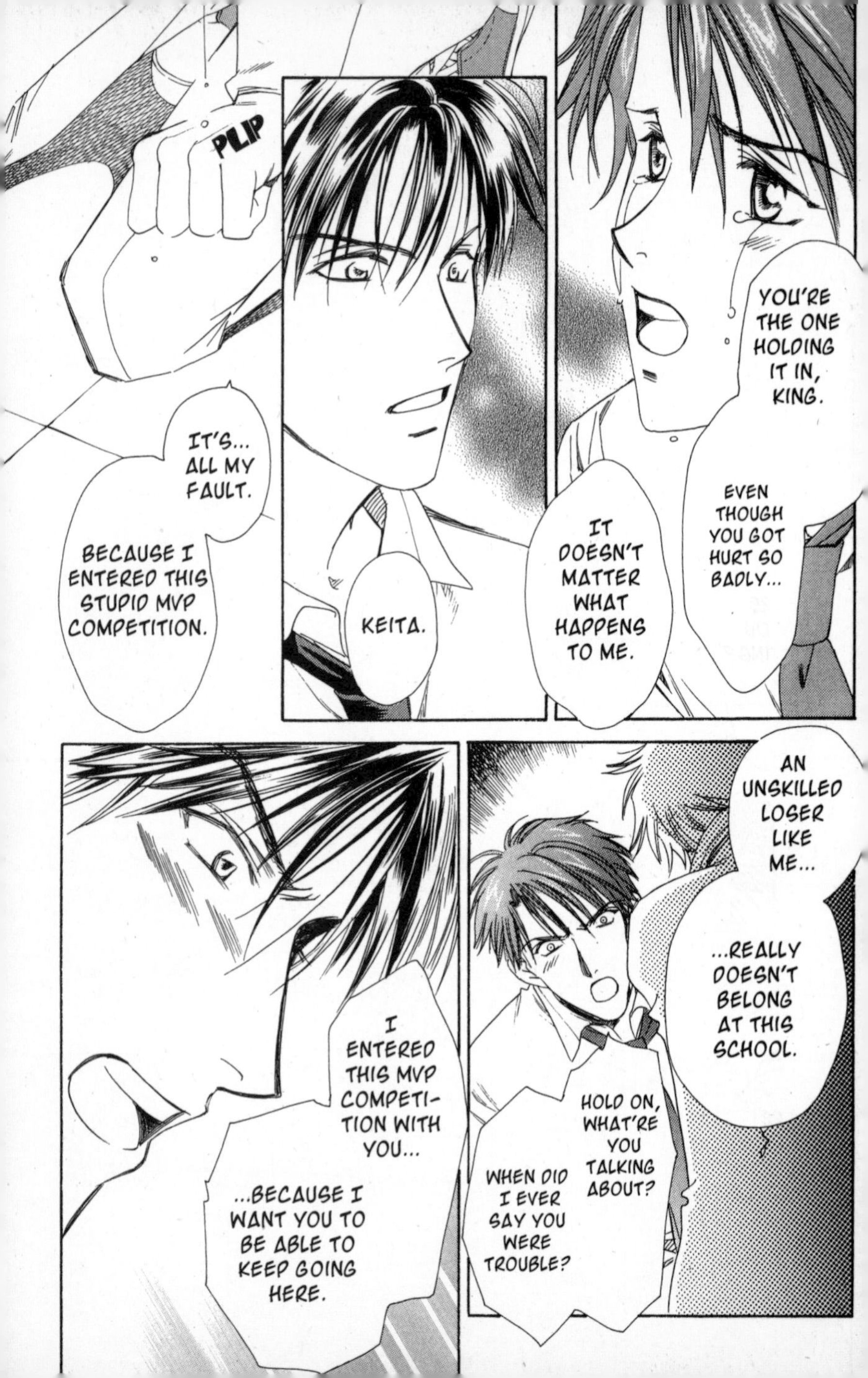
YOU'RE THE ONE HOLDING IT IN, KING.
EVEN THOUGH YOU GOT HURT SO BADLY...
IT DOESN'T MATTER WHAT HAPPENS TO ME.
KEITA.
PLIP
IT'S... ALL MY FAULT.
BECAUSE I ENTERED THIS STUDIO MVP COMPETITION.
AN UNSKILLED LOSER LIKE ME...
...REALLY DOESN'T BELONG AT THIS SCHOOL.
HOLD ON, WHAT'RE YOU TALKING ABOUT?
WHEN DID I EVER SAY YOU WERE TROUBLE?
I ENTERED THIS MVP COMPETITION WITH YOU...
...BECAUSE I WANT YOU TO BE ABLE TO KEEP GOING HERE.

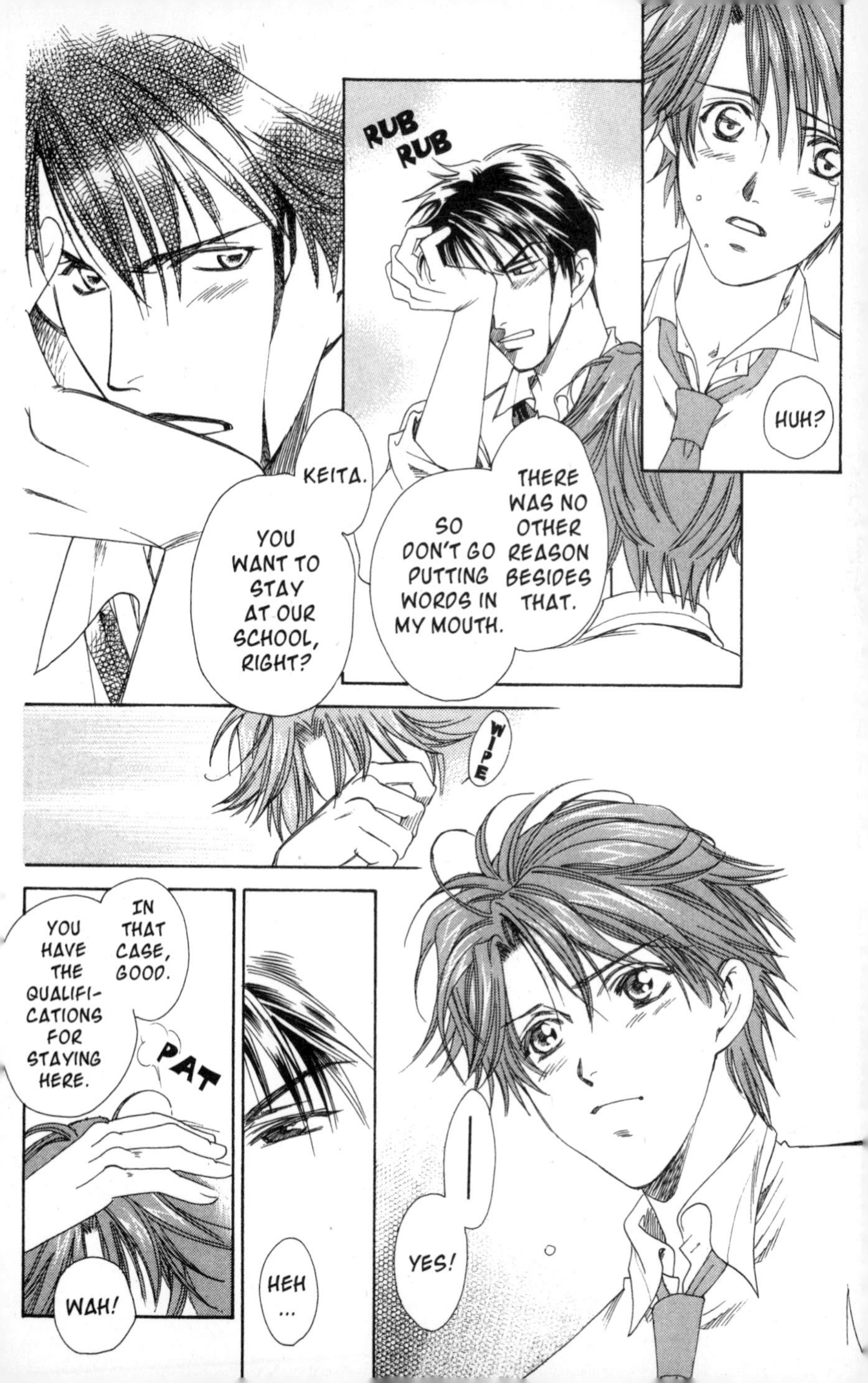
HUH?
RUB RUB
THERE WAS NO OTHER REASON BESIDES THAT.
SO DON'T GO PUTTING WORDS IN MY MOUTH.
KEITA.
YOU WANT TO STAY AT OUR SCHOOL, RIGHT?
WIPE
—
YES!
HEH ...
IN THAT CASE, GOOD.
YOU HAVE THE QUALIFI-CATIONS FOR STAYING HERE.
PAT
WAH!

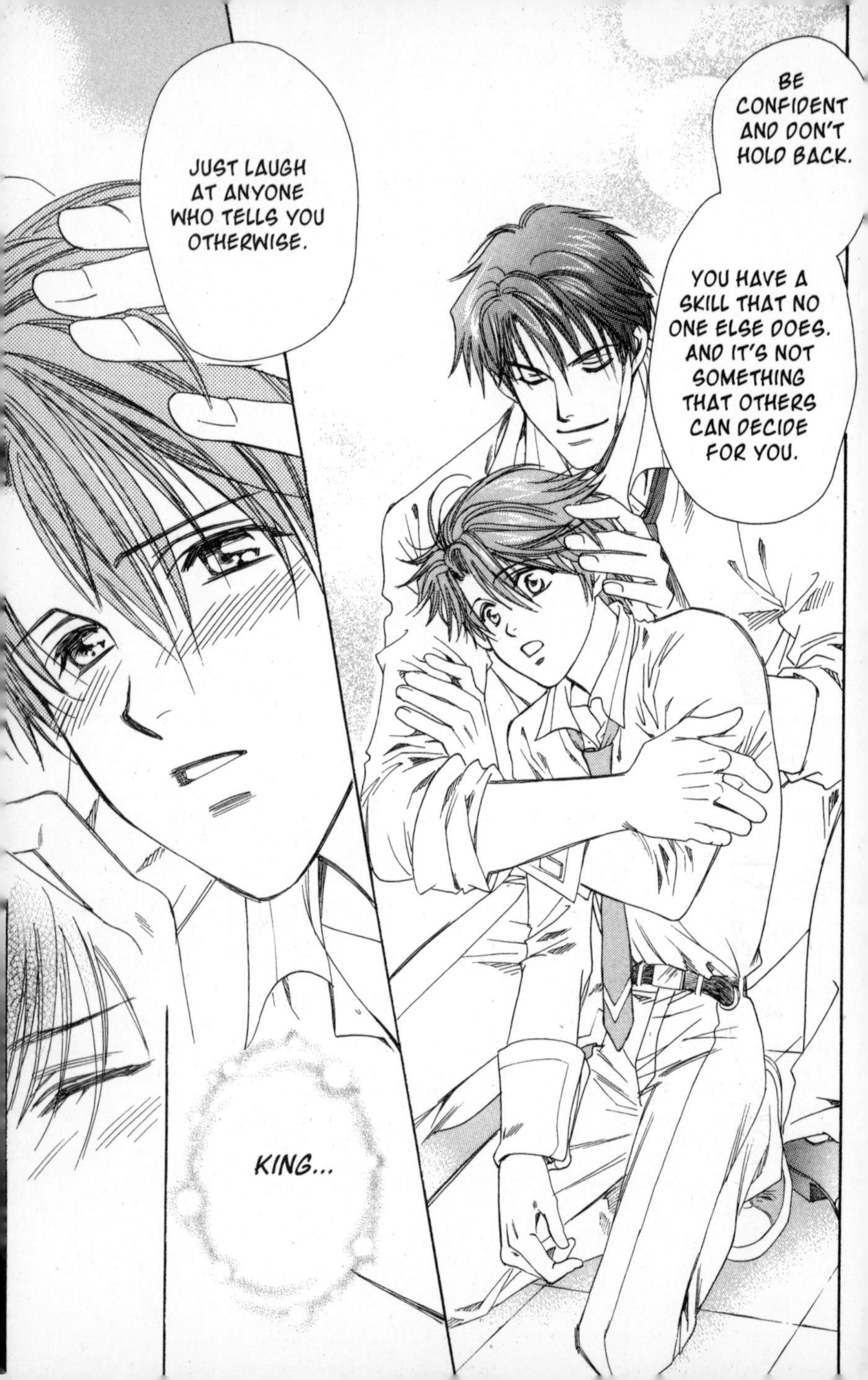
BE CONFIDENT AND DON'T HOLD BACK.
YOU HAVE A SKILL THAT NO ONE ELSE DOES. AND IT'S NOT SOMETHING THAT OTHERS CAN DECIDE FOR YOU.
JUST LAUGH AT ANYONE WHO TELLS YOU OTHERWISE.
KING...

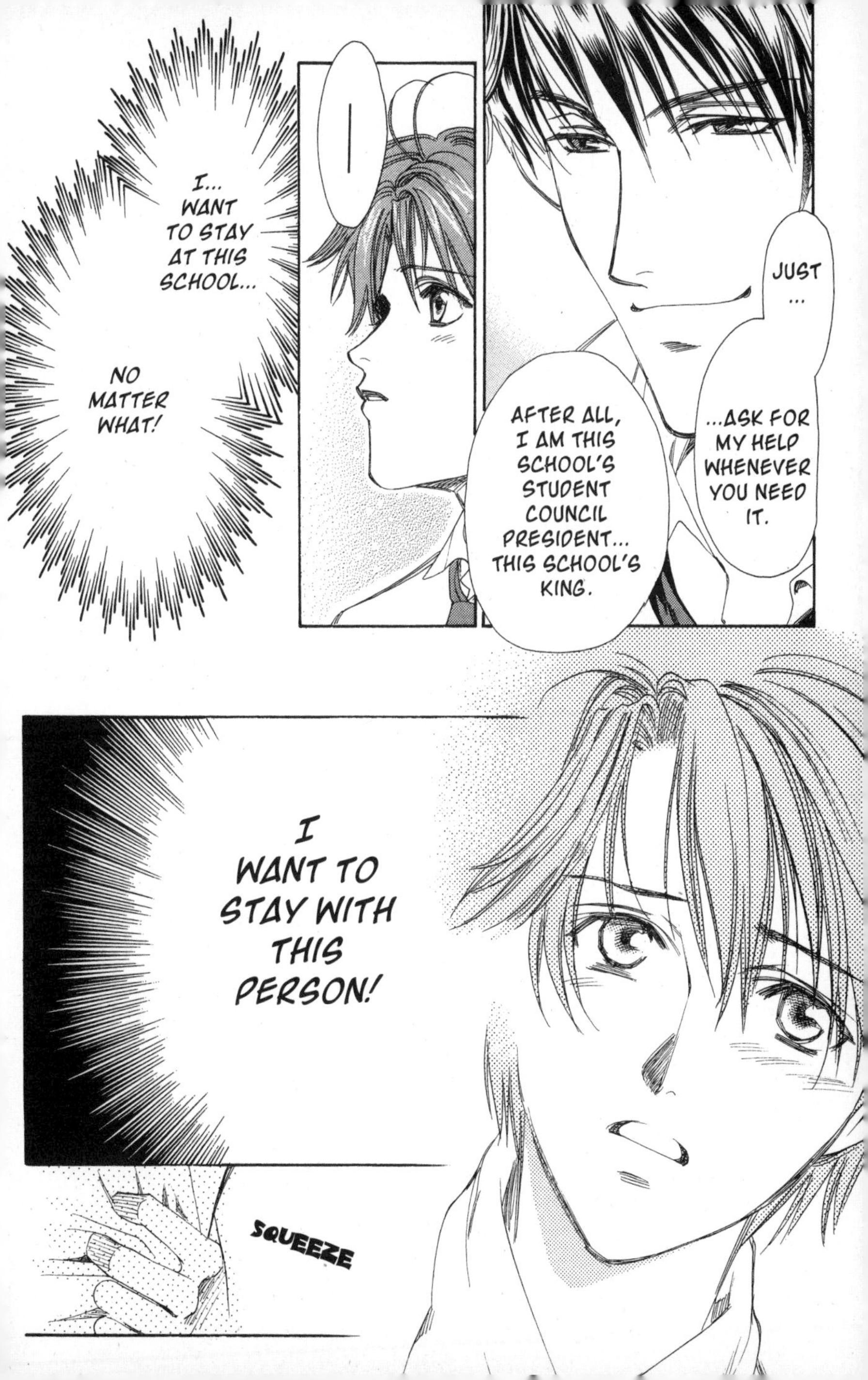
JUST ...
...ASK FOR MY HELP WHENEVER YOU NEED IT.
AFTER ALL, I AM THIS SCHOOL'S STUDENT COUNCIL PRESIDENT... THIS SCHOOL'S KING.
—
I... WANT TO STAY AT THIS SCHOOL...
NO MATTER WHAT!
I WANT TO STAY WITH THIS PERSON!
SQUEEZE

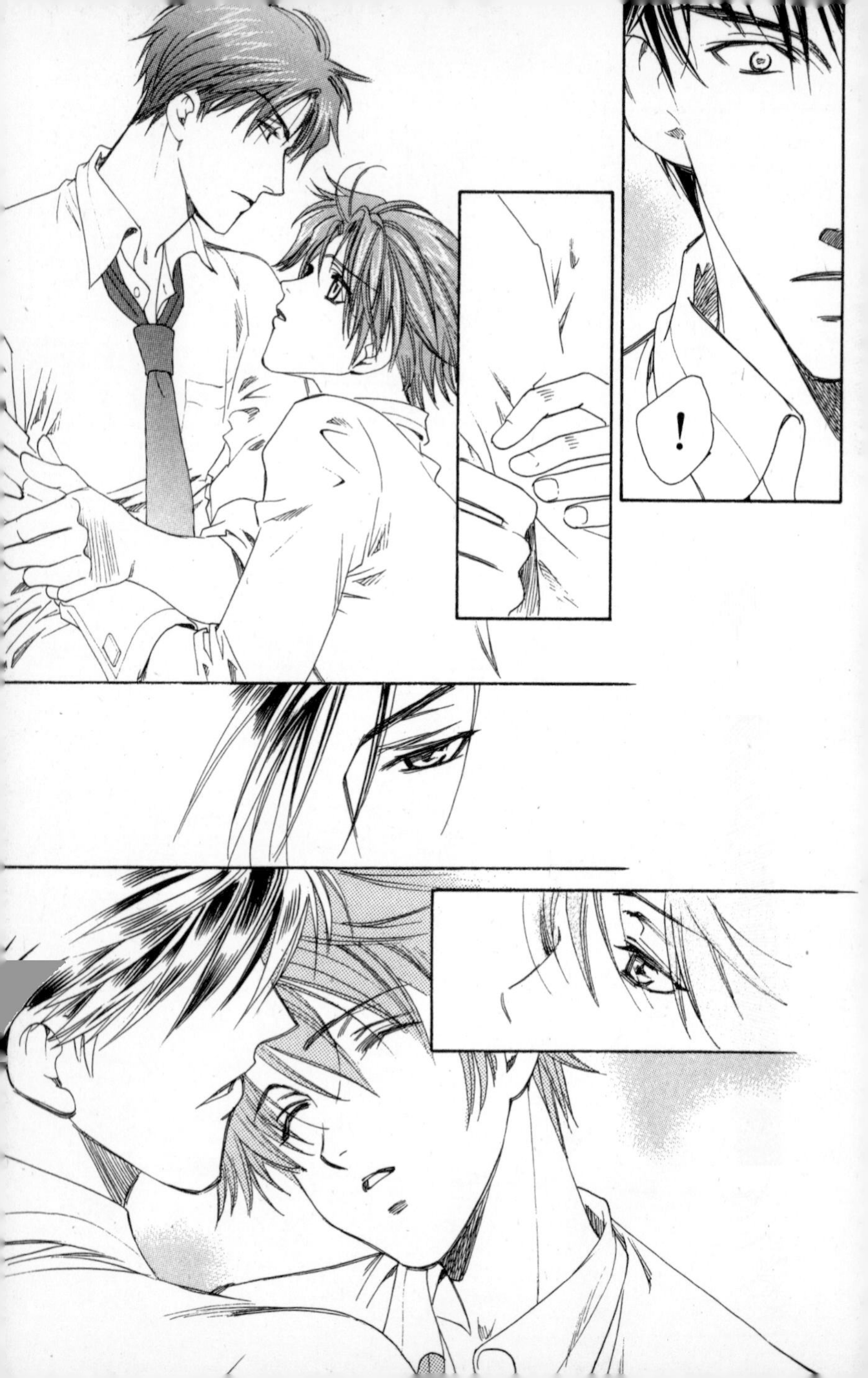
!

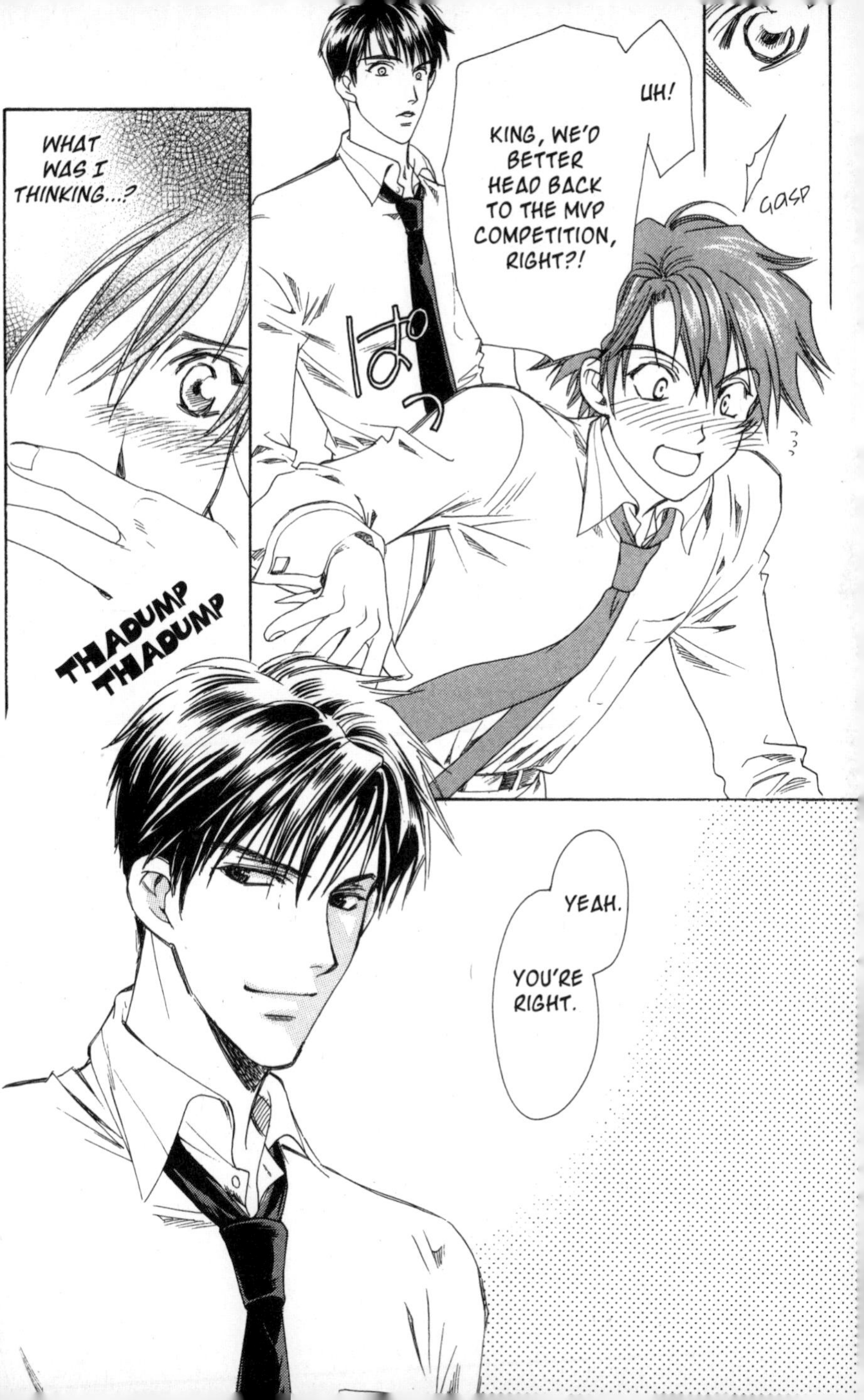
GASP
UH!
KING, WE'D BETTER HEAD BACK TO THE MVP COMPETITION, RIGHT?!
ぱっ
WHAT WAS I THINKING...?
THADUMP THADUMP
YEAH.
YOU'RE RIGHT.

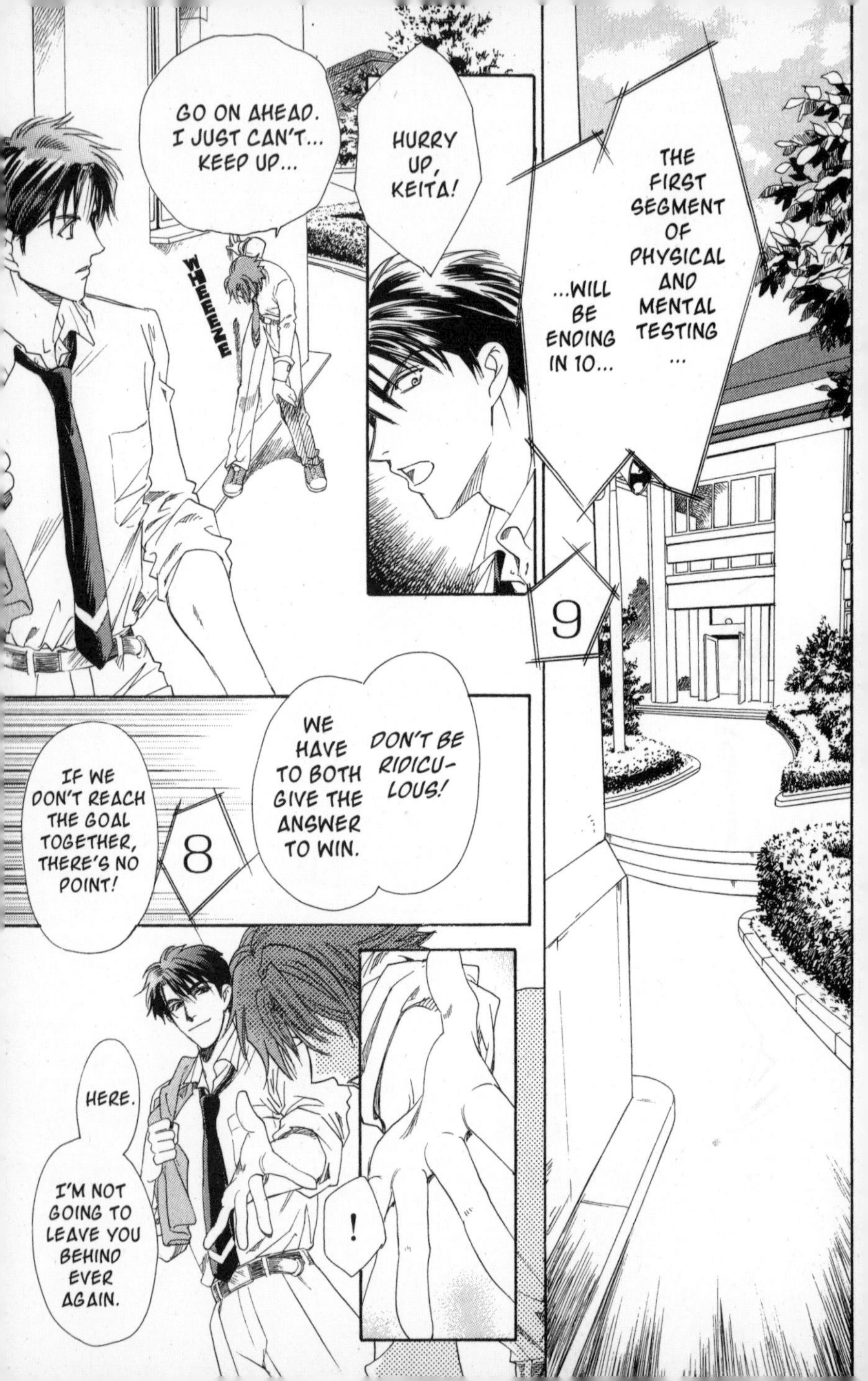
THE FIRST SEGMENT OF PHYSICAL AND MENTAL TESTING ...
...WILL BE ENDING IN 10...
HURRY UP, KEITA!
GO ON AHEAD. I JUST CAN'T... KEEP UP...
WHEEEEZE
9
DON'T BE RIDICULOUS!
WE HAVE TO BOTH GIVE THE ANSWER TO WIN.
IF WE DON'T REACH THE GOAL TOGETHER, THERE'S NO POINT!
8
!
HERE.
I'M NOT GOING TO LEAVE YOU BEHIND EVER AGAIN.

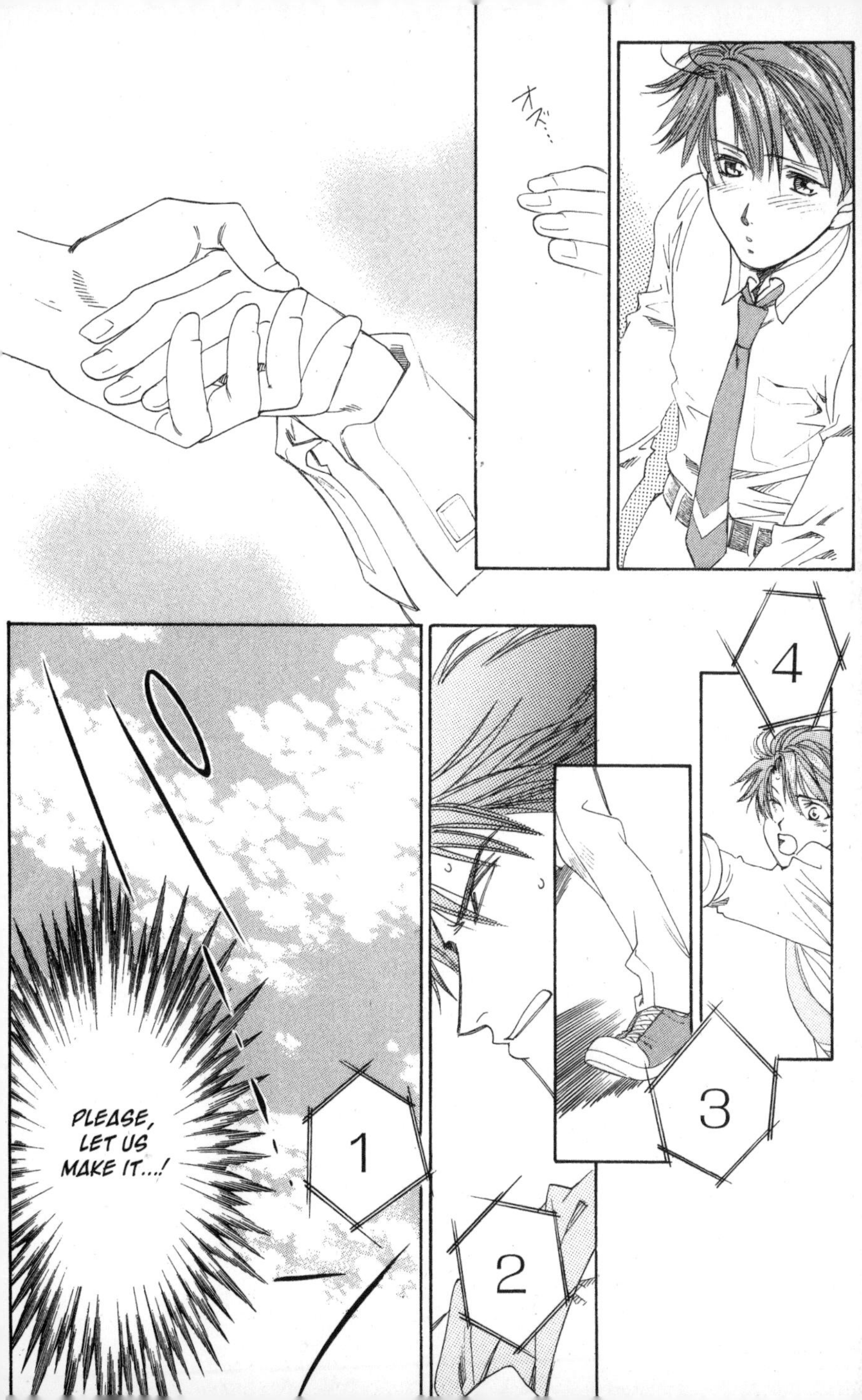

オズ…
4
3
2
1
PLEASE, LET US MAKE IT...!

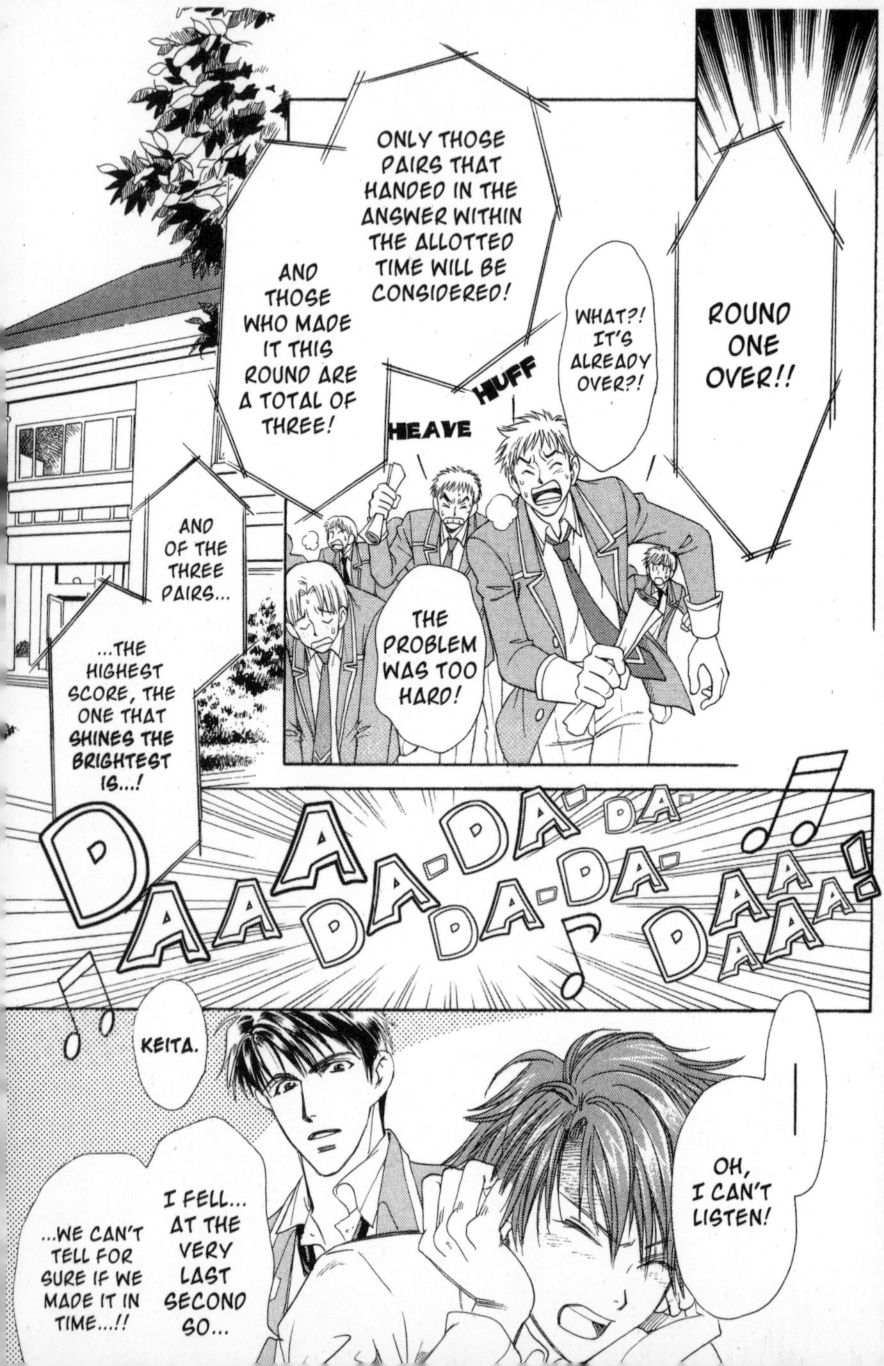
ROUND ONE OVER!!
WHAT?! IT'S ALREADY OVER?!
HUFF
HEAVE
ONLY THOSE PAIRS THAT HANDED IN THE ANSWER WITHIN THE ALLOTTED TIME WILL BE CONSIDERED!
AND THOSE WHO MADE IT THIS ROUND ARE A TOTAL OF THREE!
THE PROBLEM WAS TOO HARD!
AND OF THE THREE PAIRS...
...THE HIGHEST SCORE, THE ONE THAT SHINES THE BRIGHTEST IS...!
DAAA-DA-DA-DA-DA-DA-DAAAAA!!
OH, I CAN'T LISTEN!
KEITA.
I FELL... AT THE VERY LAST SECOND SO...
...WE CAN'T TELL FOR SURE IF WE MADE IT IN TIME...!!

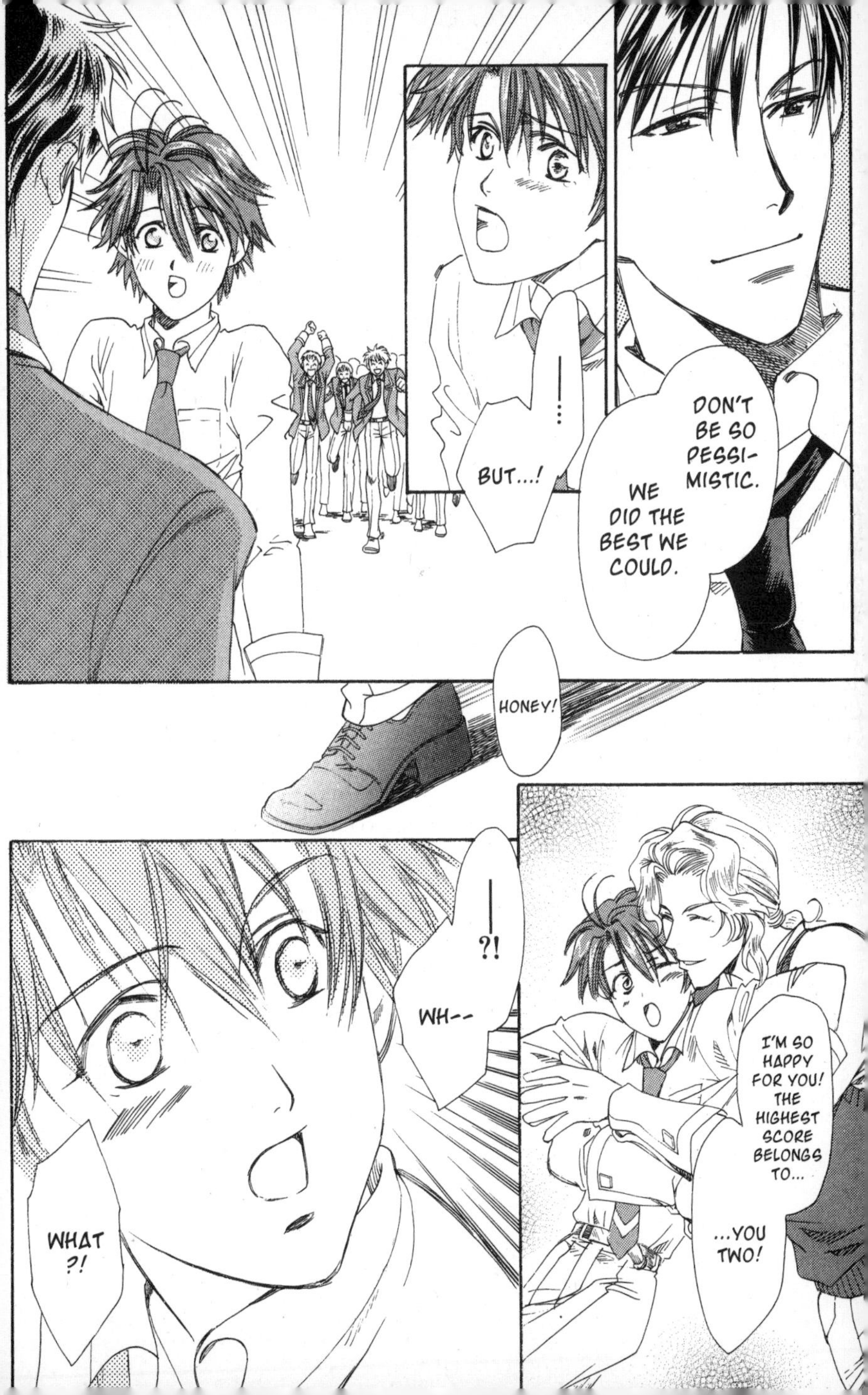
DON'T BE SO PESSIMISTIC.
WE DID THE BEST WE COULD.
—...!
BUT...!
HONEY!
I'M SO HAPPY FOR YOU! THE HIGHEST SCORE BELONGS TO...
...YOU TWO!
—?!
WH--
WHAT?!

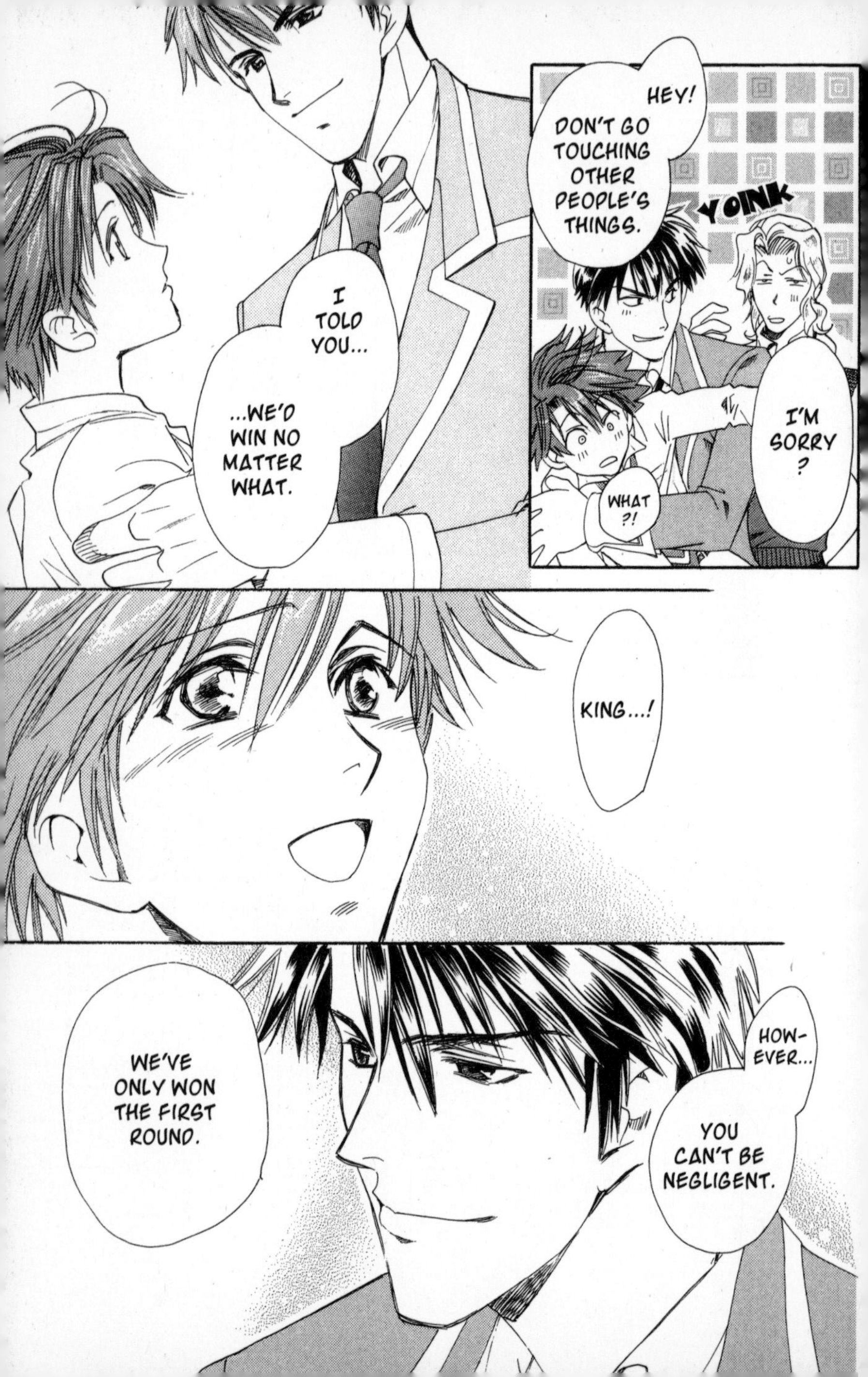
HEY! DON'T GO TOUCHING OTHER PEOPLE'S THINGS.
YOINK
I'M SORRY?
WHAT?!
I TOLD YOU...
...WE'D WIN NO MATTER WHAT.
KING...!
WE'VE ONLY WON THE FIRST ROUND.
HOW-EVER...
YOU CAN'T BE NEGLIGENT.

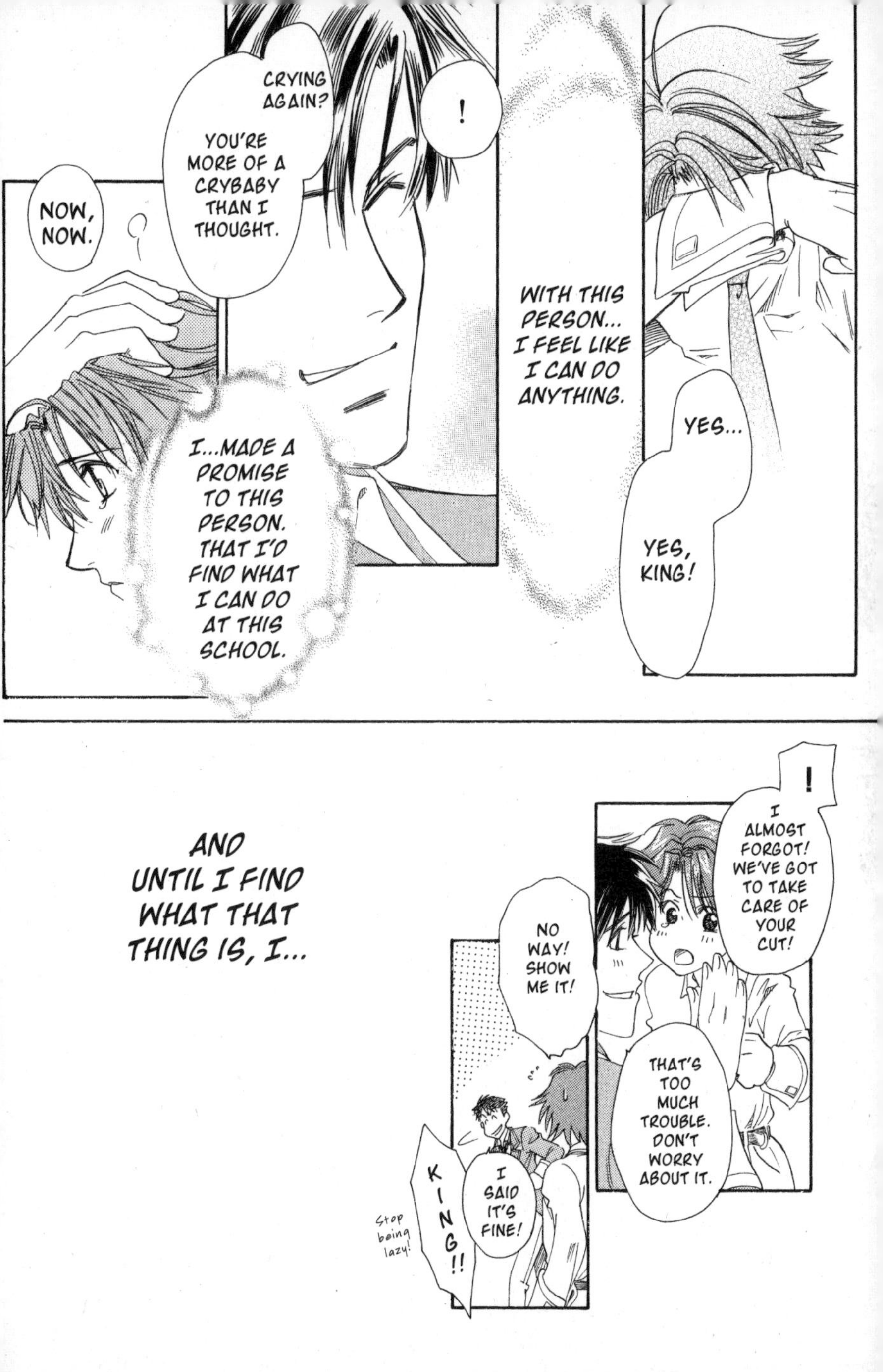
YES...
YES, KING!
WITH THIS PERSON... I FEEL LIKE I CAN DO ANYTHING.
!
CRYING AGAIN?
YOU'RE MORE OF A CRYBABY THAN I THOUGHT.
NOW, NOW.
I...MADE A PROMISE TO THIS PERSON. THAT I'D FIND WHAT I CAN DO AT THIS SCHOOL.
!
I ALMOST FORGOT! WE'VE GOT TO TAKE CARE OF YOUR CUT!
THAT'S TOO MUCH TROUBLE. DON'T WORRY ABOUT IT.
NO WAY! SHOW ME IT!
I SAID IT'S FINE!
KING!!
Stop being lazy!
AND UNTIL I FIND WHAT THAT THING IS, I...

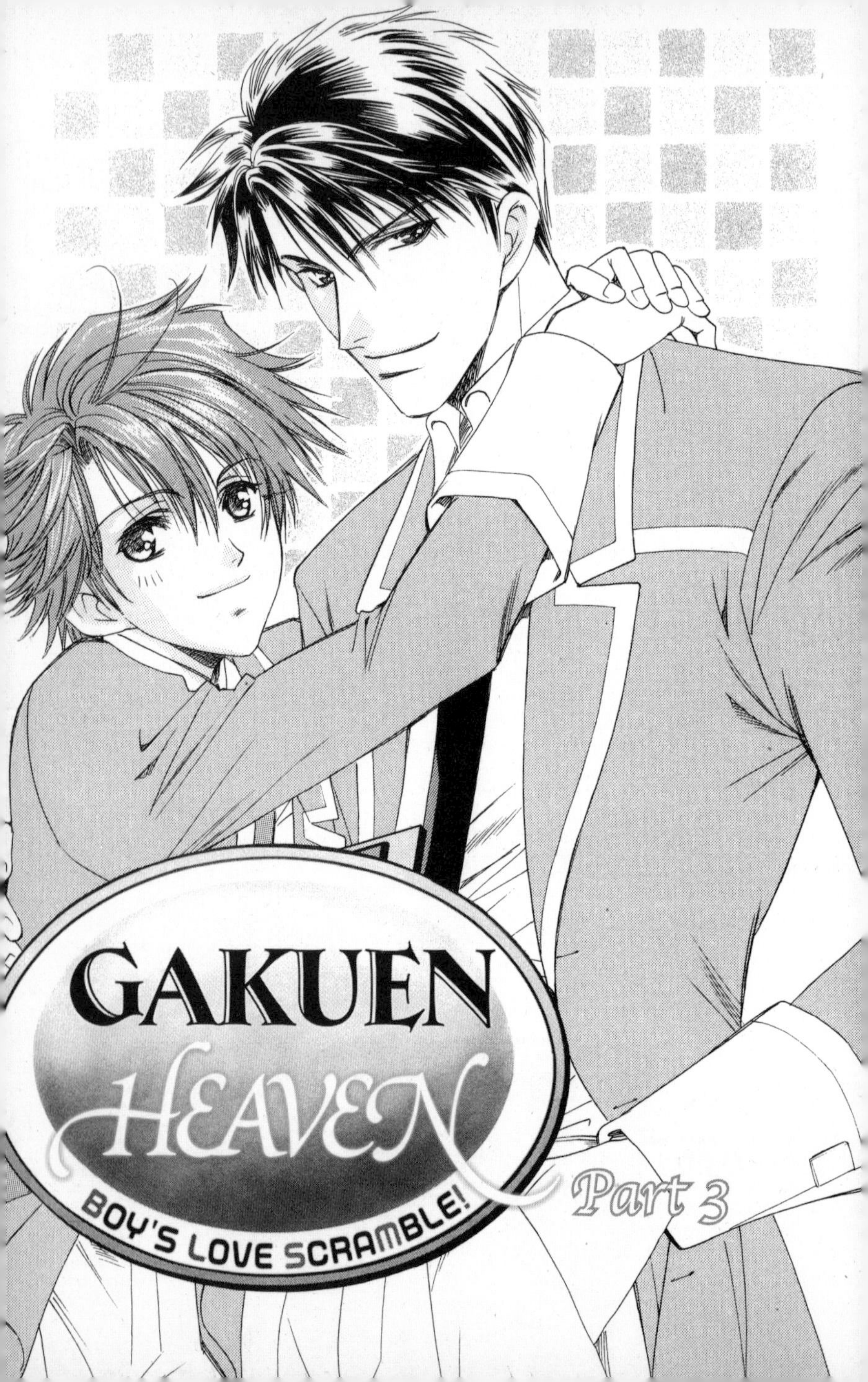
GAKUEN
HEAVEN
BOY'S LOVE SCRAMBLE!
Part 3

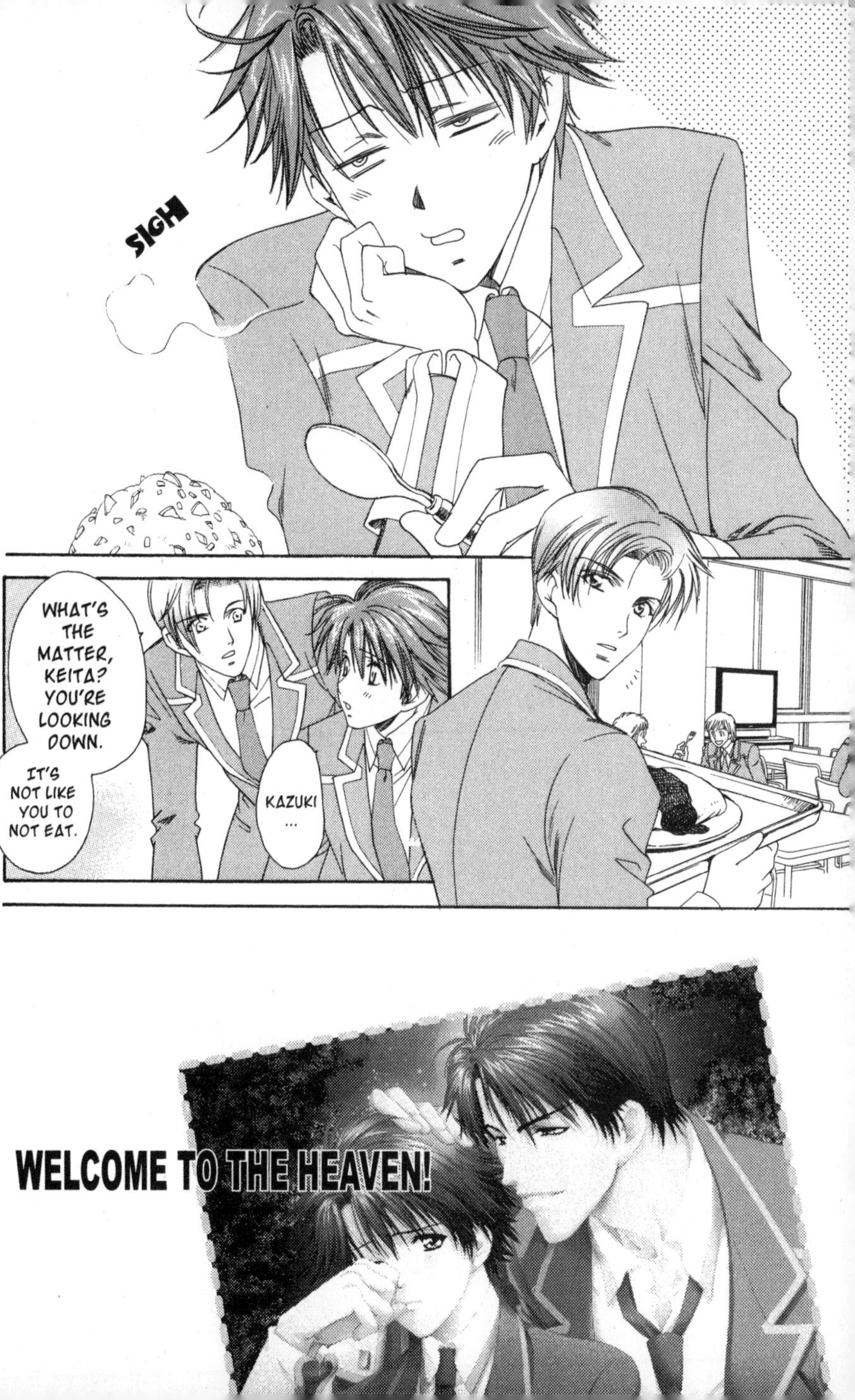
SIGH
WHAT'S THE MATTER, KEITA? YOU'RE LOOKING DOWN.
IT'S NOT LIKE YOU TO NOT EAT.
KAZUKI ...
WELCOME TO THE HEAVEN!

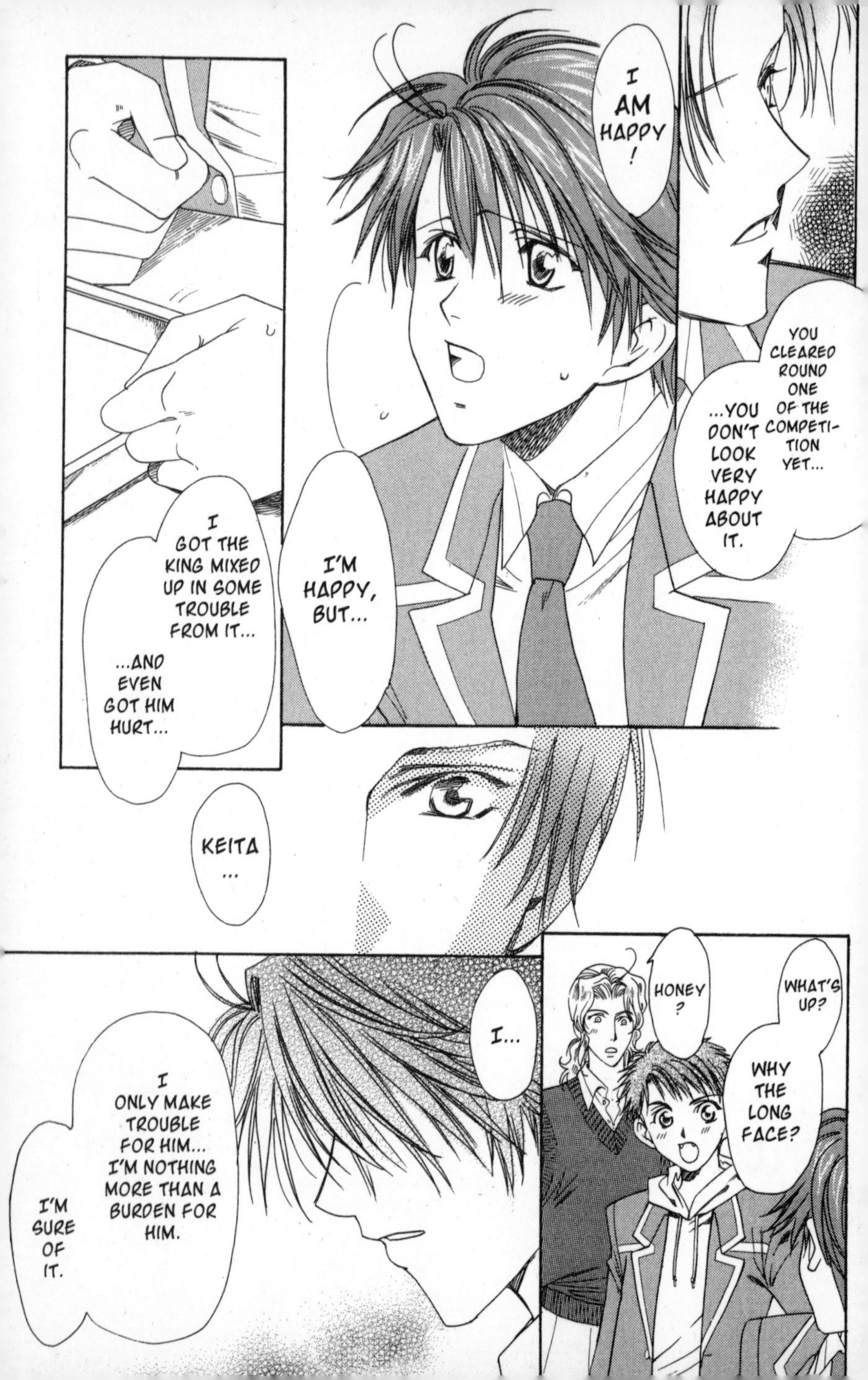
YOU CLEARED ROUND ONE OF THE COMPETITION YET...
...YOU DON'T LOOK VERY HAPPY ABOUT IT.
I AM HAPPY!
I'M HAPPY, BUT...
I GOT THE KING MIXED UP IN SOME TROUBLE FROM IT...
...AND EVEN GOT HIM HURT...
KEITA...
WHAT'S UP?
WHY THE LONG FACE?
HONEY?
I...
I ONLY MAKE TROUBLE FOR HIM... I'M NOTHING MORE THAN A BURDEN FOR HIM.
I'M SURE OF IT.

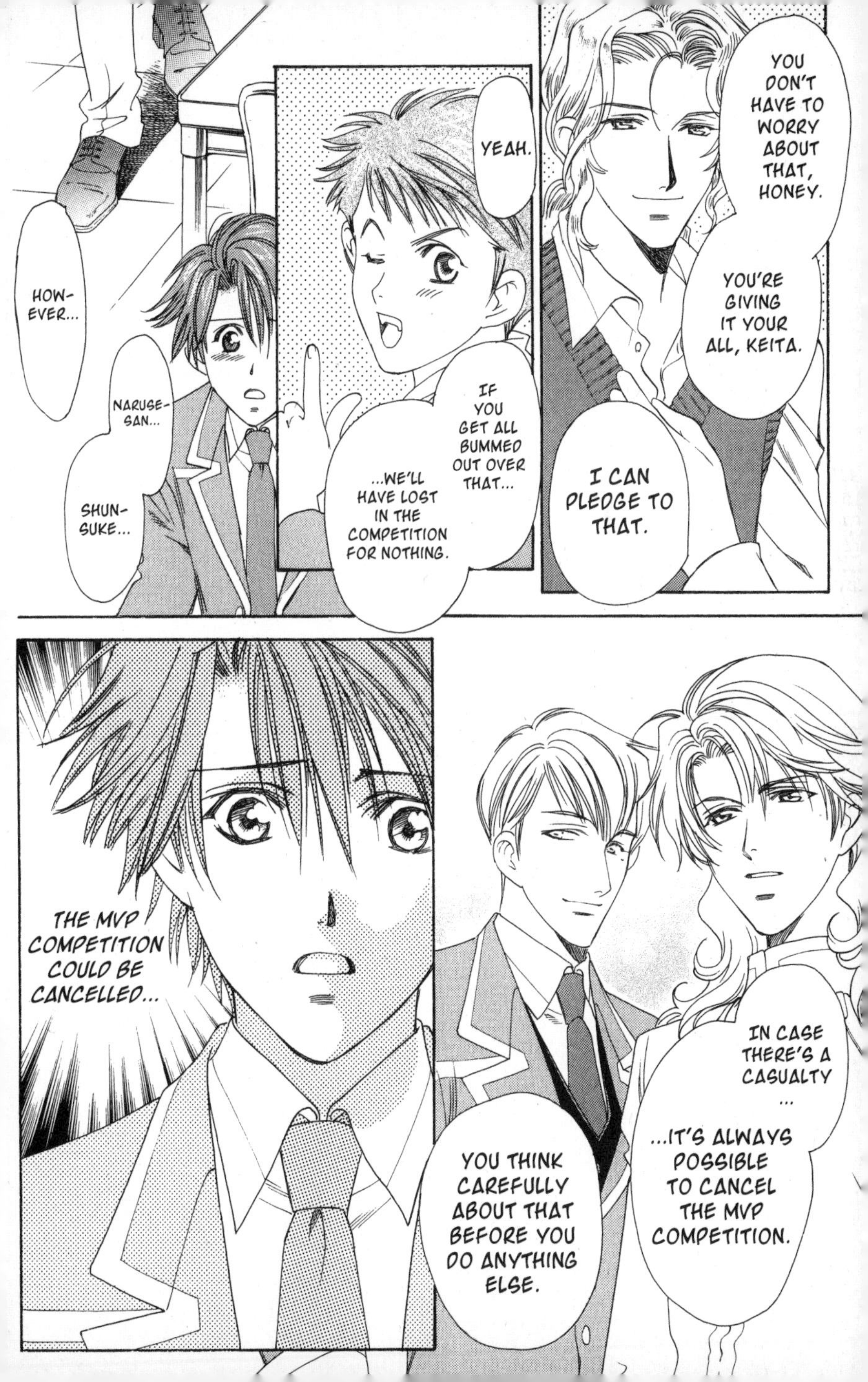
YOU DON'T HAVE TO WORRY ABOUT THAT, HONEY.
YOU'RE GIVING IT YOUR ALL, KEITA.
I CAN PLEDGE TO THAT.
YEAH.
IF YOU GET ALL BUMMED OUT OVER THAT...
...WE'LL HAVE LOST IN THE COMPETITION FOR NOTHING.
NARUSE-SAN...
SHUN-SUKE...
HOW-EVER...
IN CASE THERE'S A CASUALTY ...
...IT'S ALWAYS POSSIBLE TO CANCEL THE MVP COMPETITION.
YOU THINK CAREFULLY ABOUT THAT BEFORE YOU DO ANYTHING ELSE.
THE MVP COMPETITION COULD BE CANCELLED...

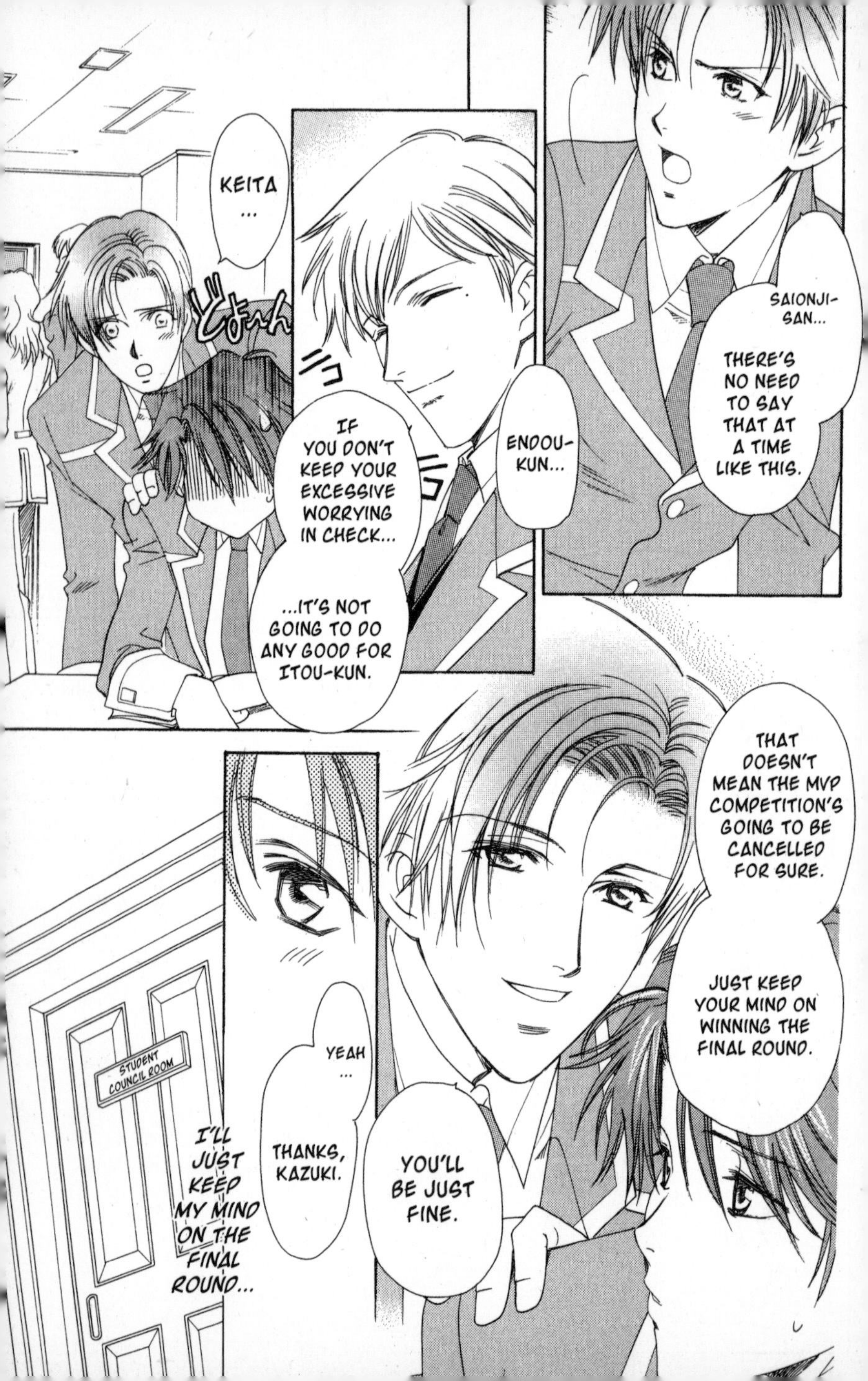
SAIONJI-SAN...
THERE'S NO NEED TO SAY THAT AT A TIME LIKE THIS.
ENDOU-KUN...
ニコ
ニコ
IF YOU DON'T KEEP YOUR EXCESSIVE WORRYING IN CHECK...
...IT'S NOT GOING TO DO ANY GOOD FOR ITOU-KUN.
KEITA ...
どよ～ん
THAT DOESN'T MEAN THE MVP COMPETITION'S GOING TO BE CANCELLED FOR SURE.
JUST KEEP YOUR MIND ON WINNING THE FINAL ROUND.
YOU'LL BE JUST FINE.
YEAH ...
THANKS, KAZUKI.
STUDENT COUNCIL ROOM
I'LL JUST KEEP MY MIND ON THE FINAL ROUND...

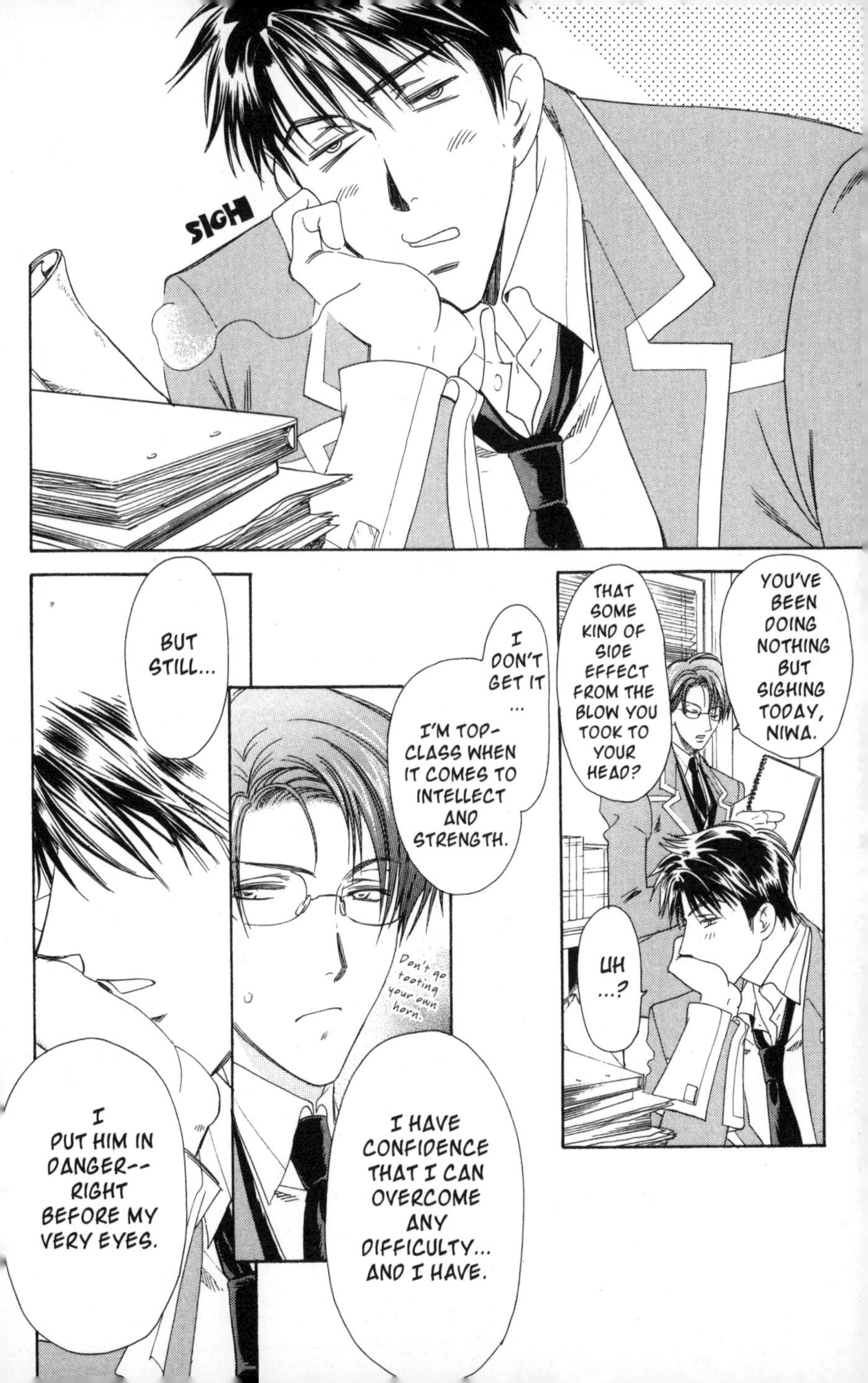
SIGH
YOU'VE BEEN DOING NOTHING BUT SIGHING TODAY, NIWA.
THAT SOME KIND OF SIDE EFFECT FROM THE BLOW YOU TOOK TO YOUR HEAD?
UH ...?
I DON'T GET IT ...
I'M TOP-CLASS WHEN IT COMES TO INTELLECT AND STRENGTH.
Don't go tooting your own horn.
I HAVE CONFIDENCE THAT I CAN OVERCOME ANY DIFFICULTY... AND I HAVE.
BUT STILL...
I PUT HIM IN DANGER-- RIGHT BEFORE MY VERY EYES.

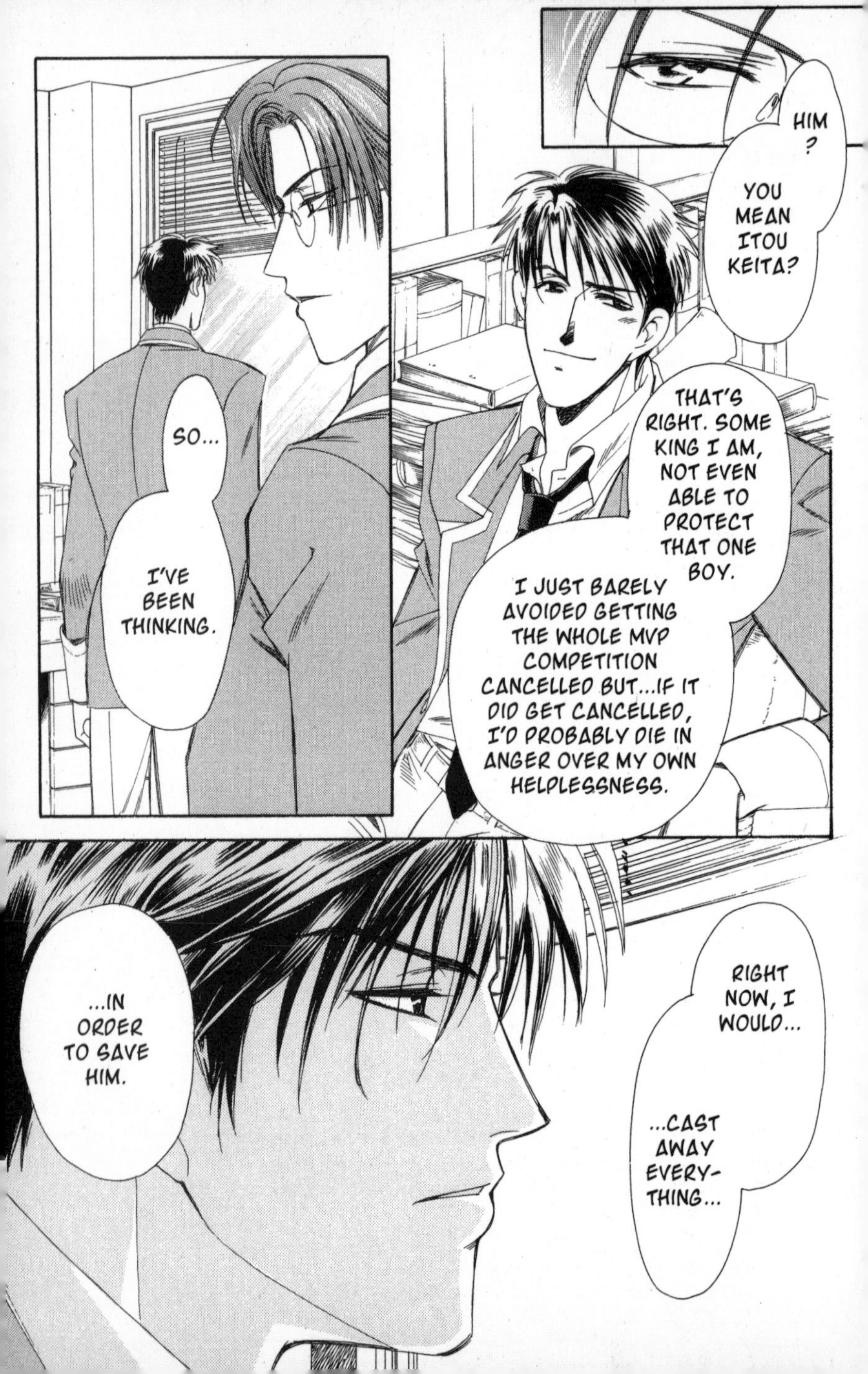
HIM?
YOU MEAN ITOU KEITA?
THAT'S RIGHT. SOME KING I AM, NOT EVEN ABLE TO PROTECT THAT ONE BOY.
I JUST BARELY AVOIDED GETTING THE WHOLE MVP COMPETITION CANCELLED BUT...IF IT DID GET CANCELLED, I'D PROBABLY DIE IN ANGER OVER MY OWN HELPLESSNESS.
SO...
I'VE BEEN THINKING.
RIGHT NOW, I WOULD...
...CAST AWAY EVERY-THING...
...IN ORDER TO SAVE HIM.

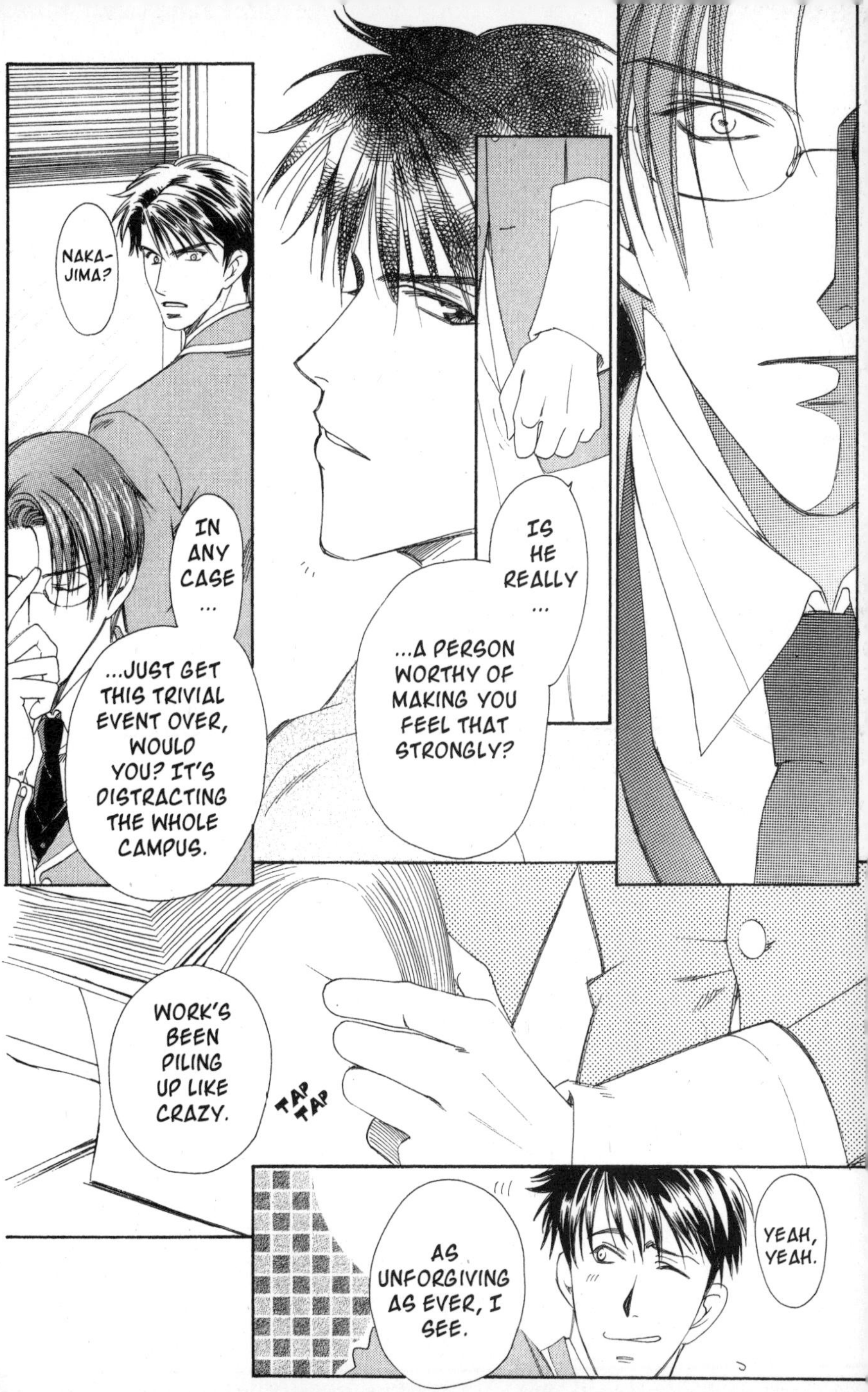
IS HE REALLY ...
...A PERSON WORTHY OF MAKING YOU FEEL THAT STRONGLY?
NAKA-JIMA?
IN ANY CASE ...
...JUST GET THIS TRIVIAL EVENT OVER, WOULD YOU? IT'S DISTRACTING THE WHOLE CAMPUS.
WORK'S BEEN PILING UP LIKE CRAZY.
TAP TAP
YEAH, YEAH.
AS UNFORGIVING AS EVER, I SEE.

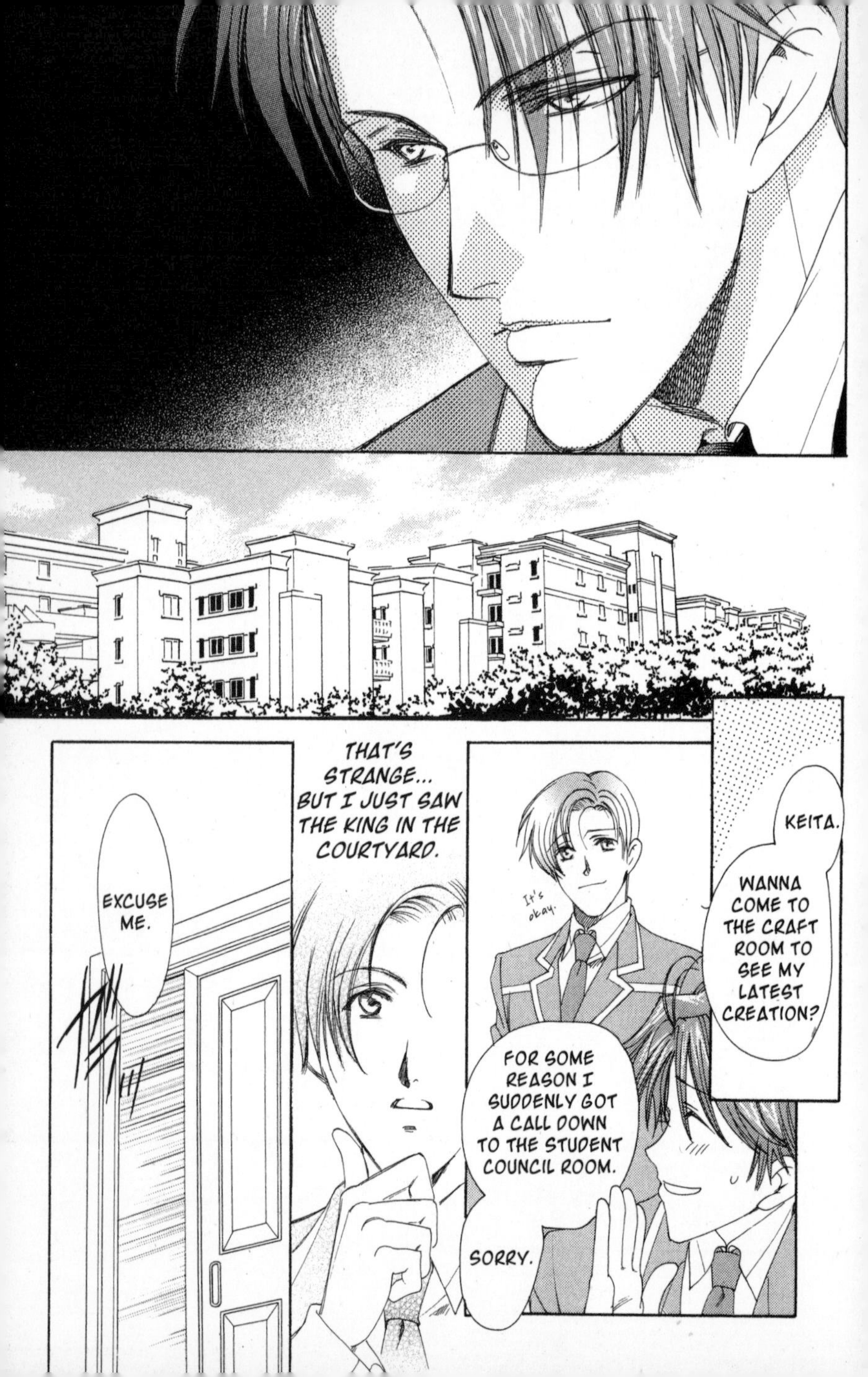
KEITA.
WANNA COME TO THE CRAFT ROOM TO SEE MY LATEST CREATION?
FOR SOME REASON I SUDDENLY GOT A CALL DOWN TO THE STUDENT COUNCIL ROOM.
SORRY.
It's okay.
THAT'S STRANGE... BUT I JUST SAW THE KING IN THE COURTYARD.
EXCUSE ME.

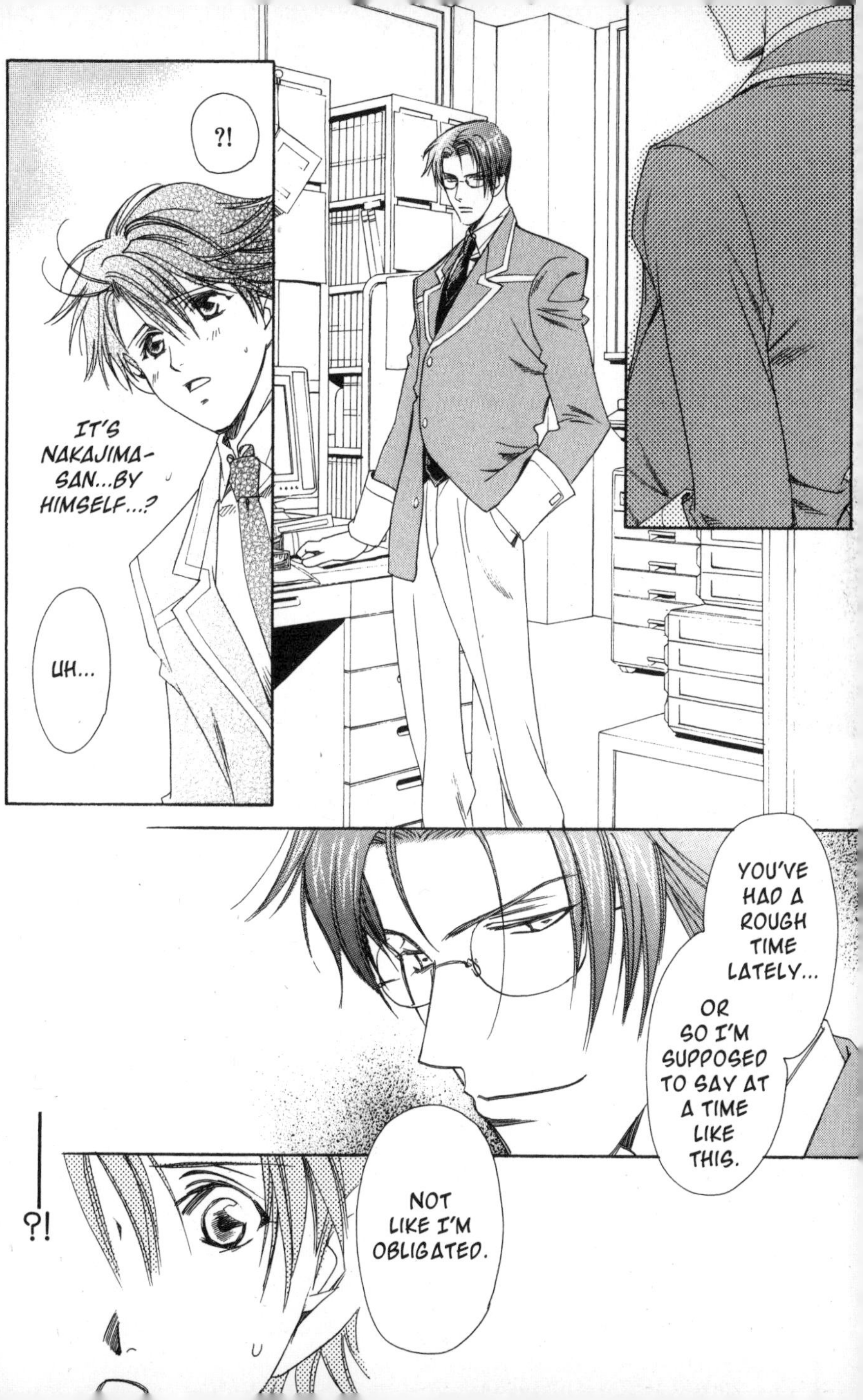
?!
IT'S NAKAJIMA-SAN...BY HIMSELF...?
UH...
YOU'VE HAD A ROUGH TIME LATELY...
OR SO I'M SUPPOSED TO SAY AT A TIME LIKE THIS.
NOT LIKE I'M OBLIGATED.
?!

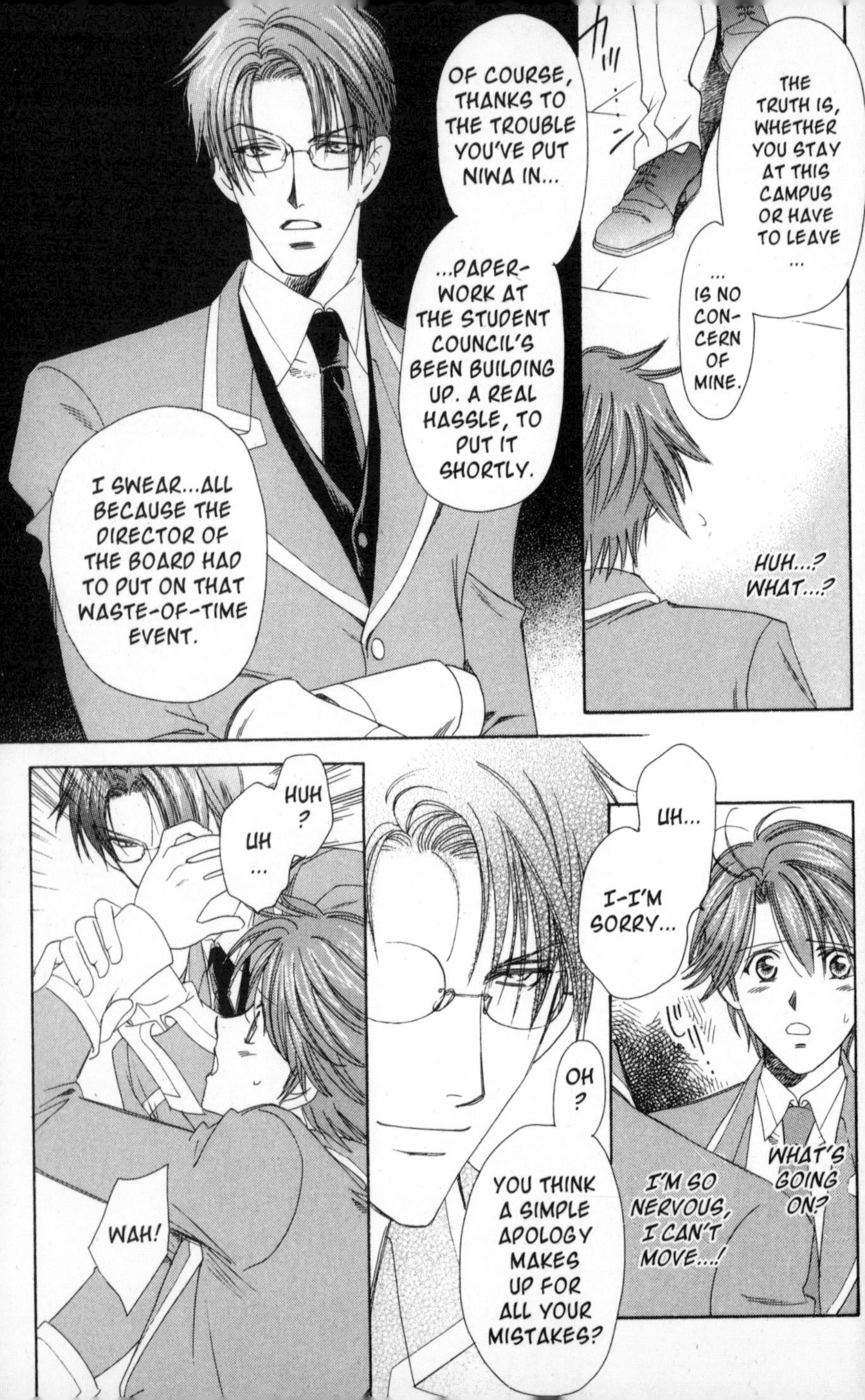
THE TRUTH IS, WHETHER YOU STAY AT THIS CAMPUS OR HAVE TO LEAVE ...
... IS NO CONCERN OF MINE.
HUH...? WHAT...?
OF COURSE, THANKS TO THE TROUBLE YOU'VE PUT NIWA IN...
...PAPER-WORK AT THE STUDENT COUNCIL'S BEEN BUILDING UP. A REAL HASSLE, TO PUT IT SHORTLY.
I SWEAR...ALL BECAUSE THE DIRECTOR OF THE BOARD HAD TO PUT ON THAT WASTE-OF-TIME EVENT.
UH...
I-I'M SORRY...
WHAT'S GOING ON?
I'M SO NERVOUS, I CAN'T MOVE...!
OH?
YOU THINK A SIMPLE APOLOGY MAKES UP FOR ALL YOUR MISTAKES?
HUH?
UH ...
WAH!

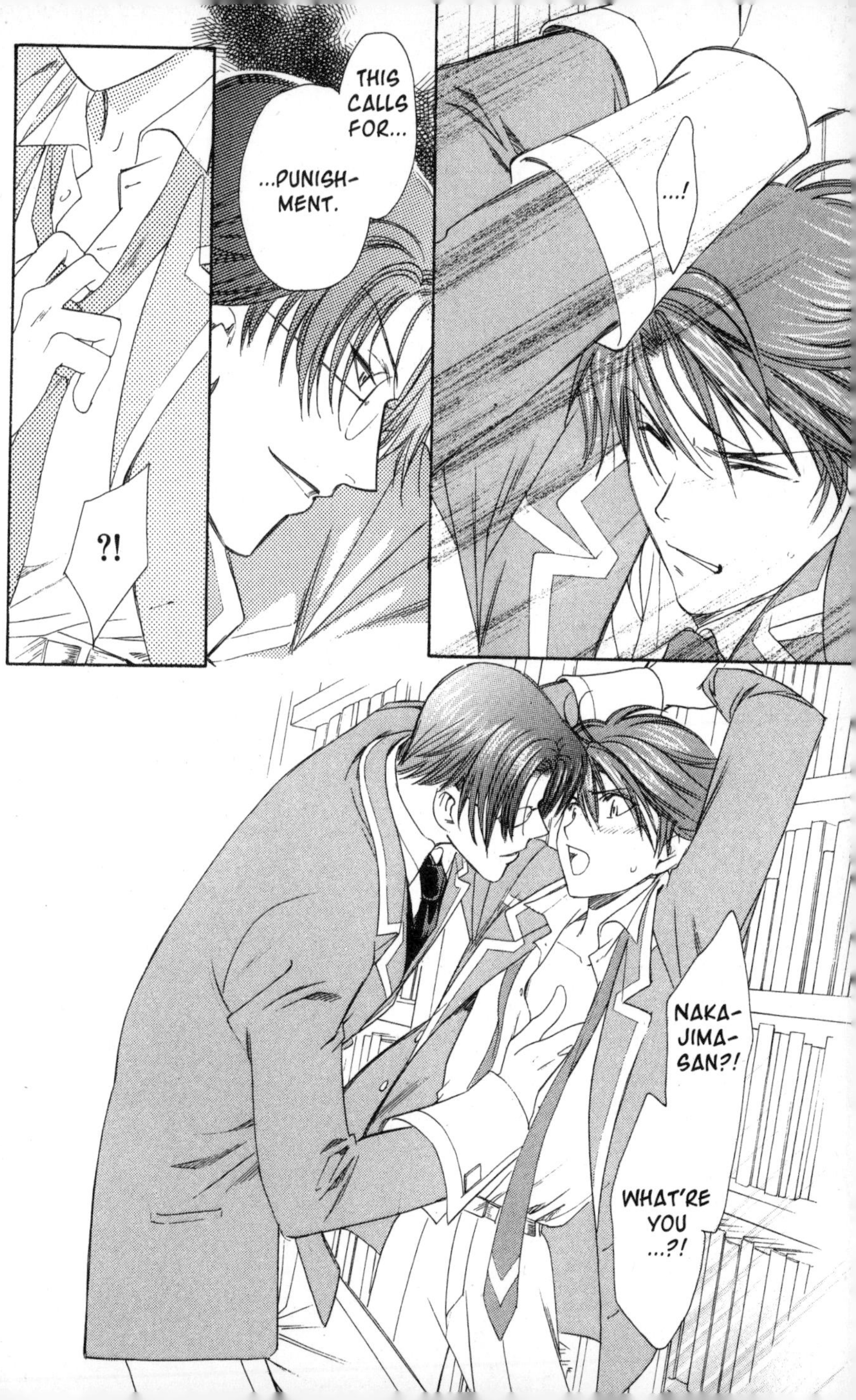
...!
THIS CALLS FOR...
...PUNISHMENT.
?!
NAKAJIMA-SAN?!
WHAT'RE YOU ...?!

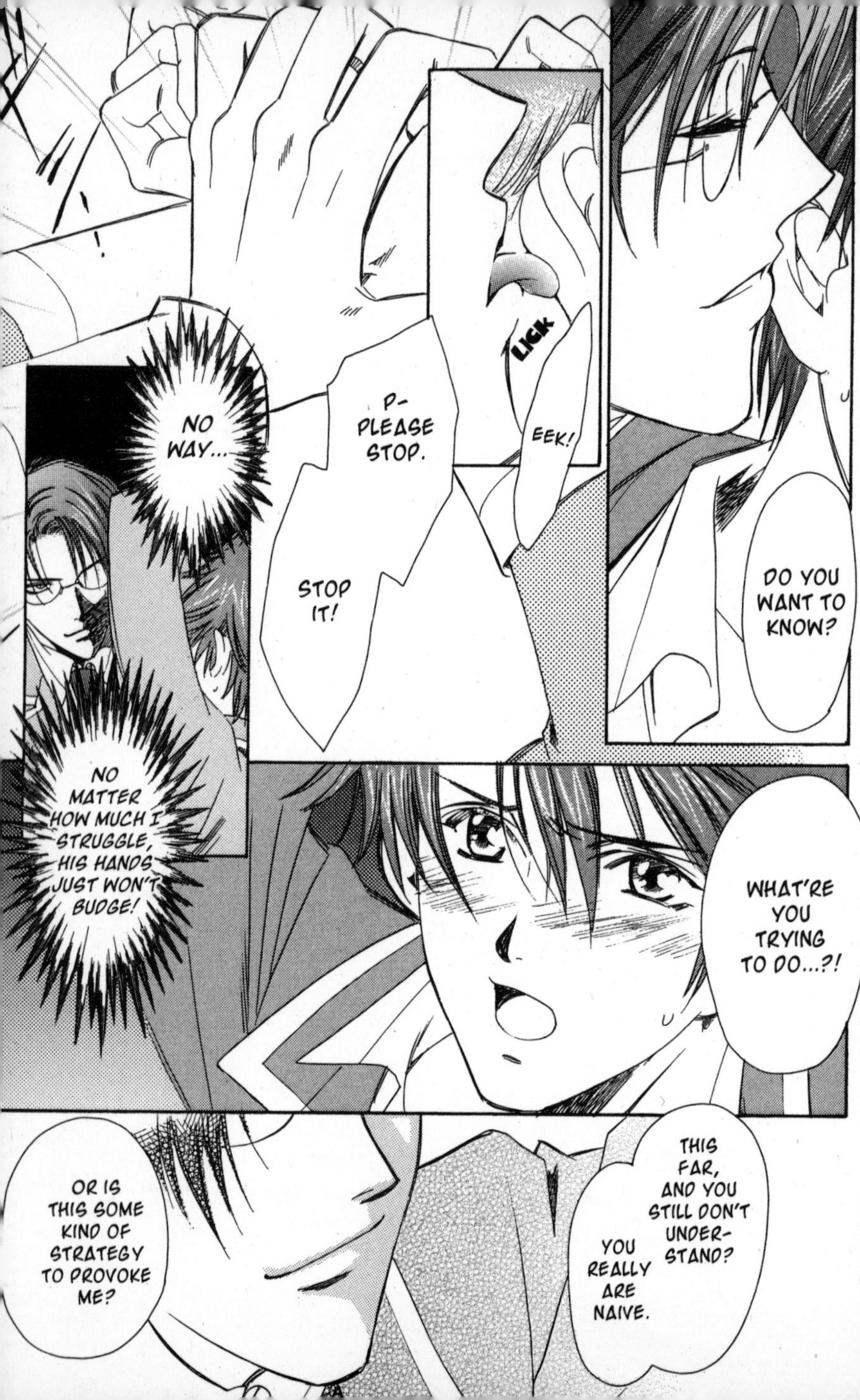
DO YOU WANT TO KNOW?
LICK
EEK!
P-PLEASE STOP.
STOP IT!
NO WAY...
NO MATTER HOW MUCH I STRUGGLE, HIS HANDS JUST WON'T BUDGE!
WHAT'RE YOU TRYING TO DO...?!
THIS FAR, AND YOU STILL DON'T UNDER-STAND?
YOU REALLY ARE NAIVE.
OR IS THIS SOME KIND OF STRATEGY TO PROVOKE ME?

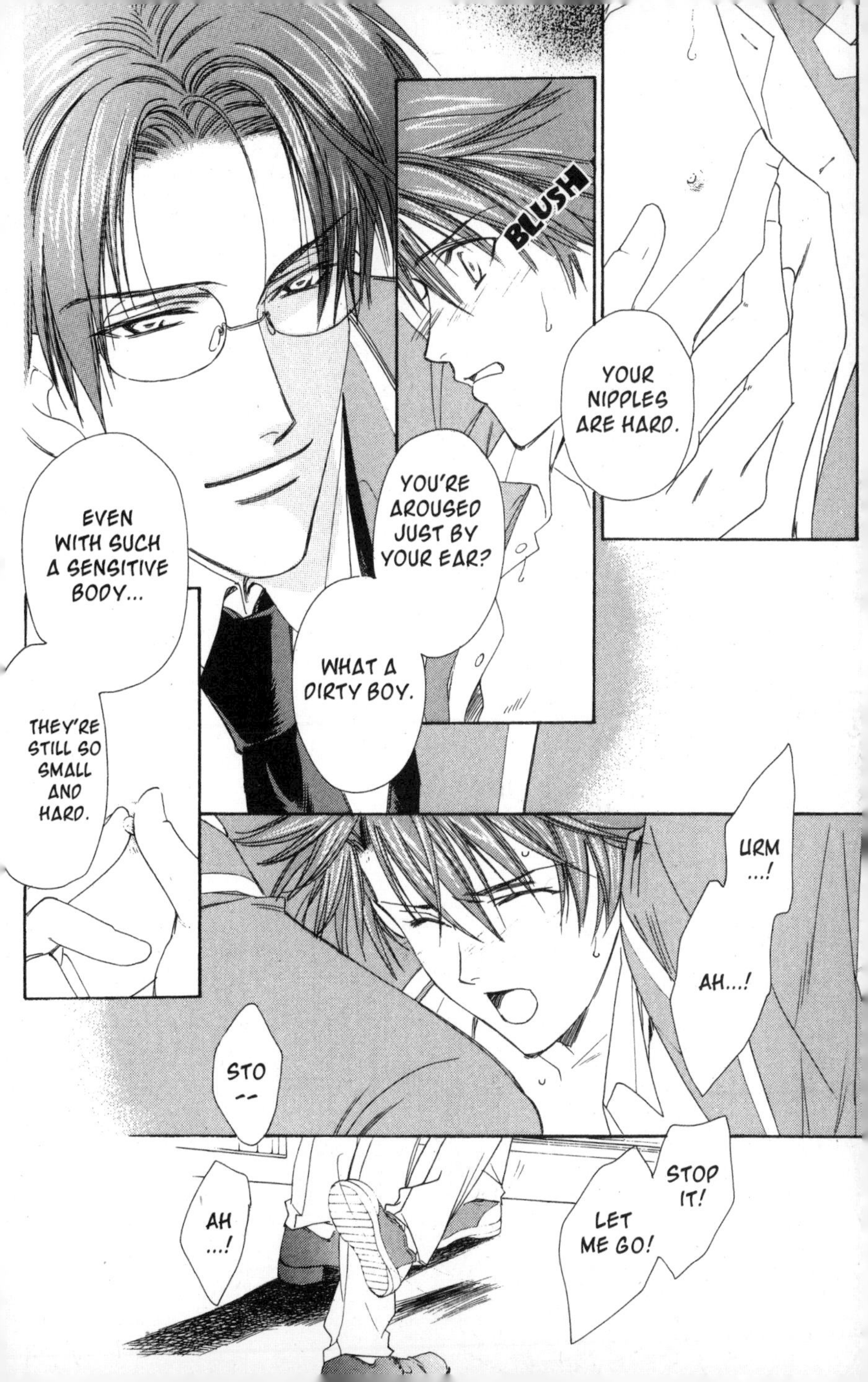
YOUR NIPPLES ARE HARD.
BLUSH
YOU'RE AROUSED JUST BY YOUR EAR?
WHAT A DIRTY BOY.
EVEN WITH SUCH A SENSITIVE BODY...
THEY'RE STILL SO SMALL AND HARD.
URM ...!
AH...!
STO --
STOP IT!
LET ME GO!
AH ...!

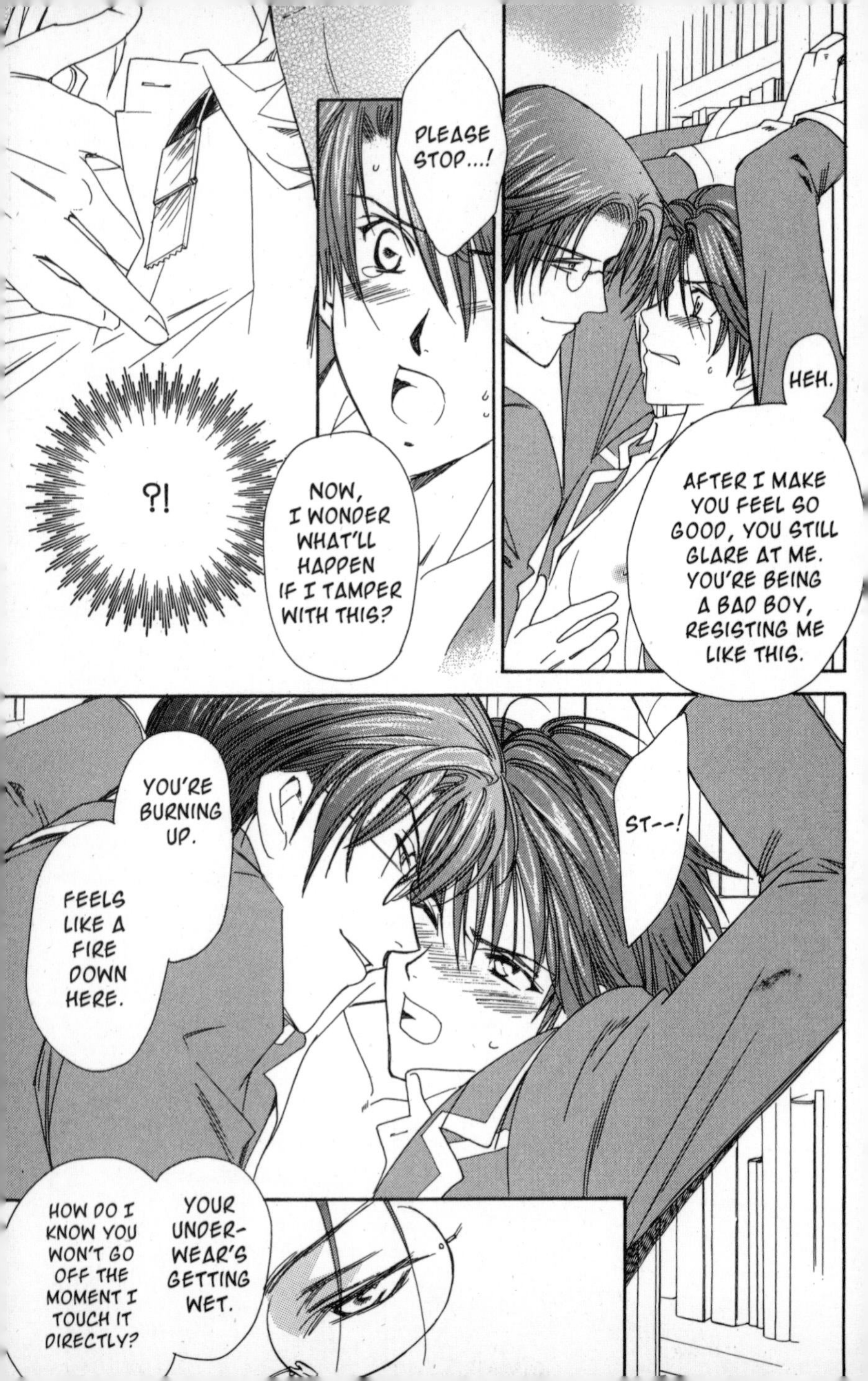
HEH.
AFTER I MAKE YOU FEEL SO GOOD, YOU STILL GLARE AT ME. YOU'RE BEING A BAD BOY, RESISTING ME LIKE THIS.
PLEASE STOP...!
NOW, I WONDER WHAT'LL HAPPEN IF I TAMPER WITH THIS?
?!
ST--!
YOU'RE BURNING UP.
FEELS LIKE A FIRE DOWN HERE.
YOUR UNDER-WEAR'S GETTING WET.
HOW DO I KNOW YOU WON'T GO OFF THE MOMENT I TOUCH IT DIRECTLY?

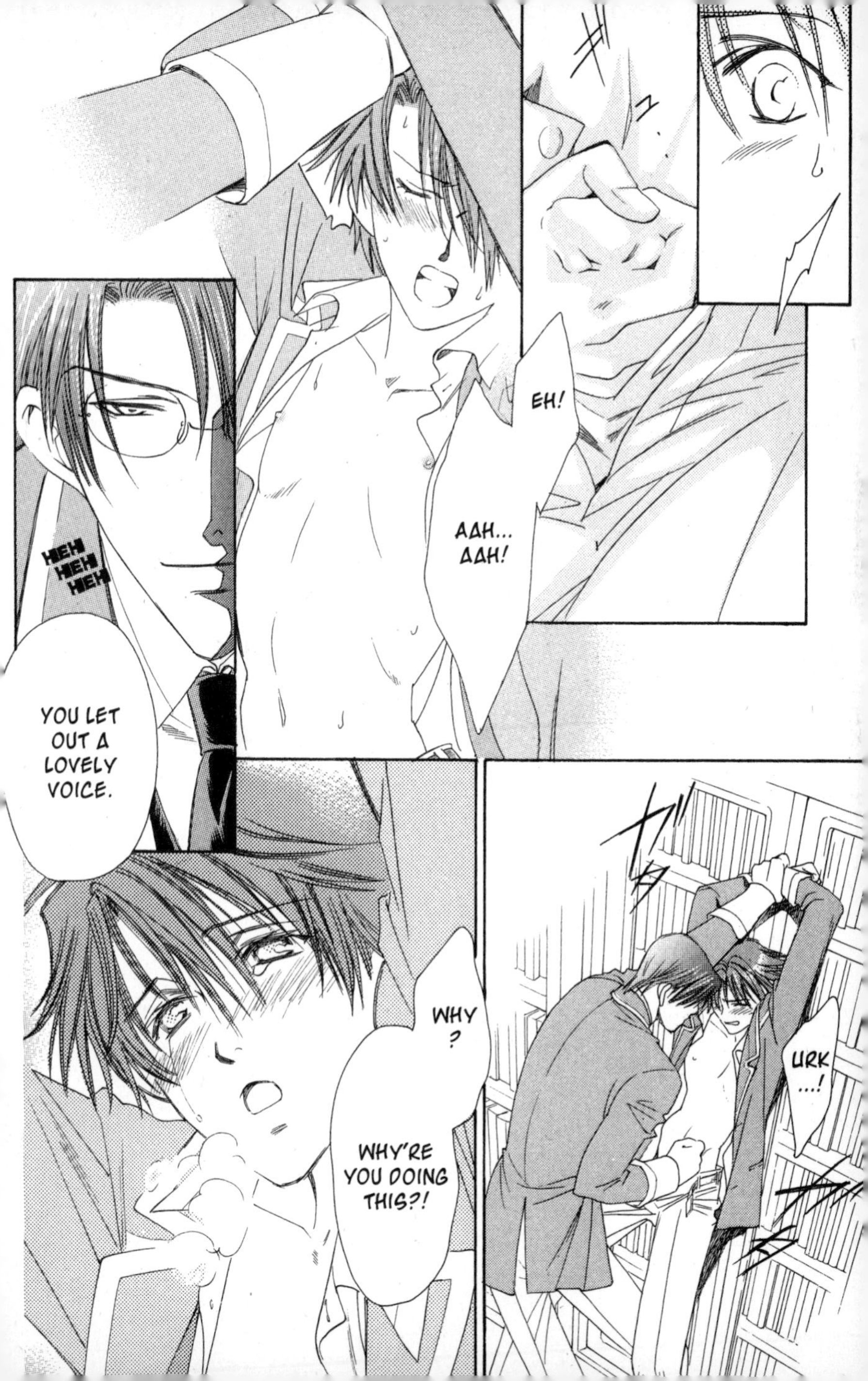
EH!
AAH... AAH!
HEH HEH HEH
YOU LET OUT A LOVELY VOICE.
URK ...!
WHY?
WHY'RE YOU DOING THIS?!

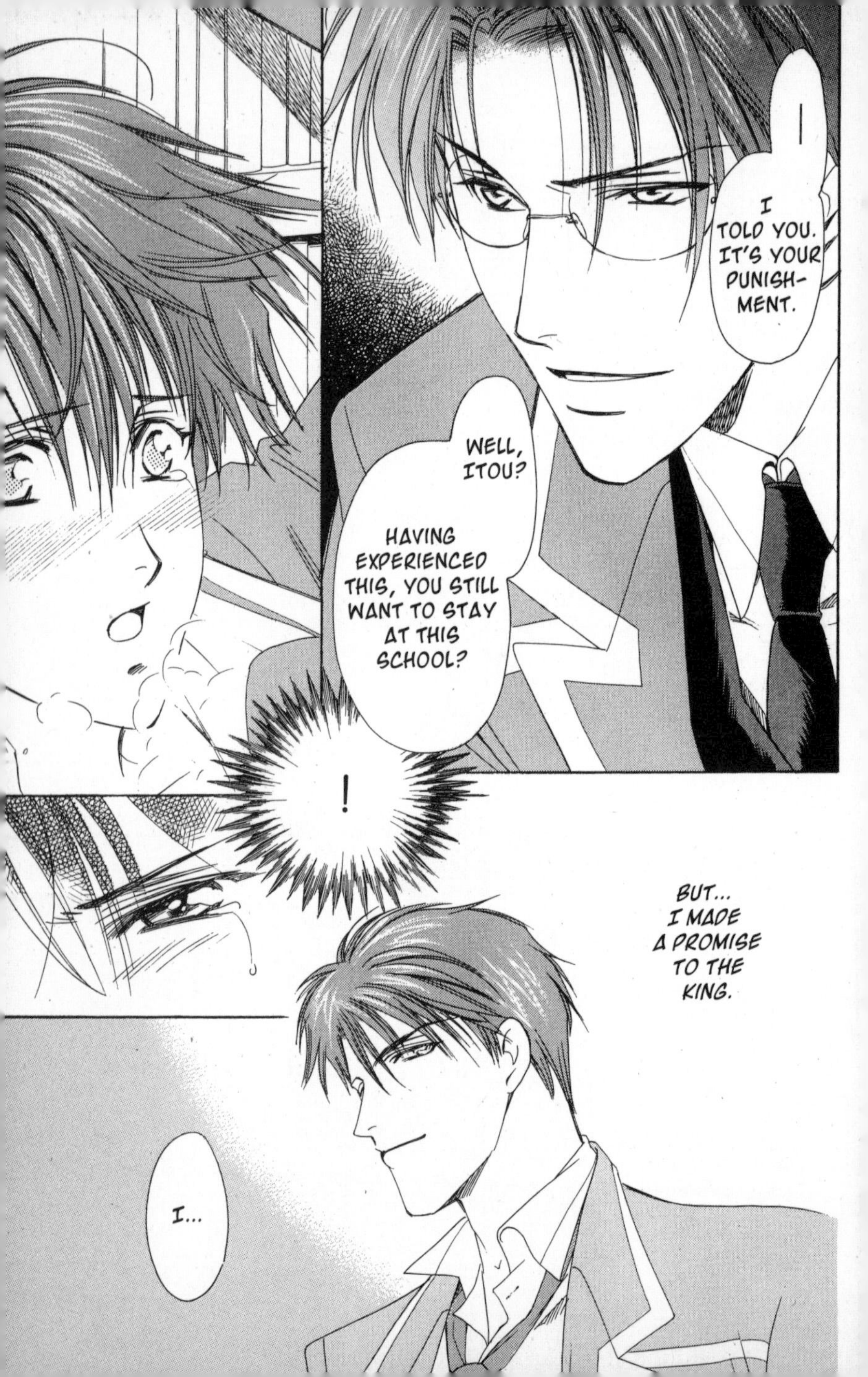
I TOLD YOU. IT'S YOUR PUNISHMENT.
WELL, ITOU?
HAVING EXPERIENCED THIS, YOU STILL WANT TO STAY AT THIS SCHOOL?
!
BUT... I MADE A PROMISE TO THE KING.
I...

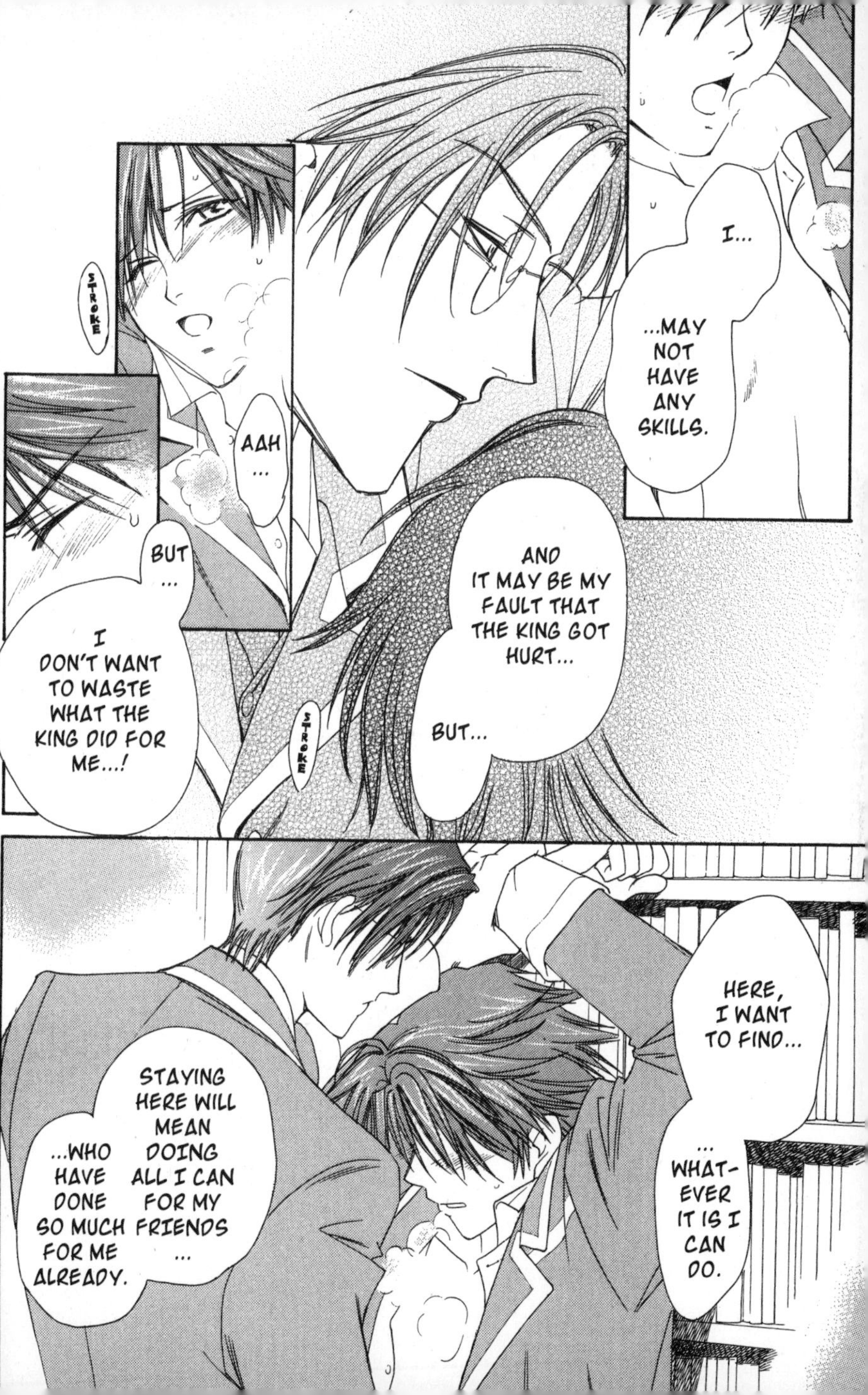
I...
...MAY NOT HAVE ANY SKILLS.
AND IT MAY BE MY FAULT THAT THE KING GOT HURT...
BUT...
STROKE
STROKE
AAH...
BUT...
I DON'T WANT TO WASTE WHAT THE KING DID FOR ME...!
HERE, I WANT TO FIND...
...WHAT-EVER IT IS I CAN DO.
STAYING HERE WILL MEAN DOING ALL I CAN FOR MY FRIENDS...
...WHO HAVE DONE SO MUCH FOR ME ALREADY.

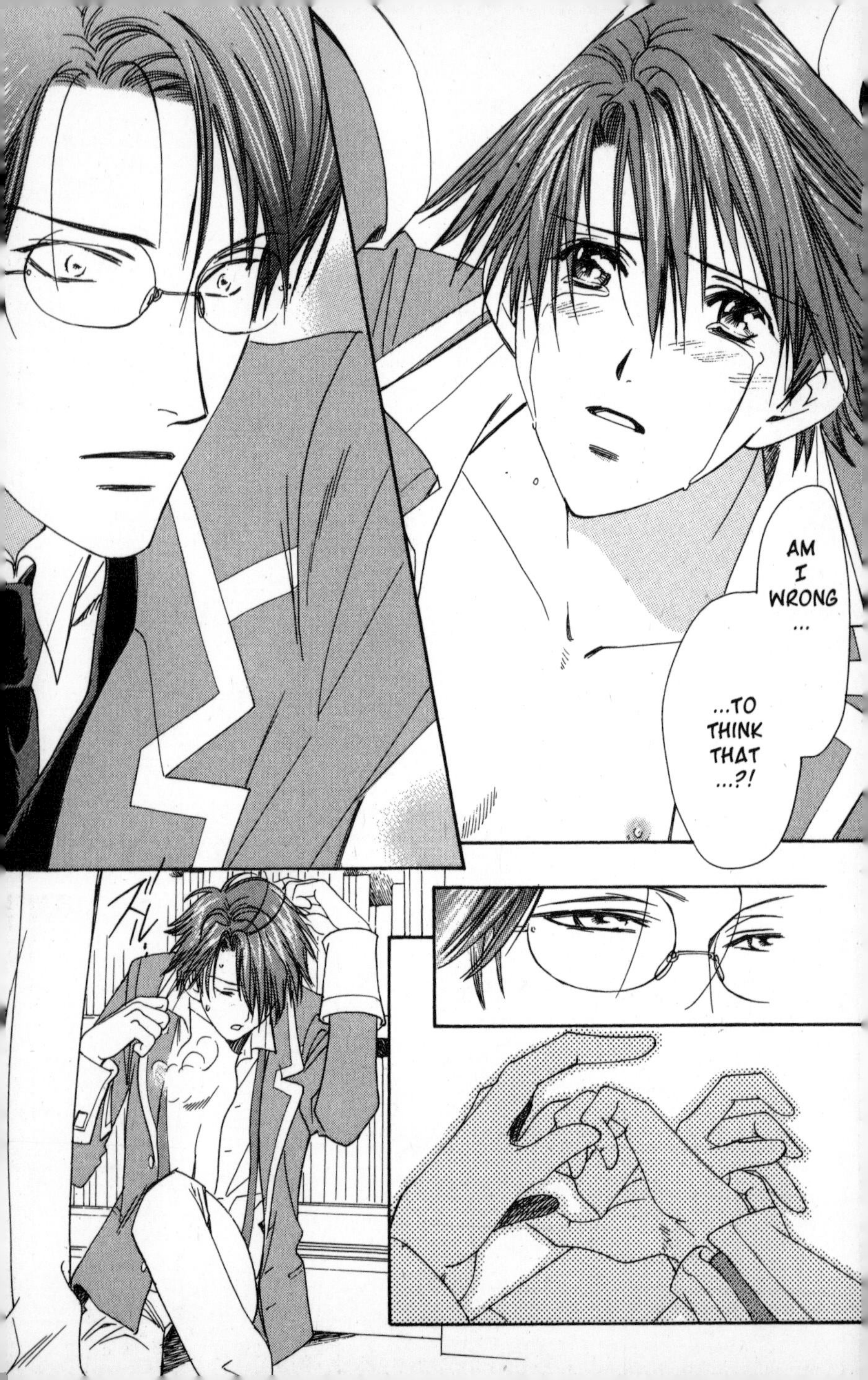
AM I WRONG ...
...TO THINK THAT ...?!

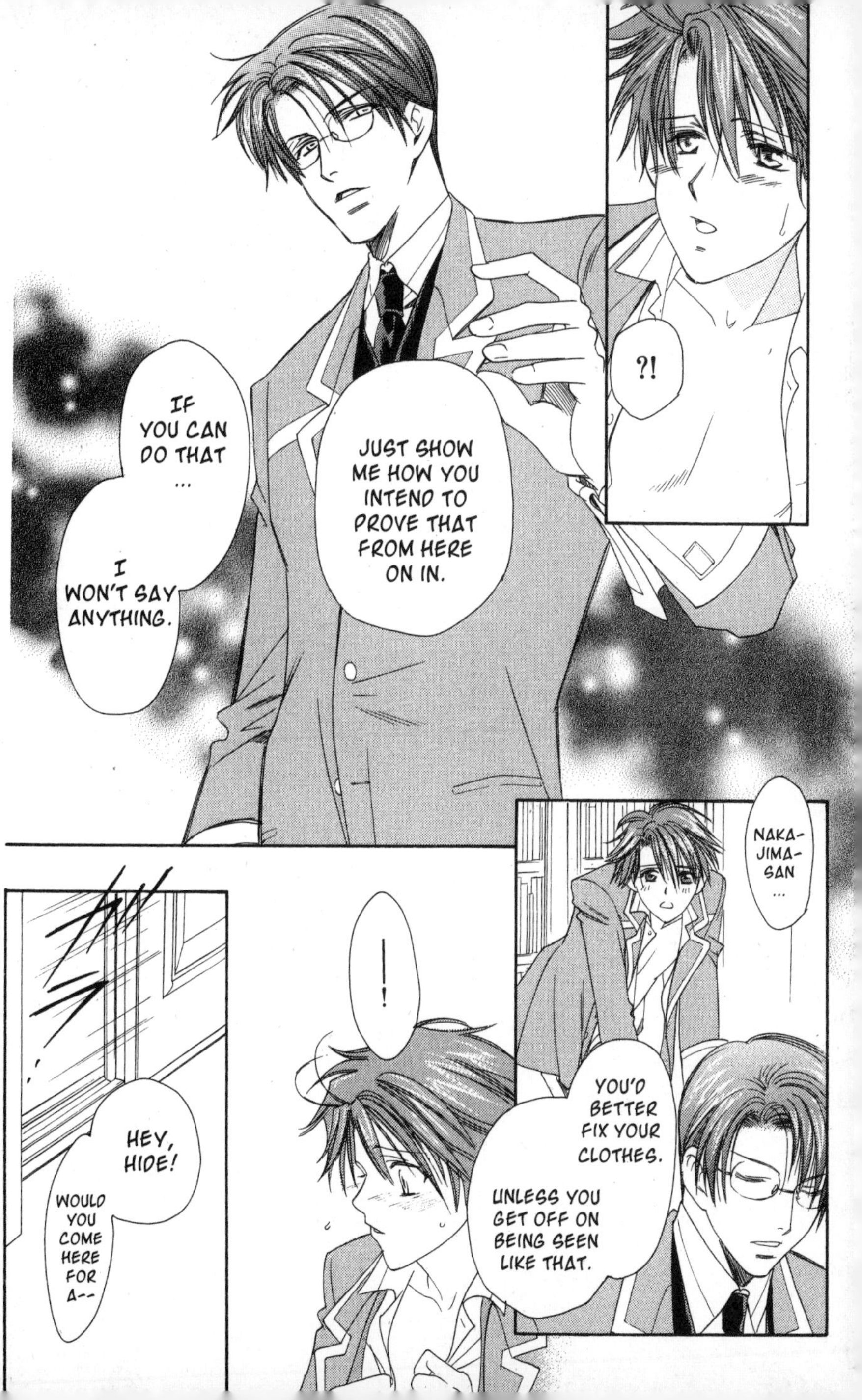
?!
JUST SHOW ME HOW YOU INTEND TO PROVE THAT FROM HERE ON IN.
IF YOU CAN DO THAT ...
I WON'T SAY ANYTHING.
NAKA-JIMA-SAN ...
YOU'D BETTER FIX YOUR CLOTHES.
UNLESS YOU GET OFF ON BEING SEEN LIKE THAT.
!
HEY, HIDE!
WOULD YOU COME HERE FOR A--

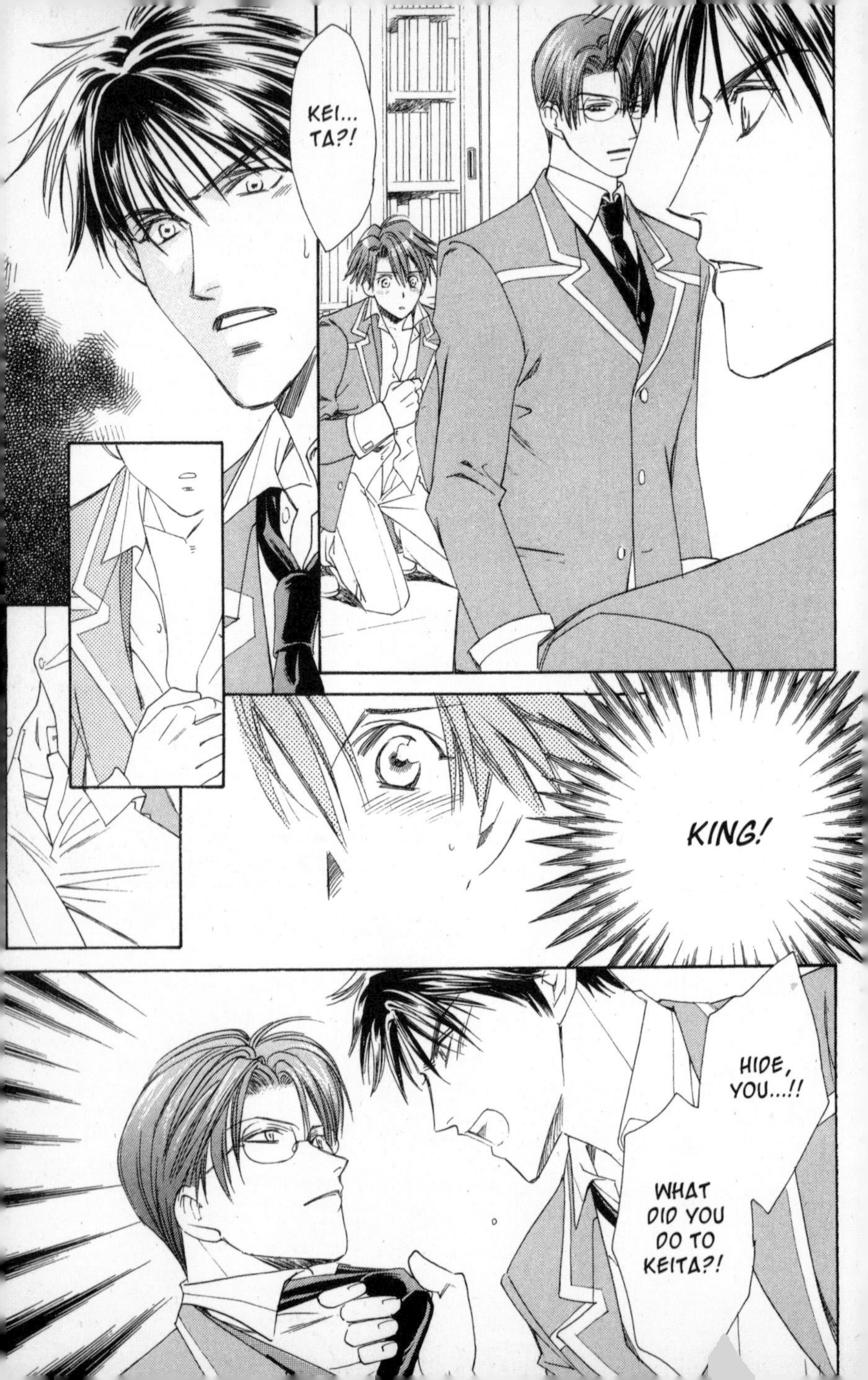
KEI... TA?!
KING!
HIDE, YOU...!!
WHAT DID YOU DO TO KEITA?!

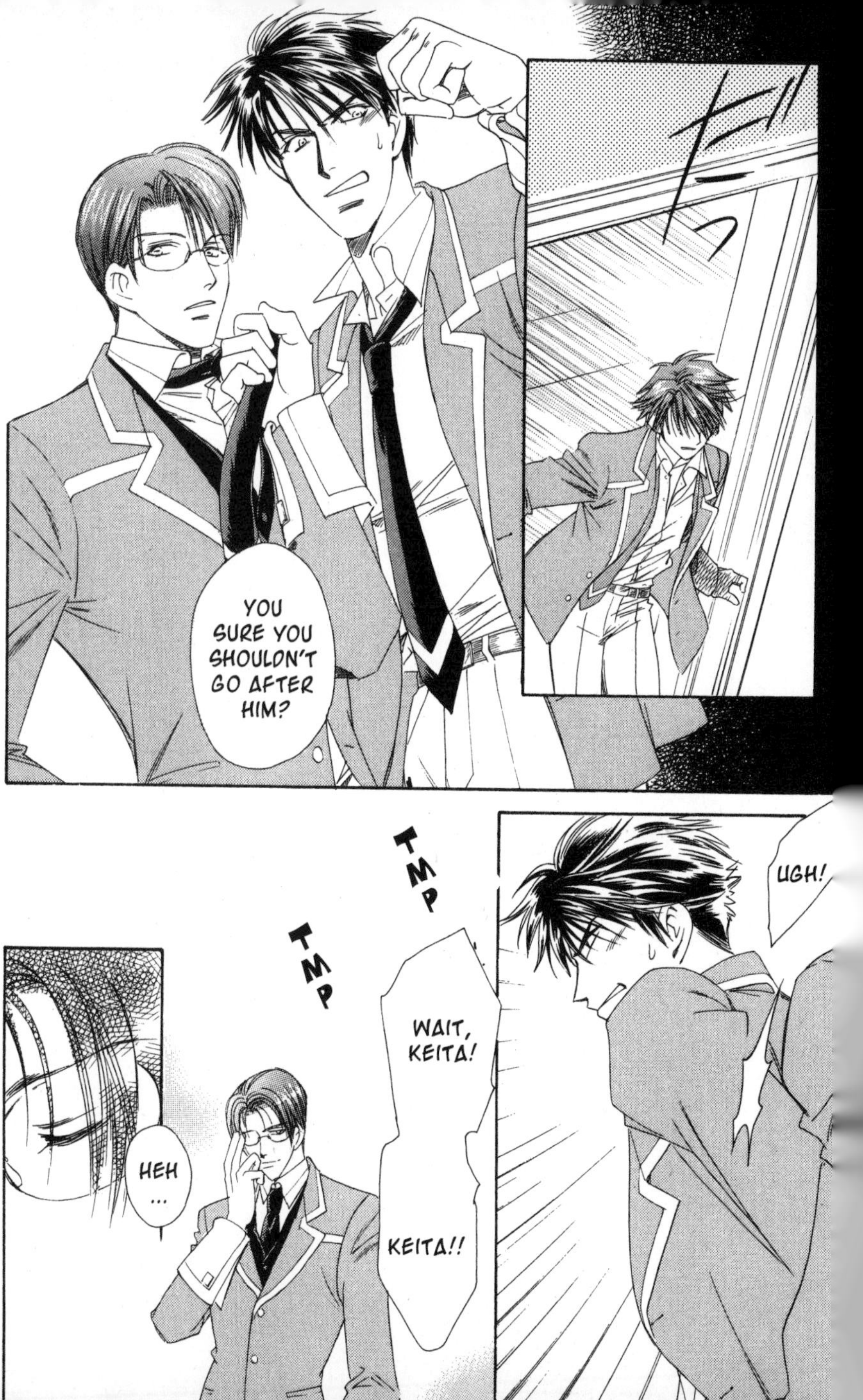
YOU SURE YOU SHOULDN'T GO AFTER HIM?
UGH!
TMP
TMP
WAIT, KEITA!
KEITA!!
HEH ...

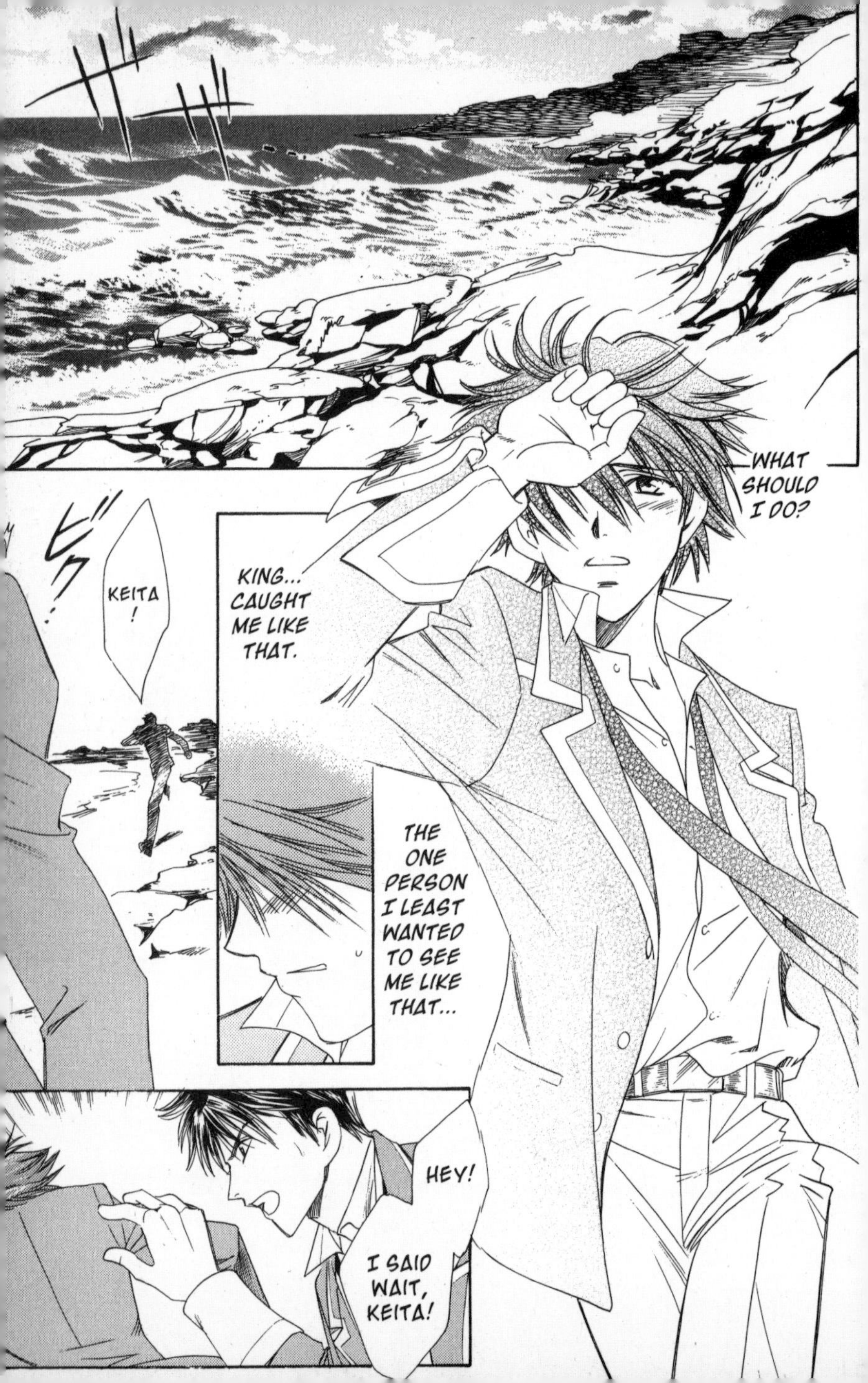
WHAT SHOULD I DO?
KING... CAUGHT ME LIKE THAT.
THE ONE PERSON I LEAST WANTED TO SEE ME LIKE THAT...
KEITA!
HEY!
I SAID WAIT, KEITA!

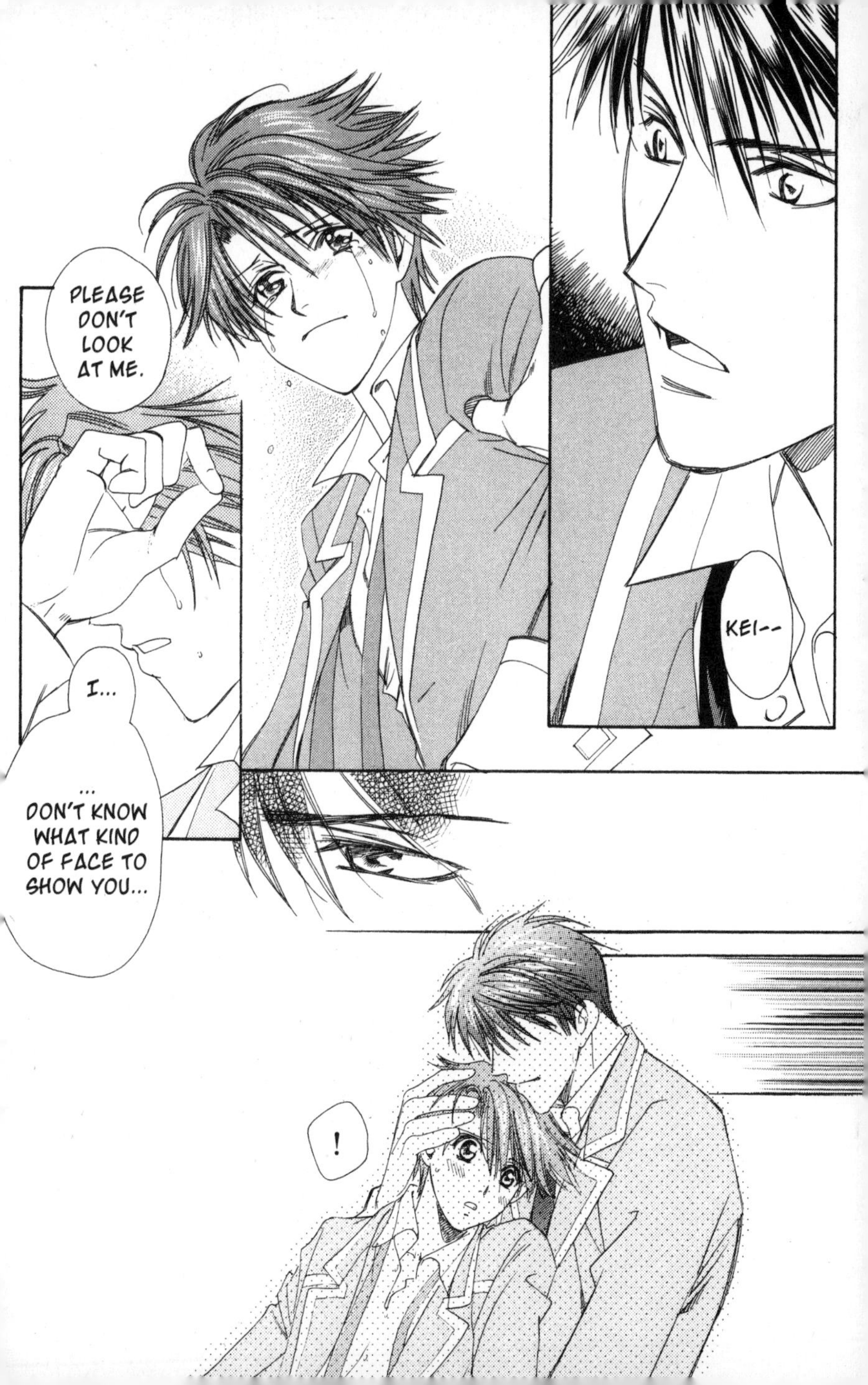
KEI--
PLEASE DON'T LOOK AT ME.
I...
... DON'T KNOW WHAT KIND OF FACE TO SHOW YOU...
!

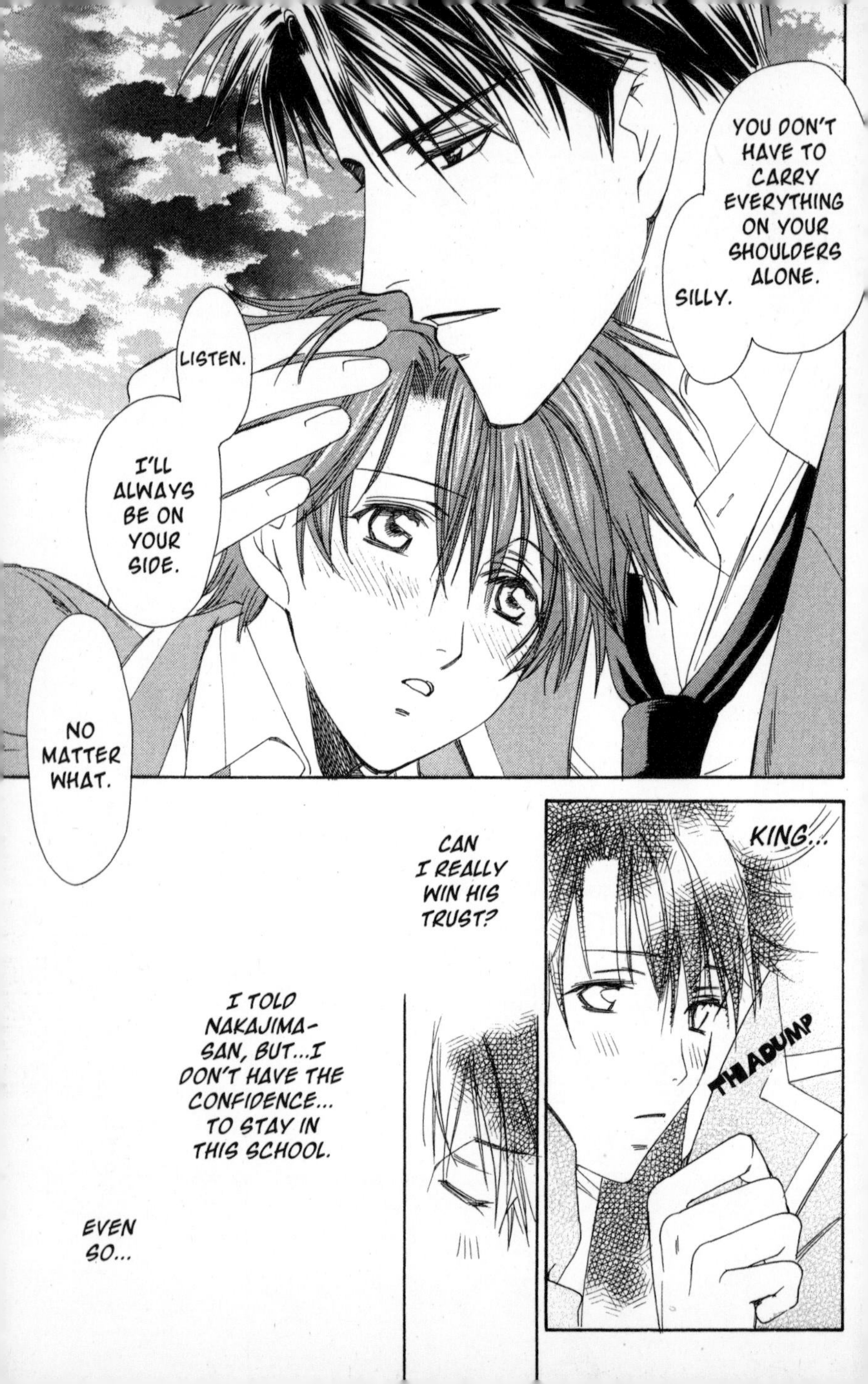
YOU DON'T HAVE TO CARRY EVERYTHING ON YOUR SHOULDERS ALONE.
SILLY.
LISTEN.
I'LL ALWAYS BE ON YOUR SIDE.
NO MATTER WHAT.
KING...
THADUMP
CAN I REALLY WIN HIS TRUST?
I TOLD NAKAJIMA-SAN, BUT...I DON'T HAVE THE CONFIDENCE... TO STAY IN THIS SCHOOL.
EVEN SO...

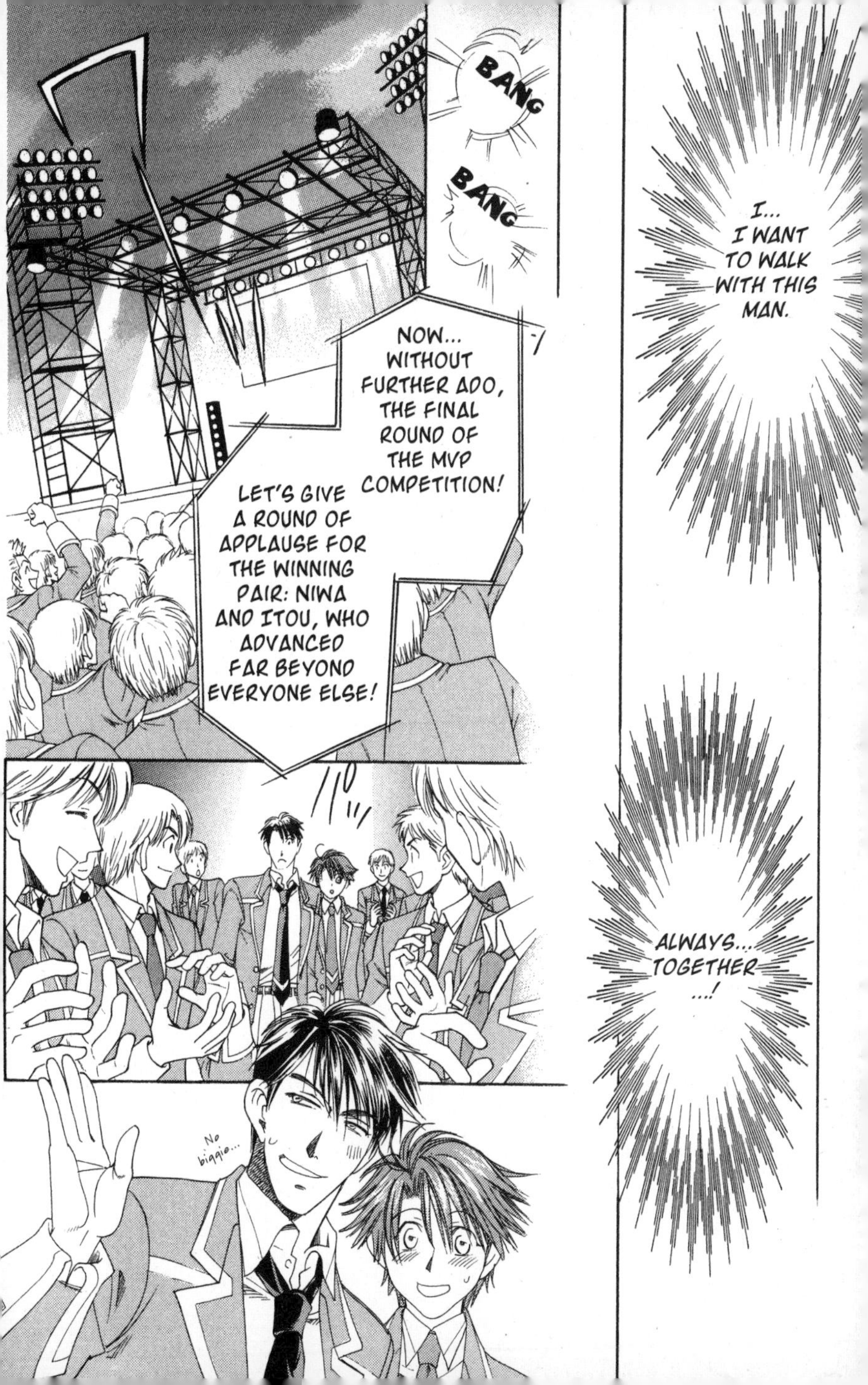

I... I WANT TO WALK WITH THIS MAN.
ALWAYS... TOGETHER ...!
BANG
BANG
NOW... WITHOUT FURTHER ADO, THE FINAL ROUND OF THE MVP COMPETITION!
LET'S GIVE A ROUND OF APPLAUSE FOR THE WINNING PAIR: NIWA AND ITOU, WHO ADVANCED FAR BEYOND EVERYONE ELSE!
No biggie...

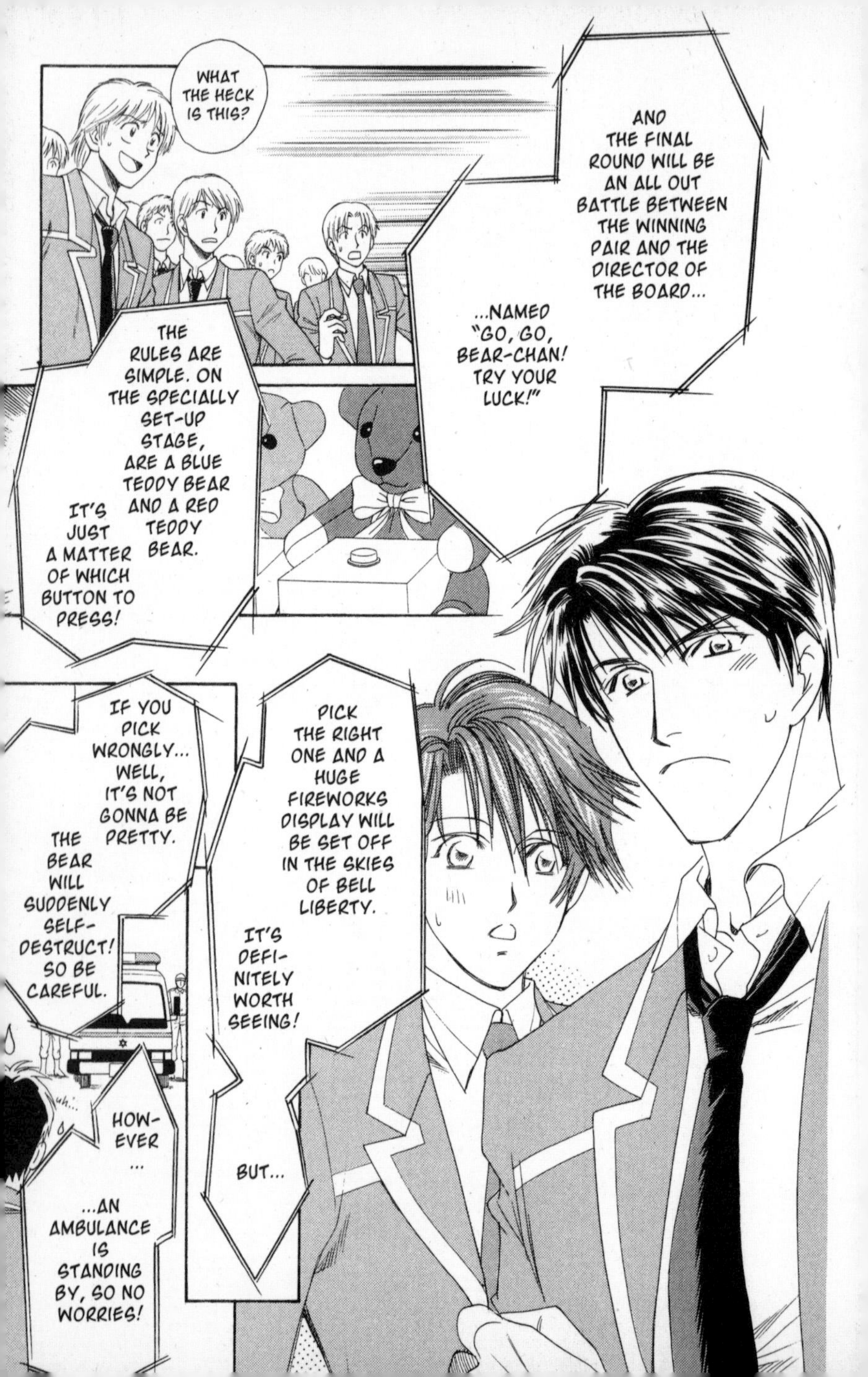
AND THE FINAL ROUND WILL BE AN ALL OUT BATTLE BETWEEN THE WINNING PAIR AND THE DIRECTOR OF THE BOARD...
...NAMED "GO, GO, BEAR-CHAN! TRY YOUR LUCK!"
WHAT THE HECK IS THIS?
THE RULES ARE SIMPLE. ON THE SPECIALLY SET-UP STAGE, ARE A BLUE TEDDY BEAR AND A RED TEDDY BEAR.
IT'S JUST A MATTER OF WHICH BUTTON TO PRESS!
PICK THE RIGHT ONE AND A HUGE FIREWORKS DISPLAY WILL BE SET OFF IN THE SKIES OF BELL LIBERTY.
IT'S DEFINITELY WORTH SEEING!
BUT...
IF YOU PICK WRONGLY... WELL, IT'S NOT GONNA BE PRETTY.
THE BEAR WILL SUDDENLY SELF-DESTRUCT! SO BE CAREFUL.
HOWEVER...
...AN AMBULANCE IS STANDING BY, SO NO WORRIES!
uh...

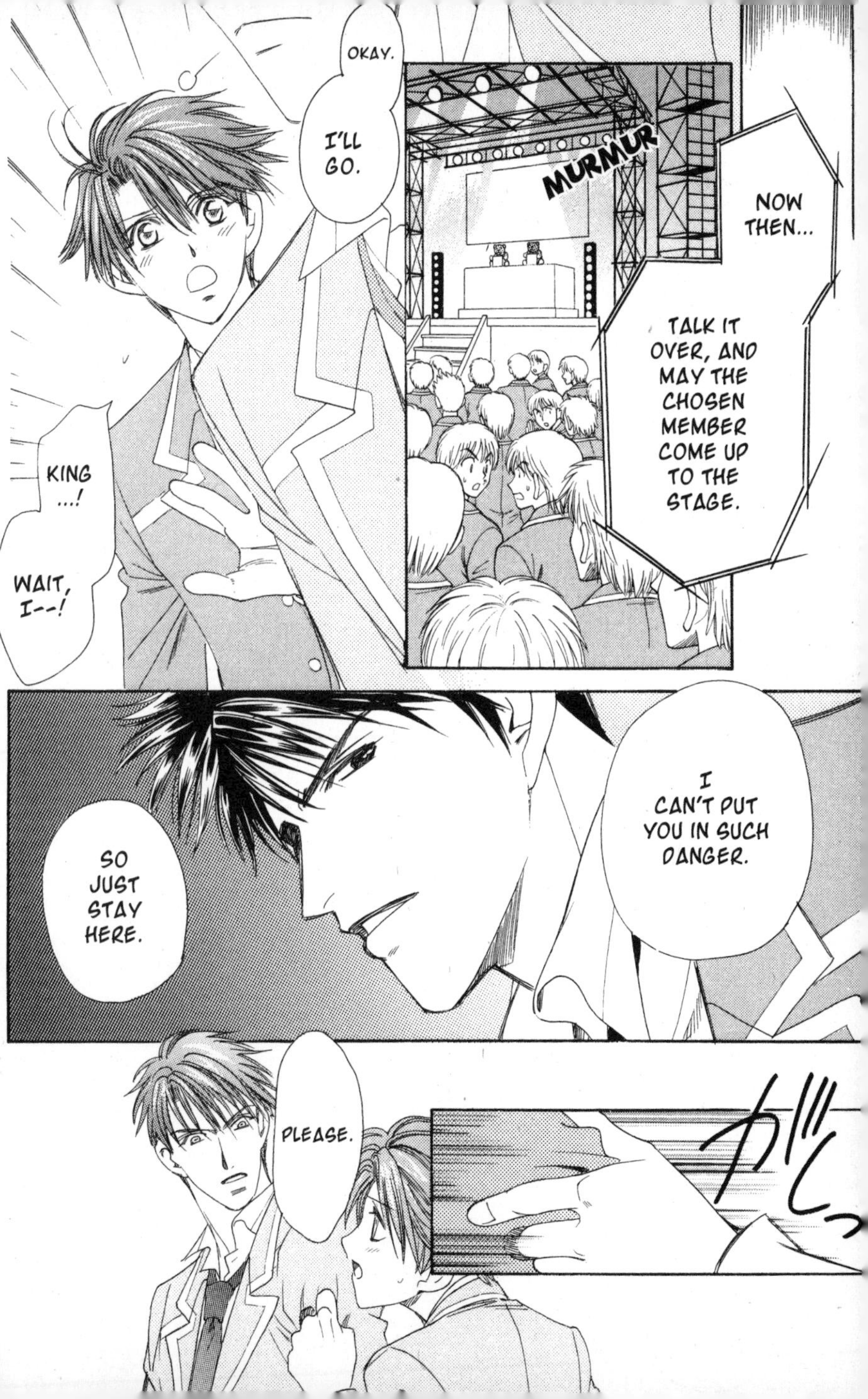
NOW THEN...
TALK IT OVER, AND MAY THE CHOSEN MEMBER COME UP TO THE STAGE.
MURMUR
OKAY.
I'LL GO.
KING ...!
WAIT, I--!
I CAN'T PUT YOU IN SUCH DANGER.
SO JUST STAY HERE.
がしっ
PLEASE.

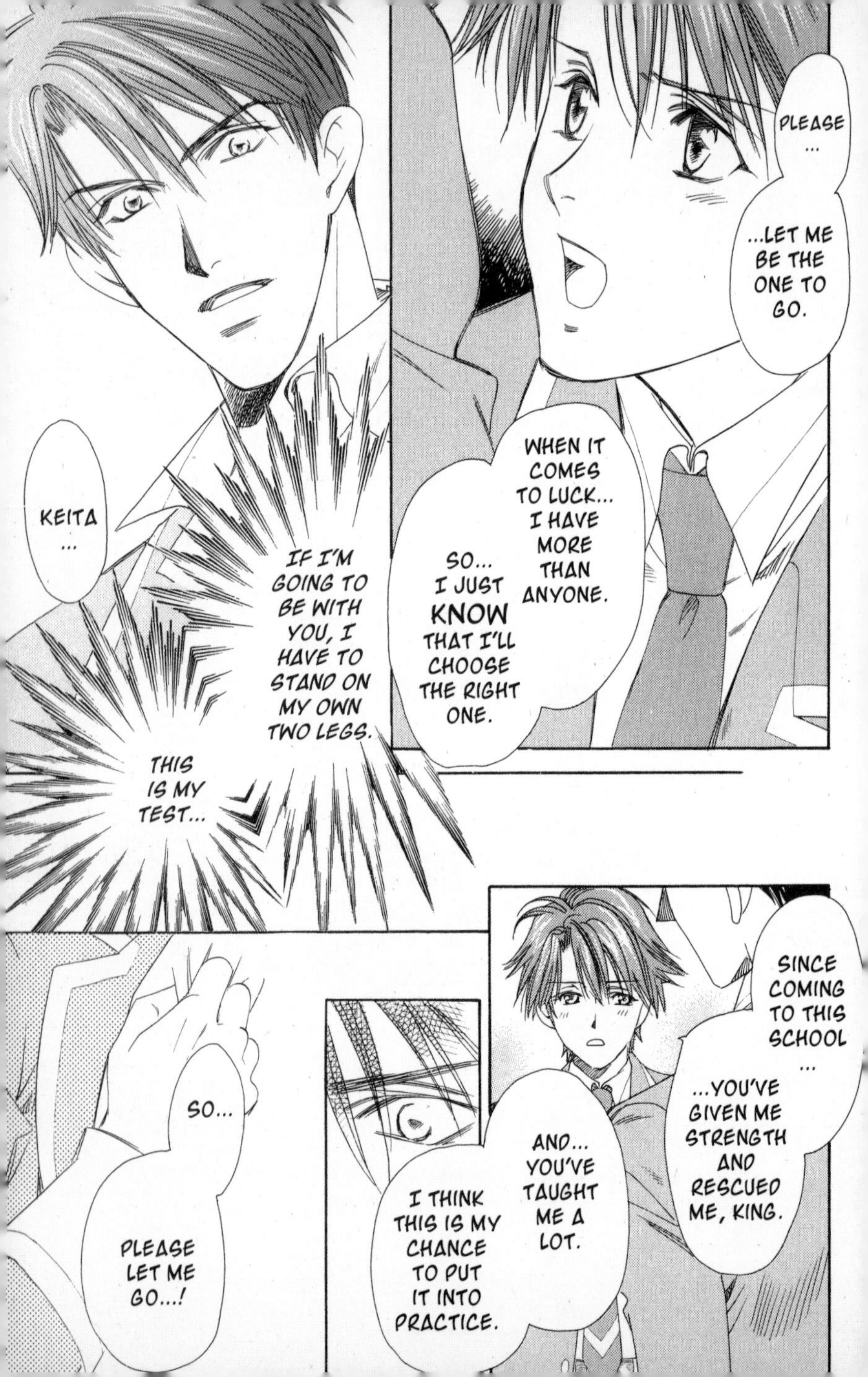
PLEASE ...
...LET ME BE THE ONE TO GO.
WHEN IT COMES TO LUCK... I HAVE MORE THAN ANYONE.
SO... I JUST **KNOW** THAT I'LL CHOOSE THE RIGHT ONE.
IF I'M GOING TO BE WITH YOU, I HAVE TO STAND ON MY OWN TWO LEGS.
THIS IS MY TEST...
KEITA ...
SINCE COMING TO THIS SCHOOL ...
...YOU'VE GIVEN ME STRENGTH AND RESCUED ME, KING.
AND... YOU'VE TAUGHT ME A LOT.
I THINK THIS IS MY CHANCE TO PUT IT INTO PRACTICE.
SO...
PLEASE LET ME GO...!

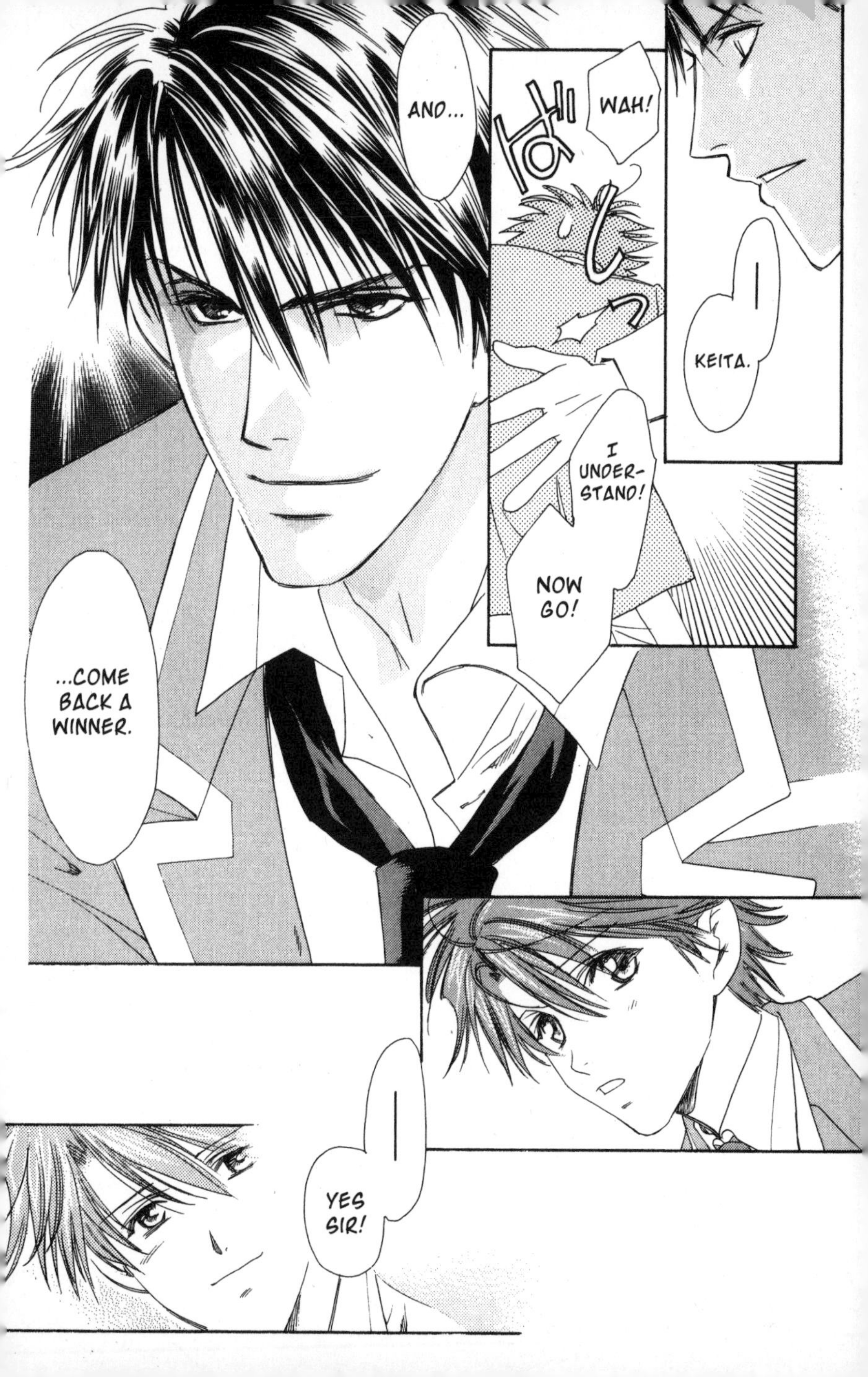
KEITA.
WAH!
ばしっ
I UNDERSTAND!
NOW GO!
AND...
...COME BACK A WINNER.
YES SIR!

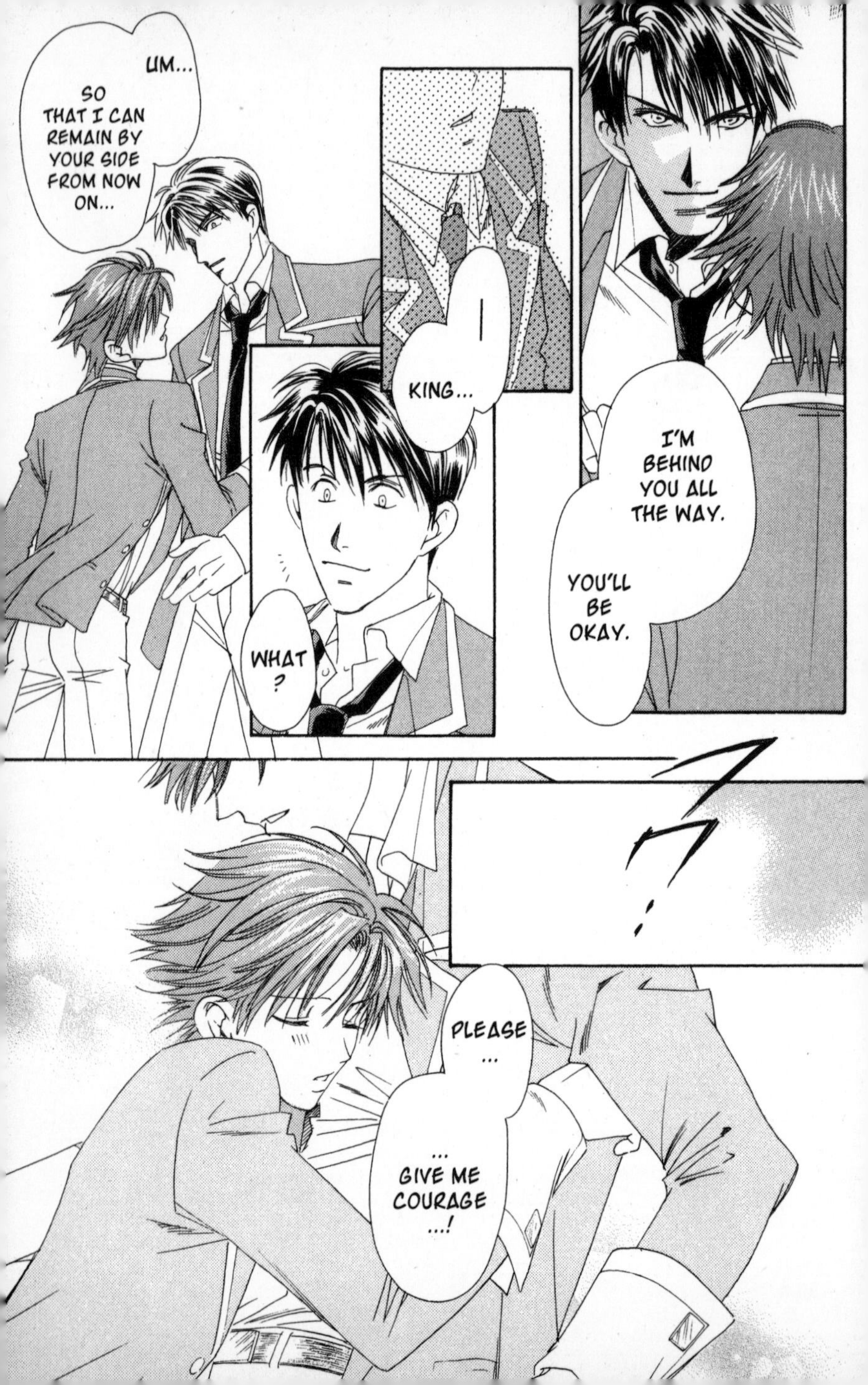
I'M BEHIND YOU ALL THE WAY.
YOU'LL BE OKAY.
KING...
WHAT ?
UM...
SO THAT I CAN REMAIN BY YOUR SIDE FROM NOW ON...
PLEASE ...
... GIVE ME COURAGE ...!

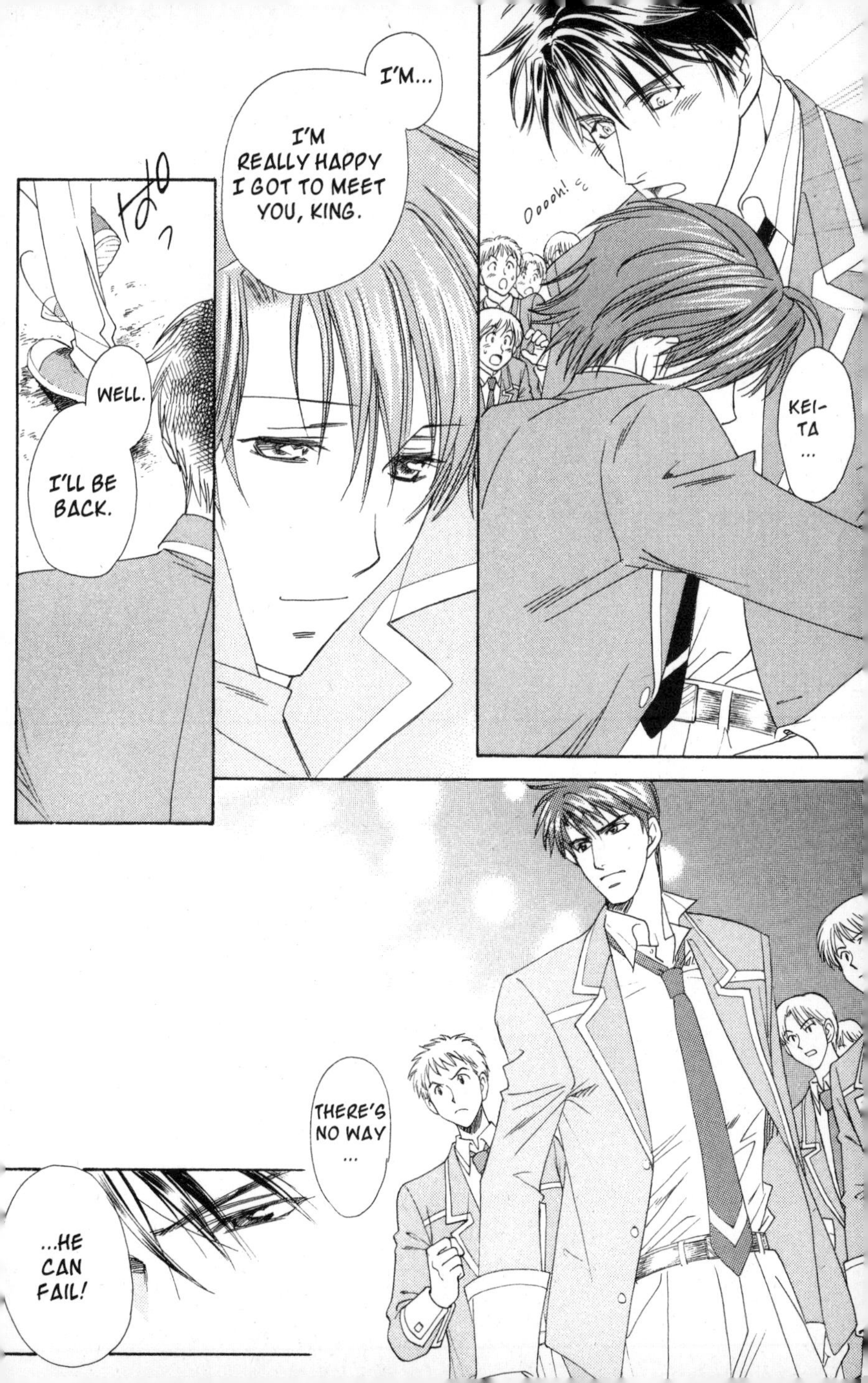
Ooooh!
KEI-TA ...
I'M...
I'M REALLY HAPPY I GOT TO MEET YOU, KING.
WELL.
I'LL BE BACK.
THERE'S NO WAY ...
...HE CAN FAIL!

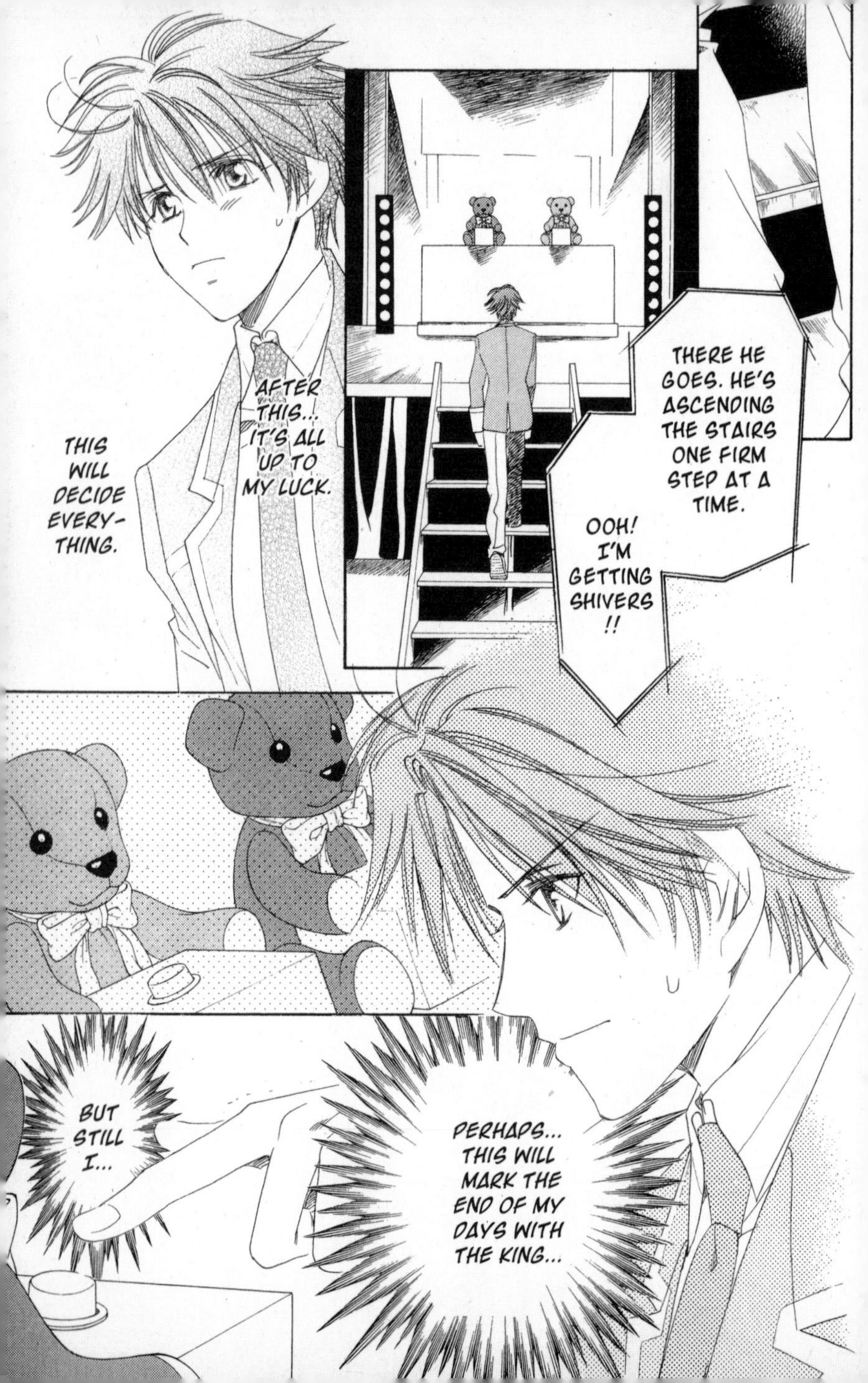
THERE HE GOES. HE'S ASCENDING THE STAIRS ONE FIRM STEP AT A TIME.
OOH! I'M GETTING SHIVERS!!
AFTER THIS... IT'S ALL UP TO MY LUCK.
THIS WILL DECIDE EVERY-THING.
PERHAPS... THIS WILL MARK THE END OF MY DAYS WITH THE KING...
BUT STILL I...

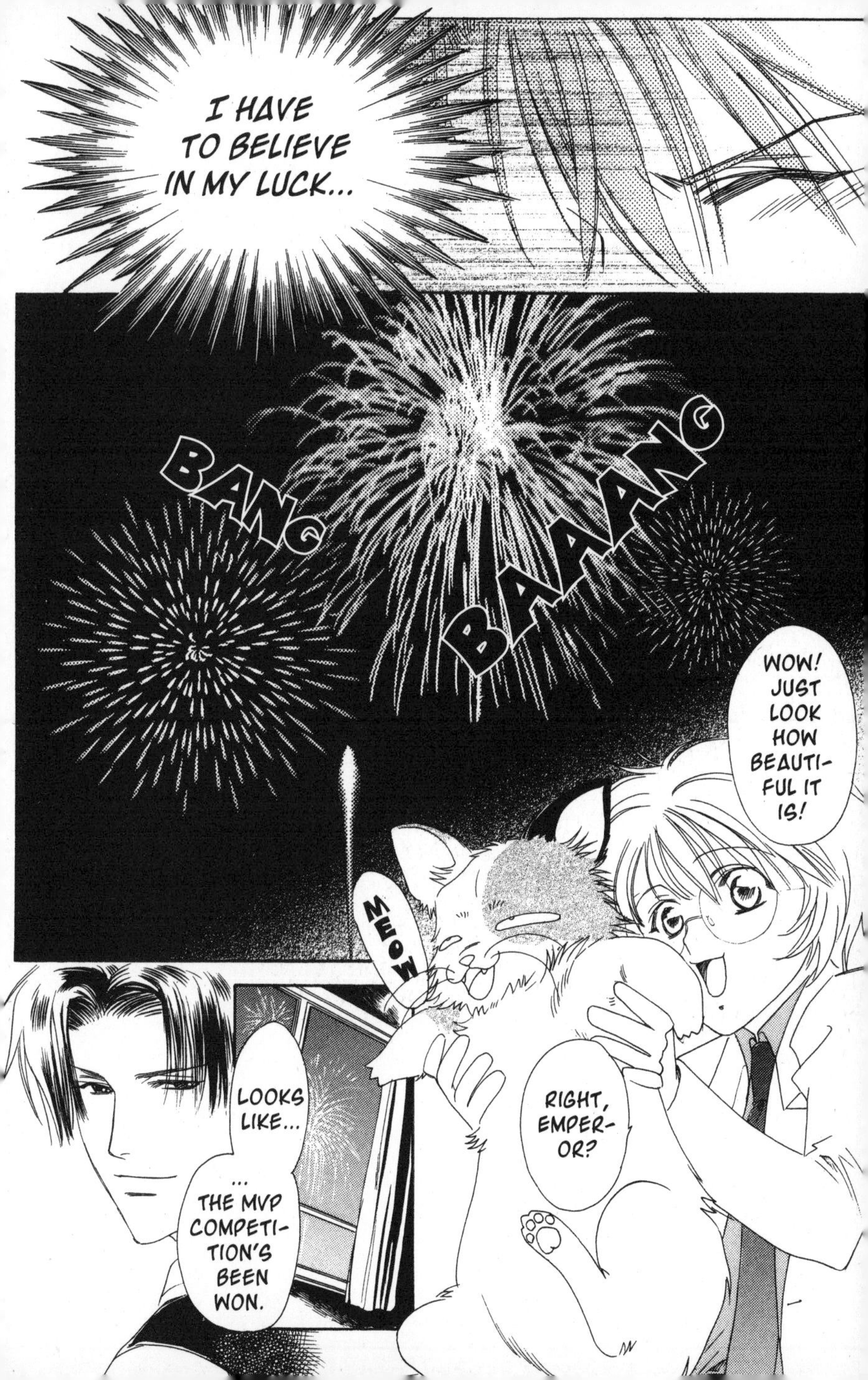
I HAVE TO BELIEVE IN MY LUCK...
BAAAANG
BANG
WOW! JUST LOOK HOW BEAUTI-FUL IT IS!
MEOW
RIGHT, EMPER-OR?
LOOKS LIKE...
... THE MVP COMPETI-TION'S BEEN WON.

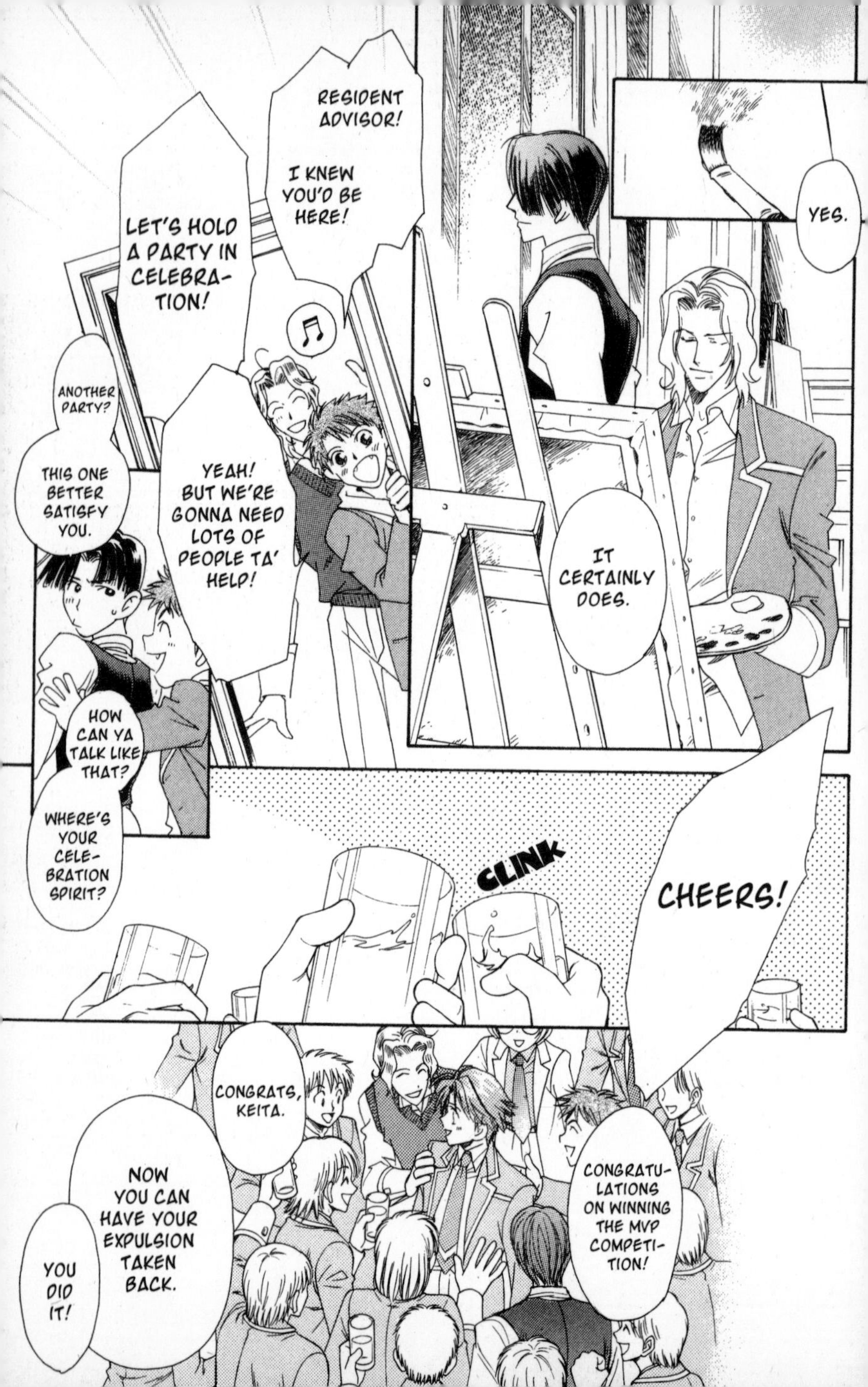
YES.
IT CERTAINLY DOES.
RESIDENT ADVISOR!
I KNEW YOU'D BE HERE!
LET'S HOLD A PARTY IN CELEBRA-TION!
YEAH! BUT WE'RE GONNA NEED LOTS OF PEOPLE TA' HELP!
ANOTHER PARTY?
THIS ONE BETTER SATISFY YOU.
HOW CAN YA TALK LIKE THAT?
WHERE'S YOUR CELE-BRATION SPIRIT?
CHEERS!
CLINK
CONGRATU-LATIONS ON WINNING THE MVP COMPETI-TION!
CONGRATS, KEITA.
NOW YOU CAN HAVE YOUR EXPULSION TAKEN BACK.
YOU DID IT!

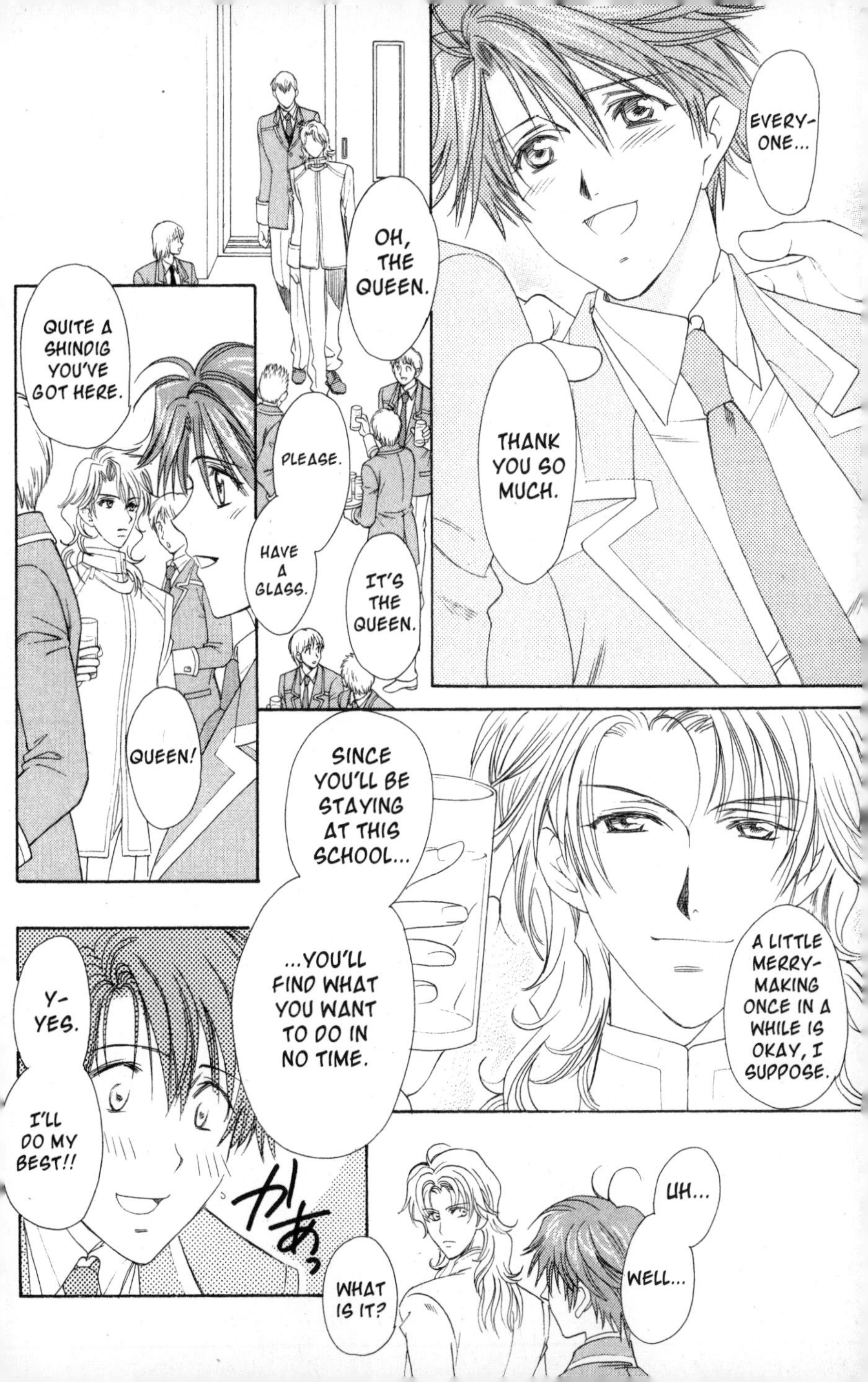
EVERY-ONE...
THANK YOU SO MUCH.
OH, THE QUEEN.
PLEASE.
HAVE A GLASS.
IT'S THE QUEEN.
QUITE A SHINDIG YOU'VE GOT HERE.
QUEEN!
A LITTLE MERRY-MAKING ONCE IN A WHILE IS OKAY, I SUPPOSE.
SINCE YOU'LL BE STAYING AT THIS SCHOOL...
...YOU'LL FIND WHAT YOU WANT TO DO IN NO TIME.
Y-YES.
I'LL DO MY BEST!!
かあっ
UH...
WELL...
WHAT IS IT?

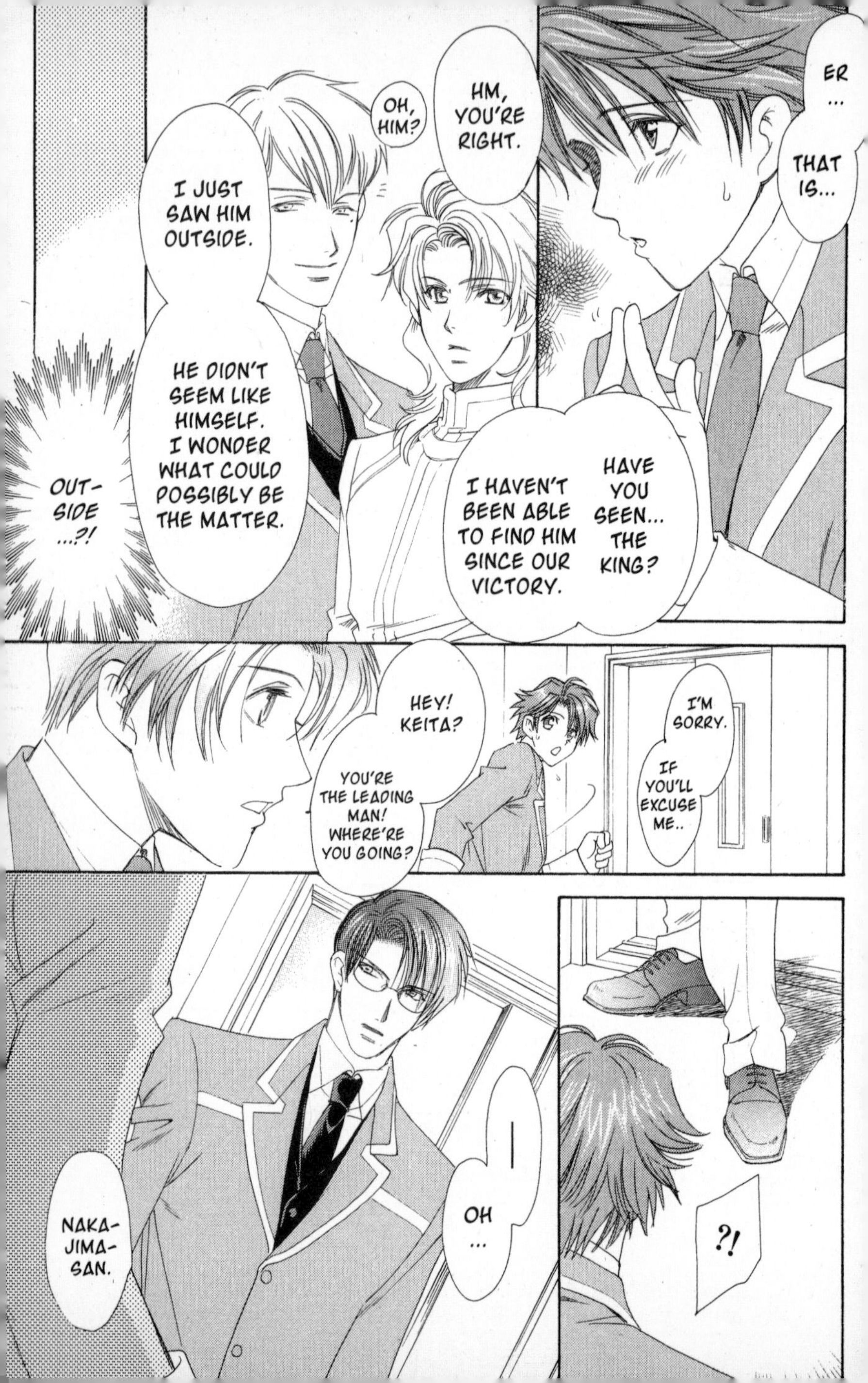
ER ... THAT IS...
HM, YOU'RE RIGHT.
OH, HIM?
HAVE YOU SEEN... THE KING?
I HAVEN'T BEEN ABLE TO FIND HIM SINCE OUR VICTORY.
I JUST SAW HIM OUTSIDE.
HE DIDN'T SEEM LIKE HIMSELF. I WONDER WHAT COULD POSSIBLY BE THE MATTER.
OUT-SIDE ...?!
I'M SORRY.
IF YOU'LL EXCUSE ME..
HEY! KEITA?
YOU'RE THE LEADING MAN! WHERE'RE YOU GOING?
?!
— OH ...
NAKA-JIMA-SAN.

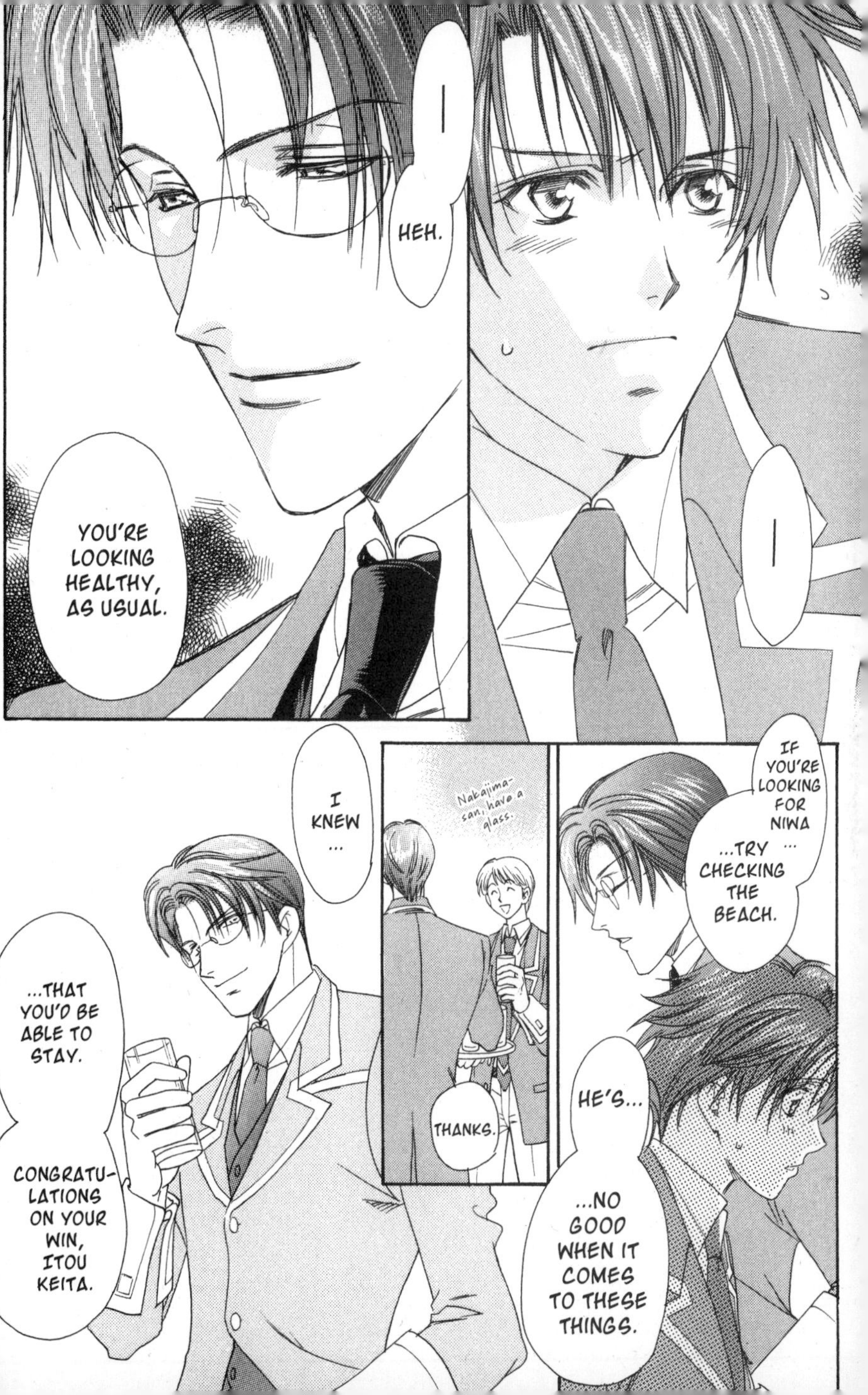
—
—
HEH.
YOU'RE LOOKING HEALTHY, AS USUAL.
IF YOU'RE LOOKING FOR NIWA ...
...TRY CHECKING THE BEACH.
HE'S...
...NO GOOD WHEN IT COMES TO THESE THINGS.
Nakajima-san, have a glass.
THANKS.
I KNEW ...
...THAT YOU'D BE ABLE TO STAY.
CONGRATU-LATIONS ON YOUR WIN, ITOU KEITA.

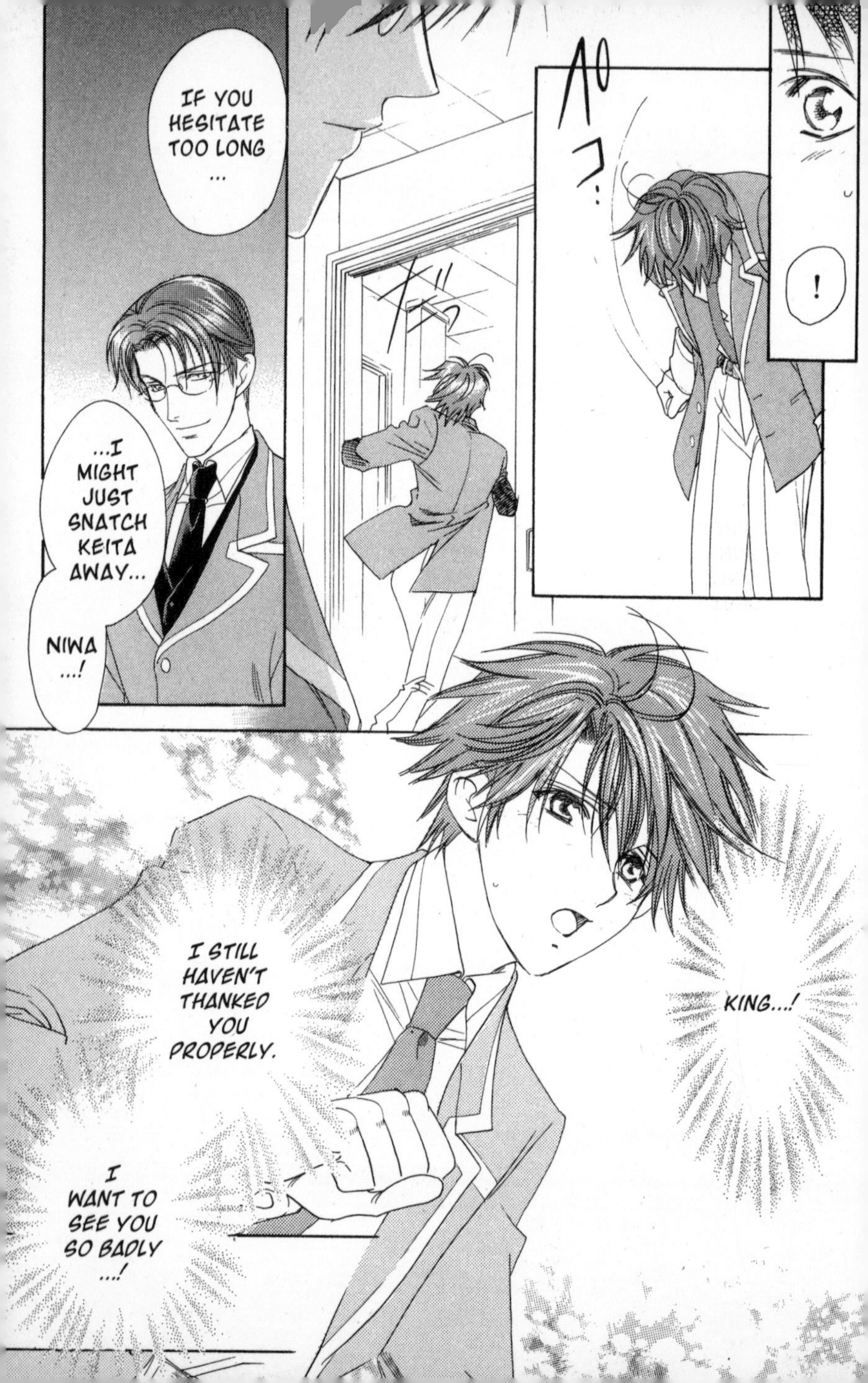
!
IF YOU HESITATE TOO LONG ...
...I MIGHT JUST SNATCH KEITA AWAY...
NIWA ...!
KING...!
I STILL HAVEN'T THANKED YOU PROPERLY.
I WANT TO SEE YOU SO BADLY ...!

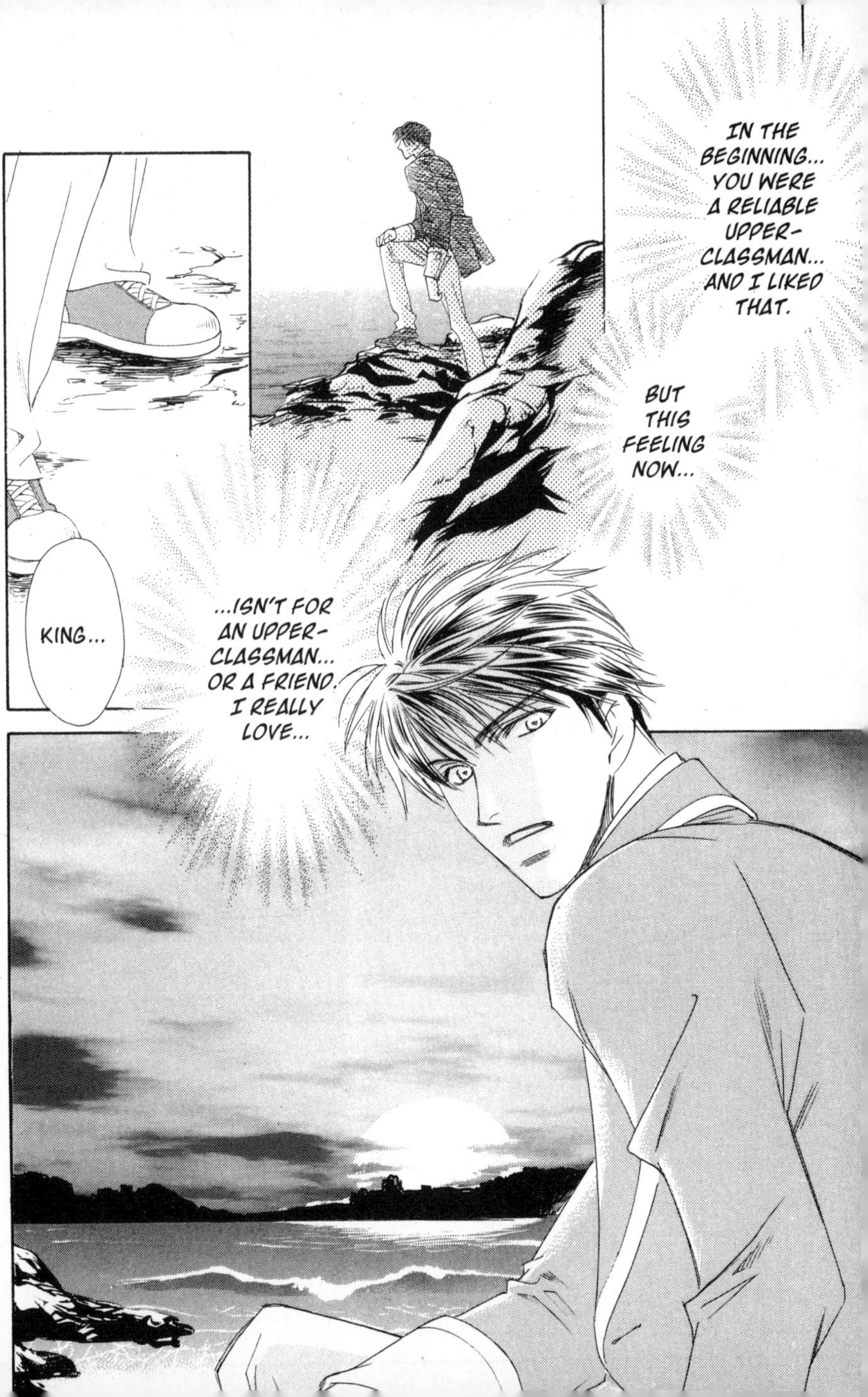
IN THE BEGINNING... YOU WERE A RELIABLE UPPER-CLASSMAN... AND I LIKED THAT.
BUT THIS FEELING NOW...
...ISN'T FOR AN UPPER-CLASSMAN... OR A FRIEND. I REALLY LOVE...
KING...

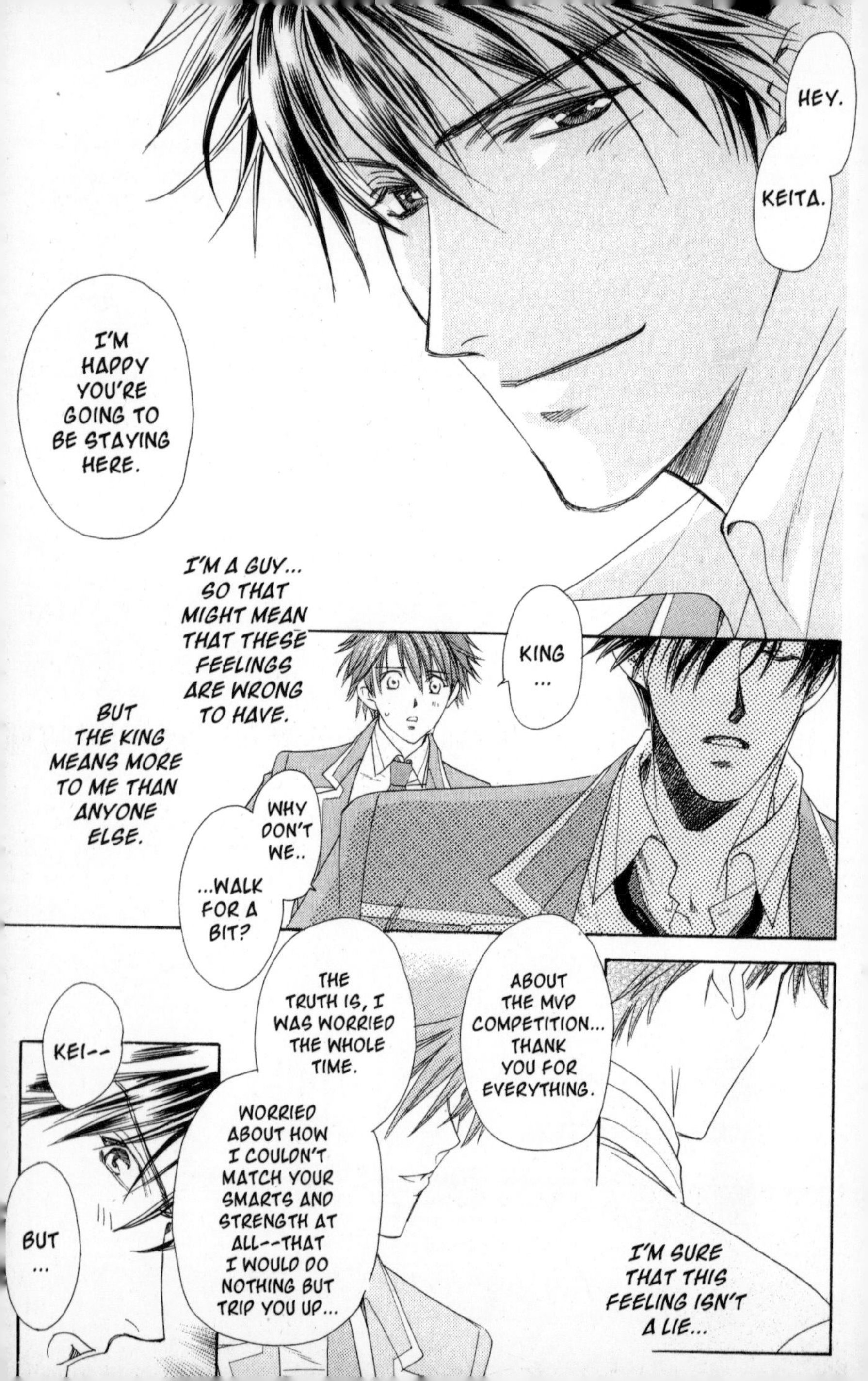
HEY.
KEITA.
I'M HAPPY YOU'RE GOING TO BE STAYING HERE.
KING ...
I'M A GUY... SO THAT MIGHT MEAN THAT THESE FEELINGS ARE WRONG TO HAVE.
BUT THE KING MEANS MORE TO ME THAN ANYONE ELSE.
WHY DON'T WE..
...WALK FOR A BIT?
ABOUT THE MVP COMPETITION... THANK YOU FOR EVERYTHING.
THE TRUTH IS, I WAS WORRIED THE WHOLE TIME.
WORRIED ABOUT HOW I COULDN'T MATCH YOUR SMARTS AND STRENGTH AT ALL--THAT I WOULD DO NOTHING BUT TRIP YOU UP...
I'M SURE THAT THIS FEELING ISN'T A LIE...
KEI--
BUT ...

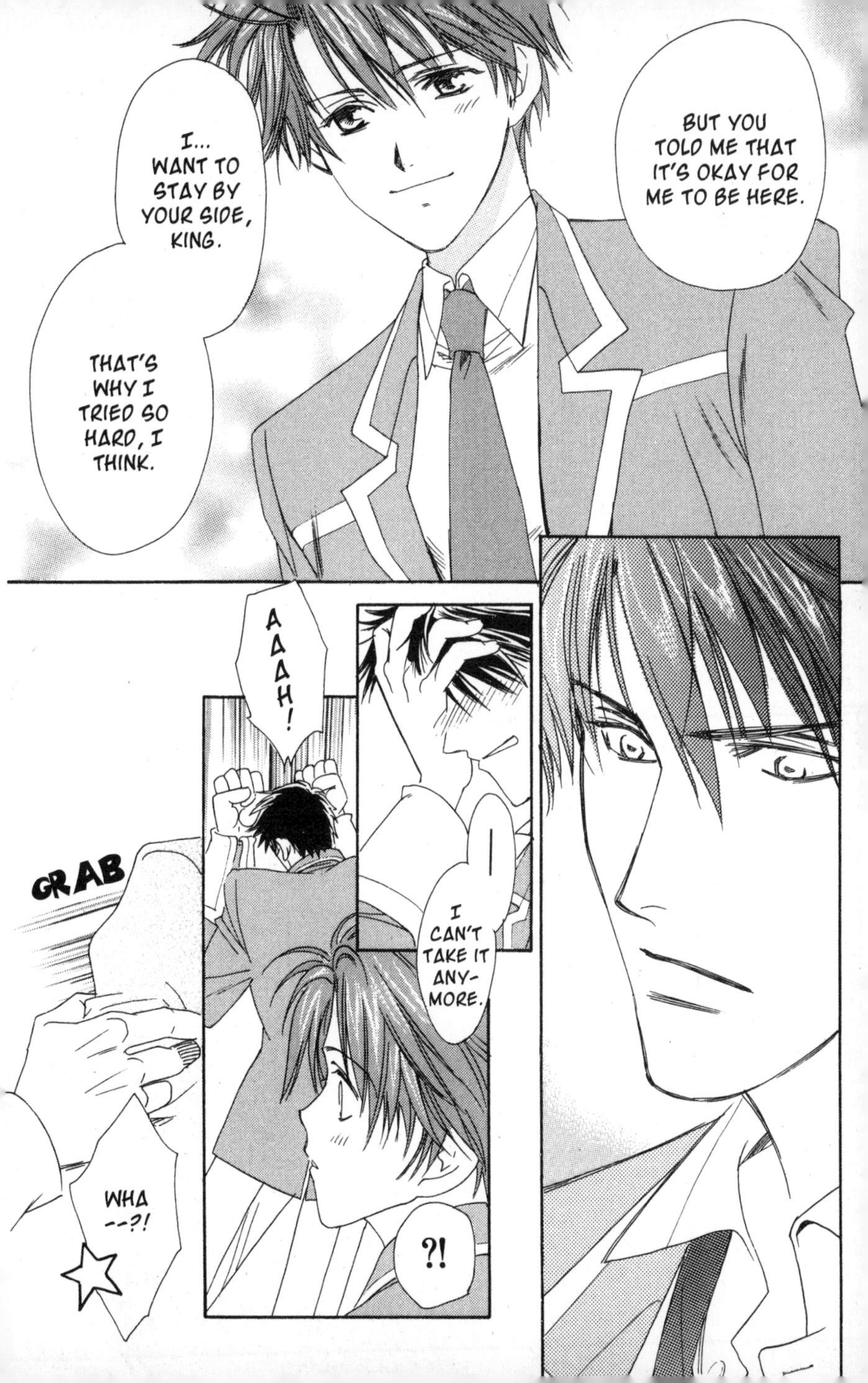

BUT YOU TOLD ME THAT IT'S OKAY FOR ME TO BE HERE.
I... WANT TO STAY BY YOUR SIDE, KING.
THAT'S WHY I TRIED SO HARD, I THINK.
I CAN'T TAKE IT ANY-MORE.
AAAH!
?!
GRAB
WHA--?!

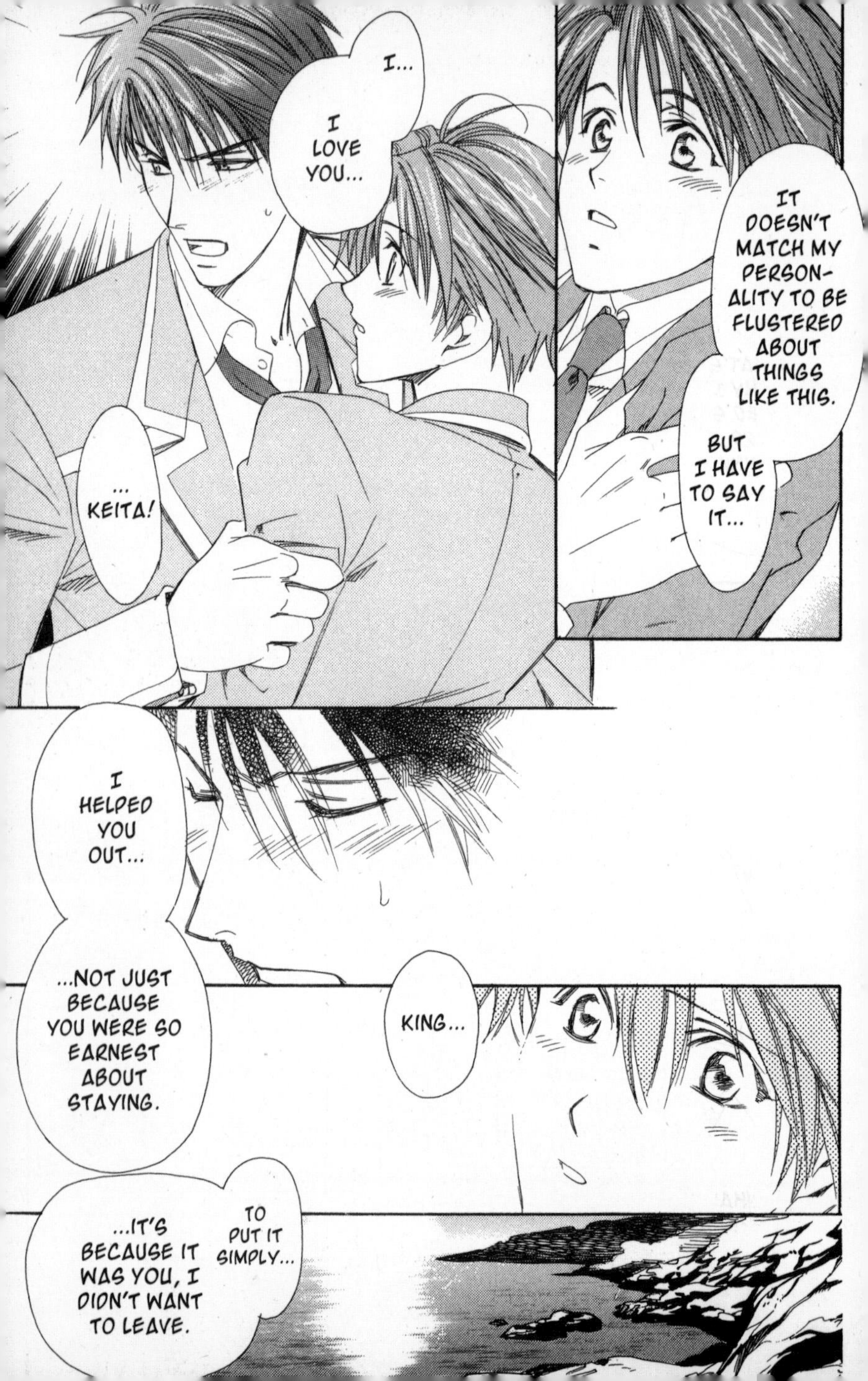
IT DOESN'T MATCH MY PERSON-ALITY TO BE FLUSTERED ABOUT THINGS LIKE THIS.
BUT I HAVE TO SAY IT...
I...
I LOVE YOU...
...KEITA!
I HELPED YOU OUT...
...NOT JUST BECAUSE YOU WERE SO EARNEST ABOUT STAYING.
KING...
TO PUT IT SIMPLY...
...IT'S BECAUSE IT WAS YOU, I DIDN'T WANT TO LEAVE.

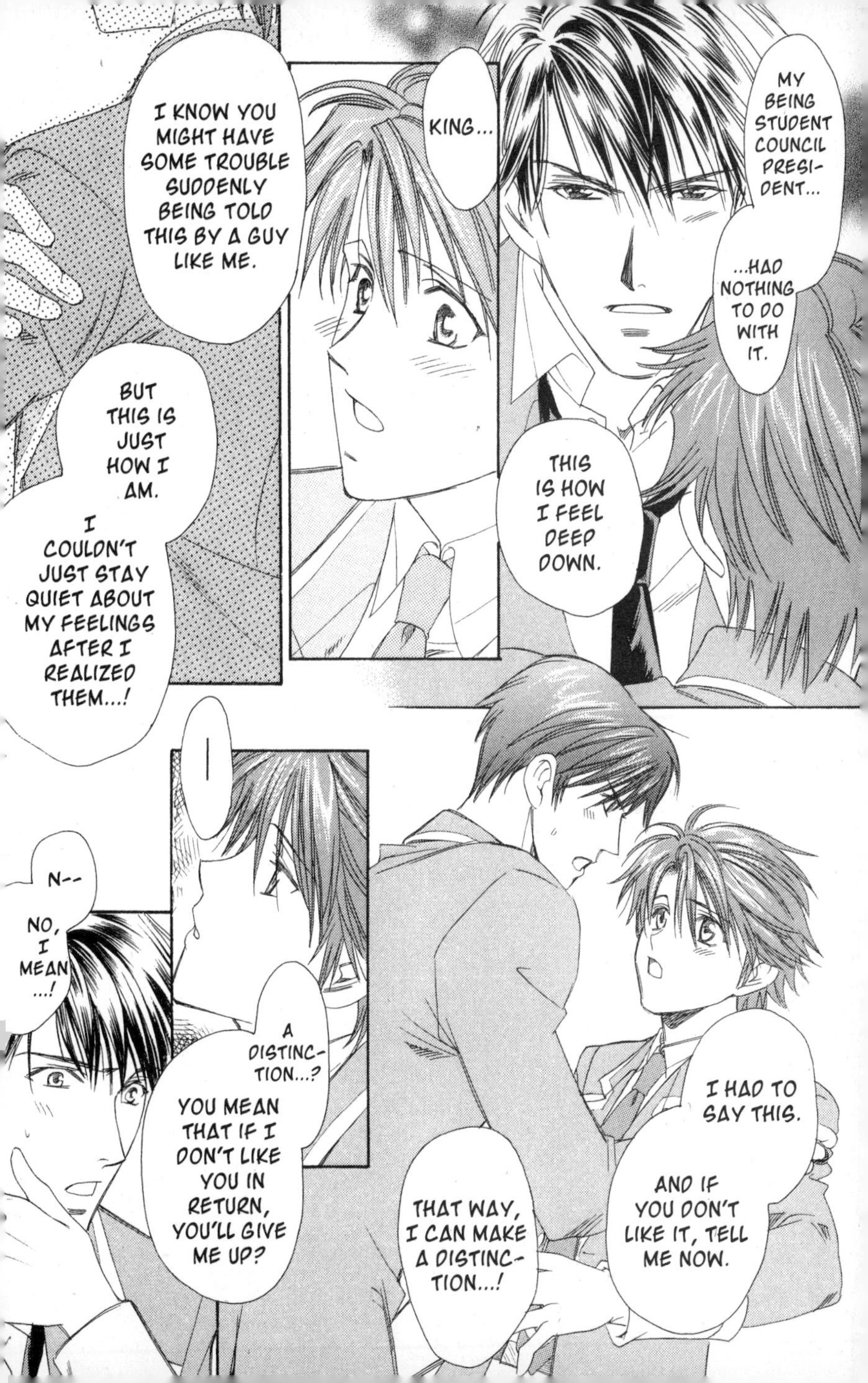
MY BEING STUDENT COUNCIL PRESI- DENT...
...HAD NOTHING TO DO WITH IT.
THIS IS HOW I FEEL DEEP DOWN.
KING...
I KNOW YOU MIGHT HAVE SOME TROUBLE SUDDENLY BEING TOLD THIS BY A GUY LIKE ME.
BUT THIS IS JUST HOW I AM.
I COULDN'T JUST STAY QUIET ABOUT MY FEELINGS AFTER I REALIZED THEM...!
I HAD TO SAY THIS.
AND IF YOU DON'T LIKE IT, TELL ME NOW.
THAT WAY, I CAN MAKE A DISTINC- TION...!
A DISTINC- TION...?
YOU MEAN THAT IF I DON'T LIKE YOU IN RETURN, YOU'LL GIVE ME UP?
N--
NO, I MEAN ...!

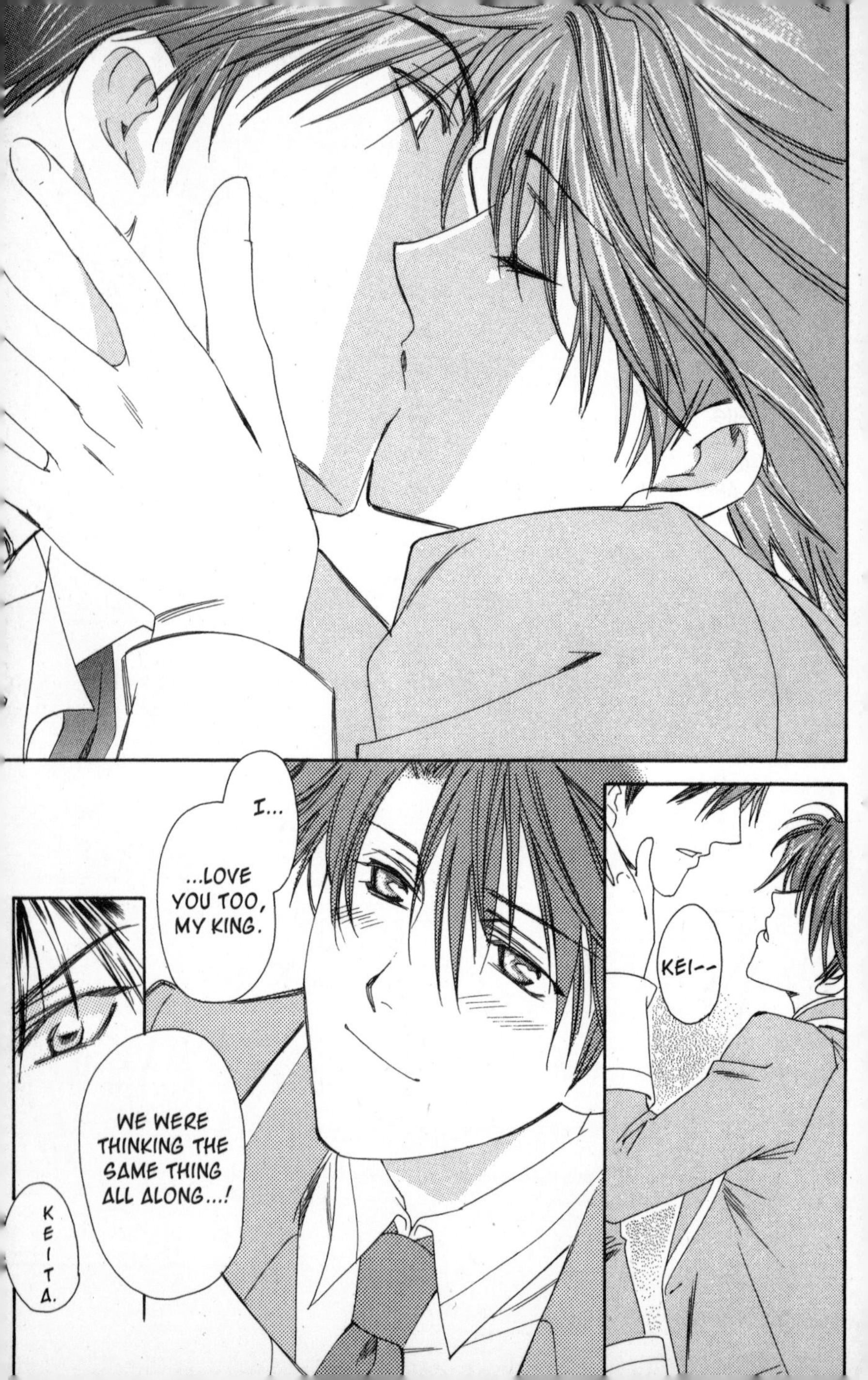
KEI--
I...
...LOVE YOU TOO, MY KING.
WE WERE THINKING THE SAME THING ALL ALONG...!
KEITA.

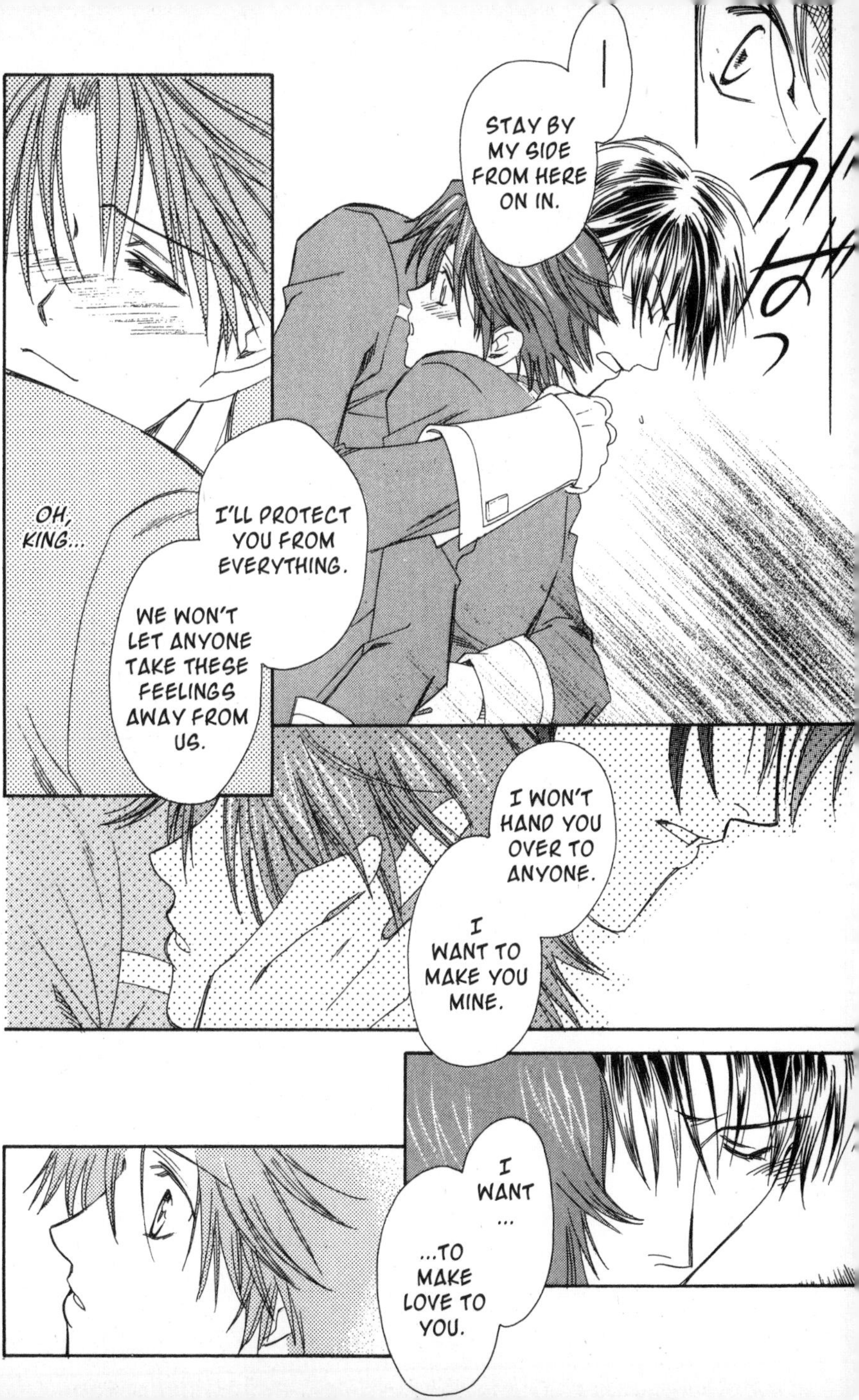
STAY BY MY SIDE FROM HERE ON IN.
I'LL PROTECT YOU FROM EVERYTHING.
WE WON'T LET ANYONE TAKE THESE FEELINGS AWAY FROM US.
OH, KING...
I WON'T HAND YOU OVER TO ANYONE.
I WANT TO MAKE YOU MINE.
I WANT ...
...TO MAKE LOVE TO YOU.

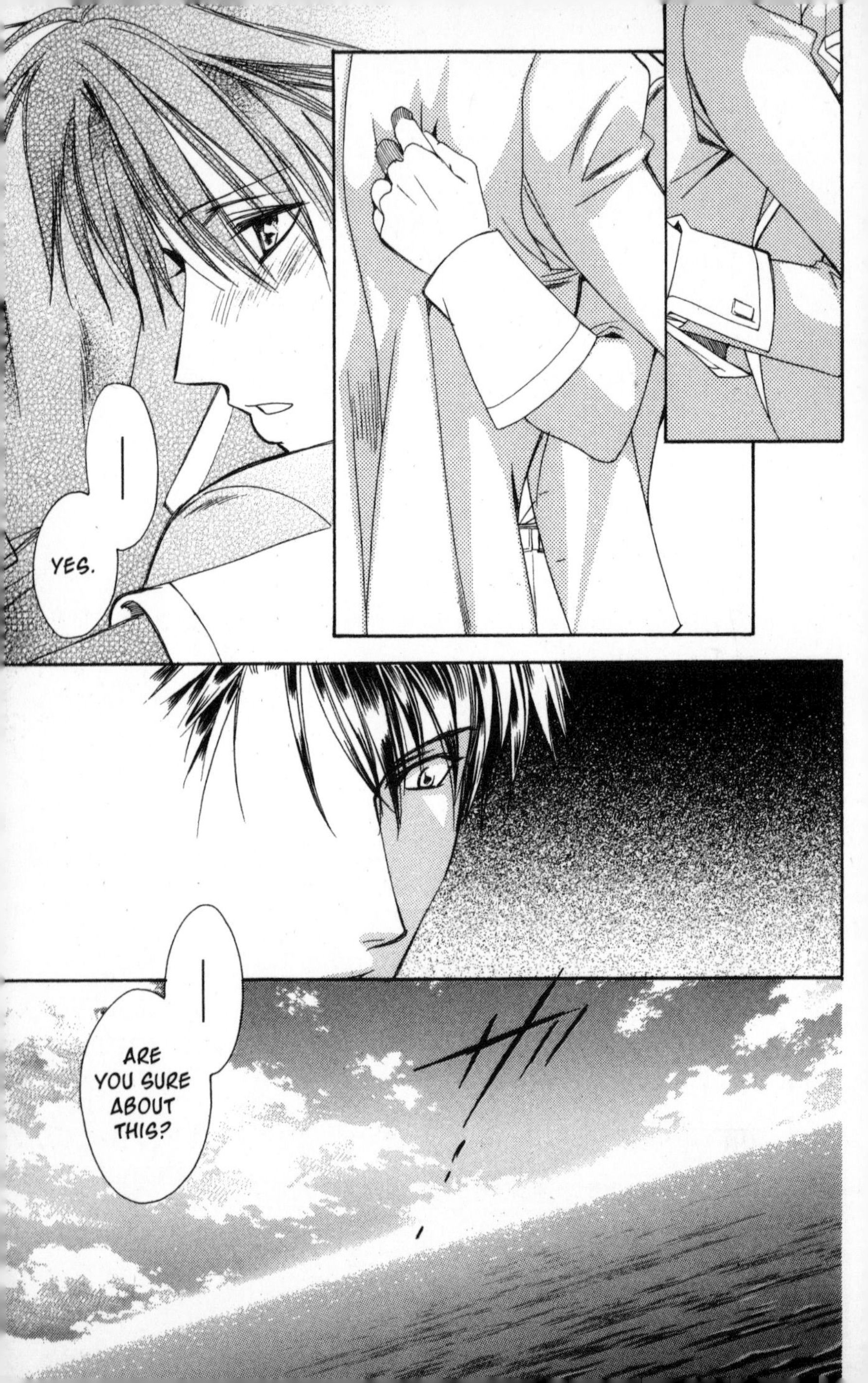
— YES.
— ARE YOU SURE ABOUT THIS?

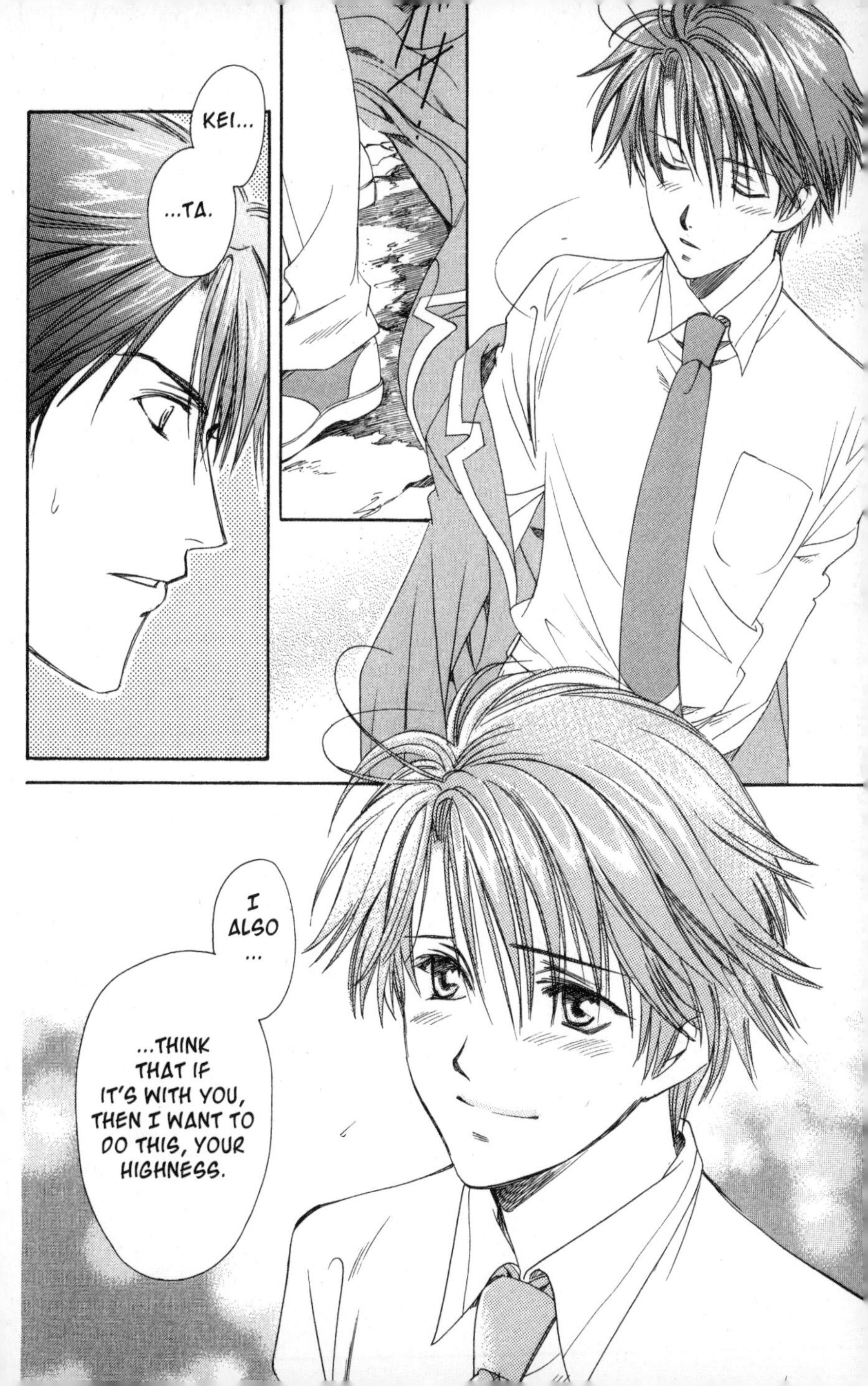
KEI...
...TA.
I ALSO ...
...THINK THAT IF IT'S WITH YOU, THEN I WANT TO DO THIS, YOUR HIGHNESS.

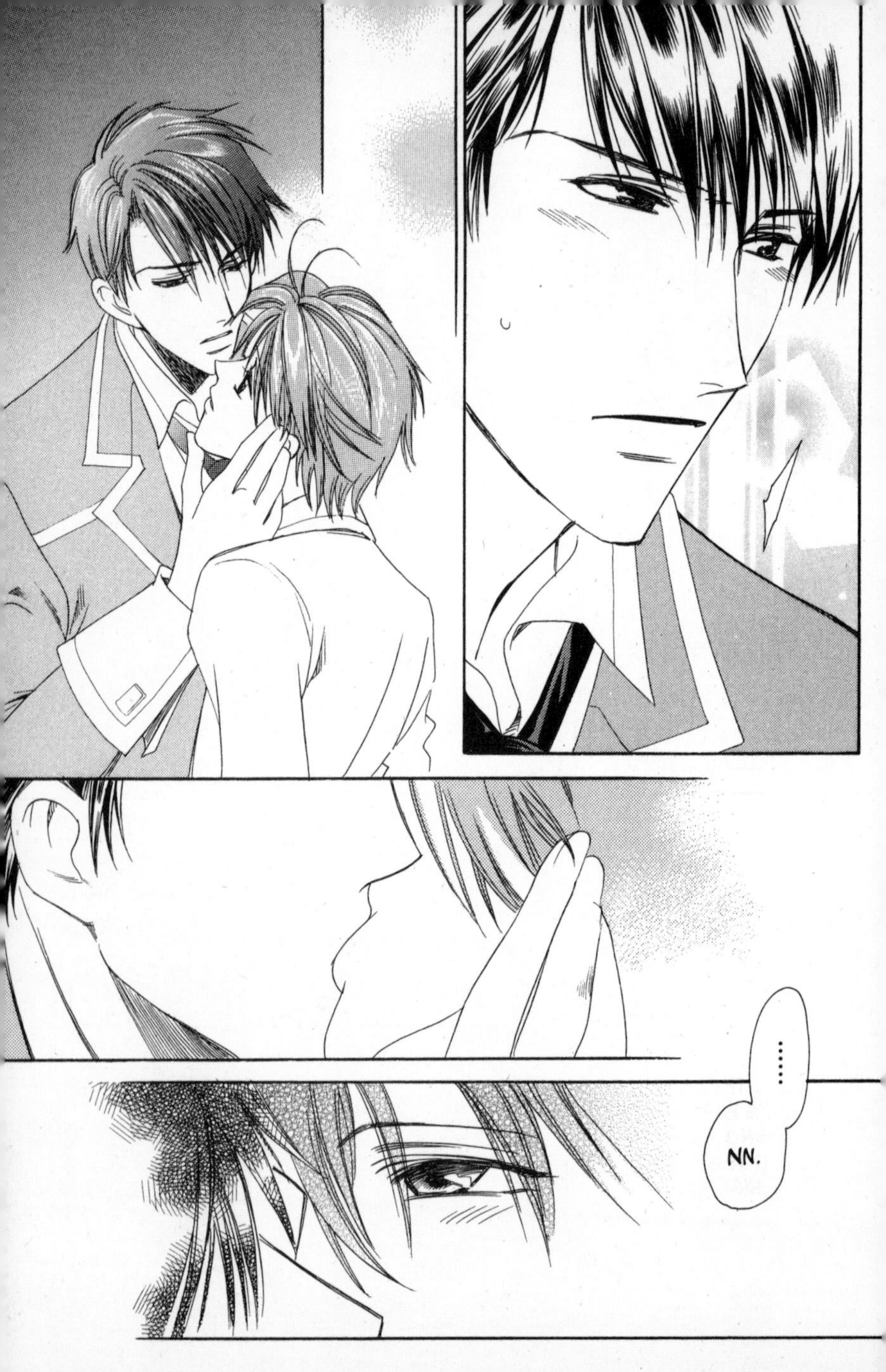
......
NN.

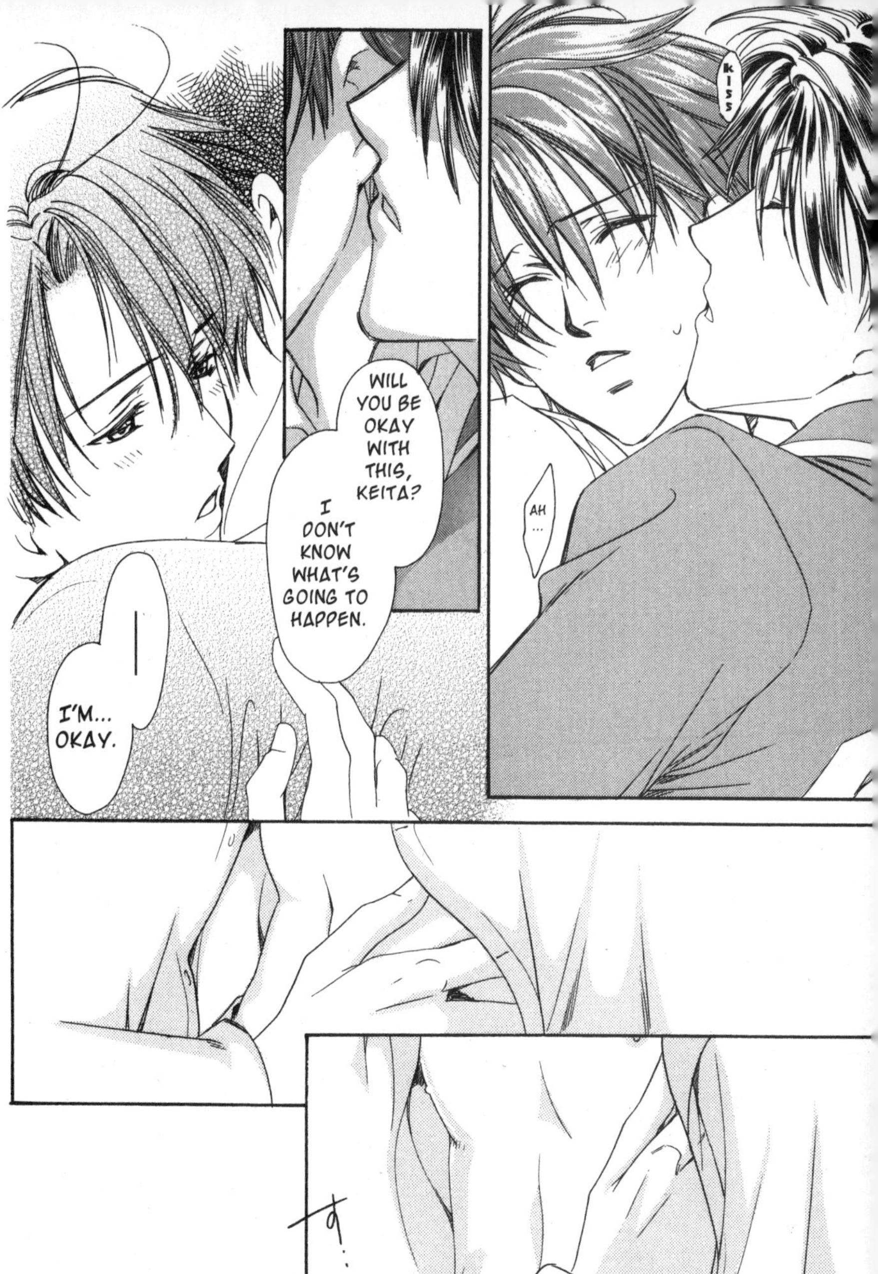
kiss
AH...
WILL YOU BE OKAY WITH THIS, KEITA?
I DON'T KNOW WHAT'S GOING TO HAPPEN.
—
I'M... OKAY.

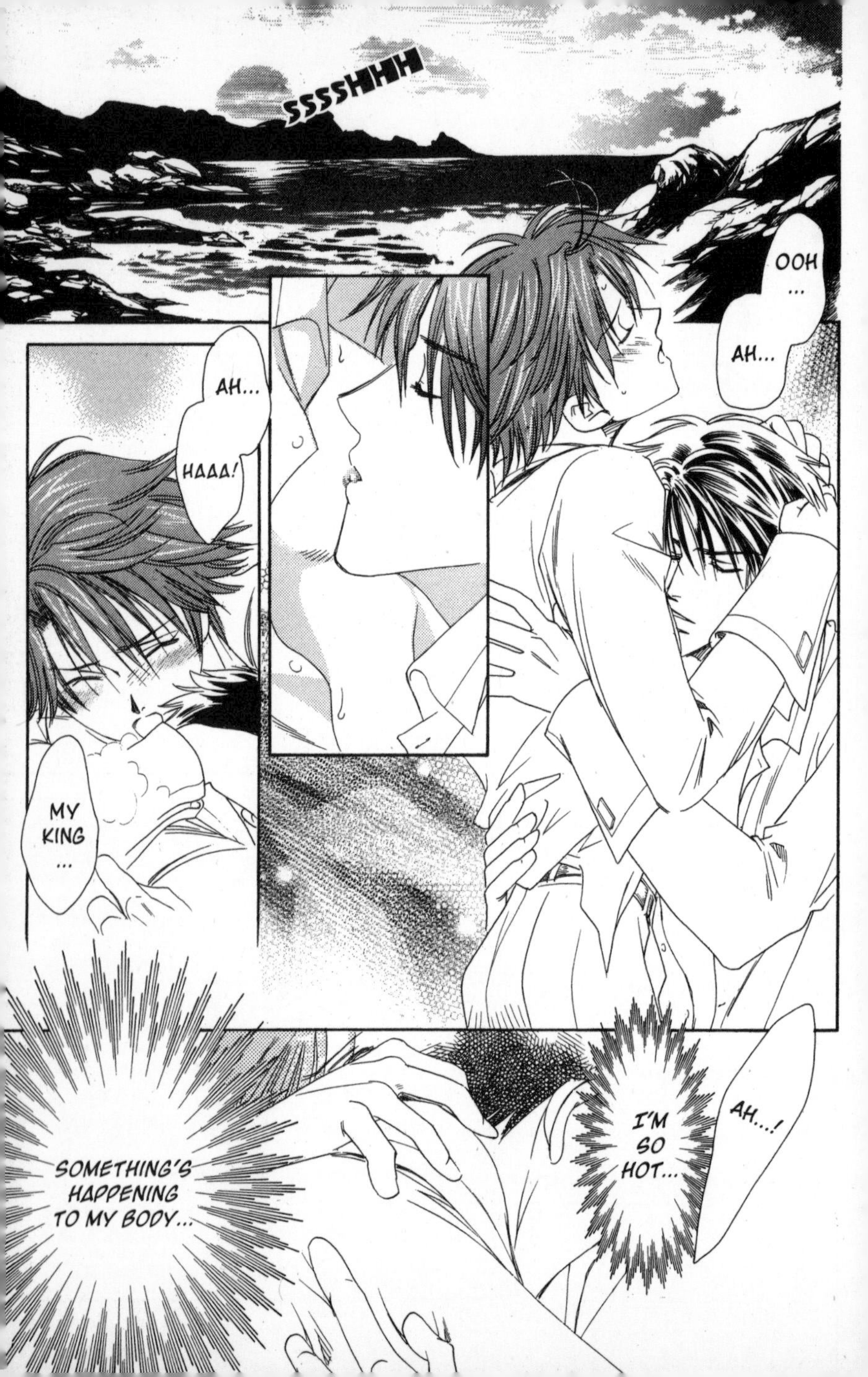
SSSSHHHH
OOH ...
AH...
AH...
HAAA!
MY KING ...
AH...!
I'M SO HOT...
SOMETHING'S HAPPENING TO MY BODY...

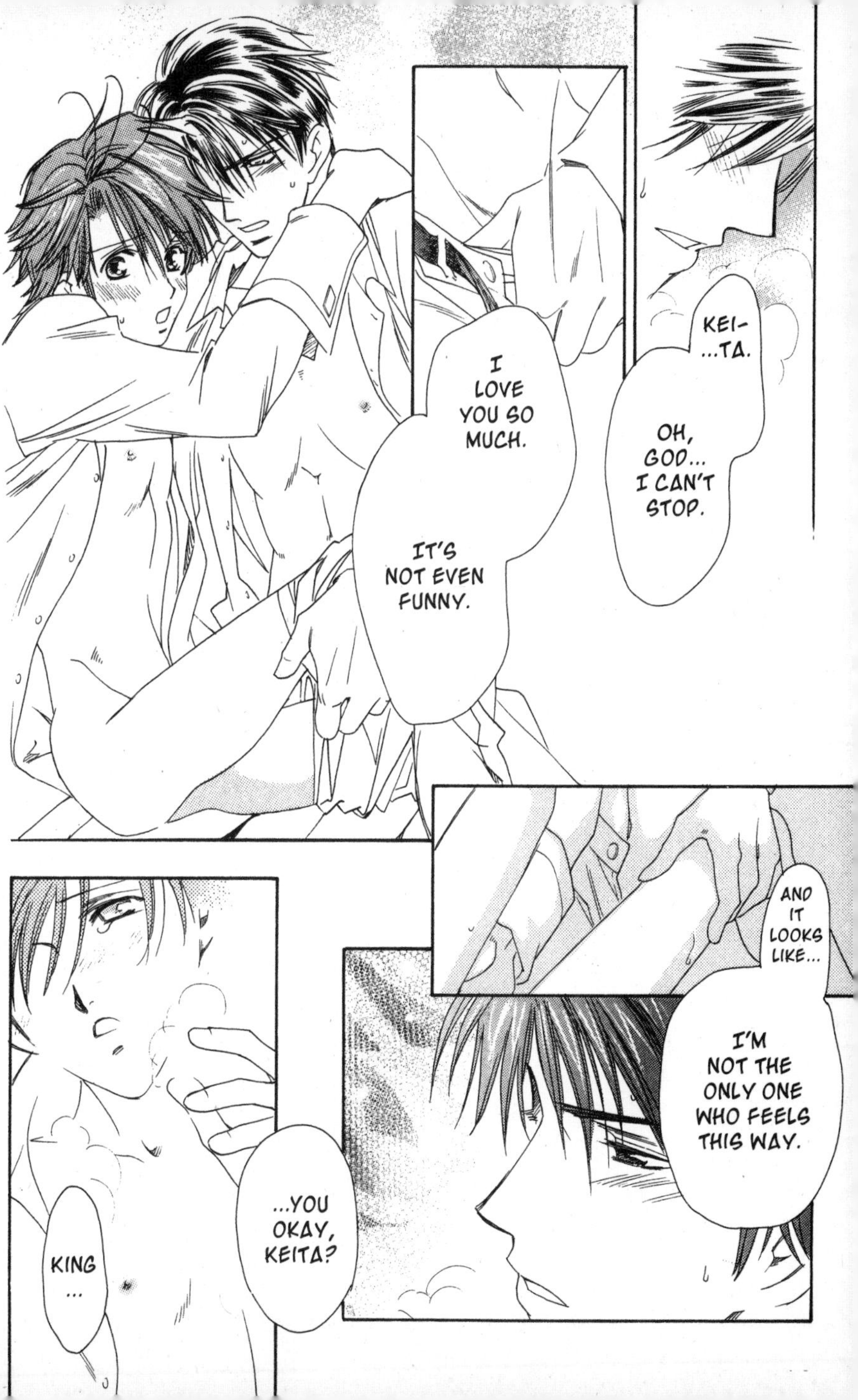
KEI-...TA.
OH, GOD... I CAN'T STOP.
I LOVE YOU SO MUCH.
IT'S NOT EVEN FUNNY.
AND IT LOOKS LIKE...
I'M NOT THE ONLY ONE WHO FEELS THIS WAY.
...YOU OKAY, KEITA?
KING ...

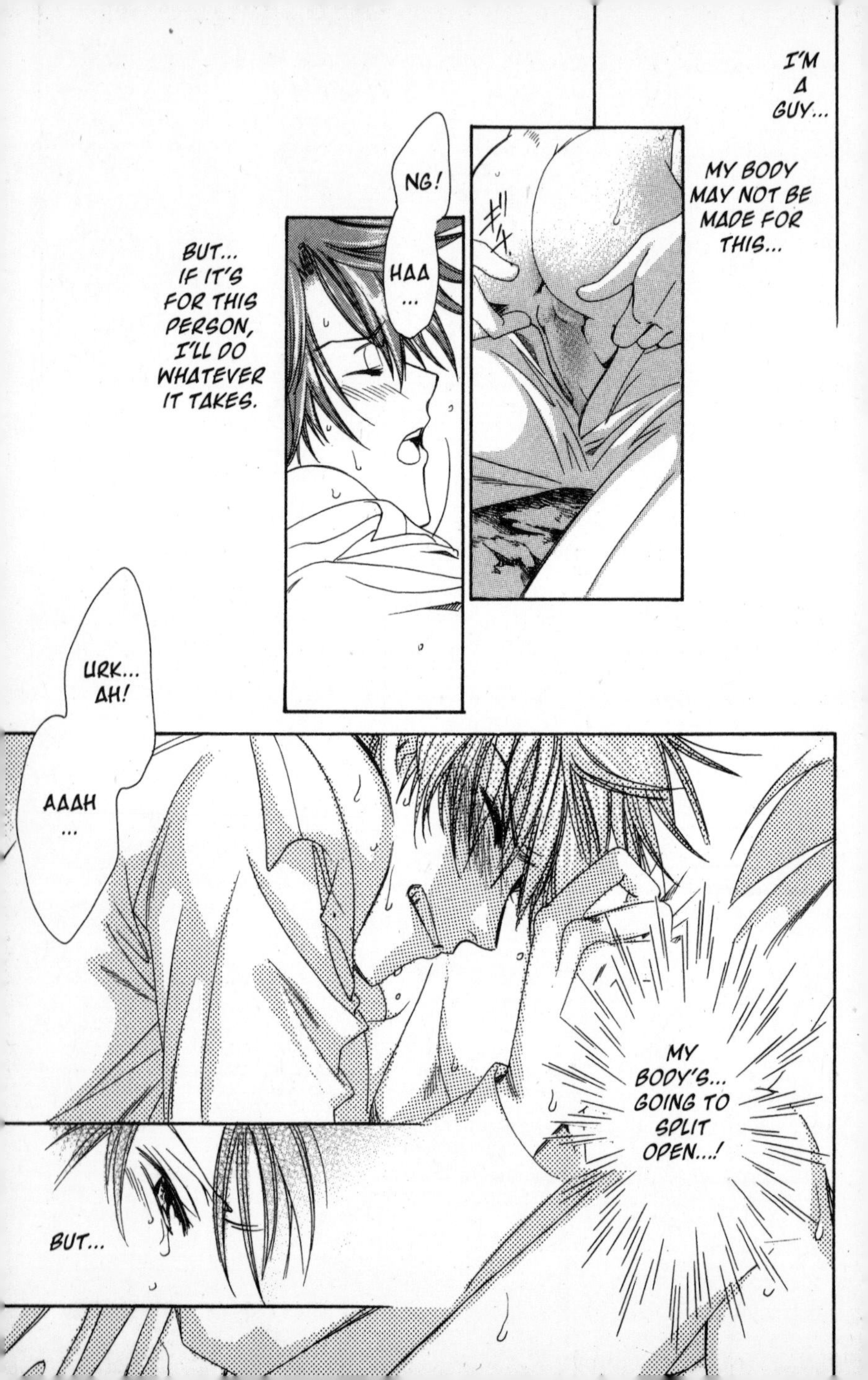
I'M A GUY...
MY BODY MAY NOT BE MADE FOR THIS...
NG!
HAA...
BUT... IF IT'S FOR THIS PERSON, I'LL DO WHATEVER IT TAKES.
URK... AH!
AAAH...
MY BODY'S... GOING TO SPLIT OPEN...!
BUT...

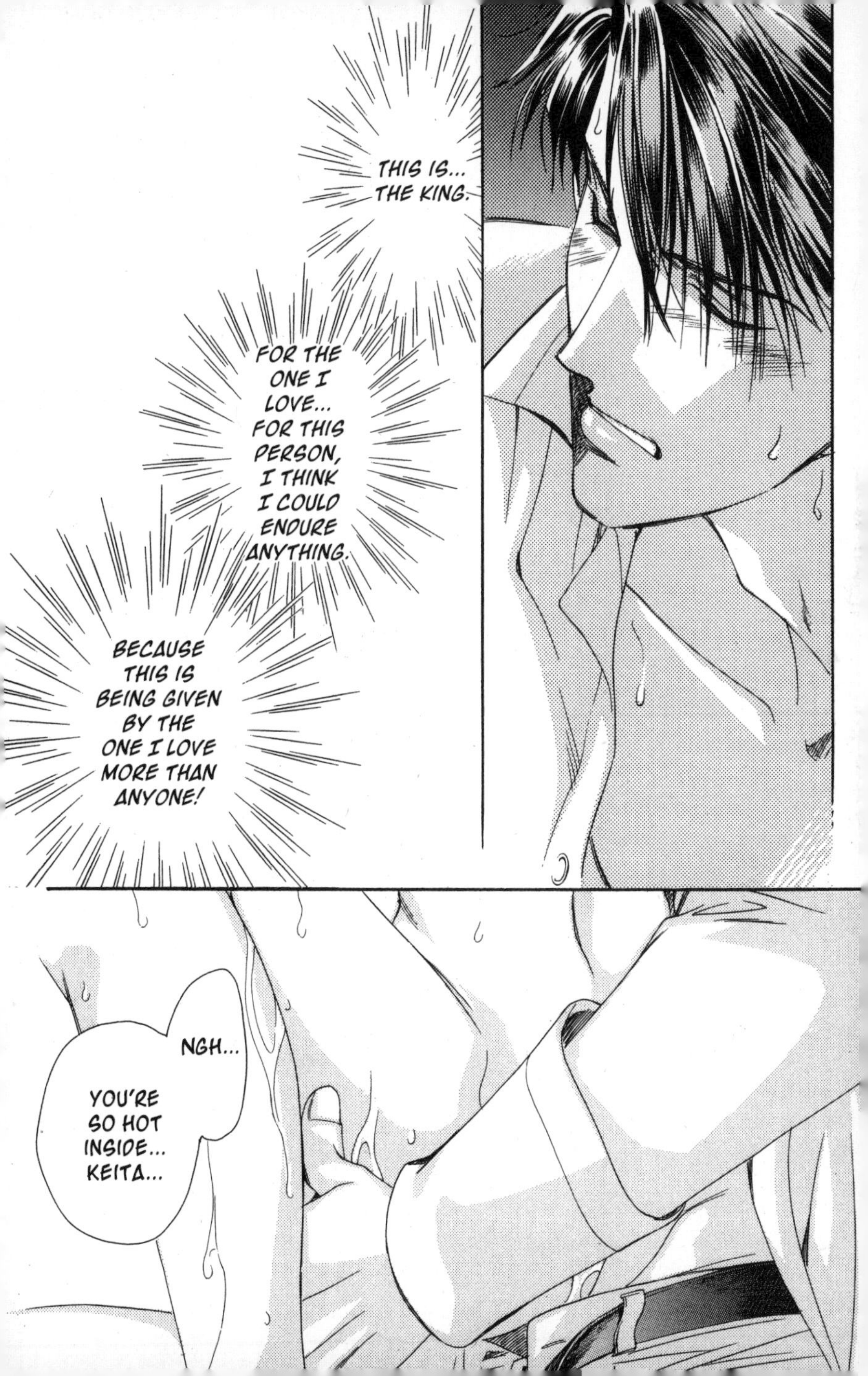
THIS IS... THE KING.
FOR THE ONE I LOVE... FOR THIS PERSON, I THINK I COULD ENDURE ANYTHING.
BECAUSE THIS IS BEING GIVEN BY THE ONE I LOVE MORE THAN ANYONE!
NGH...
YOU'RE SO HOT INSIDE... KEITA...

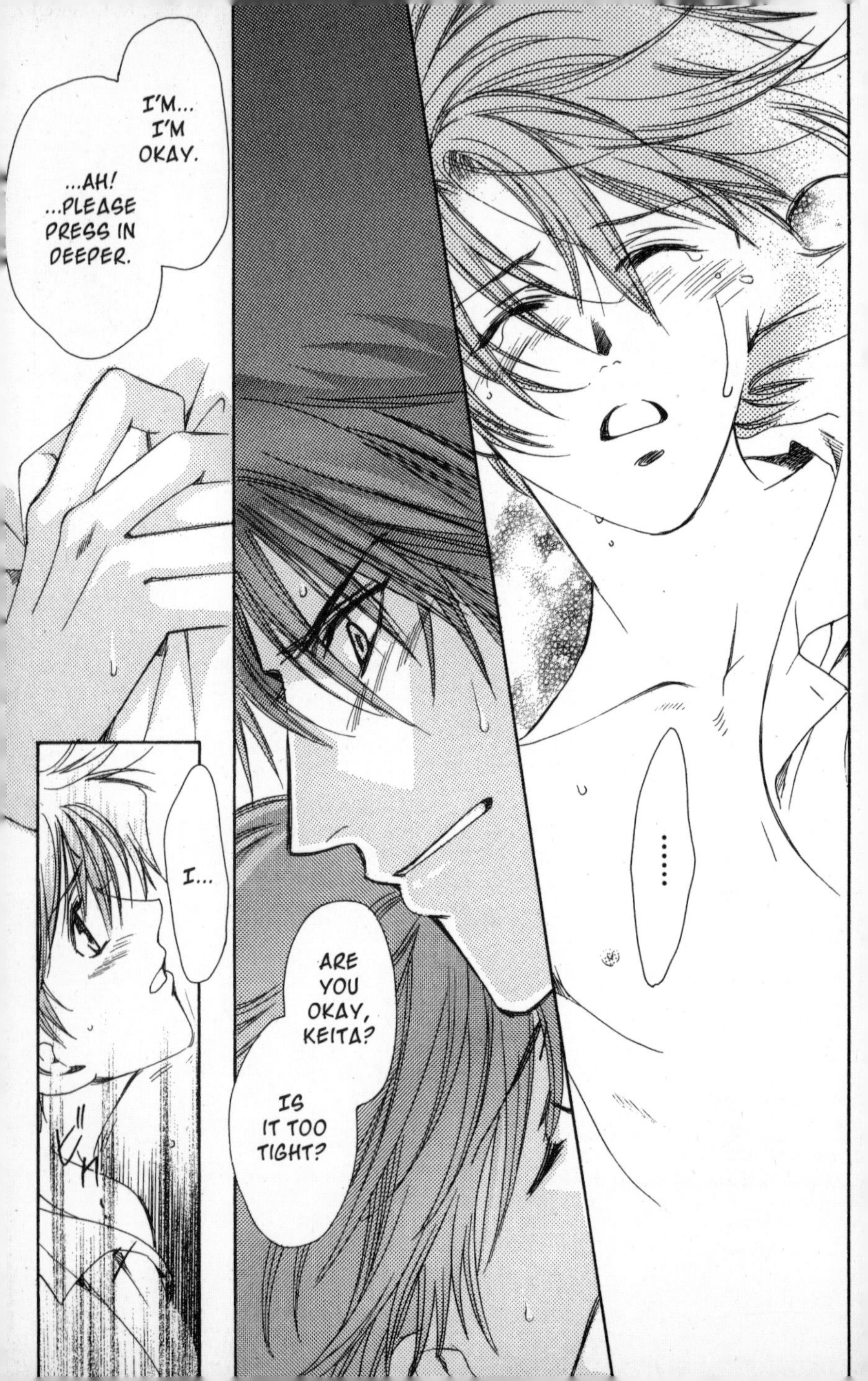
......
ARE YOU OKAY, KEITA?
IS IT TOO TIGHT?
I'M... I'M OKAY.
...AH! ...PLEASE PRESS IN DEEPER.
I...

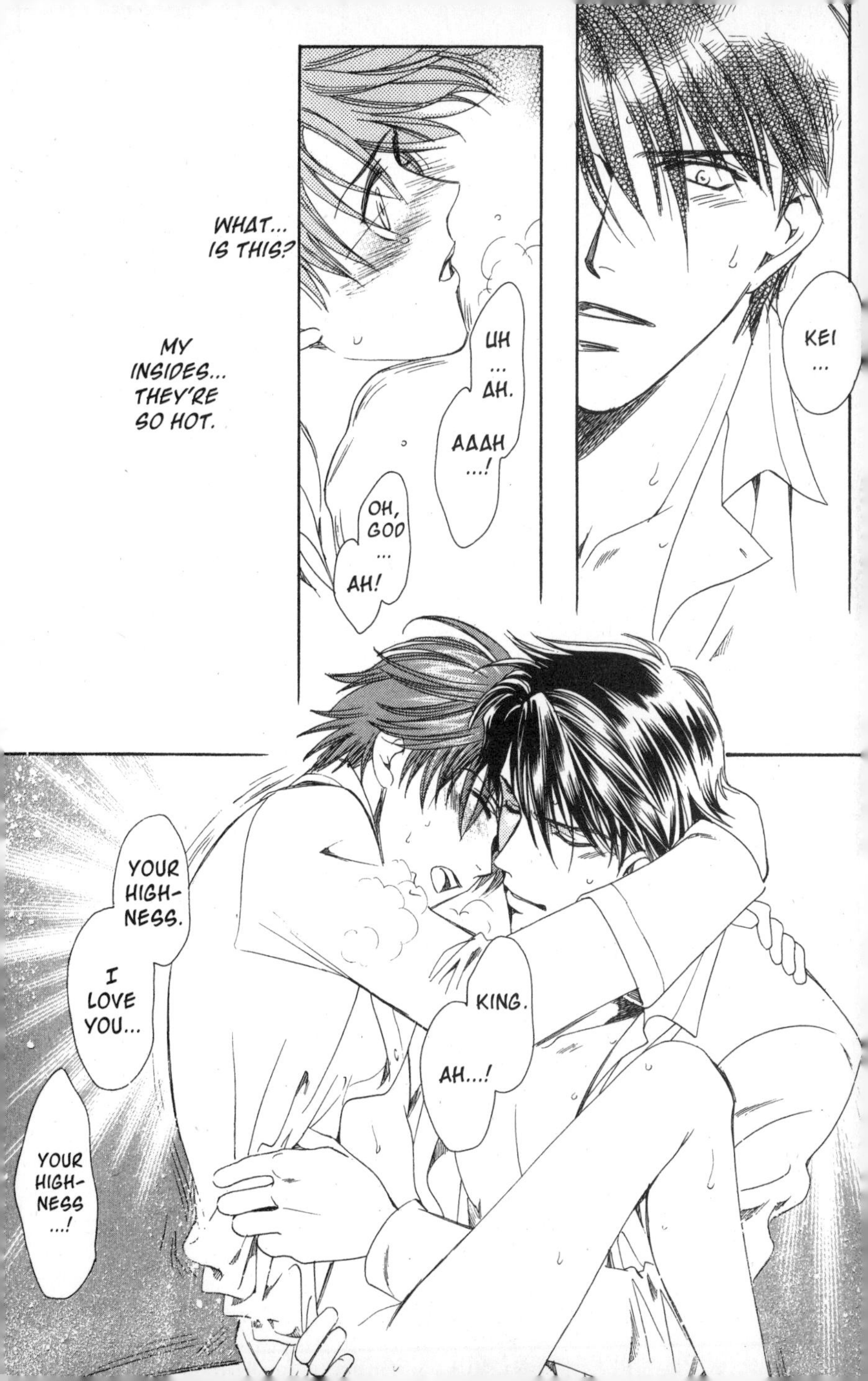
KEI ...
WHAT... IS THIS?
UH ... AH.
AAAH ...!
OH, GOD ... AH!
MY INSIDES... THEY'RE SO HOT.
KING.
AH...!
YOUR HIGH-NESS.
I LOVE YOU...
YOUR HIGH-NESS ...!

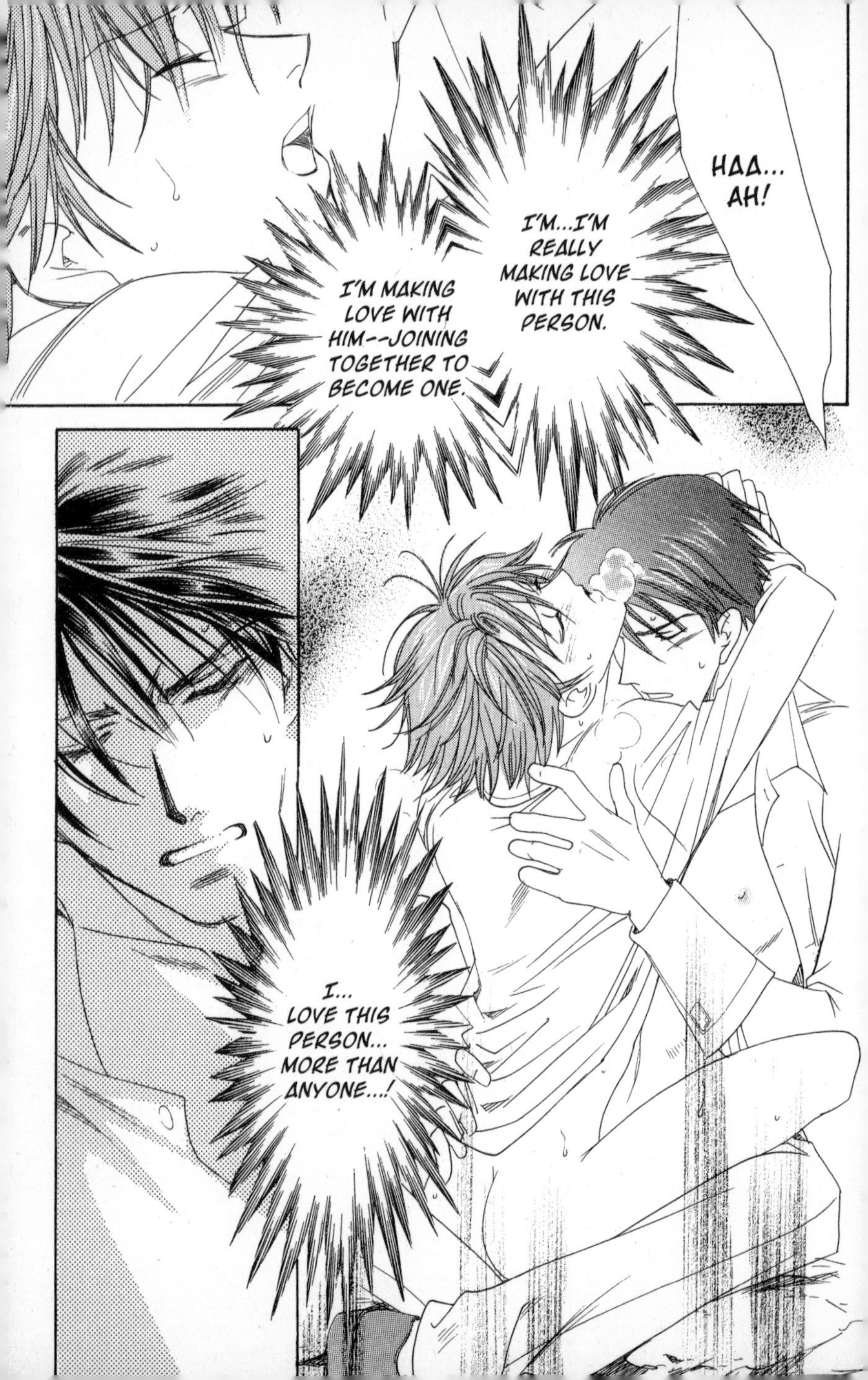
HAA... AH!
I'M...I'M REALLY MAKING LOVE WITH THIS PERSON.
I'M MAKING LOVE WITH HIM--JOINING TOGETHER TO BECOME ONE.
I... LOVE THIS PERSON... MORE THAN ANYONE...!

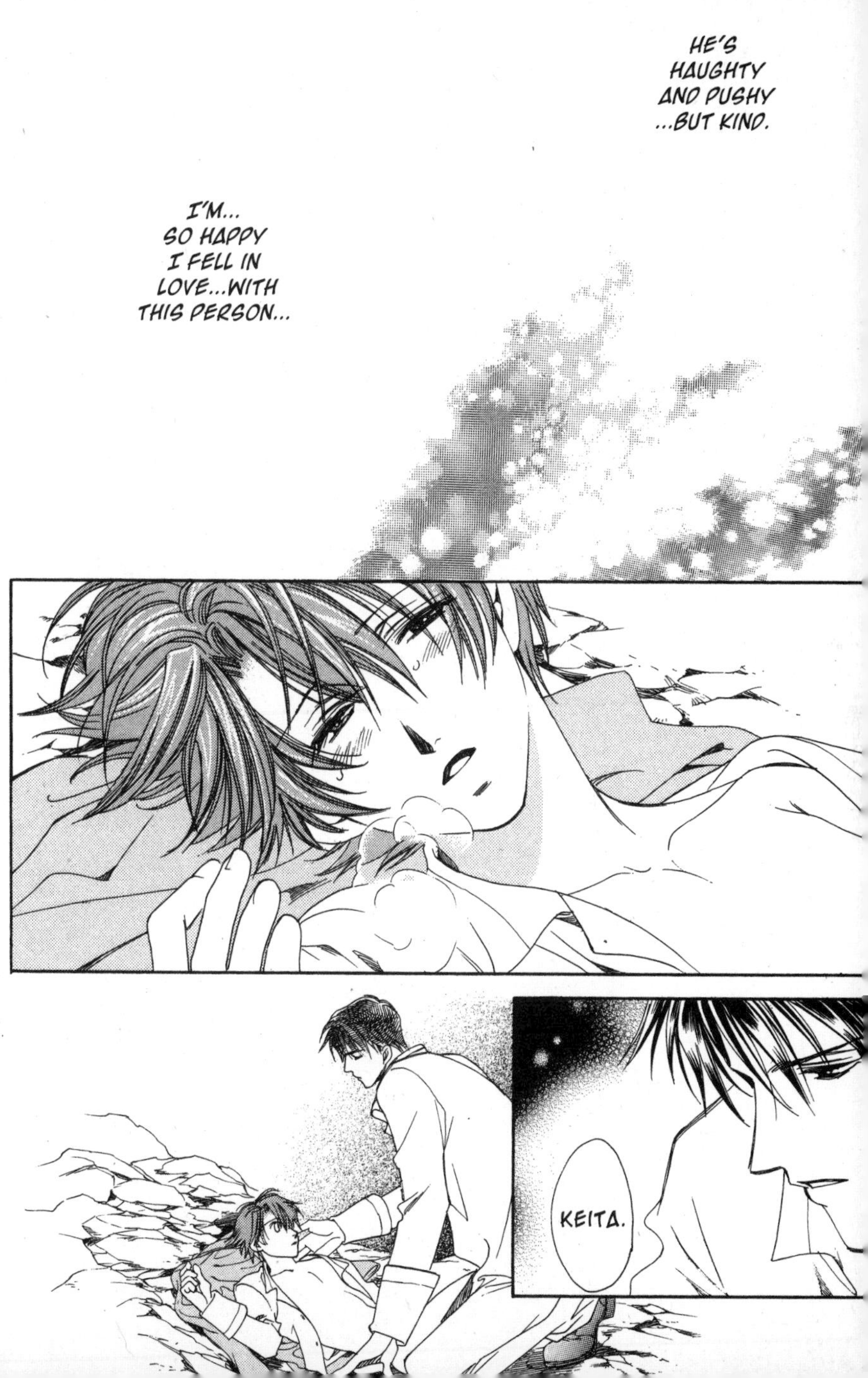
HE'S HAUGHTY AND PUSHY ...BUT KIND.
I'M... SO HAPPY I FELL IN LOVE...WITH THIS PERSON...
KEITA.

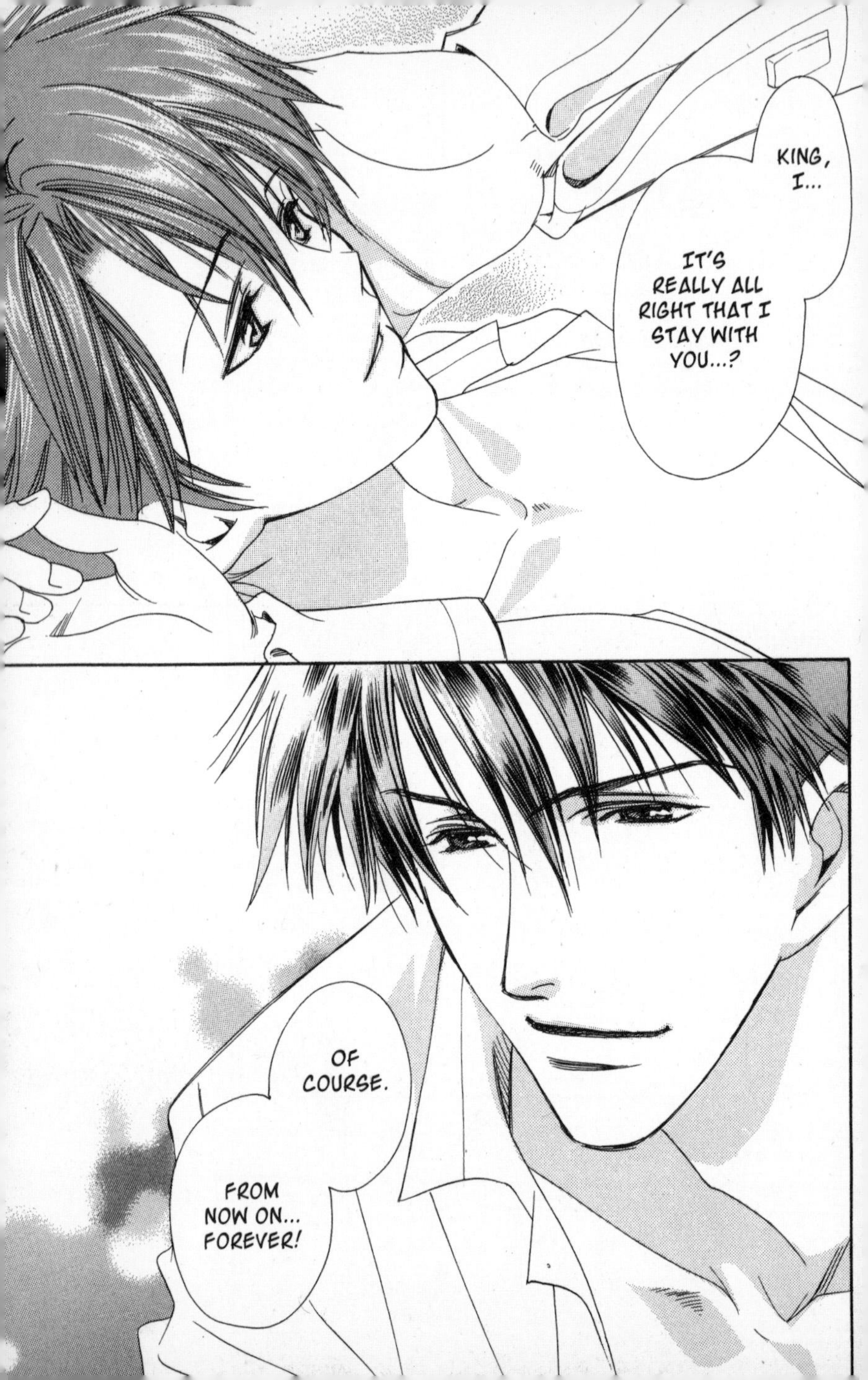
KING, I...
IT'S REALLY ALL RIGHT THAT I STAY WITH YOU...?
OF COURSE.
FROM NOW ON... FOREVER!

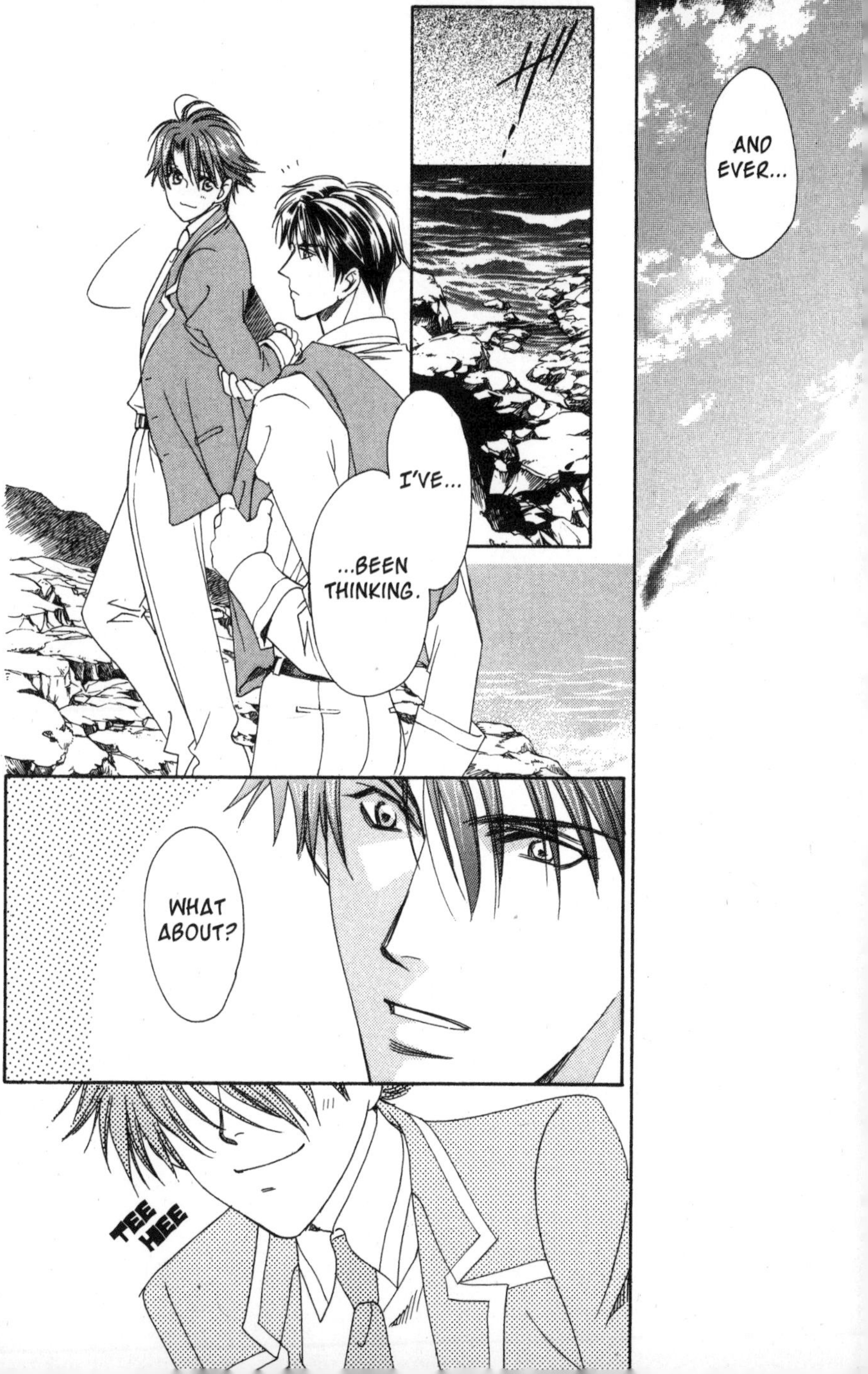
AND EVER...
I'VE...
...BEEN THINKING.
WHAT ABOUT?
TEE HEE

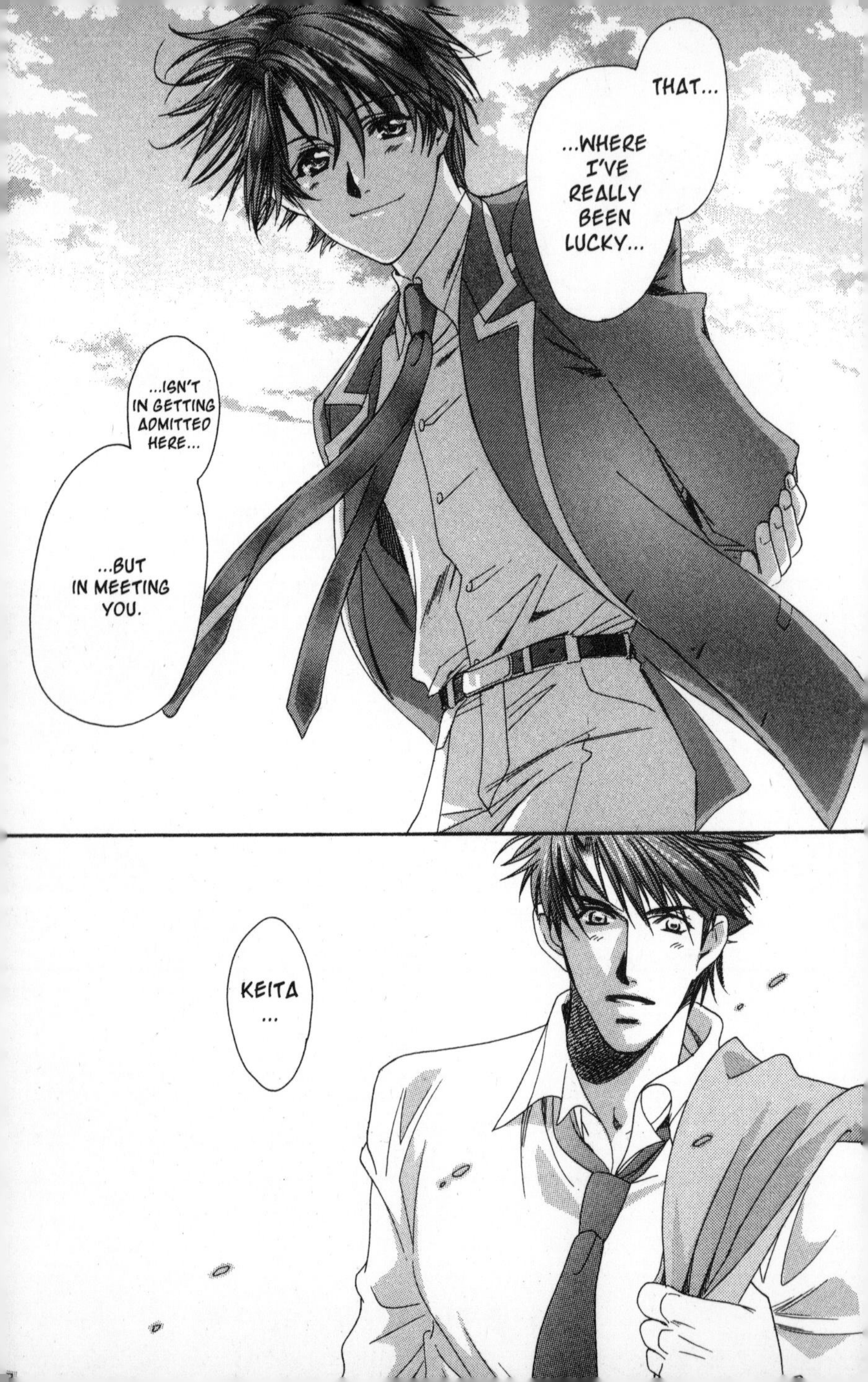
THAT...
...WHERE I'VE REALLY BEEN LUCKY...
...ISN'T IN GETTING ADMITTED HERE...
...BUT IN MEETING YOU.
KEITA ...

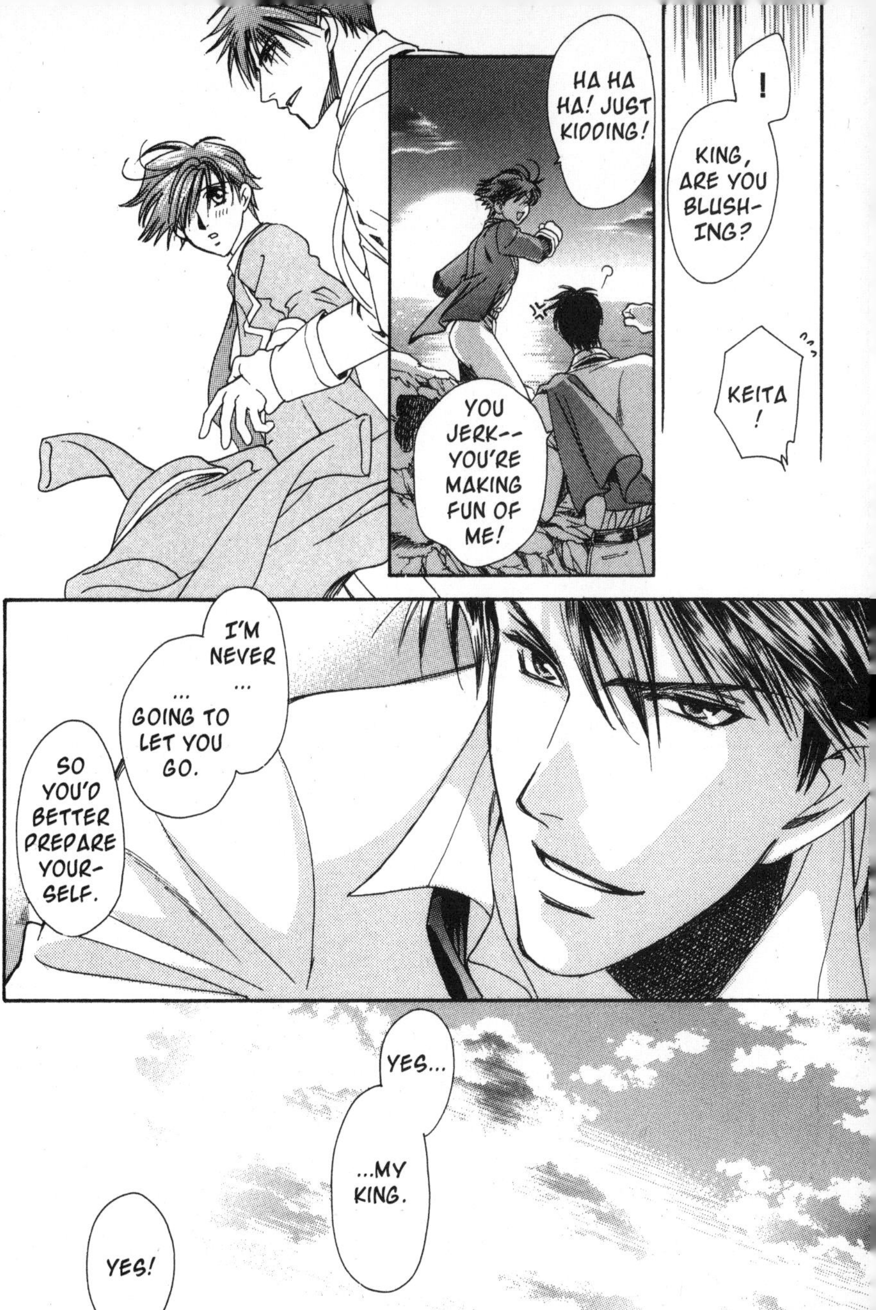
!
KING, ARE YOU BLUSH-ING?
KEITA!
HA HA HA! JUST KIDDING!
YOU JERK-- YOU'RE MAKING FUN OF ME!
I'M NEVER ...
... GOING TO LET YOU GO.
SO YOU'D BETTER PREPARE YOUR-SELF.
YES...
...MY KING.
YES!

GAKUEN HEAVEN / END ♥

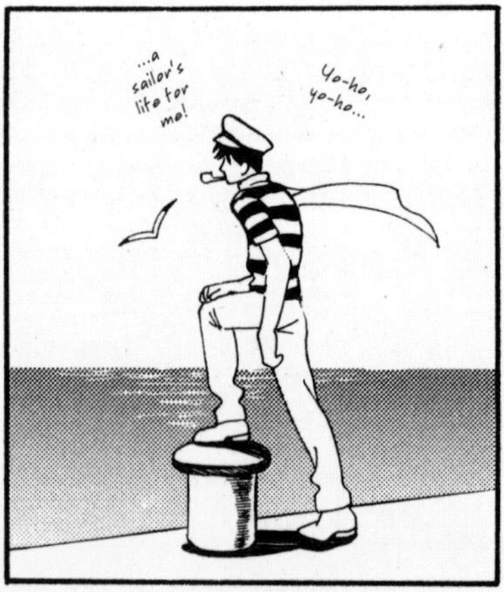
Yo-ho, yo-ho...
...a sailor's life for me!

THANK YOU FOR PICKING UP THIS BOOK. THIS IS MY FIRST TIME WITH BIBLOS.

ABOUT THREE YEARS AGO, GAKUEN HEAVEN BEGAN AS A WHIM WHEN I WAS COMMISSIONED TO DO A COVER ILLUSTRATION (BECAUSE I ACTUALLY KNEW VERY LITTLE ABOUT THE GAME). I NEVER WOULD HAVE THOUGHT IT'D STRETCH OUT FOR THIS LONG... NO, BUT REALLY I FEEL DEEPLY FOR IT. WHILE DRAWING IT, I GREW TO LOVE EACH AND EVERY CHARACTER. IN ACTUALITY, I LOVE THEM SO MUCH THAT I WANT TO WRITE ABOUT EACH ONE'S STORY.

IN THE MAGAZINE BEXBOY, THE READERS FILLED OUT A SURVEY WHERE THEY CHOSE KEITA-KUN'S PARTNER. THE RESULT WAS THE KING, SAYING THAT HE FILLED THE SEAT OF MOST SPLENDID PARTNER. WHAT CAN YOU EXPECT WITH A NICKNAME "THE KING"? SADLY ENOUGH, NAKAJIMA-SAN WAS JUST ONE STEP BELOW. SINCE IT WAS STILL SUCH A NARROW MARGIN, I MADE SURE TO INCLUDE PLENTY OF SCENES WITH HIM. I'D PLANNED ON INCLUDING ALL THE OTHERS CHARACTERS EQUALLY TOO, BUT AS I STARTED TO NEAR THE END, THE PANELS WERE TOO FEW, THE CHANCES FOR THEIR TURNS DIMINISHED, AND I ENDED UP HAVING TO LEAVE THEM OUT. SORRY...

WHEN THE STORY WAS SERIALIZED IN THE MAGAZINE, A LOT OF PEOPLE POINTED OUT THAT THE SEX SCENE WITH THE KING WAS TOO SHORT, SO IN THE FINAL VERSION YOU ARE READING NOW, I TOOK THE OPPORTUNITY TO REVISE IT THOROUGHLY (TO UTILIZE LEFT-OVER FILLER-SPACE, THE LAST PAGE OF THE MAGAZINE SERIALIZATION WAS NOTHING BUT AN AD FOR A TELEPHONE CARD). IT FEELS LIKE BOYS' LOVE USED TO HAVE AN AMATEUR STICKER ON IT, BUT HAS REALLY BLOSSOMED LATELY. WELL, I GOT TO HAVE FUN DRAWING IT, IF ANYTHING!

TO ALL THOSE WHO HELPED DRAW THIS BOOK--NAKATSUJI NAOKO-SAN, IZUMI HIJIRI-SAN, FUYUTSUKI MITSURU-SAN, KAZUKI MARI-SAN, KIYO-CHAN, AKATSUKI SHO-SAN, KITAHIRA KANA-SAN, OZAWA SACHI-SAN, MY CHIEF ODA RYOKA, HATOBA RAIKA-SAN WHO WAS IN CHARGE OF THE CG COLORING, AND MY EDITOR, A-SAMA: GOOD JOB EVERYONE! THANK YOU FROM THE BOTTOM OF MY HEART.
FOR ALL MY READERS OUT THERE, I'D BE MOST HAPPY IF YOU ENJOY THIS WORK.

FEBRUARY, 2002
HIGURI YOU

NEXT IS A SHORT SERIALIZED IN BEXBOY MAGAZINE BEFORE THE GAME WAS RELEASED! PLEASE ENJOY!

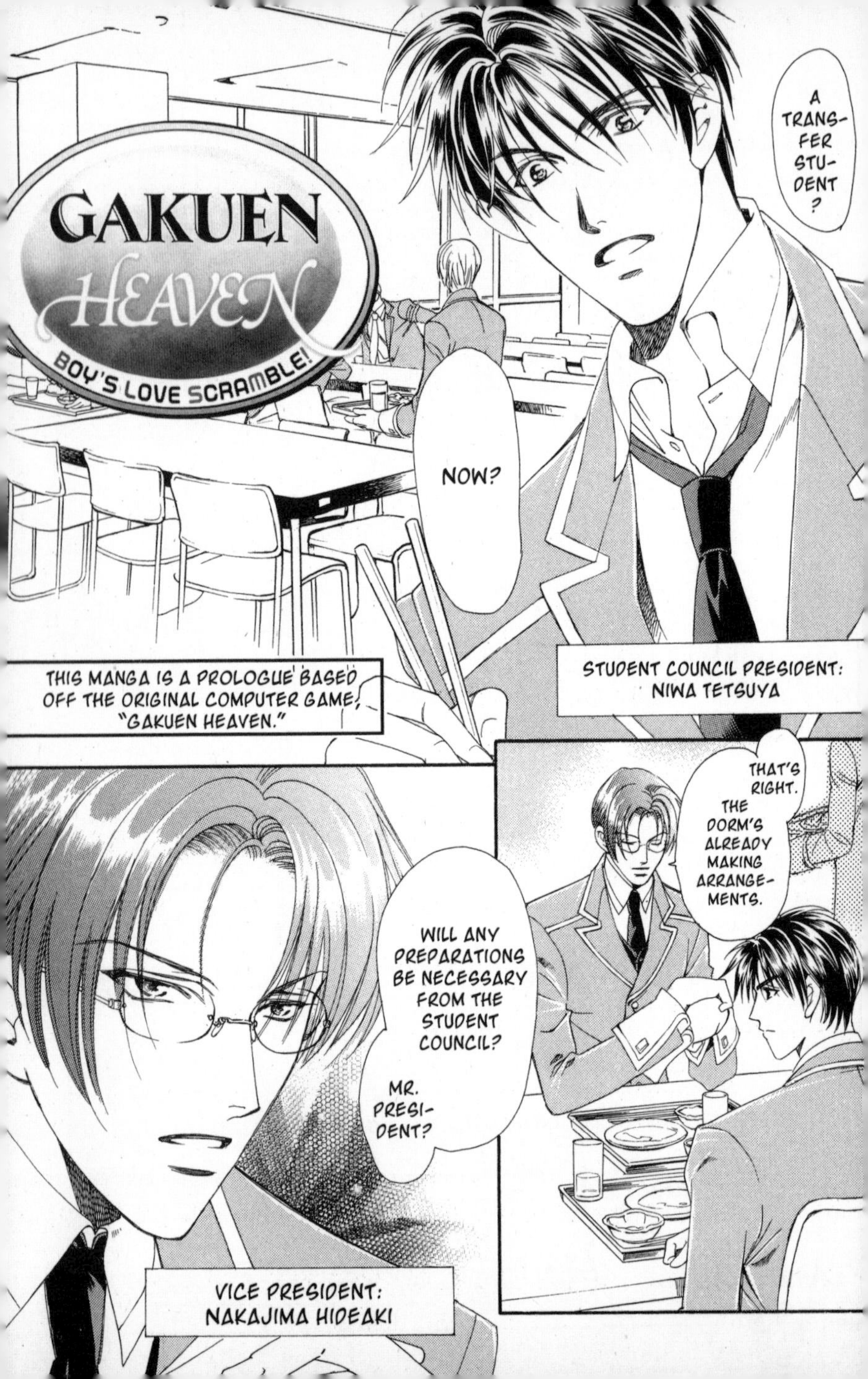
A TRANSFER STUDENT?
GAKUEN HEAVEN
BOY'S LOVE SCRAMBLE!
NOW?
STUDENT COUNCIL PRESIDENT: NIWA TETSUYA
THIS MANGA IS A PROLOGUE BASED OFF THE ORIGINAL COMPUTER GAME, "GAKUEN HEAVEN."
THAT'S RIGHT. THE DORM'S ALREADY MAKING ARRANGEMENTS.
WILL ANY PREPARATIONS BE NECESSARY FROM THE STUDENT COUNCIL?
MR. PRESIDENT?
VICE PRESIDENT: NAKAJIMA HIDEAKI

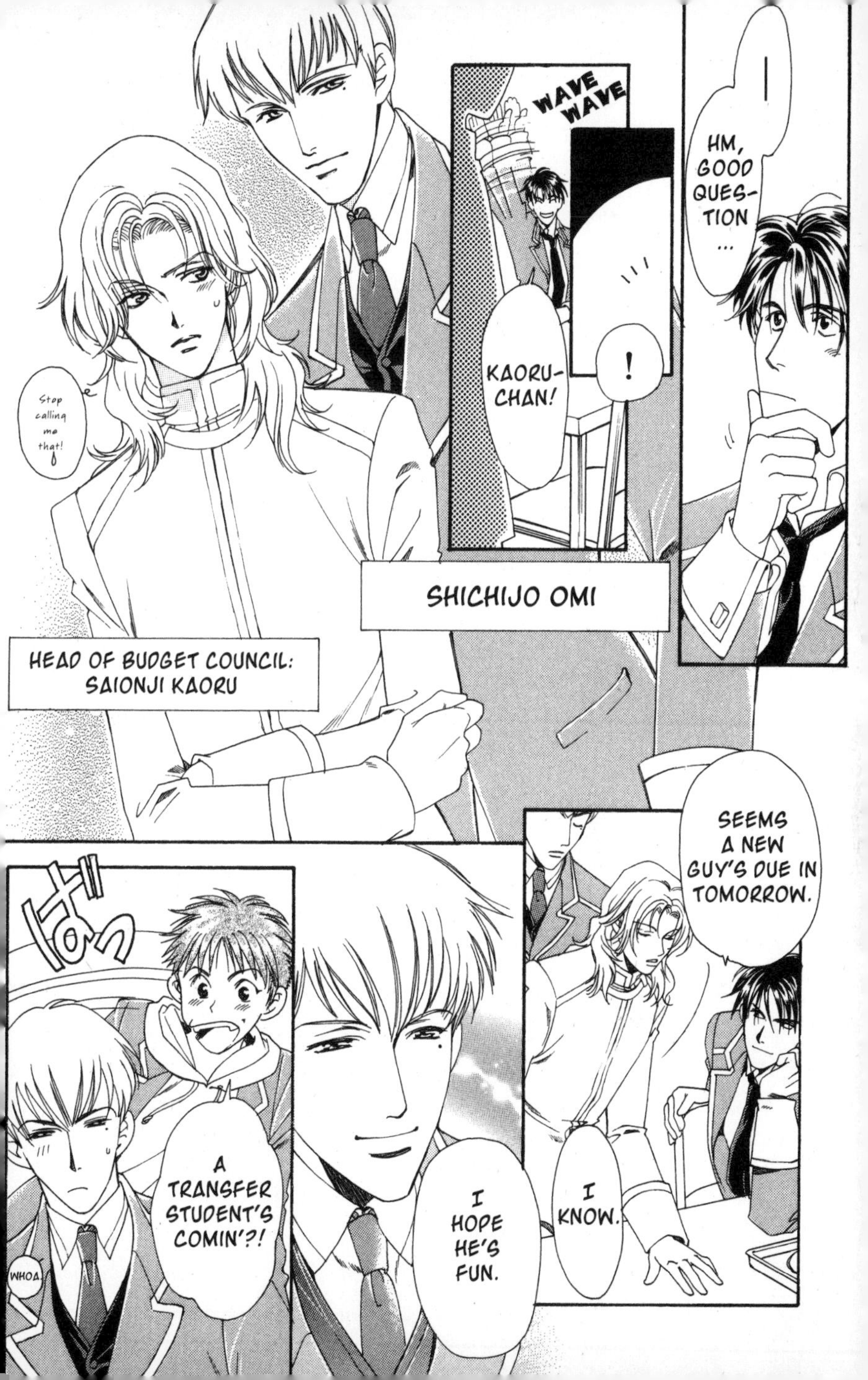
HM, GOOD QUES-TION ...
WAVE WAVE
KAORU-CHAN!
!
SHICHIJO OMI
Stop calling me that!
HEAD OF BUDGET COUNCIL: SAIONJI KAORU
SEEMS A NEW GUY'S DUE IN TOMORROW.
I KNOW.
I HOPE HE'S FUN.
ばっ
A TRANSFER STUDENT'S COMIN'?!
WHOA

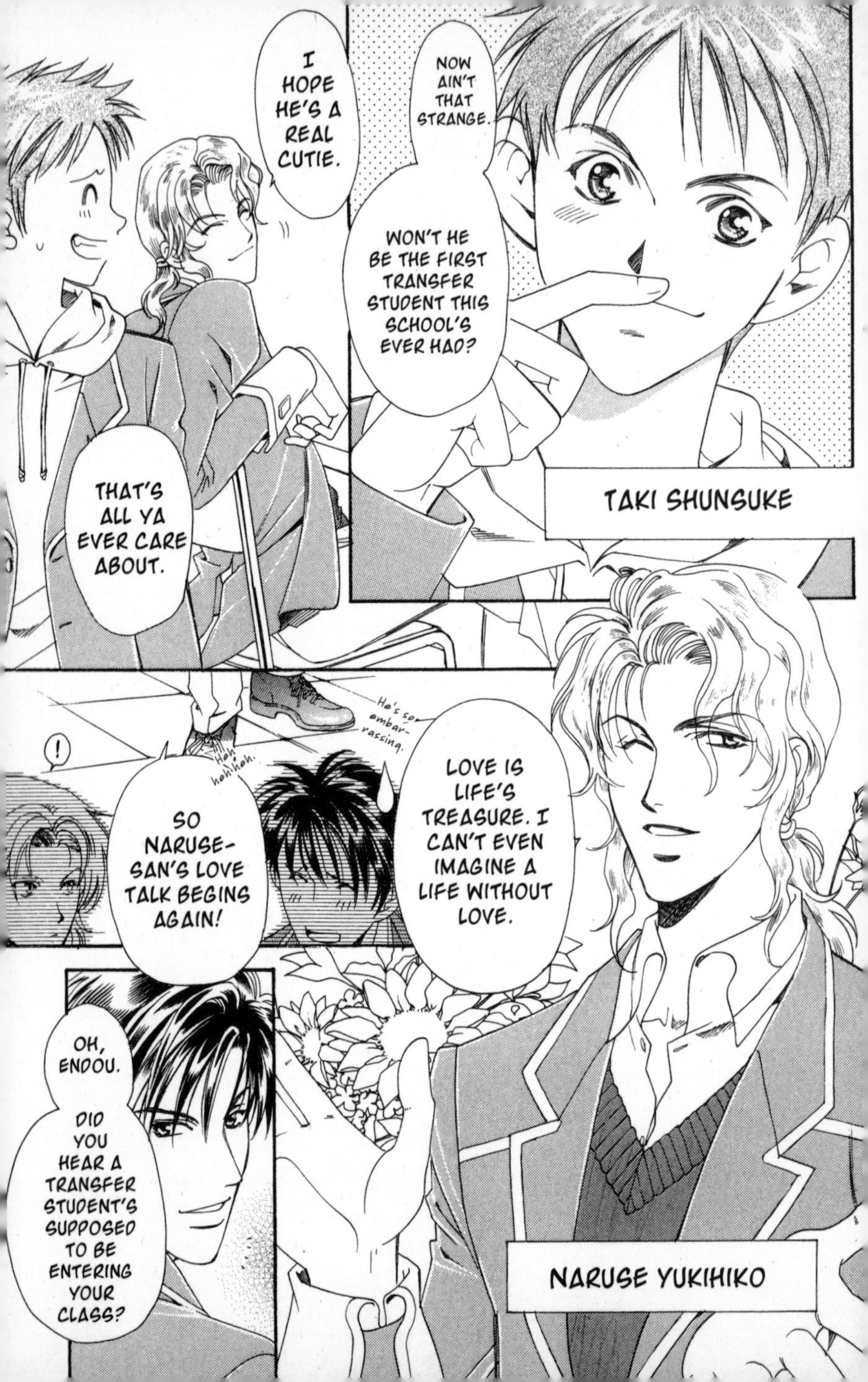
NOW AIN'T THAT STRANGE.
WON'T HE BE THE FIRST TRANSFER STUDENT THIS SCHOOL'S EVER HAD?
TAKI SHUNSUKE
I HOPE HE'S A REAL CUTIE.
THAT'S ALL YA EVER CARE ABOUT.
LOVE IS LIFE'S TREASURE. I CAN'T EVEN IMAGINE A LIFE WITHOUT LOVE.
NARUSE YUKIHIKO
He's so embarrassing.
Heh heh heh.
!
SO NARUSE-SAN'S LOVE TALK BEGINS AGAIN!
OH, ENDOU.
DID YOU HEAR A TRANSFER STUDENT'S SUPPOSED TO BE ENTERING YOUR CLASS?

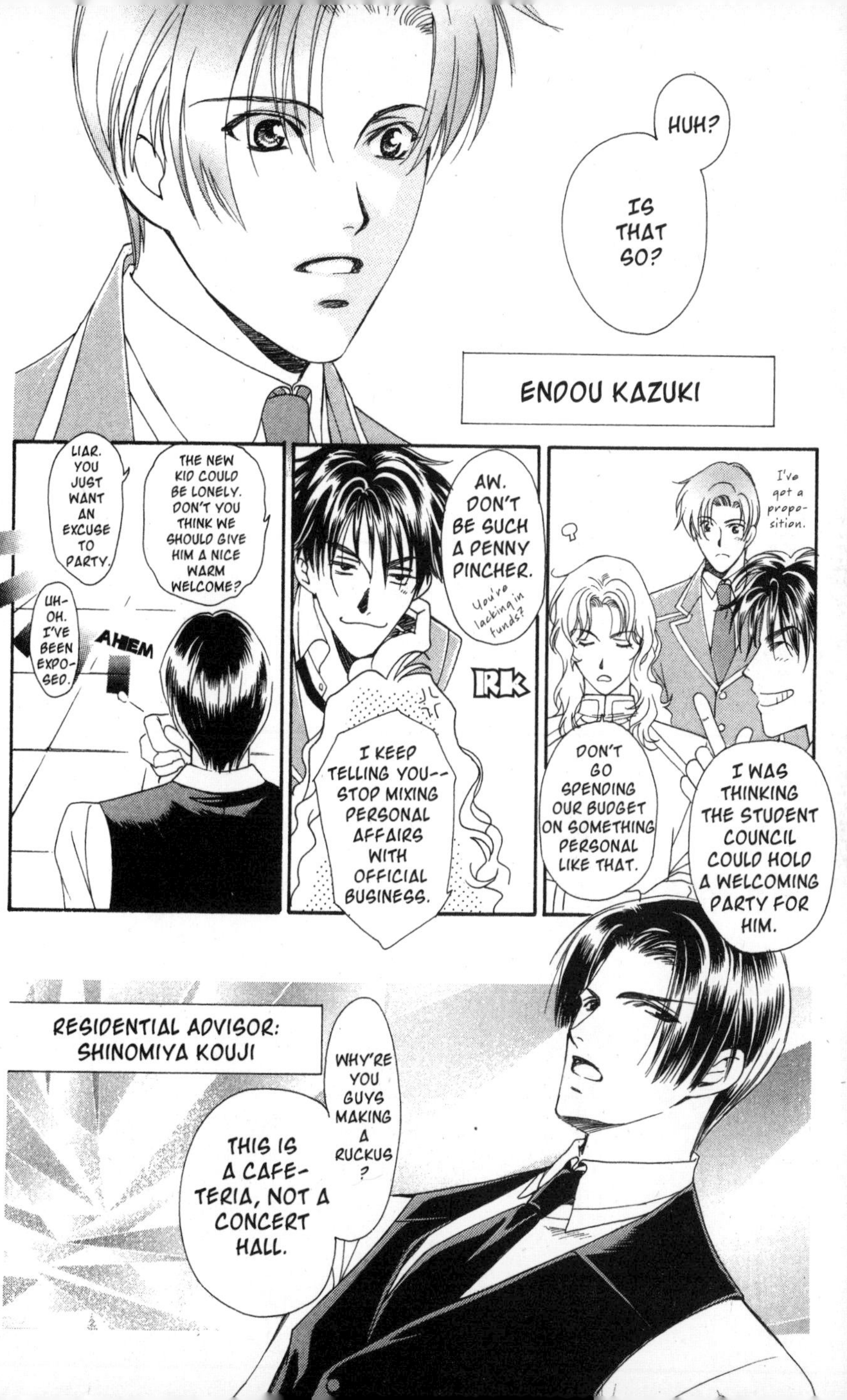

HUH?
IS THAT SO?
ENDOU KAZUKI
I've got a proposition.
I WAS THINKING THE STUDENT COUNCIL COULD HOLD A WELCOMING PARTY FOR HIM.
DON'T GO SPENDING OUR BUDGET ON SOMETHING PERSONAL LIKE THAT.
AW. DON'T BE SUCH A PENNY PINCHER.
You're lacking in funds?
IRK
I KEEP TELLING YOU-- STOP MIXING PERSONAL AFFAIRS WITH OFFICIAL BUSINESS.
THE NEW KID COULD BE LONELY. DON'T YOU THINK WE SHOULD GIVE HIM A NICE WARM WELCOME?
LIAR. YOU JUST WANT AN EXCUSE TO PARTY.
AHEM
UH-OH. I'VE BEEN EXPOSED.
WHY'RE YOU GUYS MAKING A RUCKUS?
RESIDENTIAL ADVISOR: SHINOMIYA KOUJI
THIS IS A CAFETERIA, NOT A CONCERT HALL.

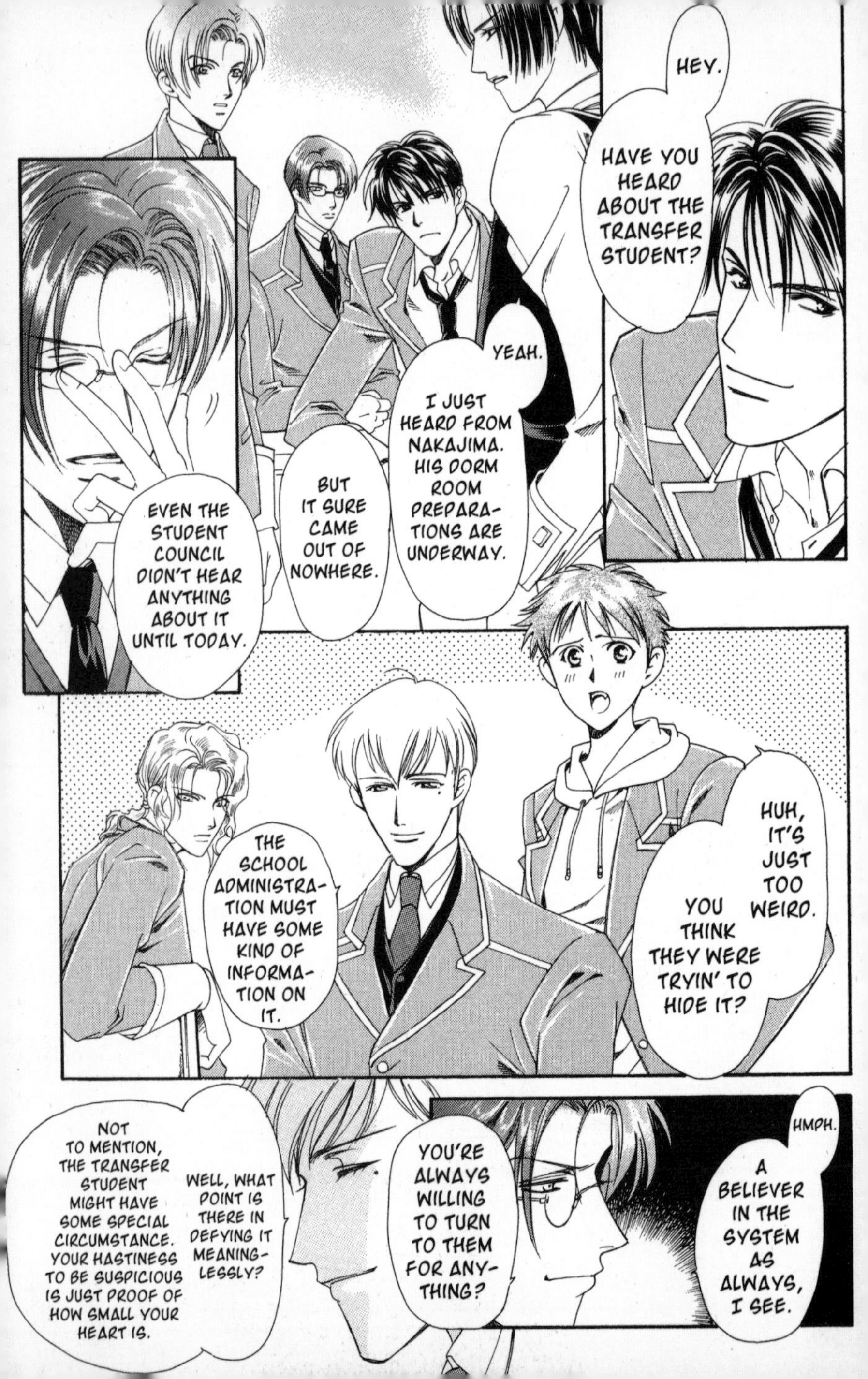
HEY.
HAVE YOU HEARD ABOUT THE TRANSFER STUDENT?
YEAH.
I JUST HEARD FROM NAKAJIMA. HIS DORM ROOM PREPARA-TIONS ARE UNDERWAY.
BUT IT SURE CAME OUT OF NOWHERE.
EVEN THE STUDENT COUNCIL DIDN'T HEAR ANYTHING ABOUT IT UNTIL TODAY.
HUH, IT'S JUST TOO WEIRD.
YOU THINK THEY WERE TRYIN' TO HIDE IT?
THE SCHOOL ADMINISTRA-TION MUST HAVE SOME KIND OF INFORMA-TION ON IT.
HMPH.
A BELIEVER IN THE SYSTEM AS ALWAYS, I SEE.
YOU'RE ALWAYS WILLING TO TURN TO THEM FOR ANY-THING?
WELL, WHAT POINT IS THERE IN DEFYING IT MEANING-LESSLY?
NOT TO MENTION, THE TRANSFER STUDENT MIGHT HAVE SOME SPECIAL CIRCUMSTANCE. YOUR HASTINESS TO BE SUSPICIOUS IS JUST PROOF OF HOW SMALL YOUR HEART IS.

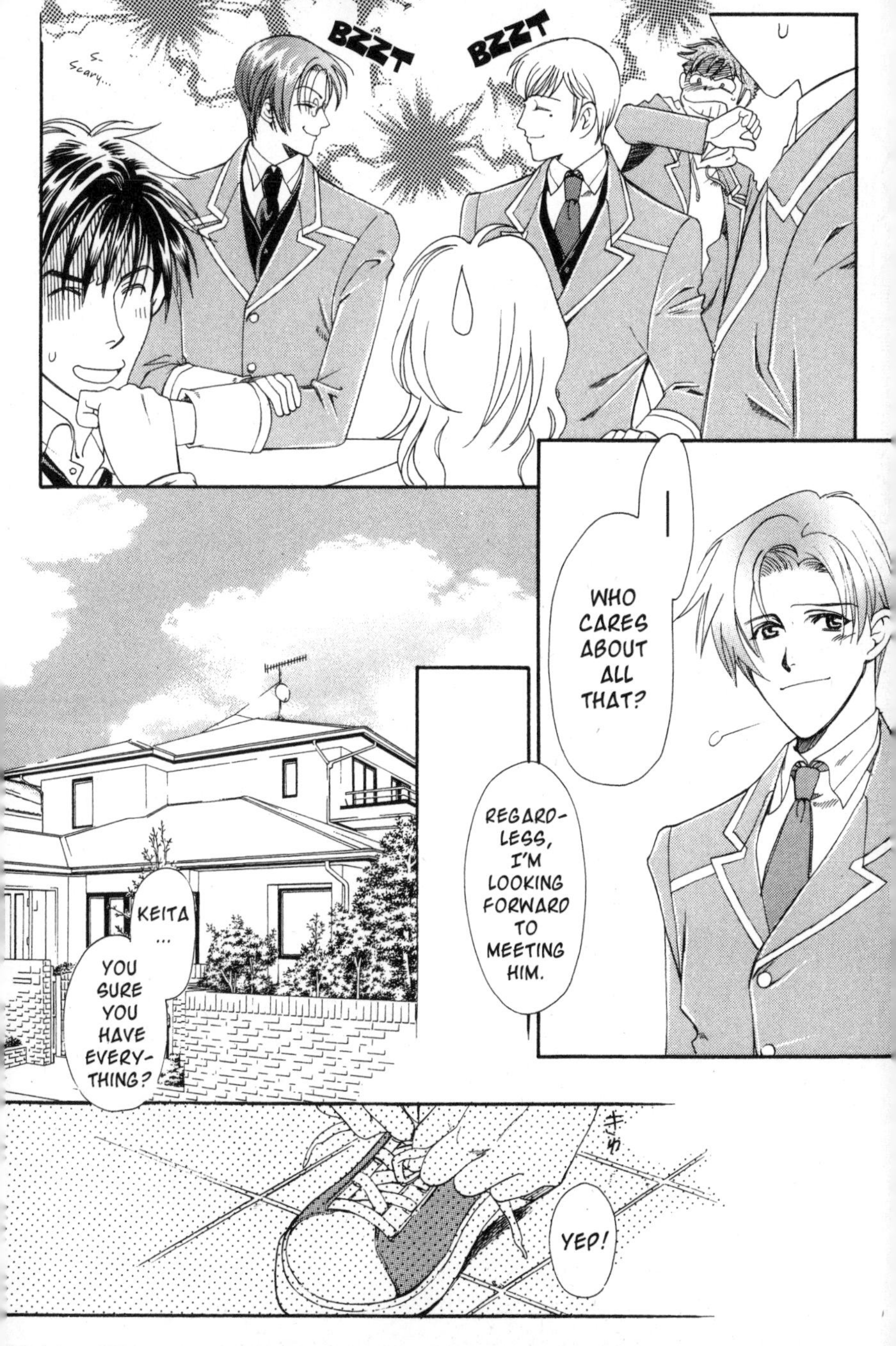
BZZT
BZZT
S-Scary...
I
WHO CARES ABOUT ALL THAT?
REGARDLESS, I'M LOOKING FORWARD TO MEETING HIM.
KEITA ...
YOU SURE YOU HAVE EVERYTHING?
きゅ
YEP!

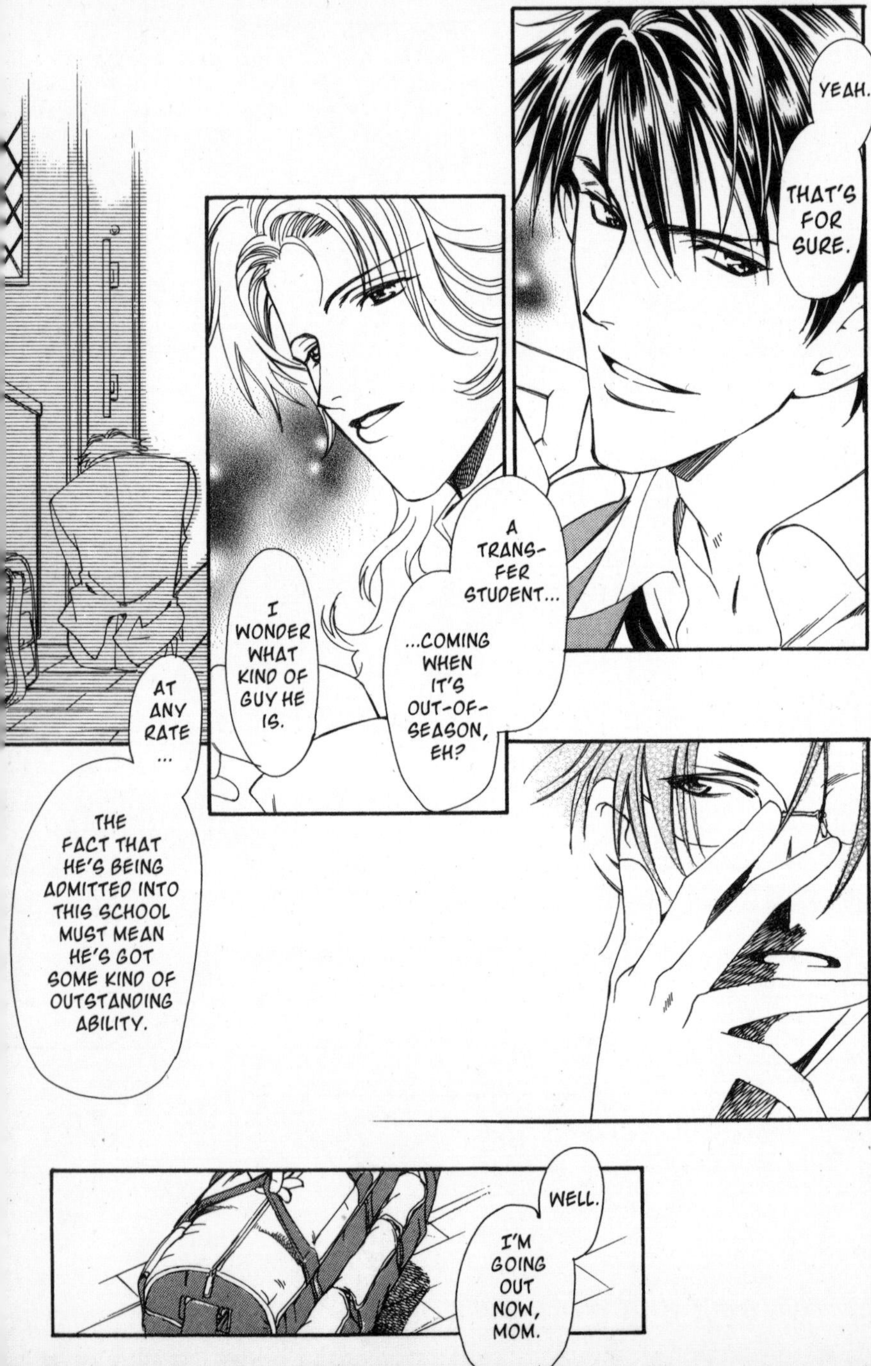
YEAH.
THAT'S FOR SURE.
A TRANSFER STUDENT...
...COMING WHEN IT'S OUT-OF-SEASON, EH?
I WONDER WHAT KIND OF GUY HE IS.
AT ANY RATE...
THE FACT THAT HE'S BEING ADMITTED INTO THIS SCHOOL MUST MEAN HE'S GOT SOME KIND OF OUTSTANDING ABILITY.
WELL.
I'M GOING OUT NOW, MOM.

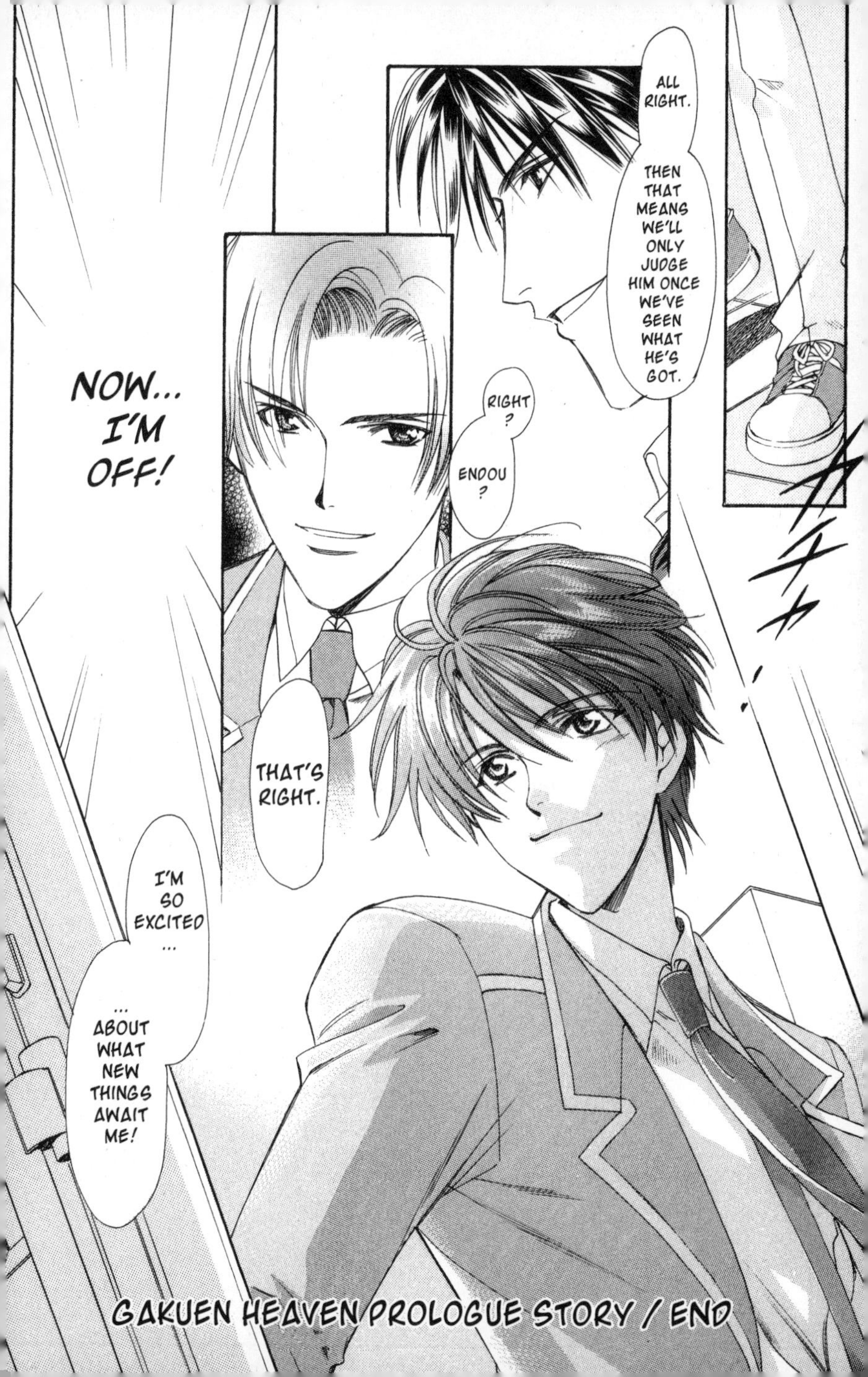

ALL RIGHT.
THEN THAT MEANS WE'LL ONLY JUDGE HIM ONCE WE'VE SEEN WHAT HE'S GOT.
RIGHT?
ENDOU?
THAT'S RIGHT.
NOW... I'M OFF!
I'M SO EXCITED...
... ABOUT WHAT NEW THINGS AWAIT ME!
GAKUEN HEAVEN PROLOGUE STORY / END

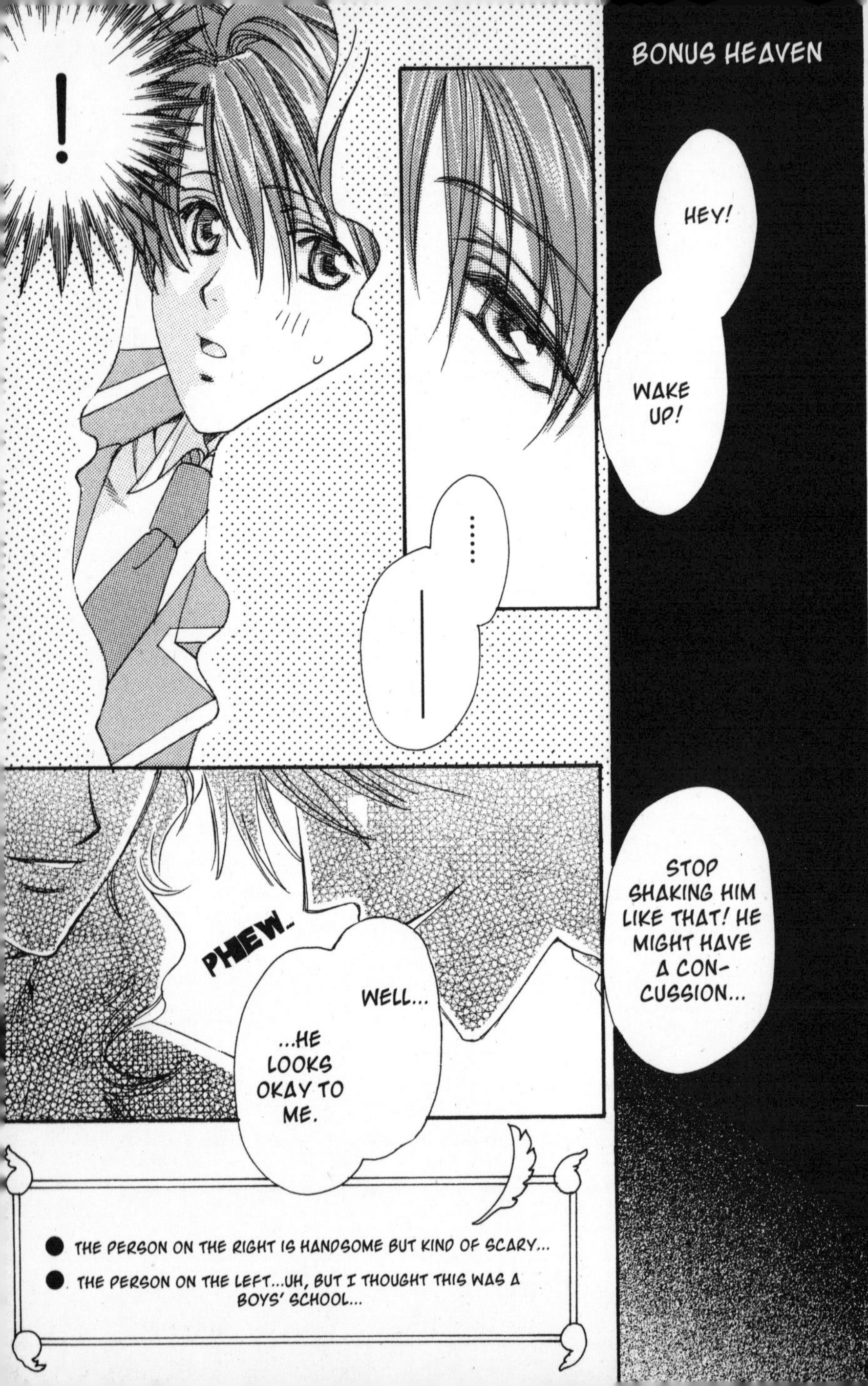
BONUS HEAVEN
HEY!
WAKE UP!
......
—
!
STOP SHAKING HIM LIKE THAT! HE MIGHT HAVE A CON-CUSSION...
PHEW..
WELL...
...HE LOOKS OKAY TO ME.
● THE PERSON ON THE RIGHT IS HANDSOME BUT KIND OF SCARY...
● THE PERSON ON THE LEFT...UH, BUT I THOUGHT THIS WAS A BOYS' SCHOOL...

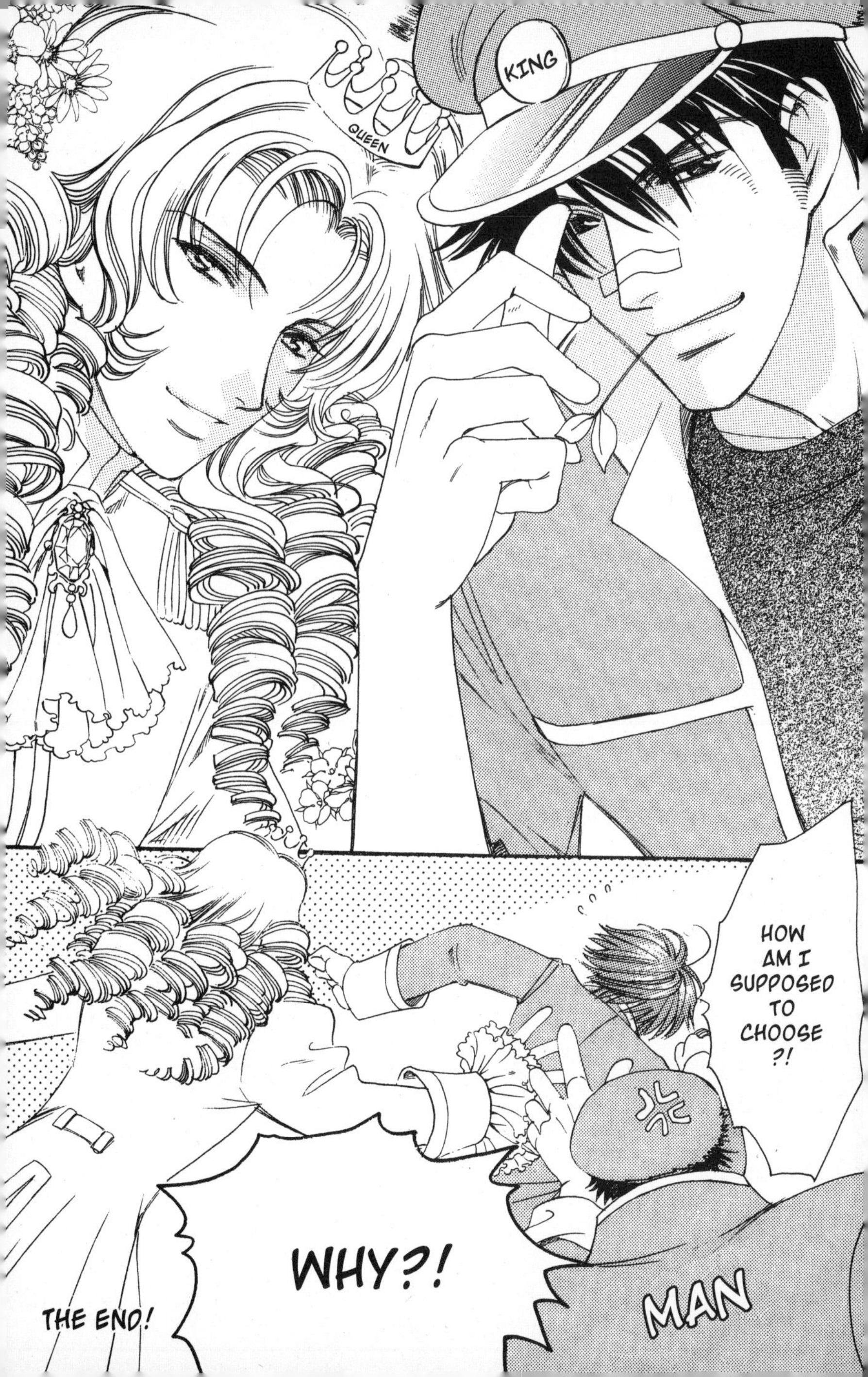
KING
QUEEN
HOW AM I SUPPOSED TO CHOOSE ?!
MAN
WHY?!
THE END!

GAKUEN HEAVEN
Art by You Higuri
Created by SPRAY
Translated by Christine Schilling

ISBN: 1-59816-708-1

First Printing: November 2006
10 9 8 7 6 5 4 3 2
Printed in the USA

This "Pure Romance" is anything but...

Passing his college entrance exams isn't the only thing Misaki has to worry about! Being romanced by a suave and older tutor is the concern, especially when the tutor in question is his brother's best friend and a famous porn novelist! Suddenly Misaki's "normal" life transforms into an educational journey filled with unfamiliar feelings and nonstop insanity.

Here's a dog that will make you beg..

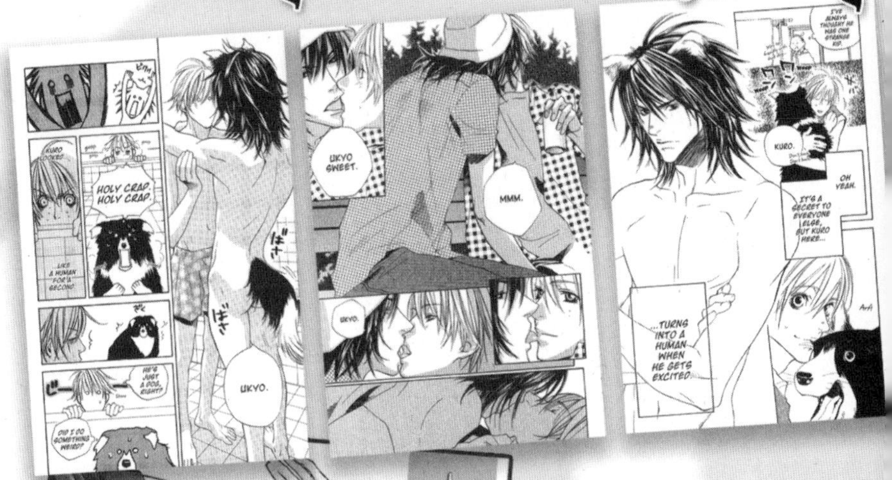

I'VE ALWAYS THOUGHT HE WAS ONE STRANGE KID.
KURO.
OH YEAH.
IT'S A SECRET TO EVERYONE ELSE, BUT KURO HERE...
...TURNS INTO A HUMAN WHEN HE GETS EXCITED.
UKYO SWEET.
MMM.
UKYO.
UKYO.
KURO LOOKS...
HOLY CRAP. HOLY CRAP.
LIKE A HUMAN FOR A SECOND.
HE'S JUST A DOG, RIGHT?
DID I DO SOMETHING WEIRD?

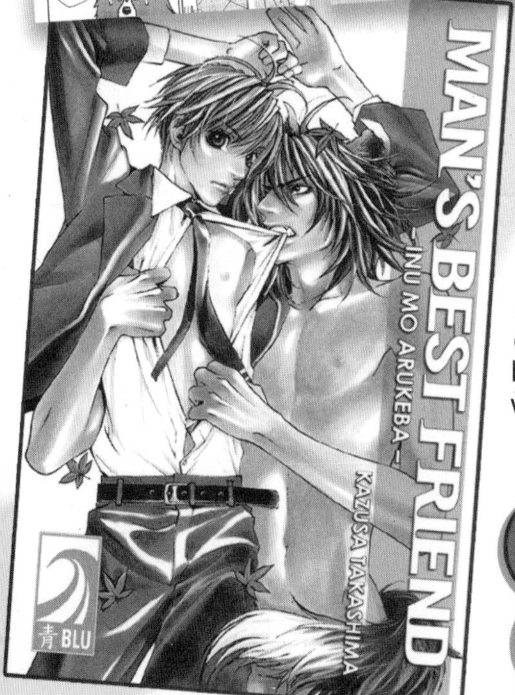

MAN'S BEST FRIEND
-INU MO ARUKEBA-
KAZUSA TAKASHIMA
青 BLU

When Ukyo rescues a stray dog and names it Kuro, he soon learns that he may have found a rare breed—his new dog can talk and magically transform into a hunky human! With his dog now taking the form of a hot man and licking him in various places, what is Ukyo to do?!

From the creator of BLU's *Wild Rock*.

FOR MATURE AUDIENCES ONLY

Price: $9.99
Available Now!

M
MATURE

青 BLU

For information about where to buy BLU MANGA titles, visit www.BLUMANGA.com

High school is difficult enough, especially when you live the shadow of your stunningly attractive older brother...

Kotori is often teased for being superficial, and with a gorgeous brother like Kujaku, you can't really blame him for thinking that looks are everything. However, once Akaiwa steps into the picture, Kotori's life is heading for a lesson in deep trust, self-confidence, and abiding love.

Suzuki Tanaka

MENKUI!

Price: $9.99
Available Now!

OT
OLDER TEEN

青 BLU

Follow the love lives of Izumi, Takamiya and others as they are brought together at a host club called "Blue Boy" that specializes in high-class male escorts. Love lines cross, chances are lost and found, and hearts are broken in this fan favorite boys' love classic.

LOVE MODE
Yuki Shimizu
1

青 BLU

In stores now! $9.99

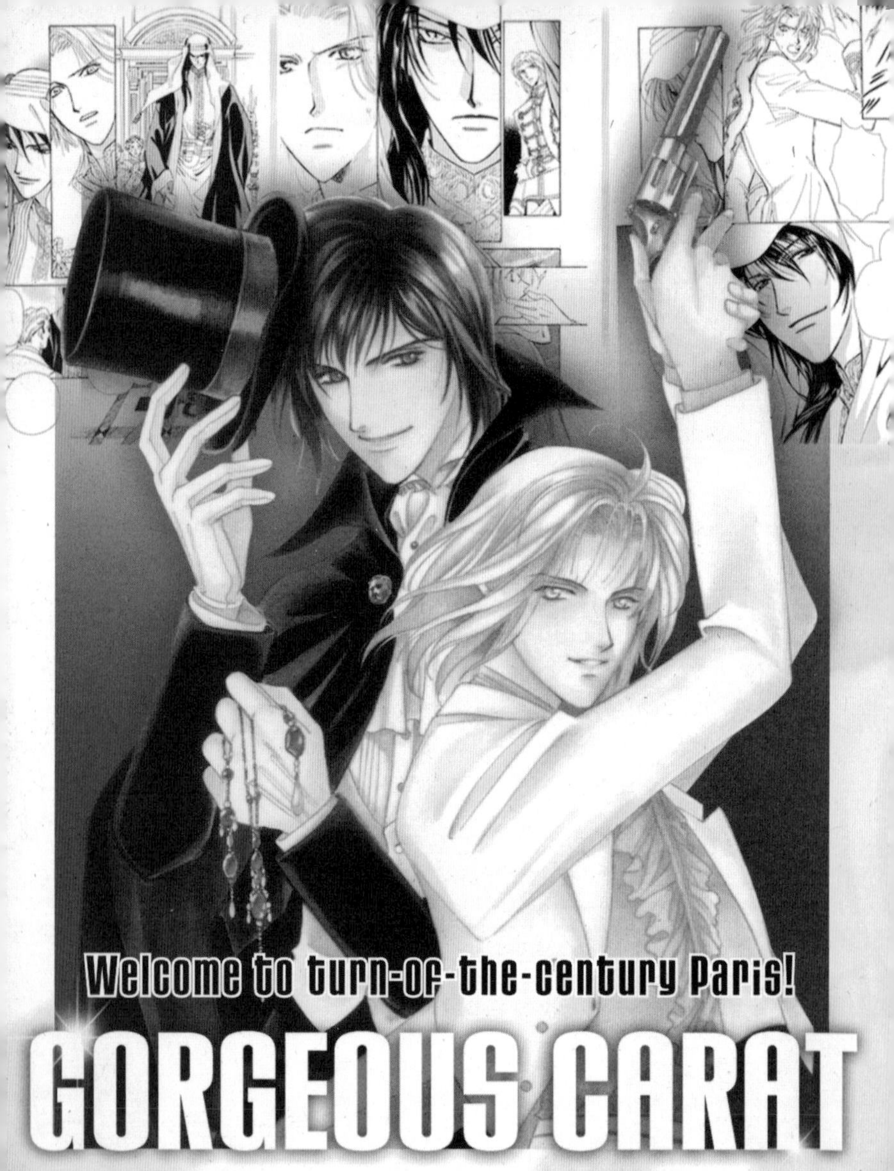

stop

blu manga are published in the original japanese format

go to the other side and begin reading